THE
GREATEST EVER
VEGETARIAN
COOKBOOK

THE GREATEST EVER VEGETARIAN COOKBOOK

Nicola Graimes

HERMES HOUSE

Publisher: Joanna Lorenz
Project Editor: Simona Hill
Designer: Jonathan Harley

Printed and bound in Hong Kong / China

1 3 5 7 9 10 8 6 4 2

ACKNOWLEDGEMENTS

The publishers would like to thank the following for their contributions to this book.

RECIPE CONTRIBUTORS
Alex Barker, Michelle Berridale-Johnson, Angela Boggiano, Carla Capalbo, Jacqueline Clark, Carole Clements, Roz
Denny, Matthew Drennan, Sarah Edmonds, Joanna Farrow, Christine France, Silvana Franco, Sarah Gates, Shirley Gill,
Shehzaid Husain, Christine Ingram, Peter Jordan, Manisha Kanani, Elizabeth Lambert Ortiz, Ruby le Bois, Lesley
Mackley, Norma MacMillan, Sue Maggs, Maggie Mayhew, Sallie Morris, Annie Nichols, Maggie Pannell, Anne Sheasby,
Hilarie Walden, Laura Washburn, Steven Wheeler, Kate Whiteman, Elizabeth Wolf-Cohen, Jenni Wright.

PHOTOGRAPHERS
William Adams-Lingwood, Karl Adamson, Edward Allwright, Steve Baxter, James Duncan, Christine France, Michelle
Garrett, Amanda Heywood, Janine Hosegood, David Jordan, Don Last, Patrick McLeavey, Thomas Odulate, Peter Reilly,
Bridget Sargeson.

STYLISTS
Madeleine Brehaut, Michelle Garrett, Katherine Hawkins, Amanda Heywood, Clare Hunt, Marion McLorman, Blake
Minton, Marian Price, Kirsty Rawlings, Judy Williams.

HOME ECONOMISTS
Hilary Guy, Jane Hartshorn, Wendy Lee, Lucy McKelvie, Jane Stevenson, Steven Wheeler.

Standard spoon and cup measures are level.

Large eggs are used unless otherwise stated.

Portion sizes: The recipes in this book are generally for four people. They can be halved or quartered, depending on the
number of servings required.

CONTENTS

INTRODUCTION	6
GENERAL REFERENCE	16
BREAKFASTS AND BRUNCHES	130
SOUPS AND APPETIZERS	158
LIGHT MEALS	212
MAIN COURSES	248
SPECIAL OCCASIONS	298
TARTS, PIES AND PIZZAS	334
SALADS	362
SIDE DISHES	400
DESSERTS, CAKES AND BAKED GOODS	448
INDEX	504

Introduction

Throughout history, every culture has used food to prevent and treat illness and disease, and promote good health. The Egyptians praised the lentil for its ability to enlighten the mind; the Ancient Greeks and Romans used honey to heal wounds; and in China, sprouted beans and grains were used to treat a wide range of illnesses, from constipation to dropsy.

However, around the time of the industrial revolution, people in Western countries came to disregard the medicinal and therapeutic properties of food, and it is only relatively recently that interest in the healing qualities of food has been revived. This renewed interest, owing to our growing concern about what we eat and drink, and our quest for good health, is spurred on by scientists who have undertaken extensive research into eating habits, and have also investigated the properties of individual foods.

Numerous studies have revealed the positive attributes of a diet that is rich in fruit and vegetables, whole grains, nuts and seeds, and beans, complemented by a moderate amount of dairy foods. Studies have shown that vegetarians suffer less from many diseases, such as obesity, cancer, heart disease, gallstones, diabetes, and constipation, that plague modern Western cultures. In fact, every scientific study comparing vegetarians with people eating a typical Western diet has found the former to be healthier and less likely to suffer from illness. Yet, vegetarianism is not just about achieving optimum health, it should also be an enjoyable and delicious way of eating.

WHAT ARE WHOLE FOODS?

Whole foods are foods to which nothing has been added or taken away. They are foods that haven't been unnecessarily processed or subjected to chemical processing, or loaded with harmful additives, colorings, or flavorings. In the narrowest sense, whole foods are specifically unrefined dried ingredients, such as grains, pulses, beans, and seeds, but in this book we have taken the liberty to expand the term to include all foods that should be included in a healthy diet. It is important to choose unrefined foods whenever you can, simply because they ensure the greatest intake of vitamins, minerals, and fiber. When food is processed, precious nutrients are taken away as a result, although there are various degrees to which this occurs. However, some would argue that a diet consisting entirely of whole foods could be decidedly brown and boring. A healthy whole foods diet should include a wide range of other ingredients to add both

Right: There is a wide range of organic produce available at health-food stores.

variety and essential nutrients. Plenty of fruit and vegetables, dairy products, fats and oils, and natural sweeteners are all needed to make whole foods palatable and appealing. And there's no reason why, if you are eating mainly whole foods, that you can't include a few refined foods. A little white flour added to a whole-wheat cake or pastry, for instance, will give a much lighter final result and will only affect the nutritional value marginally. It is not such a sin to eat white rice instead of brown, or plain pasta rather than whole-wheat occasionally, if the rest of the

Vegetarian Children

Children can thrive on a vegetarian diet as long as it is varied and balanced, and not based on foods such as chips and baked beans. Unlike adults, young children do not entirely benefit from a high-fiber, low-fat diet. They need plenty of calories and nutrients and, because they have small stomachs, require regular, small nutritious meals.

A diet based on low-fat and high-fiber foods can leads to malnutrition in young children because it does not provide sufficient nutrients and calories for growth and development. Reduced fat foods, such as skim milk and reduced-fat cheeses, lack much-needed calories, and their full-fat equivalents should be given to children under 2 years of age. High-fiber foods, such as brown rice, and whole-wheat bread and pasta, are too bulky for young children, and they become full before they have eaten enough nutrients. White bread and rice, and ordinary pasta are acceptable alternatives, provided they are eating plenty of fruit and vegetables, potatoes, cereals, beans, and lentils.

Children should avoid carbonated, caffeine and sugar-laden drinks, and drink only small amounts of juices that contain artificial sweeteners, which can cause diarrhea if consumed in excess. Children should, instead, be encouraged to drink water, milk, and diluted fruit juice.

Above: Try to eat at least three portions of fruits and vegetables a day.

dish or meal is full of nutrient-packed, high-fiber foods.

It may be a cliché, but there is more than a grain of truth in the adage, "You are what you eat." Our bodies rely and thrive on a varied nutritious diet. Yet a healthy diet is not just about boosting physical welfare. Our mental and emotional well being is equally affected by what we put on our plates. The more appetizing and appealing, the better.

ORGANIC FOODS

As food scares continue, many people are increasingly concerned about the type of food that they eat. The growing use of antibiotics, artificial additives, and chemicals, as well as the introduction of irradiation and genetically-modified foods, has added fuel to this concern. In 1995, 46 percent of fruits and vegetables analyzed in one study contained pesticide residues. A group of pesticides known as organophosphates have been a particular problem in carrots, while the results for celery are also disturbing.

People are looking for healthier, less processed foods, and the demand for organic foods is growing at a rate of about 30 percent every year. Organic foods were, until relatively recently, found only at health-food stores, but now there is an expanding range of fresh and packaged organic foods available at supermarkets. Reassuringly, every food that is labeled organic has to fulfill certain strict criteria. No artificial pesticides, fertilizers, or other chemicals can be used in the growing and/or production of organic food, and genetically-modified or irradiated ingredients are not permitted.

Traditional methods of agriculture, such as crop rotation, are used along with natural fertilizers. This preserves wildlife and minimizes pollution. Owing to their shorter shelf-life, organic fruits and vegetables are less likely to have traveled thousands of miles before reaching stores. This could mean that in the future there may be a return to locally produced, seasonal foods. Whether organic food tastes better or is higher in nutrients is open to debate, but the environment and our health will undoubtedly benefit in the long-run.

The Basic Vegetarian Whole Food Diet

We are often told to eat a balanced diet, but in the context of a vegetarian diet what does this mean? The key to good health is to eat a variety of foods that provide the right proportion of protein, carbohydrates, fiber, fat, vitamins, and minerals as well as water. The ideal diet features enough calories to provide the body with vital energy, but not an excess, which leads to weight gain. Getting this balance right is crucial to health.

When people opt for a vegetarian diet, it is not simply a matter of swapping meat and fish for cheese and eggs. Vegetarians need to ensure they eat plenty of fruit and vegetables, legumes, nuts, seeds, rice, bread, pasta, and potatoes and some dairy

Whole wheat bread (below), whole grain cereals (left), and potatoes in their skins (above) provide more nutrients in this form than if they were refined (or peeled).

foods. They should aim to eat nutrient-rich foods, rather than those that provide plenty of calories but few nutrients, such as cake and chips. The following may be a useful guide:

WHOLE-GRAINS AND POTATOES
Aim for 6–11 servings a day
This group includes cereals, such as oats, wheat, corn, millet, barley, bread, rice,

Above: Butter and margarine provide few nutrients and are laden with calories.

pasta, as well as potatoes. They should form the main part of every meal. Whole-wheat bread and pasta, brown rice, and potatoes with their skins on contain the most nutrients and provide starchy carbohydrates, fiber, protein, B complex vitamins, and minerals.

A serving equals: 1 slice of bread, ½ cup of cooked cereal, rice, or pasta or 1 medium potato.

FRUIT AND VEGETABLES
Aim for at least 5 servings a day

Fruit and vegetables provide significant amounts of vitamins, minerals, and fiber and are low in fat and calories. Cruciferous vegetables, such as broccoli, cabbage, sprouts, cauliflower, and chard, provide a powerful combination of antioxidants, which are believed to provide protection against certain cancers. Bright orange, yellow, and red fruit and vegetables are rich in the antioxidant beta carotene and vitamin C.

A serving equals: 1 medium apple, banana, or orange, a handful of cherry

Below: Peas, beans, and corn provide fiber.

Below: bean curd

tomatoes, a glass of fresh fruit juice, 1 cup of cooked vegetables, or a bowl of salad.

LEGUMES, NUTS, AND SEEDS
2–3 servings a day

Legumes, including beans, peas and lentils, bean curd and tempeh, and nuts and seeds provide valuable protein, fiber, iron, calcium, zinc, and vitamins B and E. Legumes are low in fat and provide plenty of fiber. Nuts and seeds are very nutritious but are high in fat and should be eaten in moderation.

A serving equals: a small handful of nuts and seeds, ½ cup cooked beans or 4 ounces bean curd or tempeh.

DAIRY FOODS AND NON-DAIRY ALTERNATIVES
2–3 servings a day

This group includes milk, cheese, and yogurt and provides valuable amounts of protein, calcium, and vitamins B_{12}, A, and D. These foods can be high in fat so should be eaten in moderation. Eggs are also included in this group; a maximum of 3–4 are recommended a week.

A serving equals: 1 egg, a small slice of cheese, a small glass of milk, or a small container of yogurt.

FATS, DESSERTS AND SNACKS
Eat sparingly

This diverse group includes chocolate, chips, cake, and cookies, as well as butter, margarine, and cooking oils. These foods provide few nutrients, but are laden with calories and, if eaten in excess, will lead to weight gain. Too many sugary foods can cause tooth decay.

The Essentials for Good Health

Along with water, there are six essential components for good health, which if consumed in the correct proportions, will provide the body with both sustained energy and the correct balance of nutrients required.

Below: Soluble fiber found in oats helps reduce blood cholesterol.

Carbohydrates

At one time, carbohydrates, which are made up of starches, fiber, and sugars, were considered to be fattening and less valuable than protein-rich foods. However, they are now recognized as the body's major source of energy and carbohydrate-rich foods supply a substantial amount of protein, vitamins, minerals, and fiber, with very little fat. About half the food we eat should be unrefined complex carbohydrates, such as whole-wheat cereals, whole-wheat bread and pasta, and brown rice. These high-fiber foods are broken down slowly

Below: Rice is a good source of insoluble fiber.

by the body and provide a steady supply of energy. They are preferable to sugars or simple carbohydrates because these foods are quickly absorbed into the bloodstream and give only a short-term energy boost. When feasible, opt for unrefined carbohydrates, as the refined versions, such as white flour, rice, and sugar are stripped of nutrients, including vitamins, minerals, and fiber. It's important to remember that the more carbohydrates that you eat, the more you depend on them for supplying essential nutrients.

Right: Carbohydrate-rich vegetables, such as plantains, yams, and potatoes, provide a steady supply of energy.

Fiber

Fruits, vegetables, grains, legumes, nuts, and seeds are our main source of fiber, of which there are two types: insoluble and soluble. Insoluble fiber, which is found in whole-wheat, brown rice, bran, and nuts, provides bulk to the diet and helps to combat constipation. Soluble fiber, found in legumes, vegetables, and oats, binds with toxins in the gut and promotes their

excretion, and also helps to reduce blood cholesterol. Both types of fiber reduce the risk of bowel disorders, including diverticulitis, colon and rectal cancer, and irritable bowel syndrome (although bran has been found to aggravate symptoms of IBS). Few people get enough fiber. On average we eat about 12 grams of fiber a day, but we should be consuming about 18 grams. People who want to lose weight will find that a high-fiber diet is beneficial, as it provides bulk and naturally limits the amount of food eaten.

Protein

This macro-nutrient is essential for the maintenance and repair of every cell in the body, and also ensures that enzymes, hormones, and antibodies function properly. Protein is made up of amino acids, of which there are 20, and eight of these need to be supplied by diet. A food containing all eight amino acids is known as a "complete" or high-quality protein.

How to Increase Your Fiber Intake

• Base your diet on whole-wheat bread and pasta, brown rice, and fruit and vegetables. Refined and processed foods contain less fiber and nutrients.
• Start the day with a whole-grain cereal, such as oatmeal or bran flakes.
• Eat plenty of dried fruit—add it to breakfast cereals, plain yogurt or use to make a compote.
• Add beans and lentils to salads and soups to boost their fiber content.
• Avoid peeling fruits and vegetables, if possible, as the skins contain valuable fiber.

Above: Nuts contain fat as well as protein.

For vegetarians, these include eggs and dairy products, as well as soybeans. Protein from plant sources, such as nuts, pasta, potatoes, legumes, cereals, and rice, does not usually contain all eight amino acids and are known as "incomplete" or low-quality protein. We should aim to get 10–15 percent of calories from protein.

Vegetarians are often asked where they get their protein, and lack of this nutrient can be a concern for those cutting out

Below: Buckwheat pasta is a "complete" protein.

meat and fish from their diet. Yet in reality most people eat too much protein and deficiency is virtually unheard of. In fact, an excess of protein can be detrimental, rather than beneficial to health. High-protein foods, such as dairy products and nuts, are a source of fat, and have been found to leach calcium from the body, which increases the risk of osteoporosis. It is also a common misconception that vegetarians have to meticulously combine protein foods in every meal to achieve the correct balance of amino acids. Nutritionists now believe that, provided a varied diet of grains, legumes, dairy produce, eggs, and vegetables is eaten on a daily basis, intentionally combining

Fats

A small amount of fat in the diet is essential for health. Fat not only provides vitamins A, D, and E and essential fatty acids that cannot be made in the body, but also contributes greatly to the taste, texture, and palatability of food. It contains a high number of calories, and should make up no more than 30 percent of your diet. The type of fat is as crucial as the quantity.

Saturated fat (found mainly in dairy products in the vegetarian diet) has been associated with an increased risk of cancer and coronary heart disease. Eating too much saturated fat can raise blood cholesterol levels and lead to narrowed arteries, more so than eating foods, such as eggs, that are high in cholesterol.

Left: Canola oil, which like olive and sesame oils is a monounsaturated fat and can help to reduce the levels of cholesterol in the body, also contains Omega-3 or linolenic acid, which is thought to reduce the risk of heart disease.

Unsaturated fats, both polyunsaturated and monounsaturated, can help reduce harmful "LDL" cholesterol (the type that clogs up arteries) and, importantly, increase the beneficial "HDL" cholesterol, which is thought to reduce cholesterol levels in the body. Mono-unsaturated fats, such as olive oil, sesame oil, and canola oil, are less vulnerable to oxidation than polyunsaturated fats. Polyunsaturated fats provide essential fatty acids, omega-3

and 6. Omega-3 (linolenic acid), which is found in walnuts, soybeans, wheatgerm, and canola oil, has been found to reduce the risk of heart disease, while omega-6 (linoleic acid), which is found in nuts, seeds, and oils is thought to reduce levels of blood cholesterol.

Below: All cheeses should be eaten in moderation.

How to Reduce Dietary Fat

While a vegetarian diet is often lower in fat than one based on meat, it is very easy to eat too many dairy products, oil-laden salad dressings and sauces, and high-fat ready-meals. Here are a few simple ways to reduce fat in your diet:

• Use strong, aged cheese, such as Parmesan—only a small amount is needed to add flavor to a dish.

• Try making low-fat salad dressings using miso, orange juice, yogurt, herbs, spices, or tomato juice instead of oils.

• Stir-fry foods using only a little oil. For best results make sure the wok/skillet is very hot before adding the oil.

• Avoid blended oils, as they can contain coconut or palm oil, which are both saturated fats.

• Opt for low-fat cheeses, such as cottage, ricotta, or mozzarella instead of high-fat cheeses, such as Cheddar.

• Use low-fat yogurt instead of cream in cooked recipes. Stir in a spoonful of cornstarch (mixed to a paste with a little water) to prevent the yogurt from curdling when heated.

• Choose complex carbohydrates, including potatoes, pasta, brown rice, and beans, instead of high-fat protein foods.

Above: Use naturally low-fat cheeses, such as cottage cheese, farmer's cheese, and ricotta.

Water

The importance of water is often taken for granted, yet although it is possible to survive for weeks without food, we can live for only a few days without water. Water plays a vital role in the body: it transports nutrients, regulates the body temperature, transports waste via the kidneys, and acts as a lubricating fluid. Most people do not drink enough water: it is thought that an adult requires around 10 cups per day. A shortage of water can cause headaches and loss of concentration. Soda, tea, and coffee all act as diuretics and speed up the loss of water, which causes dehydration.

Above: Eggs contain all eight essential amino acids, and are a good source of vitamin B₁₂.

Vitamins and Minerals

These nutrients are vital for good health and the functioning of our bodies, and with a few exceptions must be supplied by diet. The levels our bodies require vary depending on health, lifestyle, and age. Contrary to popular belief, vitamins and minerals do not provide energy, but assist in the release of energy provided by carbohydrates, fat, and protein.

Below: Oranges are rich in vitamin C.

How to Preserve Nutrients

The nutrients in food, particularly fruits and vegetables, are unstable and are diminished by time, preparation methods, and cooking. Leave a piece of cut fruit or a sliced potato exposed to air or soaking in water and its vitamin and mineral levels plummet. Old, wilted, or damaged produce also have reduced levels of vitamins and minerals. The following tips will ensure that you get the most from your fruit and vegetables:

• Buy fruits and vegetables that are as fresh as possible, and avoid those that have been stored under fluorescent light, as this can set off a chemical reaction that depletes nutrients.

• Buy loose fresh produce, which is much easier to check for quality than pre-packaged foods.

• Buy fruit and vegetables in small quantities, and do not keep them for too long, and remove them from plastic bags as soon as possible.

• Depending on the type of fruit or vegetable, store in a cool pantry or in the bottom of the refrigerator.

• Avoid peeling fruits and vegetables, if possible, and do not prepare them too far in advance of cooking, as nutrients such as vitamin C will be destroyed.

• Eat fruits and vegetables raw, when they are at their most nutritious.

• Avoid boiling vegetables because this method of cooking destroys water-soluble vitamins, such as thiamine and vitamins B and C. If you must boil vegetables, use as little water as possible and do not overcook them. The cooking water can also be kept and used as stock for soup.

It is not just fruit and vegetables that benefit from careful storage and handling—nuts, seeds, legumes, and grains will also be fresher and have a higher nutrient content if stored and cooked correctly.

Right: Miso contains a good amount of the water-soluble vitamin B₁₂.

Vitamins are either water-soluble or fat-soluble. Fat-soluble vitamins A, D, E, and K are stored in the liver for some time. Water-soluble vitamins, B complex and C, cannot be stored and must be replaced on a daily basis. If you drink alcohol or smoke, increase your intake of vitamin B- and C-rich foods. Of the B-complex vitamins, vegetarians should make sure they get enough B₁₂, although this shouldn't be difficult as it is

needed only in tiny amounts. It is found in dairy products, fortified breakfast cereals, yeast extract, miso, and eggs.

There are 16 essential minerals; some like calcium, are needed in relatively large amounts, while trace elements, such as selenium and magnesium, are needed in tiny quantities. Minerals have various functions, but predominantly regulate and balance the body and maintain a healthy immune system. A deficiency of iron affects one-fifth of the world's population, and vegetarians need to make a point of eating iron-rich foods.

Essential Vitamins and Minerals

VITAMIN	BEST VEGETARIAN SOURCES	ROLE IN HEALTH	DEFICIENCY
A (retinol in animal foods, beta carotene in plant foods)	*animal sources:* milk, butter, cheese, egg yolks, and margarine *plant sources:* carrots, apricots, squash, red bell peppers, broccoli, leafy greens, mango, and sweet potatoes	Essential for vision, bone growth, and skin and tissue repair. Beta carotene acts as an antioxidant and protects the immune system	Deficiency is characterized by poor night vision, dry skin, and lower resistance to infection, especially respiratory disorders
B_1 (thiamin)	Whole-grain cereals, brewer's yeast, potatoes, nuts, pulses, and milk	Essential for energy production, the nervous system, muscles, and heart. Promotes growth and boosts mental ability	Deficiency is characterized by depression, irritability, nervous disorders, loss of memory. Common among alcoholics
B_2 (riboflavin)	Cheese, eggs, milk, yogurt, fortified breakfast cereals, yeast extract, almonds, and pumpkin seeds	Essential for energy production and for the functioning of vitamin B6 and niacin, as well as tissue repair	Deficiency is characterized by lack of energy, dry cracked lips, numbness, and itchy eyes
Niacin (part of B complex)	Pulses, potatoes, fortified breakfast cereals, wheatgerm, peanuts, milk, cheese, eggs, peas, mushrooms, leafy greens, figs, and prunes	Essential for healthy digestive system, skin, and circulation. It is also needed for the release of energy	Deficiency is unusual, but characterized by lack of energy, depression, and scaly skin
B_6 (piridoxine)	Eggs, whole-wheat bread, breakfast cereals, nuts, bananas, and cruciferous vegetables, such as broccoli, cabbage, and cauliflower	Essential for assimilating protein and fat, to make red blood cells, and a healthy immune system	Deficiency is characterized by anemia, dermatitis, and depression
B_{12} (cyanocobalamin)	Milk, eggs, fortified breakfast cereals, cheese, and yeast extract	Essential for formation of red blood cells, maintaining a healthy nervous system, and increasing energy levels	Deficiency is characterized by fatigue, increase risk of infection, anemia
Folate (folic acid)	Leafy greens, fortified breakfast cereals, bread, nuts, pulses, bananas, and yeast extract	Essential for cell division; makes genetic material (DNA) for every cell. Extra is needed pre-conception and during pregnancy to protect fetus against neural tube defects	Deficiency characterized by anemia and appetite loss. Linked with neural defects in babies
C (ascorbic acid)	Citrus fruit, melons, strawberries, tomatoes, broccoli, potatoes, bell peppers, and green vegetables	Essential for the absorption of iron, healthy skin, teeth, and bones. An antioxidant that strengthens the immune system and helps fight infection	Deficiency characterized by increased susceptibility to infection, fatigue, poor sleep, and depression
D (calciferol)	Sunlight, margarine, vegetable oils, eggs, cereals, and butter	Essential for bone and teeth formation, helps the body to absorb calcium and phosphorus	Deficiency characterized by softening of the bones, muscle weakness, and anemia. Long-term shortage in children results in rickets
E (tocopherol)	Seeds, nuts, vegetable oils, eggs, whole-wheat bread, leafy greens, oats, and cereals	Essential for healthy skin, circulation, and maintaining cells—an antioxidant	Deficiency characterized by increased risk of heart attack, strokes, and certain cancers

MINERAL	BEST VEGETARIAN SOURCES	ROLE IN HEALTH	DEFICIENCY
Calcium	Milk, cheese, yogurt, leafy greens, sesame seeds, broccoli, dried figs, pulses, almonds, spinach, and watercress	Essential for building and maintaining bones and teeth, muscle function, and the nervous system	Deficiency characterized by soft and brittle bones, osteoporosis, fractures, and muscle weakness
Iron	Egg yolks, fortified breakfast cereals, leafy greens, dried apricots, prunes, pulses, whole-grains, and bean curd	Essential for healthy blood and muscles	Deficiency characterized by anemia, fatigue, and low resistance to infection
Zinc	Peanuts, cheese, whole-grains, sunflower and pumpkin seeds, pulses, milk, hard cheese, and yogurt	Essential for a healthy immune system, tissue formation, normal growth, wound healing, and reproduction	Deficiency is characterized by impaired growth and development, slow wound healing, and loss of taste and smell
Sodium	Most salt we eat comes from processed foods, such as chips, cheese, and canned foods. It is also found naturally in most foods	Essential for nerve and muscle function and the regulation of body fluid	Deficiency is unlikely but can lead to dehydration, cramps, and muscle weakness
Potassium	Bananas, milk, pulses, nuts, seeds, whole-grains, potatoes, fruits, and vegetables	Essential for water balance, normal blood pressure, and nerve transmission	Deficiency is characterized by weakness, thirst, fatigue, mental confusion and high blood pressure
Magnesium	Nuts, seeds, whole-grains, pulses, bean curd, dried figs and apricots, and green vegetables	Essential for healthy muscles, bones and teeth, normal growth, and nerves	Deficiency is characterized by lethargy, weak bones and muscles, depression, and irritability
Phosphorus	Milk, cheese, yogurt, eggs, nuts, seeds, pulses, and whole grains	Essential for healthy bones and teeth, energy production, and the assimilation of nutrients, particularly calcium	Deficiency is rare
Selenium	Avocados, lentils, milk, cheese, butter, Brazil nuts, and seaweed	Essential for protecting against free radical damage and may protect against cancer—an antioxidant	Deficiency is characterized by reduced antioxidant protection
Iodine	Seaweed and iodized salt	Aids the production of hormones released by the thyroid gland	Deficiency can lead to the formation of a goiter and a sluggish metabolism and apathy, as well as dry skin and hair
Chloride	Table salt and foods that contain table salt	Regulates and maintains the balance of fluids in the body	Deficiency is rare
Manganese	Nuts, whole-grains, pulses, bean curd, and tea	Essential component of various enzymes that are involved in energy production	Deficiency is not characterized by any specific symptoms

The Vegetarian Kitchen

This fascinating guide includes every kind of natural food, from fruit and vegetables to grains, and from dairy foods to herbs and spices. It includes essential facts about key health benefits and traditional healing qualities, as well as information on buying and storing, preparing and cooking whole foods. It is an inspiration to anyone interested in finding out more about foods that can make you live, look, and feel better.

Fruit

Perhaps the ultimate convenience food, most fruits can be simply washed and eaten and, because the nutrients are concentrated just below the skin, it is best to avoid peeling. Cooking fruit reduces valuable vitamins and minerals, so, if you can, eat it raw. Fruit is an excellent source of energy and provides valuable fiber and antioxidants, which are said to reduce the risk of heart disease and certain cancers. Thanks to modern farming methods and efficient transportation, most fruit is available all year round, although it is generally best when homegrown, organically produced, and in season.

Orchard Fruits

These fruits have a long history, spanning thousands of years, and offer an incredible range of colors and flavors. This group includes many favorites, from crisp, juicy apples, which are available all year round, to luscious, fragrant peaches—a popular summer fruit.

Apricots

APPLES

There are thousands of varieties of apple, although the choice in stores is often restricted to a mere few. Some of the most popular eating varieties are Empire. Winesap McIntosh, Granny Smith, Gala, Braeburn, and Golden and Red Delicious.

The Bramley Seedling, with its thick, shiny, green skin and tart flesh, is the most familiar cooking apple and is perfect for baking, or as the basis of apple sauce. Some lesser-known varieties, many of which have a short season, are often available from farm stores. Homegrown apples bought out of season may have spent several months in cold storage, where ripening and maturation are artificially halted. When they are taken out of storage, the apples deteriorate quickly.

Apples are delicious when they are eaten raw with their skin on. However, this versatile fruit is often used in breakfast dishes, main meals, salads, desserts, pies, and even soups. Large cooking apples are ideal puréed, stewed, and baked, but their tartness means that sugar has to be added. Some varieties of eating apple are just as good cooked and don't need any added sugar.

To preserve the maximum amount of vitamins and minerals, cook apples over low heat with little or no water. Most of the insecticides that are used on apples collect in the apple core and seeds, so, unless the apples are organic, these should be removed before cooking.

Buying and Storing: When buying apples, choose bright, firm fruits without any bruises. Organic apples are

An Apple a Day

Numerous studies have shown that eating apples regularly could reduce harmful LDL cholesterol in the body. In France, 30 middle-aged men and women were asked to add 2–3 apples a day to their diet for a month. By the end of the month, 80 percent of the group showed reduced cholesterol levels, and in half of the group the drop was more than 10 percent. Additionally, the level of good HDL cholesterol went up. Pectin, a soluble fiber found particularly in apples, is believed to be the magic ingredient.

Large cooking apples (left) and eating apples

Baked Apples

Baking is a simple and nutritious way of cooking this orchard fruit. Use cooking apples, such as Bramley.

1 Preheat the oven to 350°F. Remove the cores of the apples, then score the skin around the circumference of each to prevent the skin bursting. Place the apples in an ovenproof dish with a little water.

2 Fill the cavity of the apples with a mixture of dark brown sugar, dried fruit, and nuts. Top each with a pat of butter and bake for about 40 minutes, or until the apples are soft.

more prone to blemishes than non-organic ones, and the fruits can look a little tatty, but the taste will often be superior. Smaller apples tend to have a better flavor and texture than larger specimens. Store apples in a cool place, away from direct sunlight.

Health Benefits: The cleansing and blood-purifying qualities of apples are highly valued in natural medicine. Apples aid digestion and can remove impurities in the liver. They are a good source of vitamin C and fiber, if you eat the skin. Although low in calories, they contain fructose, a simple sugar that is released slowly to supply the body with energy and balance blood-sugar levels. People with skin problems and arthritis are said to benefit from eating apples regularly.

APRICOTS

The best apricots are sunshine gold in color and full of juice. They are delicious baked or used raw in salads.

Buying and Storing: An apricot is at its best when truly ripe. Immature fruits are hard and tasteless and never seem to attain the right level of sweetness.

Health Benefits: Extremely rich in beta carotene, minerals, and vitamin A, apricots are a valuable source of fiber.

CHERRIES

There are two types: sweet and sour. Some are best eaten raw, like the popular Bing, while others, such as Morello, are best cooked.

Buying and Storing: Choose firm, bright, glossy fruits that have fresh, green stems. Discard any that are soft or have split or damaged skin.

Glossy, red, sweet cherries

Health Benefits: Cherries stimulate and cleanse the system, removing toxins from the kidneys. They are a remedy for gout and arthritis. Cherries also contain iron, potassium, vitamins C and B, as well as beta carotene.

NECTARINES

Like a peach without the fuzzy skin, this sweet juicy fruit is named after the drink of the gods—nectar—and is delicious baked or used raw in salads.

Buying and Storing: see Peaches.

Health Benefits: When eaten raw, nectarines are especially rich in vitamin C. They aid the digestion, effectively reduce high blood pressure, and cleanse the body.

PEACHES

These summer fruits are prized for their perfume and luscious juiciness. Peaches range in color from gold to deep red, and the flesh can be orange or white.

Buying and Storing: Avoid overly soft fruit. Peaches and nectarines are extremely fragile and bruise easily, so buy when

Nectarines and peaches

slightly under-ripe. To ripen them quickly, place in a brown paper bag with an already ripened fruit. Store ripe nectarines and peaches in the fridge, but bring back to room temperature before eating.

Health Benefits: Much of the vitamin C content of a peach lies in and just under its delicate skin, so eat the fruit unpeeled. Peaches are an excellent source of the antioxidant beta carotene, which is said to lower the risk of heart disease and some forms of cancer.

PEARS

Pears have been popular for thousands of years and were extensively cultivated by both the Greeks and the Romans. Pears come into their own in the late summer and fall with the arrival of the new season's crops. Particular favorites are green and brown-skinned Conference; Williams, with its thin, yellow skin and sweet, soft flesh;

plump Comice, which has a pale yellow skin with a green tinge; and Packham, an excellent cooking pear. Like certain apples, some types of pear are good for cooking, others are best eaten raw, and a few varieties fit happily into both camps. Pears can be used in both sweet and non-sweet dishes; they are excellent in salads, and can be baked, poached in syrup, and used in pies. Pears are unlikely to cause any allergic reactions, so when cooked and puréed they make perfect food for weaning babies.

Buying and Storing: Choose firm, plump fruit that are just slightly under-ripe. Pears can ripen in a day or so and then they pass their peak very quickly, and become woolly or mushy. To tell if a pear is ripe, feel around the base of the stalk, where it should give slightly when gently pressed, but the pear itself should be firm.

Health Benefits: Despite their high water content, pears contain useful amounts of vitamin C, fiber, and potassium. In natural medicine, they are used as a diuretic and laxative. Rich in pectin and soluble fiber, pears could also be valuable in lowering harmful cholesterol levels in the body. Eating pears regularly is said to result in a clear, healthy complexion and glossy hair.

PLUMS

Ranging in color from pale yellow to dark, rich purple, plums come in many different varieties, although only a few are available in stores. They can be sweet and juicy or slightly tart; the latter are best cooked in pies and cakes, or made into a delicious jelly. Sweet plums can be eaten as they are, and are good in fruit salads, or they can be puréed and combined with custard or yogurt to make a fruit fool.

From left, Conference, Comice, and Williams pears

Plums

QUINCE

Fragrant, with a thin, yellow or green skin, these knobby fruits, which can be either apple- or pear-shaped, are always cooked. Their high pectin content means that they are good for jellies and, in Spain and France, quinces are used to make a fruit paste that is served with soft cheeses.

Buying and Storing: Look for smooth ripe fruits that are not too soft. Quinces keep well and can be stored in a bowl in your kitchen or living room. They will fill the room with their delicious scent.

Health Benefits: Quinces are rich in soluble fiber and pectin. They also calm the stomach and allay nausea.

Plums should be just firm, and not too soft, with shiny, smooth skin that has a slight "bloom." Store ripe plums in the fridge. Unripe fruits can be kept at room temperature for a few days to ripen. Plums relieve constipation and are thought to stimulate the nerves.

Yellow, pear-shaped quince

Dried Fruit

A useful source of energy, dried fruit is higher in calories than fresh fruit, and packed with vitamins and minerals. The drying process boosts the levels of vitamin C, beta carotene, potassium, and iron. Apricots and prunes are the most popular types, but dried apple rings, cherries, and peaches are also available. Sulfur, often used as a preservative in dried fruits, is best avoided, especially by people who suffer from asthma. Look for unsulfured fruit.

Pitting Fruit

1 To remove the pits from peaches, apricots, or plums, cut around the middle of the fruit down to the pit with a paring knife. Twist each half of the fruit in opposite directions.

2 Prize out the pit using the tip of the knife and discard. Rub the cut flesh with lemon juice.

Citrus Fruits

Juicy and brightly colored, citrus fruits, such as oranges, grapefruit, lemons, and limes are best known for their sweet, slightly sour juice, which is rich in vitamin C. They are invaluable in the kitchen, adding an aromatic acidity to many dishes, from soups and sauces to desserts and pies. Buy organic fruit when you can, and eat within a week or two.

ORANGES

Best eaten as soon as they are peeled, oranges start to lose vitamin C from the moment they are cut. Thin-skinned oranges tend to be the juiciest.

Popular varieties include the Navel (named after the belly button-type spot at the flower end), which contains no pits and so is good for slicing; sweet, juicy Jaffa and Valencia; and Seville, a sour orange used to make marmalade.

The outermost layer of the orange rind can be removed using a swivel vegetable peeler or paring knife. This thin rind contains aromatic oils, which give a delightful perfumed flavor to both non-sweet and sweet dishes.

Oranges

GRAPEFRUIT

The flesh of the grapefruit ranges in color from vivid pink and ruby red to white; the pink and red varieties are sweeter. Heavier fruits are likely to be juicier. Served juiced, halved, or cut into slices, grapefruit can provide a refreshing start to the day. The fruit also adds a refreshing tang to salads or a contrast to rich foods. Cooking or broiling mellows the tartness, but keep cooking times brief to preserve the nutrients. A glass of grapefruit juice before bed is said to promote sleep.

LEMONS

Both the juice and rind of this essential cooking ingredient can be used to enliven salad dressings, vegetables, marinades, sauces, and cookies. Lemon juice can also be used to prevent some fruits and vegetables from discoloring when cut. Lemons should be deep yellow in color, firm and heavy for their size, with no hint of green in the skin, as this is a sign of immaturity, while a thin, smooth skin is a sign of juicy flesh. A slice of lemon in hot water cleanses the system and invigorates the whole body. With a spoonful of honey added, a hot lemon drink is an old and trusted remedy

for alleviating colds and flu.

LIMES

Once considered to be rather exotic, limes are now widely available. Avoid fruits with a yellowing skin, as this is a sign of deterioration. The juice has a sharper flavor than that of lemons and if you substitute limes for lemons in a recipe, you will need to use less juice. Limes are used a great deal in Asian cooking and the rind can be used to flavor curries, marinades, and dips. Cilantro, chile peppers, garlic, and ginger are natural partners.

Grapefruit

Lemons

Buying and Storing:

Look for plump, firm citrus fruit that feels heavy for its size, and has a smooth thin skin; this indicates that the flesh is juicy. Fruits with bruises, brown spots, green patches (or yellow patches on limes), and soft, mushy skin should be avoided, as should dry, wrinkled specimens. Citrus fruits can be kept at room temperature for a few days but if you want to keep them longer, they are best stored in the fridge and eaten within two weeks. Most citrus fruits are waxed or sprayed with fungicides, so scrub them thoroughly to remove any residues. If you can, buy organic or unwaxed fruit.

The Powers of Vitamin C

Citrus fruit is best known for its generous vitamin C content, which is found predominantly in the flesh. An antioxidant, vitamin C has been found to thwart many forms of cancer (particularly cancer of the stomach and esophagus) by defending body cells against harmful free radicals. Free radicals attack DNA—the cell's genetic material—causing them to mutate and possibly become cancerous.

Numerous population studies have also demonstrated that a high dietary intake of vitamin C significantly reduces the risk of death from the world's greatest killers: the heart attack and stroke. It has been found both to lower harmful LDL cholesterol in the body and to raise beneficial HDL cholesterol. It does this by converting LDL cholesterol into bile acids, which are normally excreted. If vitamin C is in short supply, LDL cholesterol accumulates in the body.

The ability of vitamin C to boost the immune system by helping to fight viruses is well documented. It can be particularly beneficial for infections of the urinary tract and the herpes simplex virus. Researchers are in two minds as to whether vitamin C actually prevents colds, but they certainly agree that it can lessen the severity and length of colds and flu. It also boosts the body's ability to absorb iron from food.

Vitamin C is destroyed by heat as well as being water soluble, and is therefore easily lost in cooking. If fruits are cut some time before eating, much of their vitamin C content will also be lost.

Limes are a good source of vitamin C.

Grating Citrus Rind

1 To remove long, thin shreds of rind, use a zester. Scrape it along the surface of the fruit, applying firm pressure.

2 For finer shreds, use a grater. Rub the fruit over the fine cutters to remove the rind without any of the white pith.

Cutting Fine Strips or Julienne

1 Using a vegetable peeler, remove strips of orange rind making sure the white pith is left behind on the fruit.

2 Stack several strips of citrus rind and, using a sharp knife, cut them into fine strips or julienne.

COOK'S TIPS

• *Rolling citrus fruit firmly over a work surface or in the palms of your hands will help you extract the maximum amount of juice from the fruit.*

• *Limes and lemons will yield more juice if cut lengthwise, rather than horizontally.*

Berries and Currants

These baubles of vivid red, purple, and black are the epitome of summer and fall, although they are now likely to be found all year round. Despite their distinctive appearance and flavor, berries and currants are interchangeable in their uses—jellies and pies are the obvious choices. Interestingly, they also share health-giving qualities, including the ability to treat stomach problems and cleanse the blood, and therefore play a part in natural medicine.

STRAWBERRIES

These are the favorite summer fruits and do not need any embellishment. Serve ripe (avoid those with white or green tips) and raw, on their own, or with a little cream or some natural yogurt. Wash only if absolutely necessary and just before serving.

Health Benefits: Strawberries are rich in B complex vitamins and vitamin C. They contain significant amounts of potassium, and have good skin-cleansing properties.

RASPBERRIES

Soft and fragrant, raspberries are best served simply and unadulterated—maybe with a spoonful of natural yogurt. Those grown in Scotland are regarded as the best in the world. Raspberries are very fragile and require the minimum of handling, so wash only if really necessary. They are best eaten raw, as cooking spoils their flavor and vitamin C content.

Strawberries

Raspberries

Health Benefits: Raspberries are a rich source of vitamin C. They are effective in treating menstrual cramps, as well as cleansing the body, and removing toxins. Raspberry leaf tea is often drunk in the last few weeks of pregnancy, as it prepares the uterus for labor.

BLUEBERRIES

Dark purple in color, blueberries are very popular in the United States. When ripe, the berries are plump and slightly firm, with a natural "bloom." Avoid any that are soft and dull-skinned, and wash and dry carefully to avoid bruising. Cultivated blueberries are larger than wild ones. Both types are sweet enough to be eaten raw, but are also good cooked in pies and muffins, used for jellies, or made into a sauce to serve with nut or vegetable roasts. Unwashed blueberries will keep for up to a week in the bottom of the fridge.

Health Benefits: Numerous studies show that eating blueberries regularly can improve night vision as well as protect against the onset of cataracts and glaucoma. Blueberries are also effective in treating urinary tract infections and can improve poor circulation.

BLACKBERRIES

These are a familiar sight in early fall, growing wild in hedgerows. Cultivated blackberries have a slightly longer season and are generally much larger than the wild fruits. Juicy and plump, blackberries can vary in sweetness, which is why they are so often cooked. Wash them carefully to prevent bruising the fruits, then pat dry with paper towels. Use in pies, or make into jellies. The berries can also be lightly cooked, then puréed, and pressed through a strainer to make a sauce to serve with other fruits or ice cream. Blackberries make an ideal partner to apples and pears.

Blackberries

Cranberry Cure

A recent study reported in the Journal of the American Medical Research Association supports the long-held belief that cranberries combat cystitis and other infections of the urinary tract. It found that drinking cranberry juice reduces levels of bacteria not only in the urinary tract, but also in the bladder and kidneys.

Blueberries

Health Benefits: Blackberries are high in fiber and contain a wealth of minerals, including magnesium, iron, and calcium. They are rich in vitamin C, and are one of the best low-fat sources of vitamin E. In natural medicine, blackberries are used to cleanse the blood and they have a tonic effect. They are also used to ease stomach complaints and to treat menstrual problems. Blackberries are particularly rich in bioflavonoids, which act as antioxidants, inhibiting the growth of cancer cells and protecting against cell damage by carcinogens.

GOOSEBERRIES

A favorite fruit of Northern Europe, gooseberries are relatively rare in other parts of the world. They range from the hard and sour green type to the sweeter, softer purple variety. The skin can vary from smooth and silky to fuzzy and spiky. Slightly unripe, tart gooseberries make wonderful pies, crumbles, and jellies. Ripe, softer fruits can be puréed and mixed with cream, yogurt, or custard to make a delicious fruit fool.

Health Benefits: Rich in vitamin C, gooseberries also contain beta carotene, potassium, and fiber.

Black currants

BLACK CURRANTS, RED CURRANTS AND WHITE CURRANTS

These pretty, delicate fruits are usually sold in bunches on the stem. To remove the currants from the stalk, run the prongs of a fork down through the clusters, taking care not to damage the fruit. Wash the fruits carefully, then pat dry. Raw black currants are quite tart, but this makes

White currants

them ideal for cooking in sweet pies. They make delicious jellies, and are especially good in a traditional summer pudding when they are partnered by other berries. Sweeter white currants make a delightful addition to fruit salads.

Health Benefits: The nutritional value of currants has long been recognized. They are high in antioxidants, vitamins C and E, and carotenes. They also contain significant amounts of fiber, calcium, iron, and magnesium. In natural medicine, black currants are often used to settle stomach upsets.

Red currants

Buying and Storing: Look for firm, glossy berries and currants. Make sure that they are not squashed or moldy. Ripe fruits generally do not keep well and are best eaten on the day of purchase—store in the fridge. Unripe fruits can be kept for longer. Raspberries, blueberries, blackberries, and currants all freeze well.

Gooseberries

Fruit Purée

Soft berries are perfect for making uncooked fruit purées or coulis. Sweeten if the fruit is tart and add a splash of lemon juice to bring out the flavor.

1 To make raspberry purée, process some raspberries, with lemon juice and confectioner's sugar to taste, in a food processor or blender until smooth.

2 Press through a nylon strainer. Store in the fridge for up to two days.

Grapes, Melons, Dates, and Figs

These fruits were some of the first ever to be cultivated and are therefore steeped in history. They are available in an immense variety of shapes, colors, and sizes, and with the exception of melons, they can also be bought dried. As well as being a good source of nutrients, these fruits are high in soluble fiber.

GRAPES

There are many varieties of grape, each with its own particular flavor and character. Most are grown for wine production. Grapes for eating are less acidic and have a thinner skin than those used for wine-making. Seedless grapes are easier to eat and contain less tannin than the seeded fruit. Grapes range in color from deep purple to pale red, and from bright green to almost white. The finest eating grapes are Muscat grapes, which have a wonderful, perfumed flavor. They may be pale green or golden, or black or red. Italia grapes, another popular eating variety, have a luscious musky flavor and may be green or black. Unless they are organic, grapes should be thoroughly washed before eating as they are routinely sprayed with pesticides and fungicides.

Red and green grapes

Serve grapes with cheese, in salads, or as a topping for a pie. Before cooking them, remove the skin by blanching the grapes in boiling water for a few seconds, then peel with a small knife.

A Glass of Red Wine

According to a recent American study, phenolic is just one of the compounds found in red wine that may delay the onset of cancer. This news comes following research that wine—particularly red wine—may reduce the risk of heart disease. Nutritionally, wine is virtually worthless and should be drunk in moderation, although it may increase the absorption of iron if drunk with a meal.

Buying and Storing: Buy grapes that are plump, and fairly firm. They should be evenly colored and firmly attached to the stalk. Unwashed fruit may be stored in the fridge for up to five days.

Health Benefits: Grapes contain iron, potassium, and fiber. They are powerful detoxifiers and can improve the condition of the skin, and treat gout, liver, and kidney disorders. Research has revealed that resveratrol, a natural substance produced by grapes, can help inhibit the formation

Galia melons (front left and back), Cantaloupe melons (center), and watermelon (right)

of tumors and that purple grape juice may be even more effective than aspirin in reducing the risk of heart attacks.

MELONS

Watermelons are very low in calories because of their high water content, which is around 90 percent. They contain less vitamin C than the fragrant, orange-fleshed varieties, such as the Cantaloupe and Charentais. Avoid buying ready-cut melons, because most of the vitamins will have been lost.

Buying and Storing: Look for melons that feel heavy for their size and yield to gentle pressure at the stem end.

Health Benefits: When they are eaten on their own, melons are easy to digest and pass quickly through the system. But when they are consumed with other foods requiring a more complex digestive process, they may actually inhibit the absorption of nutrients.

FIGS

These delicate, thin-skinned fruits may be purple, brown, or greenish-gold. Delicious raw, figs can also be poached or baked. Choose unbruised, ripe fruits that yield to gentle pressure and eat on the day of purchase. If they are not too ripe, they can be kept in the fridge for a day or two. Figs are a well-known laxative and an excellent source of calcium.

DATES

Like figs, dates are one of the oldest cultivated fruits, possibly dating back as far as 50,000 BC. Fresh dates are sweet and soft and make a good natural sweetener: purée the cooked fruit, then add to cake or bread mixtures, or simply mix into natural yogurt to make a quick dessert. Dates should be plump and glossy. Medjool dates from Egypt and California have a wrinkly skin, but most other varieties are smooth. They can be stored in the fridge for up to a week. Dates are high in vitamin C and a good source of potassium and soluble fiber.

Fresh dates

Dried Vine Fruits

Currants, raisins, and golden raisins are the most popular dried fruits. Traditionally, these vine fruits are used for fruit cakes and breads, but currants and raisins are also good in non-sweet dishes. In Indian and North African cookery they are frequently used for their sweetness. Figs and dates are also popular—chopped or puréed—as an ingredient in cakes, fruit breads and pastries.

It takes about 4–5 pounds of fresh grapes to produce 1 pound of raisins or currants, while 3 pounds of fresh figs and dates produce just 1 pound of dried fruit. Although high in natural sugars, which can damage teeth if eaten to excess, dried fruit is a concentrated source of nutrients, including iron, potassium, calcium, phosphorus, vitamin C, beta carotene, and some B vitamins.

Tropical Fruit

This exotic collection of fruits ranges from the familiar bananas and pineapples to the more unusual papayas and passion fruit. The diversity in colors, shapes, and flavors is sure to excite the tastebuds.

PINEAPPLES

These distinctive-looking fruits have a sweet, exceedingly juicy, and golden flesh. Unlike most other fruits, pineapples do not ripen after picking, although leaving a slightly unripe fruit for a few days at room temperature may reduce its acidity.

Buying and Storing: Choose pineapples that have fresh green spiky leaves, are heavy for their size, and are slightly soft to the touch. Store in the fridge when ripe.

Other Tropical Fruit

Kiwi fruit, which is also known as the Chinese gooseberry, has a brown, downy skin and vivid green flesh that is peppered with tiny black seeds. It is extremely rich in vitamin C.

Passionfruit is a dark purple, wrinkly, egg-shaped fruit, which hides a pulpy, golden flesh with edible black seeds. Cut in half and scoop out the inside with a spoon. Passionfruit is rich in vitamins A and C.

Mangoes

Health Benefits: Pineapple contains an antibacterial enzyme called bromelain, which has anti-inflammatory properties and should help arthritis sufferers. It also aids digestion.

PAPAYA

Also known as pawpaw, these pear-shaped fruits come from South America. When ripe, the green skin turns a speckled yellow, and the pulp is a glorious orange-pink color. The numerous edible, small black seeds taste peppery when dried. Peel off the skin using a sharp knife or a vegetable peeler before enjoying the creamy flesh, which has a lovely perfumed aroma and sweet flavor. Ripe papaya is best eaten raw, while unripe green fruit can be used in cooking.

Health Benefits: Papaya contains an enzyme called papain, which aids the digestion,

although levels of this enzyme diminish with ripening. Skin, hair, and nails all benefit from the generous amounts of vitamin C and beta carotene found in papaya. Iron, potassium, and calcium are also present.

MANGO

The skin of these luscious, fragrant fruits can range in color from green to yellow, orange, or red. Their shape varies tremendously, too. An entirely green skin is a sign of an unripe fruit, although in Asia, these are often used in salads. Ripe fruit should yield to gentle pressure and, when cut, it should reveal a juicy, orange flesh. Preparing a mango can be awkward (see opposite). Serve sliced, or purée and use as a base for ice creams and sorbets.

Health Benefits: Rich in vitamin C and beta carotene, mangoes are also reputed to cleanse the blood.

Large and baby pineapples

Preparing Mango

Mangoes can be awkward to prepare because they have a large, flat pit that is slightly off-center. The method below produces cubed fruit. Alternatively, the mango can be peeled with a vegetable peeler and sliced around the central pit.

1 Hold the fruit with one hand and cut vertically down one side of the pit. Repeat on the opposite side. Cut away any remaining flesh around the pit.

2 Taking the two large slices, and using a sharp knife, cut the flesh into a criss-cross pattern down to the skin. Holding the mango skin side down, press it inside out, then cut the mango cubes off from the skin.

COOK'S TIP

To ripen fruit, place it in a paper bag with an already ripened fruit and leave at room temperature or in a warm place.

Papaya

BANANAS

A concentrated bundle of energy, bananas are also full of valuable nutrients. The soft and creamy flesh can be blended into smooth, sweet drinks, mashed and mixed with yogurt, or the fruits can be baked and grilled whole. Bananas also make an ideal weaning food for babies, as they rarely cause an allergic reaction.

Health Benefits: Bananas are rich in dietary fiber, vitamins, and minerals, especially potassium, which is important for the functioning of cells, nerves, and muscles, and can relieve high blood pressure. Ripe bananas soothe the stomach and are believed to strengthen the stomach lining against acid and ulcers. Their high starch content makes them a good source of sustained energy, and they are also an effective laxative. Bananas are rich in the amino acid tryptophan, which is known to lift the spirits and aid sleep.

Buying and Storing: When buying, look for fruit that is heavy for its size. Mangoes and papayas should yield to gentle pressure. Avoid overly soft or bruised fruit, or those with any hard spots. Fully ripe mangoes and papayas are best kept in the fridge. If you wish to buy ripe bananas, choose yellow (or red) fruit that are patched with brown. Bananas with patches of green can be ripened at room temperature. Don't buy completely green bananas, as these rarely ripen properly. Store bananas at cool room temperature.

Sweet, red-skinned bananas and the more familiar large and small yellow-skinned varieties

Vegetables

Vegetables offer an infinite number of culinary possibilities to the cook. The choice is immense and the growing demand for organic produce has meant that pesticide-free vegetables are now increasingly available. Vegetables are an essential component of a healthy diet and have countless nutritional benefits. They are at their best when freshly picked.

Roots and Tubers

Vegetables such as carrots, rutabagas, parsnips and potatoes, are comforting and nourishing food, and it is not surprising that they should be popular in the winter. Their sweet, dense flesh provides sustained energy, valuable fiber, vitamins, and minerals.

Fresh carrots with their green, feathery tops

CARROTS

The best carrots are not restricted to the cold winter months. Summer welcomes the slender sweet new crop, often sold with their green, feathery tops. (These are best removed after buying, as they rob the root of moisture and nutrients.) Buy organic carrots, if you can, because high pesticide residues have been found in nonorganic ones. As an added bonus, organic carrots do not need peeling.

Look for firm, smooth carrots—the smaller they are, the sweeter they are. Carrots should be prepared just before use to preserve their valuable nutrients. They are delicious raw, and can be steamed, stir-fried, roasted, or puréed.

Health Benefits: A single carrot will supply enough vitamin A for an entire day and is reputed to cut the risk of lung cancer by half, even among ex-smokers. According to one American doctor, eating an extra carrot a day could prevent 20,000 lung cancer deaths each year in the United States. This may be due to the high level of the antioxidant beta carotene that carrots contain. Beta carotene may also reduce the risk of prostate cancer in men.

Brightly Colored Vegetables

Ensure there is color in your diet. Beta carotene is just one of the carotenoids found in green, yellow, orange, and red vegetables (as well as fruit). Most carotenoids are antioxidants, which slow down or prevent cell damage from free radical oxidation in the body. Vitamins C and E are other carotenoids, along with bioflavonoids. These help to enhance the immune system, which protects us against viral and bacterial infections and boosts the body's ability to fight cancer and heart disease.

Beet

BEET

Deep, ruby-red in color, beet adds a vibrant hue and flavor to all sorts of dishes. It is often pickled in vinegar, but is much better roasted, as this emphasizes its sweet earthy flavor. Raw beet can be grated into salads or used to make relishes. It can also be added to risottos or made into delicious soups. If cooking beet whole, wash carefully, taking care not to damage the skin or the nutrients and color will leach out. Trim the stalks to about 1 inch above the root. Small beets are sweeter and more tender than larger ones.

Health Benefits: Beet has long been considered medicinally beneficial and is recommended as a general tonic. It can be used to help disorders of the blood, including anemia, it is an effective detoxifier, and, because of its high fiber content, is recommended to relieve constipation. Beet contains calcium, iron, and vitamins A and C—all at their highest levels when it is eaten raw.

CELERY ROOT

This knobby root is closely related to celery, which explains its flavor—a cross between aniseed, celery, and parsley. Similar in size to a small rutabaga, it has ivory flesh and is one of the few root vegetables that must be peeled before use. When grated and eaten raw in salads, celery root has a crunchy texture. It can also be steamed, baked in gratins, or combined with potatoes and mashed with butter or margarine and grainy mustard. It can also be used in soups and broths.

Health Benefits: Like celery, celery root is a diuretic. It also contains vitamin C, calcium, iron, potassium, and fiber.

Rutabaga contains antioxidants and other compounds that may help to prevent cancer

RUTABAGA

The globe-shaped rutabaga has pale orange flesh with a delicate sweet flavor. Trim off the thick peel, then treat in the same way as other root vegetables: grate raw into salads; dice and cook in casseroles and soups; or steam, then mash and serve as an accompaniment.

Health Benefits: Rutabagas are part of the cruciferous vegetable family, and contain compounds that are believed to have antioxidant and cancer-fighting properties. They also contain vitamins A and C.

PARSNIP

This vegetable has a sweet, creamy flavor and is delicious roasted, puréed, or steamed. Parsnips are best purchased after the first frost of the year, as the cold converts their starches into sugar, enhancing their sweetness. Scrub before use and peel only if tough. Avoid large roots, which can be woody.

Health Benefits: Parsnips are effective detoxifiers and are believed to fight some cancers. They contain vitamins C and E, iron, folic acid, and potassium.

Celery root

32 •

TURNIPS

This humble root vegetable has many
health-giving qualities, and small turnips
with their green tops intact are especially
nutritious. Their
crisp, ivory
flesh, which is
enclosed in
white, green, and
pink-tinged skin, has a
pleasant, slightly peppery
flavor, the intensity of which
depends on their size and the time of
harvesting. Small turnips can be eaten raw.
Alternatively, steam, bake, or use in
casseroles and soups.

Health Benefits: This cruciferous
vegetable is said to halt the onset of
certain cancers, particularly rectal cancer.
It is also a digestive and maintains bowel
regularity. The green tops are rich in
beta carotene and vitamin C.

POTATOES

There are thousands of potato
varieties, and many lend themselves to
particular cooking methods. Small
potatoes, such as Pink Fir Apple
and Charlotte, and new
potatoes, such as Jersey Royals, are
best steamed. They have a waxy texture,
which retains its shape after cooking,
making them ideal for salads. Main-crop
potatoes, such as Red Pontiac and Maris
Piper, are more suited to roasting, baking,
or mashing, and can be used for

Baby turnips

french fries. Discard any potatoes with
green patches as these indicate the
presence of toxic alkaloids called solanines.
  Vitamins and minerals are stored in, or
just below, the skin, so it is best to use

potatoes unpeeled. New
potatoes and special
salad potatoes need
only be scrubbed.
Potatoes are not in
themselves fattening—it is
added ingredients, such as cheese,
and the cooking method that
can add on the
calories. Steam
rather than boil, and
bake instead of frying to
retain valuable nutrients and
to keep fat levels down.

Health Benefits: Potatoes are high in
complex carbohydrates and include both
protein and fiber. They provide plenty of
sustained energy, plus vitamins B and C,
iron, and potassium.

JERUSALEM ARTICHOKES

This small knobby tuber has a sweet,
nutty flavor. Peeling can be awkward,
although scrubbing and trimming is
usually sufficient. Store in the fridge for
up to one week. Use in the same
way as potatoes—they make
good creamy soups.

Health Benefits: Jerusalem artichokes
contain vitamin C and fiber.

COOK'S TIP

*To prevent root vegetables and tubers
discoloring after preparation, immerse them
in a bowl of acidulated water—water
containing 1 tablespoon lemon juice.
Don't soak them for long because
water-soluble vitamins will
leach out into the water.*

Potatoes

RADISHES

There are several types of this peppery-flavored vegetable, which is a member of the cruciferous family. The round ruby-red variety is most familiar; the longer, white-tipped type has a milder taste. Daikon or mooli radishes are white and very long; they can weigh up to several pounds. Radishes can be used to add both flavor and a crunchy texture to salads and stir-fries. A renowned diuretic, radishes also contain vitamin C.

Jerusalem artichokes

Radishes

Daikon

HORSERADISH

This pungent root is never eaten as a vegetable. It is usually grated and mixed with cream or oil and vinegar, and served as a culinary accompaniment. It is effective in clearing blocked sinuses.

Buying and Storing: Seek out bright, firm, unwrinkled root vegetables and tubers, which do not have soft patches. When possible, choose organically grown produce, and buy in small quantities to ensure freshness. Store root vegetables in a cool, dark place.

Horseradish

Basic Vegetable Stock

Stock is easy to make at home and is a healthier option than store-bought stock. It can be stored in the fridge for up to four days. Alternatively, it can be prepared in large quantities and frozen.

INGREDIENTS

1 tablespoon olive oil

1 potato, chopped (½ cup)

1 carrot, chopped (2 tablespoons)

1 onion, chopped (⅔ cup)

1 celery stalk, chopped (1 cup)

2 garlic cloves, peeled

1 sprig of thyme

1 bay leaf

a few stalks of parsley

2½ cups water

salt and freshly ground black pepper

1 Heat the oil in a large saucepan. Add the vegetables and cook, covered, for 10 minutes, or until softened, stirring occasionally. Stir in the garlic and herbs.

2 Pour the water into the pan, bring to a boil, and simmer, partially covered, for 40 minutes. Strain, season with salt and pepper, and use as required.

Top Tuber

There are two types of the nutritious sweet potato; one has cream flesh, the other orange. The orange-fleshed variety has a higher nutritional content because it is richer in the antioxidant beta carotene, but both types contain potassium, fiber, and vitamin C, as well as providing plenty of sustained energy. Sweet potatoes are thought to cleanse and detoxify the body and can boost poor circulation. When cooked, the cream-fleshed variety has a drier texture. Both are suited to mashing, baking, and roasting.

Brassicas and Green Leafy Vegetables

This large group of vegetables boasts an extraordinary number of health-giving properties. Brassicas range from the crinkly-leafed Savoy cabbage to the small, walnut-sized Brussels sprout. Green, leafy vegetables include spinach, collard greens, and Swiss chard.

BROCCOLI

This nutritious vegetable should be a regular part of everyone's diet. Two types are commonly available: purple-sprouting, which has fine, leafy stems and a delicate head, and calabrese, the more substantial variety with a tightly budded top and thick stalk. Choose broccoli that has bright, compact flowerets. Yellowing flowerets, a limp woody stalk, and a pungent smell are an indication of overmaturity. Trim stalks before cooking, although young stems can be eaten, too. Serve raw in salads or with a dip. If you cook broccoli, steam or

Broccoli

stir-fry it to preserve the nutrients and keep the cooking time brief to retain the vivid green color and crisp texture.

Health Benefits: Broccoli is a member of the cruciferous family, which studies have shown to be particularly effective in fighting cancer of the lung, colon, and breast. Sulfur compounds, found in broccoli, stimulate the production of anti-cancer enzymes, which prevent the growth of tumors and inhibit the spread of existing tumors. Raw broccoli contains almost as much calcium as milk, and also provides plenty of B vitamins, vitamin C, iron, folate, zinc, and potassium.

CAULIFLOWER

The cream-colored compact flowerets should be encased in large, bright green leaves. To get the most nutrients from a cauliflower, eat it raw, or bake, or steam lightly. Cauliflower has a mild flavor and is delicious tossed in a vinaigrette dressing or combined with tomatoes and spices. Overcooked cauliflower is unpleasant and has a sulfurous taste.

Health Benefits: This creamy-white cruciferous vegetable has many cancer-fighting qualities, particularly against cancer of the lung and colon. Cauliflower also contains vitamin C, folate, and potassium and is used in natural medicine as a blood purifier and laxative.

Preparing Broccoli

Trim the stalks from broccoli and divide it into flowerets before using. The stems of young broccoli can be sliced and eaten, too.

Cauliflower

The Crucial Role of Phytochemicals

Cruciferous vegetables, such as broccoli, cabbages, kohlrabi, radishes, cauliflowers, Brussels sprouts, watercress, turnips, kale, bok choy, mustard greens, collard greens, chard, and rutabaga, are all packed with phytochemicals, which numerous studies have shown can fight off various forms of cancer. These are a group of compounds found in varying amounts in all fruit and vegetables, but particularly in cruciferous vegetables.

Phytochemicals are believed to provide an anticarcinogenic cocktail, which plays a crucial role in fighting disease by stimulating the body's enzyme defences against cancer-inducing substances. Eating cruciferous vegetables on a regular basis—

Kohlrabi (below left); Chinese cabbages and cavalo nero (below); and cauliflower, Savoy cabbage, Brussels sprouts, spinach leaves, broccoli, and kale (right) are packed with phytochemicals

at least three or four times a week— may halve the risk of lung, colon, breast, ovary, uterus, or prostate cancer.

According to a senior British researcher, phytochemicals may be found to be as important as antioxidants in fighting disease. Phytochemicals include compounds such as carotenoids, selenium, fiber, isothiocyanates, indoles, phenols, tocopherols, bioflavonoids, and protease inhibitors.

CABBAGE

Frequently overcooked, cabbage is best eaten raw, or cooked until only just tender. There are several different varieties: Savoy cabbage has substantial, crinkly leaves with a strong flavor and is perfect for stuffing; firm white and red cabbages can be shredded and used raw in salads (as can Chinese cabbage); while bok choy is best cooked in stir-fries or with noodles.

Health Benefits: Studies show that eating cabbage more than once a week can reduce the likelihood of colon cancer in men by about 65 percent. Raw or juiced cabbage is particularly potent and has antiviral and antibacterial qualities as well. Cabbage is thought to speed up the metabolism of estrogen in women and this may provide protection against cancer of the breast and uterus. It is a valuable source of vitamins C and E, beta carotene, folate, potassium, thiamine, and fiber.

Cabbage

Mixed Cabbage Stir-fry

Stir-frying is a quick method of cooking
that retains much of the vitamins and
minerals that are lost during boiling.
When cabbage is cooked in this way, it
remains crisp and keeps its vivid color.

INGREDIENTS

1 tablespoon peanut or
   sunflower oil
1 large garlic clove, chopped
1-inch piece fresh ginger root, chopped
5 cups mixed cabbage leaves, such as
   Savoy, white, cavalo nero, or
   bok choy, finely shredded
2 teaspoons soy sauce
1 teaspoon clear honey
1 teaspoon toasted sesame oil (optional)
1 tablespoon sesame seeds, toasted

1 Heat the oil in a wok or large, deep
skillet, then sauté the garlic and ginger
for about 30 seconds. Add the cabbage
and stir-fry for 3–5 minutes, until tender,
tossing frequently.

2 Stir in the soy sauce, honey, and
sesame oil and cook for 1 minute.
Sprinkle with sesame seeds and serve.

Health Benefits: Brussels sprouts contain
significant amounts of vitamin C, folate,
iron, potassium, and some B vitamins.
Because they are a cruciferous vegetable,
sprouts can help prevent certain cancers.

Buying and Storing: Seek out bright, firm
brassicas with no signs of discoloration or
wilting. Avoid cauliflowers that have black
spots or yellowing leaves. Ensure cabbages
have a heavy heart. Chinese cabbages
should be compact and heavy for their
size with bright, undamaged leaves.
Choose small Brussels sprouts with tightly
packed leaves. Store cabbages and
Brussels sprouts in a cool, dark place for
up to a week. Broccoli and cauliflower
should be stored in the fridge for only
2–3 days. Chinese cabbage and bok choy
don't keep well. Store in the salad drawer
of the fridge and use within 1–2 days.

Preparing Brussels Sprouts

1 Peel away any outer damaged leaves
from the Brussels sprouts.

2 Before cooking, cut a cross in the
base of each sprout, so that they
cook quickly and evenly.

BRUSSELS SPROUTS

These are basically miniature cabbages
that grow on a long tough stalk. They have
a strong nutty flavor. The best are small
with tightly packed leaves—avoid any
that are very large or turning yellow or
brown. Sprouts are sweeter when
picked after the first frost.
They are best cooked
very lightly, so either
steam or, better still,
stir-fry to keep their green
color and crisp texture, as well
as to retain the vitamins and minerals.

Brussels sprouts

GREEN LEAFY VEGETABLES

For years we have been told to eat up our greens and now we are beginning to learn why. Research into their health benefits has indicated that eating dark green leafy vegetables, such as spinach, collard greens, chard, and kale, on a regular basis may protect us against certain forms of cancer.

Kale

Spinach

This dark, green leaf is a superb source of cancer-fighting antioxidants. It contains about four times more beta carotene than broccoli. It is also rich in fiber, which can help to lower harmful levels of LDL cholesterol in the body, reducing the risk of heart disease and stroke. Spinach does contain iron, but not in such rich supply as was once thought. Furthermore, spinach contains oxalic acid, which inhibits the absorption of iron and calcium in the body. However, eating spinach with a vitamin-C-rich food will increase absorption. Spinach also contains vitamins C and B_6, calcium, potassium, folate, thiamine, and zinc. Nutritionally, it is most beneficial when eaten raw in a salad, but it is also good lightly steamed, then chopped and added to omelets.

Spinach

Swiss chard

A member of the beet family, Swiss chard has large, dark leaves and thick, white, orange or red edible ribs. It can be used in the same way as spinach, or the stems may be cooked on their own. Swiss chard is rich in vitamins and minerals, although, like spinach, it contains oxalic acid.

Spinach beet

Similar to Swiss chard, this form of the beet plant is grown only for its leaves, which have a sweet, mild flavor. Use in the same way as spinach.

Collard greens

These leafy, dark green young cabbages are full of flavor. Rich in vitamin C and beta carotene, collard greens contain indoles, one of the phytochemicals that are thought to protect the body against breast and ovarian cancer.

Buying and Storing: Green, leafy vegetables do not keep well—up to 2 or 3 days at most. Eat soon after purchase to enjoy them at their best. Look for brightly colored, undamaged leaves that are not showing any signs of yellowing or wilting. Wash the leaves thoroughly in cold water before use and eat them raw, or cook lightly, either by steaming or stir-frying to preserve their valuable nutrients.

Spinach beet

Mixed Swiss chard

Collard greens

Pumpkins and Squashes

Widely popular in the United States, Africa, Australia, and the Caribbean, pumpkins and squashes come in a tremendous range of shapes, colors, and sizes. Squashes are broadly divided into summer and winter types: cucumbers and zucchini fall into the summer category, while pumpkins, butternut, and acorn squashes are winter varieties.

Pumpkins

WINTER SQUASHES

These have tough skins, dense, fibrous flesh, and large seeds. Most winter squashes can be used in both sweet and non-sweet dishes.

Acorn squash

This small to medium-size squash has an attractive, fluted shape and looks rather like a large acorn—hence its name. The orange flesh has a sweet flavor and slightly dry texture, and the skin color ranges from golden to dark green. Its large seed cavity is perfect for stuffing.

Butternut squash

A large, pear-shaped squash with a golden brown skin and vibrant orange flesh. The skin is inedible and should be removed along with the seeds. Roast, bake, mash, or use in soups or casseroles. The flesh has a rich, sweet, creamy flavor when cooked and makes a good substitute for pumpkin.

Pumpkins

These are native to America and they are synonymous with Thanksgiving. Small pumpkins have sweeter, less fibrous flesh than the larger ones, which are perhaps best kept for making into lanterns. Deep orange in color, pumpkin can be used in both sweet and non-sweet dishes, such as pies, soups, casseroles, soufflés, and even ice cream. Avoid boiling pumpkin as it can become waterlogged and soggy. The seeds are edible and highly nutritious.

SUMMER SQUASHES

Picked when still young, these have thin edible skins and tender, edible seeds. Their delicate flesh cooks quickly.

Pattypan squash

These pretty, baby squashes resemble mini flying saucers. They are similar in taste to a zucchini and are best steamed or roasted. They may be yellow or bright green, and although they can be expensive to buy, there is no waste. Pattypan squash will keep for a only few days in the fridge.

Zucchini

The most widely available summer squash, zucchini have the most flavor when they are small and young; the flavor diminishes when they are old and the seeds toughen. Young zucchini have a glossy, bright green skin and creamy colored flesh. Extremely versatile, they can be steamed, grated raw into salads, stir-fried, griddled, puréed, or used in soups and casseroles. Their deep yellow flowers are a delicacy and are perfect for stuffing.

Butternut, acorn, and pattypan squashes

Zucchini

39

Squash

The grown-up equivalent of zucchini, this squash has a pleasant, mild flavor and is best baked either plain or with a stuffing. Spices, chile peppers, and tomatoes are particularly good flavorings.

Cucumbers

Probably cultivated as long ago as 10,000 BC, cucumbers were popular vegetables with the Greeks and the Romans. The long, thin, smooth-skinned variety is most familiar. Their refreshing, mild flavor makes cucumbers perfect to use raw in salads or thinly sliced as a sandwich filling. However, they can also be pickled and cooked in other ways, such as steaming, baking, or stir-frying.

Buying and Storing: Look for firm, bright, unblemished vegetables that are heavy for their size. Winter squash can be kept for several weeks if stored whole in a cool, dry place. Once cut, they should be kept in the fridge and eaten as soon as possible. Summer squash don't keep as well and should be stored in the fridge for only a few days.

Health Benefits: Summer squash are effective diuretics and their potassium content means they are beneficial for those with high blood pressure. Pumpkins are also a diuretic, as well as a laxative, and like other winter squashes, contain high amounts of vitamin E, beta carotene, and potassium. Beta carotene and vitamin E are antioxidants and are believed to reduce the risk of certain cancers. Summer squashes contain less beta carotene. Because of their high water content, all squash are low in calories.

Peeling Pumpkin

1 Cut the pumpkin in half using a large sharp knife and scoop out the seeds and fibrous parts with a spoon.

2 Cut the pumpkin into large chunks, then cut the skin using a sharp knife.

Roasting Squash

1 Preheat the oven to 400°F. Cut the squash in half, scoop out the seeds and place the squash cut side down on an oiled cookie sheet.

2 Bake for 30 minutes, or until the flesh is soft. Serve in the skin, or remove the flesh and mash with butter.

Cucumber

Shoot Vegetables

This highly prized collection of vegetables, each honored with a distinctive flavor and appearance, ranges from the aristocratic asparagus to the flowerbud-like globe artichoke.

FENNEL

Florence fennel is closely related to the herb and spice of the same name. The short, fat bulbs have a similar texture to celery and are topped with edible feathery fronds. Fennel has a mild aniseed flavor, which is most potent when eaten raw. Cooking tempers the flavor, giving it a delicious sweetness. When using fennel raw, slice it thinly or chop roughly and add to salads. Alternatively, slice or cut into wedges and steam, or brush with olive oil and roast, or cook on a griddle. Fennel is at its best when it is fresh and should be eaten as soon as possible. It can, however, be stored in the fridge for a few days.

Asparagus

Health Benefits:

Fennel is a diuretic and also has a calming and toning effect on the stomach. It is low in calories and contains beta carotene and folate, which is known to reduce the risk of spina bifida in the unborn child. Fennel seeds are good for the digestion.

ASPARAGUS

Highly valued since Roman times, asparagus has been cultivated commercially since the 17th century. There are two main types: white asparagus is picked just before it sprouts above the surface of the soil; while green-tipped asparagus is cut above the ground and develops its color when it comes into contact with sunlight. It takes three years to grow a crop from seed, which may account for its expense. Before use, scrape the lower half of the stalk with a vegetable peeler, then trim off the woody end.

Briefly poach whole spears in a skillet containing a little boiling salted water, or tie the spears in a bundle and boil upright in an asparagus boiler or tall pan. Asparagus is delicious served with melted butter, or dipped into mayonnaise or vinaigrette. It can also be roasted in a little olive oil and served with a sprinkling of sea salt to bring out the flavor.

Health Benefits: Asparagus was used as a medicine long before it was eaten as a food. It is a rich source of vitamin C and also has diuretic and laxative properties. It contains the antioxidant glutathione, which has been found to prevent the formation of cataracts in the eyes.

White and red Belgian endive

Preparing Fennel

Cut the fennel bulb in half lengthwise, then either cut into quarters or slice thinly.

Fennel

BELGIAN ENDIVE

This shoot has long, tightly packed leaves. There are two kinds, white and red. Red Belgian endive has a more pronounced flavor, while the white variety has crisper leaves. The crisp texture and slightly bitter flavor means that it is particularly good in salads. It can also be steamed or braised, although in cooking, sadly, the red-leaf

Health Benefits: Globe artichokes are a good source of vitamins A and C, fiber, iron, calcium, and potassium. In natural medicine, they are used to treat high blood pressure.

Buying and Storing: When buying shoot vegetables, always choose the freshest-looking specimens. Asparagus spears should have firm stalks. Belgian endive should be neither withered nor brown at the edges—the best white variety is sold wrapped in blue paper to keep out the sunlight and to prevent it from turning green and bitter. Fennel bulbs should be crisp and white with fresh fronds. Globe artichokes should have tightly closed, stiff leaves and the stalk attached.

Store all these vegetables in the salad drawer of the fridge. Asparagus, Belgian endive, and fennel should be eaten within 2–3 days; globe artichokes will keep for up to a week; and celery will keep for about 2 weeks if very fresh when purchased.

Left: Globe artichokes, celery, and Belgian endive

variety fades to brown. Before use, remove the outer leaves and wash thoroughly, then trim the base. In natural medicine, Belgian endive is sometimes used to treat gout and rheumatism. It is also a digestive and liver stimulant, and good for a spring tonic.

CELERY

Like asparagus, celery was once grown primarily for medicinal reasons. Serve raw, steam, or braise. Celery leaves have a tangy taste and are also useful for adding flavor to stocks. Low in calories, but rich in vitamin C and potassium, celery is a recognized diuretic and sedative.

GLOBE ARTICHOKES

Once cooked, the purple-tinged leaves of globe artichokes have an exquisite flavor. They are eaten with the fingers by dipping each leaf into garlic butter or vinaigrette dressing, then drawing each leaf through the teeth and eating the fleshy part. The heart is then dipped in the butter or dressing and eaten with a knife and fork.

Preparing Globe Artichokes

1 Hold the top of the artichoke firmly and using a sharp knife, remove the stalk, and trim the base so that the artichoke sits flat.

2 Using a sharp knife or scissors, trim off and discard the tops of the leaves and cut off the pointed top.

3 Cook the artichokes in a pan of boiling, lightly salted water for 35–45 minutes, until a leaf can be pulled out easily. Drain upside down.

4 Pull out the central leaves, then scoop out the hairy choke with a teaspoon, and discard.

Vegetable Fruits

By cultivation and use, tomatoes, eggplant, and bell peppers are all vegetables, but botanically they are classified as fruit. Part of the nightshade family, they have only relatively recently become appreciated for their health-giving qualities.

Tomatoes

TOMATOES

There are dozens of varieties to choose from, which vary in color, shape, and size. The egg-shaped plum tomato is perfect for cooking as it has a rich flavor and a high proportion of flesh to seeds—but it must be used when fully ripe. Too often, store-bought tomatoes are bland and tasteless because they have been picked too young. Vine-ripened and cherry tomatoes are sweet and juicy and are good in salads or uncooked sauces. Large beefsteak tomatoes have a good flavor and are also excellent for salads. Sun-dried tomatoes add a rich intensity to sauces, soups, and stews. Genetically engineered tomatoes are now sold in some countries, but at present they are only sold canned as a concentrated paste. Check the label before buying.

EGGPLANT

The dark-purple, glossy-skinned eggplant is the most familiar variety, although it was the small, ivory-white egg-shaped variety that originally inspired the name eggplant. There is also the bright-green pea eggplant that is used in Asian cooking, and a pale-purple Chinese eggplant. Known in the Middle East as "poor man's caviar," eggplants give substance and flavor to spicy casseroles and tomato-based bakes, and are delicious roasted, griddled, and

Eggplant

Buying and Storing:
Look for deep-red fruit with a firm, yielding flesh. Tomatoes that are grown and sold locally will have the best flavor. To improve the flavor of a slightly hard tomato, leave it to ripen fully at room temperature. Avoid refrigeration because this stops the ripening process and adversely affects the taste and texture of the tomato.

Health Benefits: Vine-ripened tomatoes are higher in vitamin C than those picked when they are still green. They are also a good source of vitamin E, beta carotene, magnesium, calcium, and phosphorus. Tomatoes contain the bioflavonoid lycopene, which is believed to prevent some forms of cancer by reducing the harmful effects of free radicals.

Peeling and Seeding Tomatoes

Tomato seeds can give sauces a bitter flavor. Removing them and the tomato skins will also give a smoother end result.

2 Lift out the tomatoes with a slotted spoon, rinse in cold water to cool slightly, and peel away the skin.

1 Immerse the tomatoes in boiling water and leave for about 30 seconds—the base of each tomato can be slashed to make peeling easier.

3 Cut the tomatoes in half, then scoop out the seeds, and remove the hard core. Dice or roughly chop the flesh according to the recipe.

puréed into garlic-laden dips. It is not essential to salt eggplant to remove any bitterness; however, this method prevents the absorption of excessive amounts of oil during frying.

Buying and Storing: When buying, look for small to medium-size eggplant, which have sweet, tender flesh. Large specimens with a shriveled skin are overmature and are likely to be bitter and tough. Store in the fridge for up to two weeks.

Health Benefits: An excellent source of vitamin C, eggplant also contain moderate amounts of iron and potassium, calcium, and B vitamins. They also contain bioflavonoids, which help prevent strokes and reduce the risk of certain cancers.

Bird's eye chile peppers

Serrano chile peppers

Habanero chile peppers

Red and green chile peppers

Jalapeño chile peppers

CHILE PEPPERS

Native to America, this member of the capsicum family now forms an important part of many cuisines, including Indian, Thai, Mexican, South American, and African. There are more than 200 different types of chile pepper, ranging from the long, narrow Anaheim to the lantern-shaped and incredibly hot Habanero. Red chile peppers are not necessarily hotter than green ones—but they will probably have ripened for longer in the sun. The heat in chiles comes from capsaicin, a compound found in the seeds, white membranes, and, to a lesser extent, in the flesh. Chile peppers range in potency from the mild and flavorful to the blisteringly hot, Dried chiles tend to be hotter than fresh. Smaller chiles, such as Bird's eye chiles, contain more seeds and membrane, which makes them more potent than larger ones. It is

important to wash your hands after using chile peppers as they can irritate the skin and eyes.

Buying and Storing: Choose unwrinkled firm chile peppers and store in the fridge.

Health Benefits: Chile peppers contain more vitamin C than an orange and are a good source of beta carotene, folate, potassium, and vitamin E. They stimulate the release of endorphins, the body's "feel-good" chemicals and are a powerful decongestant, helping to open sinuses and air passages. Chiles stimulate the body and improve circulation, but if eaten to excess, can irritate the stomach.

Chile Boost

For an instant uplift, sprinkle some dried crushed chile on your food. The chile will stimulate the release of endorphins, which are the body's "feel-good" chemicals.

Handle chile peppers with care, as they can irritate the skin and eyes. Wear gloves when preparing chiles.

Avocados

Although avocados have a high fat content, the fat is monounsaturated, and is thought to lower blood cholesterol levels in the body. Avocados also contain valuable amounts of vitamins C and E, and iron, potassium, and manganese. They are said to improve the condition of the skin and hair.

Once cut, avocados should be brushed with lemon or lime juice to prevent discoloration. They are usually eaten raw. Avocado halves can be dressed with a vinaigrette, or filled with sour cream sprinkled with cayenne pepper, or hummus. Slices or chunks of avocado are delicious in salads. In Mexico, where they grow in abundance, there are countless dishes based on avocados. Guacamole is the best known, but they are also used in soups and stews.

BELL PEPPERS

Like chiles, bell peppers are also members of the capsicum family. They range in color from green through to orange, yellow, red, and even purple. Green bell peppers are fully developed, but not completely ripe, which can make them difficult to digest. They have refreshing, juicy flesh with a crisp texture. Other colors of bell peppers are more mature, have sweeter flesh, and are more digestible than less ripe green ones.

Roasting or charbroiling bell peppers will enhance their sweetness. They can also be stuffed, sliced into salads, or steamed.

Buying and Storing: Choose bell peppers that are firm and glossy with unblemished skin, and store in the fridge for up to a week.

Health Benefits: Bell peppers contain significant amounts of vitamin C, as well as beta carotene, some B complex vitamins, calcium, phosphorus, and iron.

Peeling Bell Peppers

1 Roast the bell peppers under a hot broiler for 12–15 minutes, turning regularly until the skin chars and blisters.

2 Alternatively, place on a cookie sheet and roast in an oven preheated to 400°F for 20–30 minutes, until blackened and blistered.

3 Put the bell peppers in a plastic bag and let cool—the steam will encourage the skin to peel away easily.

4 Peel away the skin, then slice in half. Remove the core and scrape out any remaining seeds. Slice or chop according to the recipe.

Bell peppers

Pods and Seeds

While most of these vegetables are delicious eaten fresh, many of them—peas, corn, and fava and green beans, for example—can also be bought frozen. High in nutritional value, these popular vegetables can be enjoyed all year. Other types of pea include snow peas and sugar snap peas, which can be eaten whole—pod and all.

Above, clockwise from top left: String beans, fine green beans, snow peas, fava beans, peas, and (center) baby corn cobs

PEAS

Peas are one of the few vegetables that taste just as good when frozen. Because freezing takes place soon after picking, frozen peas often have a higher nutritional value than fresh. Another advantage is that frozen peas are readily available all year round. Peas in the pod have a restricted availability and their taste diminishes if not absolutely fresh, because their sugars rapidly turn to starch. However, when they are at the peak of freshness, peas are delicious and have a delicate, sweet flavor. Pop them from the pod and serve raw in salads or steam lightly. Delicious cooked with fresh mint, peas also make satisfying purées and soups, and can be added to risottos and other rice dishes.

FAVA BEANS

When young and fresh these beans are a delight to eat. Tiny pods can be eaten whole; simply trim them, and then slice.

Usually, however, you will need to shell the beans, as their skins can become tough. Elderly beans are often better skinned after they are cooked. Fava beans can be eaten raw or lightly cooked.

GREEN BEANS

Green, string, and thin beans are eaten pod and all. They should be bright green and crisp-textured. Simply trim and lightly cook or steam them. Serve green beans hot, or let cool slightly

Corn

and serve them as a warm salad with a squeeze of fresh lemon juice or with a vinaigrette dressing.

Buying and Storing: Look for bright green, smooth, plump pods and keep in the fridge for no more than a day or two.

Health Benefits: Peas and beans are good sources of protein and fiber. They are rich in vitamin C, iron, thiamine, folate, phosphorous, and potassium.

CORN

Corn cobs are best eaten soon after picking, before their natural sugars start to convert into starch when the flavor fades and the kernels toughen. Remove the green outer leaves and cook whole or slice off the kernels with a sharp knife. Baby corn cobs can be eaten raw, and are good in stir-fries.

Buying and Storing: Look for very fresh, plump kernels that show no signs of discoloration, wrinkling, or drying and eat soon after purchase. If you do not intend to eat them immediately, store in the coolest part of the fridge.

Health Benefits: Corn is a good carbohydrate food and is rich in vitamins A, B, and C, and fiber. It contains useful amounts of iron, magnesium, phosphorus, and potassium. Baby corn is high in folate, which is essential for maintaining the immune system.

The Onion Family

Onions and garlic are highly prized as two of the oldest remedies known to man. Both contain allicin, which has been found to stimulate the body's antioxidant mechanisms, raising levels of beneficial HDL cholesterol and combating the formation of clogged arteries. Additionally, these vegetables are indispensable in cooking. The wide variety of onions can be enjoyed raw or cooked and, with garlic, add flavor to a huge range of non-sweet dishes.

ONIONS

Every cuisine in the world includes onions in one form or another. They are an essential flavoring, offering a range of taste sensations, from the sweet and juicy red onion and powerfully pungent white onion to the light and fresh scallion. Pearl onions and shallots are the babies of the family. Tiny pearl onions are generally pickled, while shallots are good roasted with their skins on, when they develop a caramel sweetness. Yellow onions are most common and are highly versatile.

Buying and Storing: When buying, choose onions that have dry, papery skins and are heavy for their size. They will keep for 1–2 months stored in a cool, dark place.

Health Benefits: Numerous studies highlight the healing powers of the onion. It is a rich source of quercetin, a potent antioxidant that has been linked to preventing stomach cancer. Eating half a raw onion a day is said to thin the blood, lower the LDL cholesterol, and raise beneficial HDL cholesterol by about 30 percent. This means that cholesterol is transported away from the arteries, reducing the risk of heart disease and stroke. Whether raw or cooked, onions are antibacterial and antiviral, helping to fight off colds, relieve bronchial congestion, asthma, and hay fever. They are also good for people with arthritis, rheumatism, and gout.

GARLIC

For centuries, this wonder food has been the focus of much attention, and is praised for its medicinal powers, which range from curing toothache to warding off evil demons. The flavor of garlic is milder when whole or sliced; crushing or chopping releases the oils, making the flavor stronger. Slow-cooking also tames the pungency of garlic, although it still affects the breath.

Onion and Garlic Cures
Onions have been used in all kinds of traditional remedies.
• In the past, babies were often given a teaspoonful of onion infusion for colic: a slice of onion would be infused in hot water for a few minutes, and the water let cool.
• Raw garlic can relieve symptoms of food poisoning. It has been shown to kill bacteria, even those that are resistant to antibiotics. Some people say that garlic keeps old age at bay.

Buying and Storing: Most garlic is semi-dried to prolong its shelf life, yet the cloves should still be moist and juicy. Young garlic, which is available in early summer, has a long green stem and soft white bulb. It has a fresher flavor than semi-dried garlic, but can be used in the same ways. Pungency varies, but the general rule when buying garlic is: the smaller the bulb, the more potent the flavor. If stored in a cool, dry place and not in

Above: Scallions, red onions, shallots, and white onions

Leeks

the fridge,
garlic will keep for up to about eight weeks. If the air is damp, garlic will sprout, and if it is too warm, the cloves will eventually turn to gray powder.

Health Benefits: Garlic tops the American National Cancer Institute's list as a potential cancer-preventive food. Although the antiviral, antibacterial, and antifungal qualities of garlic are most potent when eaten raw, cooking does not inhibit its anti-cancer, blood-thinning, and decongestant capabilities. Studies show that eating 2–3 garlic cloves a day reduces by half the probability of a subsequent heart attack in previous heart patients. Garlic has also been found to lower blood cholesterol, reduce high blood pressure, boost the immune system, act as an anti-inflammatory, lift mood, and have a calming effect. It should be eaten on a daily basis.

Below: Garlic bulbs and cloves

LEEKS

Like onions and garlic, leeks have a very long history. They grow in all sorts of climates and are known to have been eaten and enjoyed by the ancient Egyptians, Greeks, and Romans. Leeks are very versatile, having their own distinct, subtle flavor. They are less pungent than onions, but are still therapeutically beneficial. Excellent in soups and casseroles, leeks can also be used as a pie filling or in tarts, or simply steamed and served hot with a light, creamy sauce, or cooled slightly and dressed with a vinaigrette. They are also delicious sliced or shredded and then stir-fried with a little garlic and ginger.

Commercially grown leeks are usually about 10 inches long, but you may occasionally see baby leeks, which are very tender and are best steamed.

Buying and Storing: Choose firm leeks with bright green leaves. Avoid those without their roots, as they deteriorate more quickly. Leeks will keep for up to a week in the salad drawer of the fridge.

Health Benefits: Leeks have the same active constituents as onions, but in smaller amounts. They also contain vitamins C and E, iron, folate, and potassium.

Cleaning Leeks

Leeks need meticulous cleaning to remove any grit and earth that may hide between the layers of leaves. This method will ensure that the very last tiny piece of grit will be washed away.

1 Cut off the root, then trim the top of the green part and discard. Remove any tough or damaged outer leaves.

2 Slash the top green part of the leek into quarters and rinse the leek well under cold running water, separating the layers to remove any hidden dirt. Slice or leave whole, depending on the recipe.

Mushrooms

Thanks to their rich earthiness, mushrooms add substance and flavor to all sorts of dishes. There are more than 2,000 edible varieties, but only a tiny proportion are readily available. These fall into three camps: common cultivated mushrooms, like the button; wild varieties that are now cultivated, such as the shiitake; and the truly wild types that have escaped cultivation, such as the morel.

Cultivated mushrooms come in a wide variety of sizes

BUTTON, CAP, AND FLAT MUSHROOMS

The most common cultivated variety of mushrooms, these are actually one type in various stages of maturity. The button mushroom is the youngest and has, as its name suggests, a tight, white, button-like cap. It has a mild flavor and can be eaten raw in salads. Cap mushrooms are slightly more mature and larger in size, while the flat mushroom is the largest and has dark, open gills. Flat mushrooms have the most prominent flavor and are good broiled or baked on their own, or stuffed.

Below: Field blewitts

Chanterelles

Below: Crimini (left) and portabello mushrooms

CRIMINI MUSHROOMS

The brown-capped crimini mushroom looks similar to the cultivated button, but has a more assertive, nutty flavor.

PORTABELLO MUSHROOMS

Similar in appearance to the cultivated flat mushroom, the portabello is simply a large crimini mushroom. It has a rich flavor and a meaty texture and is good broiled.

FIELD MUSHROOMS

This wild mushroom has an intense, rich flavor. It is ideal for broiling and stuffing.

CHANTERELLES

This egg-yolk-colored mushroom has a pretty, funnel shape and a fragrant but delicate flavor. Also known as the girolle, it is sold fresh in season and dried all year round. If buying fresh, eat as soon as possible and wipe rather than wash, as the skin is very porous. Sauté, bake, or add to sauces.

FIELD BLEWITTS

This wild mushroom is now widely cultivated in caves in Britain, Switzerland, and France. It has a thick, lilac-blue stem,

Dried and fresh cèpes

which is topped with
a smooth, whitish cap.
When cooked, field blewitts have a
dense, meaty texture.

CEPES

This wild mushroom, which is also known
by its Italian name, porcini, has a tender,
meaty texture and woody flavor. Dried
cèpes are used for their rich flavor.

MORELS

Slightly sweet-flavored mushrooms with a
distinctive, pointed, honeycomb cap and a
hollow stalk, morels can be awkward to
clean. They are costly to buy fresh because
they have a short season, but can be
bought dried.

ENOKI MUSHROOMS

These Japanese mushrooms have a pretty,
tiny cap on an elegant, long stalk. Sold in
clusters, enoki have a
slightly lemony flavor.
Use in stir-fries or eat
raw in salads.

Morels

Dried Mushrooms

These are a useful stand-by and have
a rich, intense flavor. To reconstitute
dried mushrooms, soak them in
boiling water for 20–30 minutes,
depending on the variety and size of
mushroom, until tender. Drain and
rinse well to remove any grit
and dirt. Dried mushrooms
often require longer cooking
than fresh ones.

Shiitake Mushrooms

In Asia, these mushrooms are
recommended for a long and healthy
life, and research has shown that they
have antiviral properties that stimulate
the immune system. Shiitake
mushrooms may help lower blood
cholesterol, even curtailing some of
the side effects of saturated fat. They
have also been found to halt the later
stages of certain cancers.

OYSTER MUSHROOMS

Now cultivated and widely available,
oyster mushrooms have an attractive
shell-shaped cap and thick stalk. They are
usually pale, gray-brown, although yellow
and pink varieties are also available.

Buying and Storing: Buy mushrooms that
smell and look fresh. Avoid ones with
damp, slimy patches and any that are
discolored. Store in a
paper bag in the
fridge for up
to 4 days.

Health Benefits: Mushrooms do not
contain a wealth of nutrients but they are
a useful source of vitamins B_1 and B_2,
potassium, iron, and niacin.

Cleaning Mushrooms: Before use, wipe
mushrooms with damp paper towels and
trim the stem. Wild mushrooms often
harbor grit and dirt and may need to be
rinsed briefly under cold running water,
but dry thoroughly. Never soak
mushrooms or they will become soggy.
Peeling is not usually necessary.

Oyster mushrooms

Salad Greens

It is only a few years since the most exotic lettuce available was the crisp-textured iceberg. Today, salad greens come in a huge variety of shapes, sizes, colors, and flavors, from bitter-tasting chicory to peppery arugula and red-leaf lollo rosso. Making a mixed leaf salad has never been so easy, or the result so delicious.

Left, clockwise from left: chicory, oak leaf, romaine, butterhead, and iceberg lettuces

LETTUCES

Cultivated for thousands of years, lettuces were probably first eaten as a salad vegetable during Roman times. Nutritionally, lettuce is best eaten raw, but it can be braised, steamed, or made into a soup. Large-leaf varieties can be used to wrap around a filling.

Butterhead lettuce

This soft-leaf lettuce has an unassuming flavor and is good as a sandwich-filler.

Romaine lettuce

Known since Roman times, the romaine lettuce has long, sturdy leaves and a strong flavor. Little gem is a baby version and has firm, densely packed leaves.

Iceberg lettuce

This lettuce has a round, firm head of pale green leaves with a crisp texture. Like the butterhead, it has a mild, slightly bitter flavor and is best used as a garnish. It is reputed to be one of the most highly chemically treated crops, so choose organic iceberg lettuces if you can.

Oak leaf

This attractive lettuce has red-tinged, soft-textured leaves with a slightly bitter flavor. In salads, combine with green lettuces for a contrast of tastes and textures.

Lollo rosso

The pretty, frilly leaves of lollo rosso are green at the base and a deep, fall red around the edge. Its imposing shape means it is best mixed with other leaves if used in a salad, or as a base for roasted vegetables. Lollo biondo is a pale green version.

Chicory

Also known as frisée, chicory has spiky, ragged leaves that are dark green on the outside and fade to an attractive pale yellow-green towards its center. It has a distinctive bitter flavor that is enhanced by a robust dressing.

Radicchio

Mâche

Mâche

Also known as corn salad, this tiny lettuce has a cluster of small, rounded, velvety leaves with a delicate flavor. Serve on its own or mix with other salad greens.

SALAD GREENS

A great variety of different salad greens is now readily available.

Radicchio

A member of the chicory family, radicchio has deep red, tightly packed leaves that have a bitter peppery flavor. It is good in salads and can be sautéed or roasted.

Arugula

Classified as a herb, arugula is a popular addition to salads, or it can be served as a starter with thin shavings of Parmesan cheese. It has a strong, peppery flavor, which is more robust when wild. Lightly steamed arugula has a milder flavor than the raw leaves, but it is equally delicious.

Sorrel

The long pointed leaves of sorrel have a refreshing, sharp flavor that is best when mixed with milder tasting leaves. It contains oxalic acid which, when cooked, inhibits the absorption of iron. Sorrel is an effective diuretic.

Watercress

The hot, peppery flavor of watercress complements milder tasting leaves and is classically combined with fresh orange. It does not keep well and is best used within two days of purchase. Watercress is a member of the cruciferous family and shares its cancer-fighting properties.

Sorrel

Buying and Storing: Salad greens are best when they are very fresh and do not keep well. Avoid leaves that are wilted, discolored, or shriveled. Store in the fridge, unwashed, for between 2 days and 1 week, depending on the variety. As salad greens are routinely sprayed with pesticides, they should be washed thoroughly, but gently, to avoid damaging the leaves, and then dried in a dish towel. Better still, choose organically grown produce.

Health Benefits: Although all types of salad greens are about 90 percent water, they contain useful amounts of vitamins and minerals, particularly folate, iron, and the antioxidants, vitamin C and beta carotene. The outer, darker leaves tend to be more nutritious than the paler leaves in the center. More importantly, like other green, leafy vegetables, their antioxidant content has been found to guard against the risk of many cancers. Salad greens are usually eaten raw, when the nutrients are at their strongest. Lettuce is reputed to have a calming, sedative effect.

Watercress

Herbs

Herbs have been highly prized by natural practitioners for centuries because, in spite of their low nutritional value, they possess many reputed healing qualities. In cooking, herbs can make a significant difference to the flavor and aroma of a dish and they have the ability to enliven the simplest of meals. Fresh herbs can easily be grown at home in the garden, or in a pot, or window box.

Chives and bay leaves

BASIL

This delicate aromatic herb is widely used in Italian and Thai cooking. The leaves bruise easily, so are best used whole or torn, rather than cut with a knife. Basil is said to have a calming effect on the stomach, easing constipation, nausea, and cramps, and aiding digestion.

BAY LEAVES

These dark-green, glossy leaves are best left to dry for a few days before use. They have a robust, spicy flavor and are an essential ingredient in bouquet garni. Studies show that bay has a restorative effect on the digestive system.

CHIVES

A member of the onion family, chives have a milder flavor and are best used as a garnish, snipped over egg or potato dishes, or added to salads or tarts. Like onions, chives are an antiseptic and act as a digestive.

CILANTRO

Warm and spicy, cilantro is popular in Indian and Thai curries, stir-fries, and salads. It looks similar to flat leaf parsley, but its taste is completely different. It is often sold with its root intact. The root has a more intense flavor than the leaves and can be used in curry pastes. Cilantro

Basil

Using Dried Herbs

Although fresh herbs have the best flavor and appearance, dried herbs can be a convenient and useful alternative, especially in the winter months when some fresh herbs are not available.

• A few herbs, such as basil, dill, mint, and parsley do not dry well, losing most of their flavor.

• Oregano, thyme, marjoram, and bay retain their flavor when dried and are useful substitutes for fresh.

• Dried herbs have a more concentrated flavor than fresh, so much less is required—usually a third to a half as much as fresh.

• When using dried herbs in cooking, always allow sufficient time for them to rehydrate and soften.

• Dried herbs do little for uncooked dishes, but are useful for flavoring marinades, and are good in slow-cooked stews and soups.

• When buying dried herbs, they should look bright, not faded. Because light spoils their flavor and shortens shelf-life, store in sealed, airtight jars in a cool, dark place.

Cilantro

marinades and is a good partner for mustard. An attractive herb with delicate, wispy leaves, add to dishes just prior to serving as its mild flavor diminishes with cooking. Dill is a popular herb for settling the stomach and is thought to reduce flatulence. It is also said to be mildly soporific and, in the form of gripe water, is sometimes given to babies to relieve gas and colic.

is an effective digestive, easing indigestion and nausea. It is also said to act as a tonic for the heart.

DILL

The mild, yet distinctive, aniseed flavor of dill goes well with potatoes, zucchini, and cucumber. It makes a good addition to creamy sauces and can be added to a wide variety of egg dishes. It can also be used as a flavoring for dressings and

Dill

Pesto

Freshly made pesto, spooned over warm pasta or spread over bread and topped with a round of goat cheese, makes a perfect quick supper. It is usually made with basil, but other herbs, such as arugula, cilantro, or parsley, can be substituted. The pine nuts can also be replaced with walnuts, cashew nuts or pistachios.

INGREDIENTS

1 cup fresh basil leaves
2 garlic cloves, crushed
1/2 cup pine nuts
1/2 cup olive oil, plus extra
  for drizzling
4 tablespoons freshly grated
  Parmesan cheese
salt and freshly ground black pepper

1 Place the basil, garlic, and pine nuts in a food processor or blender and process until finely chopped.

2 Gradually add the olive oil and then the Parmesan, and blend to a coarse purée. Season to taste. Spoon into a lidded jar, then pour in the extra olive oil to cover. Use at once or store in the fridge.

Freezing Herbs

This is an excellent method of preserving fresh delicate herbs, such as basil, chives, dill, tarragon, cilantro, and parsley. The herbs will lose their fresh appearance and texture when frozen, but are still suitable for use in cooking. They will keep for up to 3 months in the freezer.

• Half-fill ice-cube trays with chopped herbs and top up with water. Freeze, then place the cubes in freezer-bags. The frozen cubes can be added to soups, stews, and stocks, and heated until they melt.

• Place whole sprigs or leaves, or chopped herbs in freezer bags, expel any air and tightly seal.

• Freeze herb sprigs or leaves on trays. When the herbs are frozen, transfer them carefully to freezer-bags, expel any air, seal tightly, and return to the freezer.

• Pack chopped fresh herbs in plastic containers and freeze. Scatter straight into soups and stews.

54 •

Kaffir lime leaves

MINT

The most familiar types are spearmint and peppermint, but there are other distinctly flavored varieties, such as apple, lemon, and pineapple mint, which are worth looking for, and make a refreshing drink when infused in boiling water. Mint is used as a flavoring in a wide variety of dishes, from stuffings to fruit salads. It is a vital ingredient in the Middle Eastern salad, tabbouleh, and is also mixed with unsweetened yogurt to make raita, a soothing accompaniment to hot curries. It is a traditional cure for nausea and indigestion and is also effective in stimulating and cleansing the system.

KAFFIR LIME LEAVES

These attractive glossy, green leaves are commonly used in Asian cuisines, lending a tantalizing citrus aroma and flavor to a wide variety of dishes. They are available fresh from Asian stores, or dried from large supermarkets. The fruit resembles a knobby lime and its rind, which is rich in vitamin C, is used grated in Thai and Indonesian curries. The leaves can be used as a digestive.

MARJORAM

Closely related to oregano, marjoram has a slightly sweeter flavor. It goes well in Mediterranean-style vegetable dishes, such as ratatouille, or in casseroles, and tomato sauces, but should be added at the last minute, as its flavor diminishes when heated. It also makes a good addition to a marinade. Marjoram improves the circulation and relieves stomach pains.

LEMON BALM

This herb makes a refreshing tea and is good in any sweet or non-sweet dish that uses lemon juice. It has antibacterial, antiviral, and antidepressant qualities. The calming and sedative attributes of lemon balm are beneficial for those suffering from stress or nervous exhaustion.

Lemon balm, marjoram, mint, and oregano

OREGANO

This is a wild variety of marjoram, but has a more robust flavor that goes well with tomato-based dishes. Oregano can relieve digestive problems.

PARSLEY

There are two types of parsley: flat leaf and curly. Both taste relatively similar, but the flat leaf variety is preferable in cooked dishes. Parsley is an excellent source of vitamin C, iron, and calcium. Chewing parsley after eating garlic or onions can neutralize the smell and freshen breath.

Parsley

ROSEMARY

Wonderfully aromatic, rosemary is traditionally used in meat dishes, but it can also add a smoky flavor to hearty bean and vegetable dishes. Rosemary has a reputation for invigorating the circulation, and for relieving headaches and respiratory problems.

SAGE

The leaves of this herb, which may be silver-gray or purple, have a potent aroma and only a small amount is needed. Sage is commonly added to meat dishes but, if used discreetly, it is delicious with beans, cheese, lentils, and in stuffings. Sage was used medicinally before it found its way into the kitchen and is regarded as a tonic for the stomach, kidneys, and liver.

Rosemary and s[...]

Thyme

THYME

This robustly flavored aromatic herb is good in tomato-based recipes, and with roasted vegetables, lentils, and beans. It is also an essential ingredient in a bouquet garni. Thyme aids the digestion of fatty foods and works as a powerful antiseptic.

TARRAGON

A popular herb in French cooking, tarragon has an affinity with all egg- and cheese-based dishes. The short, slender-leaf French variety has a warm, aniseed flavor and is considered to be superior to Russian tarragon. Tarragon has diuretic properties and can relieve indigestion. Infused in a herbal tisane, it can soothe sore throats and promote restful sleep.

Buying and Storing: Fresh herbs are widely available, sold loose, in packets, or growing in pots. The packets do not keep for long and should be stored in the fridge. Place stems of fresh herbs in a half-filled jar of water and cover with a plastic bag. Sealed with a rubber band, the herbs should keep in the fridge for a week. Growing herbs should be kept on a sunny windowsill. If watered regularly, and not cut too often, they will keep for months.

Drying Herbs

Bay, rosemary, sage, thyme, and marjoram all dry well, but other more delicate herbs, such as basil, cilantro, and parsley are better used fresh. Pick herbs before they flower, preferably on a sunny morning after the dew has dried. Avoid washing them—instead brush with a pastry brush or wipe with a dry cloth. Tie the herbs in bunches and hang them upside down in a warm, dark place. The leaves should be dry and crisp after a week. Leave the herbs in bundles or strip the leaves from the stems and store in airtight jars.

Making Herbal Infusions

Infusions, or tisanes, are made from steeping fresh herbs in boiling water. They can be used as a medicinal gargle or refreshing healthy drink. Peppermint tea is an excellent remedy for indigestion or irritable bowel syndrome and is best drunk after a meal.

To make peppermint tea: pour boiling water over fresh peppermint leaves. Cover the bowl and leave to stand for about 10 minutes, then strain the liquid into a cup and drink.

Tarragon

Sprouted Seeds, Pulses, and Grains

Sprouts are quite remarkable in terms of nutritional content. Once the seed (or pulse, or grain) has germinated, the nutritional value rises dramatically. There are almost 30 percent more B vitamins and 60 percent more vitamin C in the sprout than in the seed, pulse, or grain. Supermarkets and health food stores sell a variety of sprouts, but to grow them at home all you need is a jar, some cheesecloth, and a rubber band.

MUNG BEAN SPROUTS

The most commonly available bean sprouts, these are popular in Chinese and Asian cooking, where they are used in soups, salads, and stir-fries. They are fairly large, with a crunchy texture and a delicate flavor.

ALFALFA SPROUTS

These tiny, wispy white sprouts have a mild, nutty flavor. They are best eaten raw to retain their crunchy texture.

Mung bean sprouts

WHEAT BERRY SPROUTS

Sprouts grown from wheat berries have a crunchy texture and sweet flavor, and are excellent in breads. If they are left to grow, the sprouts will become wheatgrass, a powerful detoxifier that is is usually made into a juice.

Alfalfa sprouts

GARBANZO BEAN SPROUTS

Sprouts grown from garbanzos have a nutty flavor and add substance to dishes.

LENTIL SPROUTS

These sprouts have a slightly spicy, peppery flavor and thin, white shoots. Use only whole lentils: split ones won't sprout.

ADZUKI BEAN SPROUTS

These fine wispy sprouts have a sweet nutty taste. Use in salads and stir-fries.

Sprouting Seeds, Pulses, and Grains

Larger pulses, such as garbanzo beans, take longer to sprout than small beans, but they are all easy to grow and are usually ready to eat in three or four days. Store sprouts in a covered container in the fridge for 2–3 days.

2 The next day, pour away the water through the cheesecloth and fill the jar with water again. Shake gently, then turn the jar upside down, and drain thoroughly. Leave the jar on its side in a warm place, away from direct sunlight.

I Wash 3 tablespoons seeds, pulses, or grains thoroughly in water, then place in a large jar. Fill the jar with lukewarm water, cover with a piece of cheesecloth, and fasten securely with a rubber band. Let stand in a warm place overnight.

3 Rinse the seeds, pulses or grains three times a day, until they have grown to the desired size. Make sure they are drained thoroughly to prevent them turning rancid. Remove from the jar, rinse well, and remove any ungerminated beans.

> **How to Use Bean Sprouts**
> • Sprouted pulses and beans have a denser more fibrous texture, while sprouts grown from seeds are lighter. Use a mixture of the three for a variety of tastes and textures.
> • Mung bean sprouts are often used in Asian food, particularly stir-fries, and require little cooking.
> • Alfalfa sprouts are good as part of a sandwich filling as well as in salads. They are not suited to cooking.
> • Sprouted grains are good in breads, adding a pleasant crunchy texture. Knead them in after the first rising, before shaping the loaf.
> • Use garbanzo bean and lentil sprouts in casseroles and bakes.

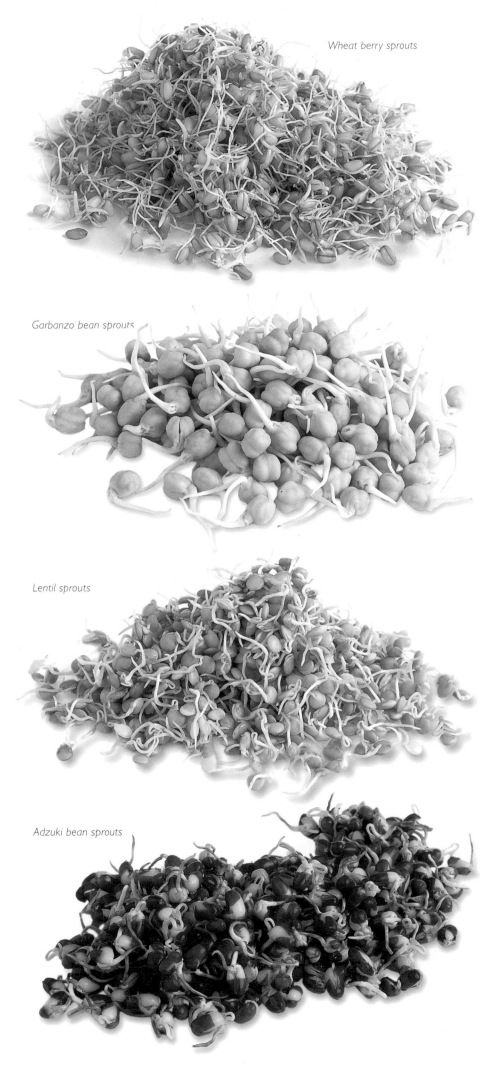

Wheat berry sprouts

Garbanzo bean sprouts

Lentil sprouts

Adzuki bean sprouts

Buying and Storing: If you can, choose fresh, crisp sprouts with the seed or bean still attached. Avoid any that are slimy or musty-looking. Sprouts are best eaten on the day they are bought, but if fresh they will keep, wrapped in a plastic bag in the fridge, for 2–3 days. Rinse and pat dry before use.

Health Benefits: Sprouted seeds, pulses, and grains supply rich amounts of protein, B complex vitamins, and vitamins C and E, potassium, and phosphorus which, due to the sprouting process, are in an easily digestible form. In Chinese medicine, sprouts are highly valued for their ability to cleanse and rejuvenate the system.

Tips on Sprouting
• Use whole seeds and beans, as split ones will not germinate.
• Regular rinsing with fresh water and draining is essential when sprouting to prevent the beans from turning rancid and moldy.
• Cover the sprouting jar with cheesecloth to allow air to circulate and to let water in and out.
• After two or three days, the jar can be placed in sunlight to encourage the green pigment chlorophyll and increase the sprout's magnesium and fiber content.
• Soybean and garbanzo bean sprouts need to be rinsed four times a day.
• Keen sprouters may wish to invest in a special sprouting container that comes with draining trays.

Sprouting container

Sea Vegetables

The West has only relatively recently acknowledged the extraordinary variety and remarkable health benefits of sea vegetables, which have been an essential part of the Asian diet for centuries. Sea vegetables are highly versatile and can be used as the main component of a dish, to add texture and substance, or as a seasoning. Some sea vegetables, such as wakame, hijiki, and kombu (or kelp), can be used in soups, stews, and stir-fries, while others, such as agar-agar and carrageen, are used as a setting agent in molds, mousses, and cheesecakes.

Laver

Toasting Nori

Nori can be toasted over a burner until it is very crisp. The sheets can then be crumbled between the fingers and used as a garnish for soups, salads, or stir-fries. Take care when you are toasting the nori sheets that you do not scorch them—or your fingers.

1 Hold a sheet of nori with a pair of tongs about 2 inches above a warm burner for about 1 minute, moving it around so it toasts evenly and turns bright green and crisp.

2 Leave the nori sheet to cool for a few moments, then crumble. Sprinkle over salad, or use to garnish soups or stir-fries.

NORI

This useful sea vegetable has a delicate texture and mild flavor. It is sold in thin purple-black sheets, which turn a pretty, translucent green when toasted or cooked. It is one of the few sea vegetables that does not require soaking. Nori is processed by being chopped, flattened, and dried on frames, like paper. In Japanese cooking, the sheets are used to wrap delicate, small packages of vinegared rice and vegetables that are eaten as sushi. Once toasted and crisp, nori is crumbled and used as a garnish.

LAVER

A relation of nori, which grows outside Japan, laver is commonly found around the shores of Britain. Unlike Japanese nori, it is not cultivated. Laver is used in traditional regional cooking—particularly in Wales, Scotland, and Ireland. It is cooked into a thick dark purée, which can be spread on hot toast or mixed with oatmeal to make the Welsh delicacy, laverbread. It can also be added to sauces and stuffings. Available ready-cooked in cans from health food stores, laver has a stronger flavor than nori and a higher concentration of vitamins and minerals.

Nori sheets and flakes

Arame

ARAME

Sold in delicate, black strips, arame has a mild, slightly sweet flavor. If you haven't tried sea vegetables before, it is a good one to start with. It needs to be soaked before using in stir-fries or salads, but if using in moist or slow-cooked dishes, such as noodles and soups, it can be added straight from the packet. Arame has been used to treat female disorders and is recommended for high blood pressure. It is rich in iodine, calcium, and iron.

Preparing Arame

Soaking and cooking times vary depending on how the arame is to be used.

1 Rinse the arame in a strainer under cold, running water, then place in a bowl and cover with cold water. Leave to soak for 5 minutes—it should double in volume. Drain and place in a saucepan.

2 Add fresh water and bring to a boil. Simmer for 20 minutes until tender.

WAKAME

This sea vegetable is often confused with its relative, kombu, because it looks very similar until it is soaked, when it changes color from brown to a delicate green. Wakame has a mild flavor and is one of the most versatile sea vegetables. Soak briefly and use in salads and soups, or toast, crumble, and use as a condiment. It is rich in calcium and vitamins B and C.

KOMBU

Known as kelp in the West, kombu is now farmed. It is a brown sea vegetable and is usually sold dried in strips, although in Japan it is available in a multitude of forms. It has a very strong flavor and is used in slowly cooked dishes, soups, and stocks—it is an essential ingredient in the Japanese stock, dashi. A small strip of kombu added to beans while they are cooking will soften them and increase their digestibility, as well as their nutritional value. Kombu is richer in iodine than other sea vegetables, and also contains calcium, potassium, and iron.

Kombu or kelp

Wakame

Hijiki

Dulse is rich in several minerals—potassium, iodine, phosphorus, iron, and manganese.

HIJIKI

This sea vegetable looks similar to arame, but is thicker and has a slightly stronger flavor. Once soaked, hijiki can be sautéed or added to soups and salads, but it does require longer cooking than most sea vegetables. It expands considerably during soaking, so only a small amount is needed. It is particularly rich in calcium and iron.

DULSE

A purple-red sea vegetable, dulse has flat fronds, which have a chewy texture and spicy flavor when cooked. For hundreds of years, dulse was popular in North America and northern Europe and was traded on both sides of the Atlantic. It needs to be soaked until soft before adding to salads, noodle dishes, soups, and vegetable dishes. It can also be toasted and crumbled to make a nourishing garnish.

AGAR-AGAR

The vegetarian equivalent to the animal-derived gelatin, agar-agar can be used as a setting agent in both sweet and non-sweet dishes. Known as kanten in Japan, it can be bought as flakes or strands, both of which need to be dissolved in water before use. Agar-agar has a neutral taste and its gelling abilities vary according to the other ingredients in a dish, so you may need to experiment, if substituting it for gelatin in a recipe, to achieve the best results. It is more effective than gelatin, so only a small amount is needed. It is said to be an effective laxative.

Using Agar-agar to Make Jelly

Agar-agar can be used in place of gelatin; 1/4oz agar-agar flakes will set about 2 1/2 cups liquid.

1 Place 1/4oz agar-agar flakes in a saucepan with 1 1/4 cups cold water; let soak for 15 minutes.

2 Bring to a boil, then simmer for a few minutes, until the flakes dissolve. Stir in 1 1/4 cups fresh orange juice. Pour into a mold and set aside to cool, then chill in the fridge until set.

Dulse

Carrageen (left) and agar-agar flakes

CARRAGEEN

This fern-like seaweed, also known as Irish moss, is found along the Atlantic coasts of America and Europe. Like agar-agar, it has gelling properties, but produces a softer set, making it useful for molds and mousses and as a thickener in soups and stews. It is used for treating colds and bronchial problems as well as digestive disorders.

Buying and Storing: Sea vegetables are usually sold dried and will keep for months. Once the packet is opened, transfer the sea vegetables to an airtight jar. Fresh sea vegetables may be stored in the fridge, but will remain fresh for only 1–2 days. Rinse well before use.

Health Benefits: The health benefits of sea vegetables have been recognized for centuries and range from improving the luster of hair and clarity of the skin to reducing cholesterol levels in the body. Sea vegetables are particularly rich in the antioxidant beta carotene. They contain some of the B complex vitamins, and significant amounts of the major minerals, such as calcium, magnesium, potassium, phosphorus, and iron, as well as useful amounts of trace elements, such as selenium, zinc, and iodine.

The rich mineral content of sea vegetables benefits the nervous system, helping to reduce stress. It also boosts the immune system, aiding the metabolism,

while the iodine content prevents goiter and helps thyroid function. Research shows that alginic acid found in some seaweeds, notably kombu, arame, hijiki, and wakame, binds with heavy metals, such as cadmium, lead, mercury, and radium, in our intestines and helps to eliminate them.

COOK'S TIP

Some sea vegetables simply need washing and soaking for a few minutes before serving or adding to dishes; others require prolonged soaking and cooking before they are tender enough to eat. Most expand considerably after soaking, so only a small amount is required.

Rolled Sushi with Mixed Filling

INGREDIENTS
1½ cups sushi rice
4 sheets nori seaweed, for rolling
soy sauce and gari (ginger pickles), to serve

FOR THE MIXED VINEGAR
8 teaspoons rice vinegar
4½ teaspoons sugar
⅔ teaspoon sea salt

FOR THE FILLING
4 large dried shiitake mushrooms
7½ teaspoons soy sauce
1 tablespoon each of mirin, sake or dry white wine, and sugar
1 small carrot, quartered lengthwise
½ cucumber, quartered lengthwise, seeds removed

Makes 32 pieces

1 Cook the rice in salted boiling water, then drain. Meanwhile, heat the ingredients for the mixed vinegar. Let the vinegar cool, then add to the hot cooked rice. Stir well with a spatula, fanning the rice constantly—this gives the rice an attractive glaze. Cover with a damp cloth and let cool. Do not put in the fridge, as this will make the rice harden.

2 To make the filling, soak the dried shiitake mushrooms in scant 1 cup water for 30 minutes; drain, reserving the soaking water, and remove their stems. Pour the reserved soaking water into a saucepan and add the remaining filling ingredients (except the cucumber), then simmer for 4–5 minutes. Remove the carrot and set aside. Continue cooking until all the liquid has evaporated, then thinly slice the shiitake mushrooms and set aside for the filling.

3 Place a bamboo mat (makisu) on a chopping board. Lay a sheet of nori, shiny side down, on the mat.

4 Spread a quarter of the prepared, dressed rice over the nori, using your fingers to press it down evenly. Leave a ½-inch space at the top and bottom. Place a quarter of each of the filling ingredients—the sliced mushrooms, carrot, and cucumber—across the middle of the layer of rice.

5 Carefully hold the nearest edge of the nori and the mat, then roll up the nori using the mat as a guide to make a neat tube of rice with the filling ingredients in the middle. Roll the rice tightly to ensure that the grains stick together and to keep the filling in place. Roll the sushi off the mat and make three more rolls in the same way.

6 Using a wet knife, cut each roll into eight pieces and stand them upright on a platter. Wipe the blade and rinse it under cold water between cuts to prevent the rice from sticking. Serve soy sauce and gari with the sushi.

Cereal Grains

Grains have been cultivated throughout the world for centuries. The seeds of cereal grasses, they are packed with concentrated goodness and are an important source of complex carbohydrates, protein, vitamins, and minerals. The most popular types of grain, such as wheat, rice, oats, barley, and corn or maize, come in various forms, from whole grains to flours. Inexpensive and readily available, grains are incredibly versatile and should form a major part of our diet.

Wheat

Wheat is the largest and most important grain crop in the world and has been cultivated since 7,000 BC.

The wheat kernel comprises three parts: bran, germ, and endosperm. Wheat bran is the outer husk, while wheat germ is the nutritious seed from which the plant grows. Sprouted wheat is an excellent food, highly recommended in cancer prevention diets. The endosperm, the inner part of the kernel, is full of starch and protein and forms the basis of wheat flour. In addition to flour, wheat comes in various other forms.

Wholewheat berries

Wheatgrass

WHEAT BERRIES

These are whole wheat grains with the husks removed and they can be bought in health food stores. Wheat berries may be used to add a sweet, nutty flavor and chewy texture to breads, soups, and stews, or can be combined with rice or other grains. Wheat berries must be soaked overnight, then cooked in boiling salted water until tender. If they are left to germinate, the berries sprout into wheatgrass, a powerful detoxifier and cleanser (see below).

WHEAT BRAN

Wheat bran is the outer husk of the wheat kernel and is a by-product of white flour production. It is very high in soluble dietary fiber, which makes it nature's most effective laxative. Wheat bran makes a healthy addition to bread doughs, breakfast cereals, cakes, muffins, and cookies, and it can also be used to add substance to stews and bakes.

Wheatgrass—a Natural Healer

Grown from the wholewheat grain, wheatgrass has been recognized for centuries for its general healing qualities. When juiced, it is a powerful detoxifier and cleanser and is a rich source of B vitamins and vitamins A, C, and E, as well as all the known minerals. Its vibrant green color comes from chlorophyl (known as "nature's healer"), which works directly on the liver to eliminate harmful toxins. It is also reputed to have anti-aging capabilities.

Once it is juiced, wheatgrass must be consumed within 15 minutes, preferably on an empty stomach. Some people may experience nausea or dizziness when drinking the juice for the first time, but this will soon disappear.

Wheat germ

Wheat flakes

Bulgur wheat

way as wheat berries (although it cooks in less time), or as an alternative to rice and other grains. When cooked, it has a slightly sticky texture and pleasant crunchiness. Serve it as an accompaniment, or use in salads and pilaffs.

BULGUR WHEAT

Unlike cracked wheat, this grain is made from cooked wheat berries, which have the bran removed, and are then dried and crushed. This light, nutty grain is simply soaked in water for 20 minutes, then drained—some manufacturers specify cold water, but boiling water produces a softer grain. It can also be cooked in boiling water until tender. Bulgur wheat is the main ingredient in the Middle Eastern salad, tabbouleh, where it is combined with chopped parsley, mint, tomatoes, cucumber, and onion, and dressed with lemon juice and olive oil.

Cooking Wheat Berries

Wheat berries make a delicious addition to salads, and they can also be used to add texture to breads and stews.

1 Place the wheat berries in a bowl and cover with cold water. Soak overnight, then rinse thoroughly and drain.

2 Place the wheat berries in a pan with water. Bring to a boil, then cover, and simmer for 1–2 hours, until tender, replenishing with water when necessary.

WHEAT FLAKES

Steamed and softened berries that have been rolled and pressed are known as wheat flakes or rolled wheat. They are best used on their own or mixed with other flaked grains in porridge, as a base for muesli, or to add nutrients and substance to breads and cakes.

WHEAT GERM

The nutritious heart of the whole wheat berry, wheat germ is a rich source of protein, vitamins B and E, and iron. It is used in much the same way as wheat bran and lends a pleasant, nutty flavor to breakfast cereals and porridge. It is available toasted or untoasted. Store wheat germ in an airtight container in the fridge as it can become rancid if kept at room temperature.

CRACKED WHEAT

This is made from crushed wheat berries and retains all the nutrients of wholewheat. Often confused with bulgur wheat, cracked wheat can be used in the same

SEMOLINA

Made from the endosperm of durum wheat, semolina can be used to make a hot milk pudding or it can be added to cakes, cookies, and breads to give them a pleasant grainy texture.

COUSCOUS

Although this looks like a grain, couscous is a form of pasta made by steaming and drying cracked durum wheat. Couscous is popular in North Africa, where it forms the basis of a national dish of the same name. Individual grains are moistened by hand, passed through a strainer, and then steamed in a couscousière, suspended over a bubbling vegetable stew, until light

Semolina

Cooking Couscous

Traditionally, the preparation of couscous is a time-consuming business, requiring lengthy steaming. The couscous found in most stores nowadays, however, is precooked, which cuts the preparation time drastically.

I Place the couscous in a large bowl, add enough boiling water to cover and leave for 10 minutes, or until all the water has been absorbed. Separate the grains, season and mix in a pat of butter.

2 Alternatively, moisten the grains and place in a cheesecloth-lined steamer. Steam for 15 minutes, or until the grains are tender and fluffy.

and fluffy. Nowadays, the couscous that is generally available is the quick-cooking variety, which simply needs soaking, although it can also be steamed or baked. Couscous has a fairly bland flavor, which makes it a good foil for spicy dishes.

WHEAT FLOUR

This is ground from the whole grain and may be whole wheat or white, depending on the degree of processing. Stone-ground flour is high in a protein called gluten, which makes it ideal for bread making, while soft flour is lower in gluten but higher in starch and is better for light

cakes and pastries. Durum wheat flour comes from one of the hardest varieties of wheat and is used to make pasta. Most commercial white flour is a combination of soft and hard wheat, which produces an all-purpose flour.

Because the refining process robs many commercial flours of most of their nutrients, the lost vitamins and minerals are synthetically replaced. When buying flour, look for brands that are unbleached and organically produced, as these have fewer chemical additives. Nutritionally, stone-ground whole wheat flour is the best buy because it is largely unprocessed

Couscous

Wheat flour (left) and malted brown flour, which contains flour from malted wheat grains. Stone-ground versions are available

Celiac Disease

This is caused by an allergy to gluten, a substance found in bread, cakes, pastries, and cereals, It is estimated that millions of people suffer from the disease, many without diagnosis. Symptoms may include anemia, weight loss, fatigue, depression, and diarrhea. Wheat, rye, barley, and oats are the main culprits and sufferers are usually advised to remove these completely from their diet. Rice, soy, buckwheat, quinoa, millet, and corn are gluten-free substitutes.

and retains all the valuable nutrients. It produces slightly heavier breads, cakes, and pastries than white flour, but can be combined with white flour to make lighter versions, although, of course, the nutritional value will not be so high.

SEITAN

Used as a meat replacement, seitan is made from wheat gluten and has a firm, chewy texture. It can be found in the chiller cabinet of health food stores. Seitan has a neutral flavor that benefits from marinating. Slice or cut into chunks and stir-fry, or add to stews and pasta sauces during the last few minutes of cooking time. Seitan does not need to be cooked for long, just heated through.

Buying and Storing: Buy wheat-based foods from stores with a high turnover of stock. Wheat berries can be kept for around 6 months, but whole wheat flour should be used within 3 months, as its oils turn rancid. Always decant grains into airtight containers and store in a cool, dark place. Wheat germ deteriorates very quickly at room temperature and should be stored in an airtight container in the fridge for no more than a month.

Health Benefits: Wheat is most nutritious when it is unprocessed and in its whole form. (When milled into white flour, wheat loses a staggering 80 percent of its nutrients.) Wheat is an excellent source of dietary fiber, the B vitamins, and vitamin E, as well as iron, selenium, and zinc. Fiber is the most discussed virtue of whole wheat and most of this is concentrated in the bran. Eating one or more spoonfuls of bran a day is recommended to relieve constipation. Numerous studies show fiber to be effective in inhibiting colon and rectal cancer, varicose veins, hemorrhoids, and obesity. Phytoestrogens found in wholegrains may also ward off breast cancer. On the negative side, wheat is also a well-known allergen and triggers celiac disease, a gluten intolerance.

Seitan

Rice

Throughout Asia, a meal is considered incomplete without rice. It is a staple food for over half the world's population, and almost every culture has its own repertoire of rice dishes, ranging from risottos to pilaffs. What's more, this valuable food provides a good source of vitamins and minerals, as well as a steady supply of energy.

White and brown long grain rice

Jasmine fragrant rice

LONG GRAIN RICE

The most widely used type of rice is long grain rice, where the grain is five times as long as it is wide. Long grain brown rice has had its outer husk removed, leaving the bran and germ intact, which gives it a chewy nutty flavor. It takes longer to cook than white rice, but contains more fiber, vitamins, and minerals. Long grain white rice has had its husk, bran, and germ removed, taking most of the nutrients with them, and leaving a bland-flavored rice that is light and fluffy when cooked. It is often whitened with chalk, talc, or other preservatives, so rinsing is essential. Easy-cook long grain white rice, sometimes called parboiled or converted rice, has been steamed under pressure. This process hardens the grain and makes it difficult to overcook, and some nutrients are transferred from the bran and germ into the kernel during this process. Easy-cook brown rice cooks more quickly than normal brown rice.

JASMINE RICE

This rice has a soft, sticky texture and a delicious, mildly perfumed flavor—which accounts for its other name, fragrant rice. It is a long grain rice that is widely used in Thai cooking, where its delicate flavor tempers strongly spiced food.

Cooking Long Grain Brown Rice

There are many methods and opinions on how to cook rice. The absorption method is one of the simplest and retains valuable nutrients, which would otherwise be lost in cooking water that is drained away.

Different types of rice have different powers of absorption, however the general rule of thumb for long grain rice is to use double the quantity of water to rice. For example, use 1 cup of rice to 2 cups of water. 1 cup long grain rice is sufficient for about four people as an accompanying side dish.

1 Rinse the rice in a strainer under cold, running water. Place in a heavy-based saucepan and add the measured cold water. Bring to a boil, uncovered, then reduce the heat, and stir the rice. Add salt to taste, if you wish.

2 Cover the pan with a tight-fitting lid. Simmer for 25–35 minutes, without removing the lid, until the water is absorbed and the rice tender. Remove from the heat and let stand, covered, for 5 minutes before serving.

Red rice

Wild rice

RED RICE

This rice comes from the Camargue in France and has a distinctive chewy texture and a nutty flavor. It is an unusually hard grain, which although it takes about an hour to cook, retains its shape. Cooking intensifies its red color, making it a distinctive addition to salads and stuffings.

WILD RICE

This is not a true rice, but an aquatic grass grown in North America. It has dramatic, long, slender brown-black grains that have a nutty flavor and chewy texture. It takes longer to cook than most types of rice—35–60 minutes, depending on whether you like it chewy or tender—but you can reduce the cooking time by soaking it in water overnight. Wild rice is extremely nutritious. It contains all eight essential amino acids and is particularly rich in lysine. It is a good source of fiber, low in calories, and gluten free. Use in stuffings, serve plain, or mix with other rices in pilaffs and rice salads.

BASMATI RICE

This is a slender, long grain rice, which is grown in the foothills of the Himalayas. It is aged for a year after harvest, giving it a characteristic light, fluffy texture and aromatic flavor. Its name means "fragrant."

Both white and brown types of basmati rice are available. Brown basmati contains more nutrients, and has a slightly nuttier flavor than the white variety. Widely used in Indian cooking, basmati rice has a cooling effect on hot and spicy curries. It is also excellent for biryanis and for rice salads, when you want very light, fluffy separate grains.

White and brown basmati rice

Quick Ways to Flavor Rice

• Cook brown rice in vegetable stock with sliced dried apricots. Sauté an onion in a little oil and add ground cumin, coriander, and fresh chopped chile, then mix in the cooked rice.

• Add raisins and toasted almonds to saffron-infused rice.

Valencia rice

Quick Ways to Flavor Risotto

• When making risotto, replace a quarter of the vegetable stock with red or white wine.

• Add a bay leaf, the juice and zest of a lemon, or a lemon grass stalk, and cardamom pods to the cooking water.
• Saffron adds a yellow color to risotto rice. Add a few strands to the vegetable stock.

VALENCIA RICE

Traditionally used for making Spanish paella, this short grain rice is not as sturdy as risotto rice and needs to be handled with care because it breaks down easily. The best way of cooking paella is to leave the rice unstirred once all the ingredients are in the pan.

RISOTTO RICE

To make Italian risotto, it is essential that you use a special, fat, short grain rice. Arborio rice, which originates from the Po Valley region in Italy, is the most widely sold variety of risotto rice, but you may also find varieties such as Carnaroli and Vialone Nano in specialty stores. When cooked, most rice absorbs around three times its weight in water; risotto rice can absorb nearly five times its weight, and the result is a creamy grain that still retains a slight bite.

Above, clockwise from left: Arborio, carnaroli, and vialone nano risotto rice

Making a Simple Risotto

A good risotto, which is creamy and moist with tender grains that retain a slight bite, is easy to make. The secrets are to use the correct type of rice (arborio, carnaroli, or vialone nano); to add the cooking liquid gradually—it should be completely absorbed by the rice before the next ladleful is added; and to stir the risotto frequently to prevent the grains from sticking.

INGREDIENTS

1 tablespoon olive oil
small pat of butter
1 onion, finely chopped (½ cup)
1 ¾ cups risotto rice
5 cups hot vegetable stock
⅔ cup freshly grated
   Parmesan cheese
salt and freshly ground black pepper

SERVES 4

Variations

• Add finely chopped cooked (not pickled) beet toward the end of the cooking time to give the rice a vibrant pink color and slight sweetness.
• To make mushroom and broccoli risotto, sauté 2 cups sliced or chopped flat mushrooms with the onion. Blanch 2 cups broccoli flowerets for 3 minutes, until tender, and add toward the end of cooking time.

1 Heat the oil and butter in a large, heavy-based pan, then cook the onion for 7 minutes, until soft, stirring occasionally. Add the rice and stir to coat the grains in the hot oil and butter.

2 Add a quarter of the stock and cook over low to medium heat, stirring frequently, until the liquid is absorbed. Add more stock, a little at a time, stirring, until all the liquid is added and absorbed.

3 After about 20 minutes, the grains will be creamy, but still retain a bite. Turn off the heat, stir in the Parmesan, and check the seasoning. Add salt and pepper to taste and serve immediately.

Japanese Rice Products

The Japanese are extremely resourceful when it comes to exploiting the vast potential of rice.

Sake This spirit is Japan's national drink; it can also be used in cooking.

Mirin Sweet rice wine that is delicious in marinades and non-sweet dishes, and is a key ingredient in teriyaki.

Rice vinegar Popular throughout Asia, this ranges in color from white to brown. Japanese rice vinegar has a mild, mellow flavor. The Chinese version is much harsher.

Amasake A healthful rice drink made by adding enzymes from fermented rice to wholegrain pudding rice. It has a similar consistency to soy "milk" and can be flavored. Amasake may be used for baking or to make creamy desserts. It is also an excellent and easily digestible weaning food.

Right, clockwise from top left: amasake, mirin, rice vinegar, and sake.

PUDDING RICE

This rounded, short grain rice is suitable for milk puddings and rice desserts. The grains swell and absorb a great deal of milk during cooking, which gives the pudding a soft, creamy consistency. Brown pudding rice is also available.

GLUTINOUS RICE

This rice is almost round in shape and has a slightly sweet flavor. Despite its name, the rice is gluten-free. The grains stick together when cooked owing to their high starch content, making the rice easier to eat with chopsticks.

Glutinous rice, which can be either white, black, or purple, is used in many Southeast Asian countries to make sticky, creamy puddings. In China, white glutinous rice is often wrapped in lotus leaves and steamed to make a popular dim sum dish.

Pudding rice

White and black glutinous rice

JAPANESE SUSHI RICE

Similar to glutinous rice, this is mixed with rice vinegar to make sushi. Most sushi rice eaten in the West is grown in California.

Sushi rice

Buying and Storing: To ensure freshness, always buy rice from stores that have a regular turnover of stock. Store in an airtight container in a cool, dry, dark place to keep out moisture and insects. Wash before use to remove any impurities. Cooked rice should be cooled quickly, then chilled, and reheated thoroughly before serving.

Health Benefits: Rice is a valuable source of complex carbohydrates and fiber. In its whole form, it is a good source of B vitamins. White rice is deprived of much of its nutrients because the bran and germ have been removed. The starch in rice is absorbed slowly, keeping blood-sugar levels on an even keel and making it an important food for diabetics. Research shows that rice may benefit sufferers of psoriasis. It can also be used to treat digestive disorders, calm the nervous system, prevent kidney stones, and reduce the risk of bowel cancer. However, the phytates found in brown rice can inhibit the absorption of iron and calcium.

Quick Ideas for Rice

Rice can be served plain, but it is also good in one-dish meals, marrying well with a host of exotic flavorings and simple storecupboard ingredients.

• To make a Middle-Eastern inspired rice dish, cook long grain brown rice in vegetable stock, then stir in some toasted slivered almonds, pieces of dried date and fig, cooked garbanzo beans, and chopped fresh mint.

• For a simple pullao, gently fry a finely chopped onion in sunflower oil with cardamom pods, a cinnamon stick, and cloves, then stir in basmati rice. Add water, infused with a pinch of saffron, and cook until tender. Toward the end of the cooking time, add golden raisins and cashew nuts, then garnish with chopped cilantro.

Rice Products

Rice flakes These are made by steaming and rolling whole or white grains. They are light and quick-cooking, and can be added raw to muesli or used to make porridge, creamy puddings, bread, cookies, and cakes.

Rice bran Like wheat and oat bran, rice bran comes from the husk of the grain kernel. It is high in soluble dietary fiber and useful for adding texture and substance to bread, cakes and cookies, and stews.

Rice flour Often used to make sticky Asian cakes and sweets, rice flour can also be used to thicken sauces. Because rice flour does not contain gluten, cakes made with it are rather flat. It can be combined with wheat flour to make cakes and bread, but produces a crumbly loaf. Rice powder is a very fine rice flour, found in Asian stores.

Right, clockwise from top left: rice bran, rice flour, rice powder, and rice flakes.

Other Grains

Wheat and rice are undoubtedly the most widely used grains, yet there are others, such as oats, rye, corn, barley, quinoa, and spelt, that should not be ignored because they provide variety in our diet and are packed with nutrients. Grains come in many forms, from whole grains to flour, and are used for baking, breakfast cereals, and cooked dishes.

OATS

Available rolled, flaked, as oatmeal, or oatbran, oats are warming and sustaining when cooked. Like rye, oats are a popular grain in northern Europe, particularly Scotland, where they are commonly turned into hot oatmeal, oatcakes, and pancakes.

Whole oats are unprocessed with the nutritious bran and germ remaining intact. Oat groats are the hulled, whole kernel, while rolled oats are made from groats that have been heated and pressed flat. Quick-cooking rolled oats have been precooked in water and then dried, which diminishes their nutritional value. Medium oatmeal is best in cakes and breads, while fine is ideal in pancakes, and fruit and milk drinks. Oat flour is gluten-free and has to be mixed with other flours that contain gluten to make leavened bread. Oat bran can be sprinkled over breakfast cereals and mixed into any kind of yogurt.

Health Benefits: Oats are perhaps the most nutritious of all the grains. Recent research has focused on the ability of oat bran to reduce blood cholesterol (sometimes with dramatic results), while beneficial HDL cholesterol levels increase. For best results, oat bran should be eaten daily at regular intervals.

High in fiber, oats are an effective laxative and also feature protease inhibitors, a combination that has been found to inhibit certain cancers. Oats also

Below, clockwise from top left: Rolled oats, oatmeal, whole oats and oat bran

Rye: grain and flour

contain vitamin E and some B vitamins, as well as iron, calcium, magnesium, phosphorus, and potassium.

RYE

The most popular grain for bread-making in Eastern Europe, Scandinavia, and Russia, rye flour produces a dark, dense, and dry loaf that keeps well. It is a hardy grain, which grows where most others fail—hence its popularity in colder climates. Rye is low in gluten and so rye flour is often mixed with high-gluten wheat flours to create lighter textured breads, the color of which is sometimes intensified using molasses. The whole grain can be soaked overnight, then cooked in boiling water until tender, but the flour, with its robust, full flavor and grayish color, is the most commonly used form. The flour ranges from dark to light, depending on whether the bran and germ have been removed.

Health Benefits: Rye is a good source of vitamin E and some B vitamins, as well as protein, calcium, iron, phosphorus, and potassium. It is also high in fiber, and is used in natural medicine to help to strengthen the digestive system.

CORN

Although we are most familiar with yellow corn or maize, blue, red, black, and even multicolored varieties can also be found. It is an essential storecupboard ingredient in the United States, the Caribbean, and Italy, and comes in many forms.

Masa harina

Maize meal, or masa harina, is made from the cooked whole grain, which is ground into flour and commonly used to make the Mexican flat bread, tortilla.

Cornmeal

The main culinary uses for cornmeal are cornbread, a classic, southern American bread, and polenta, which confusingly is both the Italian name for cornmeal as well as a dish made with the grain. Polenta (the cooked dish) is a thick, golden dish, which is often flavored with butter and cheese

Making Polenta

Polenta makes an excellent alternative to mashed potato. It needs plenty of seasoning and is even better with a pat of butter and cheese, such as Parmesan, Gorgonzola, or Taleggio. Serve with stews or casseroles.

1 Pour 4 cups water into a heavy-based saucepan and bring to a boil. Remove from the heat.

2 In a steady stream, gradually add 1½ cups instant polenta and mix constantly with a balloon whisk to avoid any lumps forming.

3 Return the pan to the heat and cook, stirring continuously with a wooden spoon, until the polenta is thick and creamy and starts to come away from the sides of the pan—this will take only a few minutes if you are using instant polenta.

4 Season to taste with salt and plenty of ground black pepper, then add a generous pat of butter and mix well. Remove from the heat and stir in the cheese, if using.

Clockwise from top left: Blue and yellow cornmeal, cornstarch, popcorn, masa harina, and polenta

or chopped herbs. Once cooked, polenta can also be left to cool, then cut into slabs and fried, grilled, or griddled until golden brown. It is delicious with roasted vegetables. Ready-to-slice polenta is available from some supermarkets.

Polenta grain comes in various grades, ranging from fine to coarse. You can buy polenta that takes 40–45 minutes to cook or an "instant" part-cooked version that can be cooked in less than 5 minutes.

In the Caribbean, cornmeal is used to make puddings and dumplings.

Cornstarch
This fine white powder is a useful thickening agent for sauces, soups, and casseroles. It can also be added to cakes.

Hominy
These are the husked whole grains of corn. They should be cooked in boiling water until softened, then used in stews and soups, or added to cakes and muffins.

Grits
Coarsely ground, dried yellow or white corn is known as grits. Use for pancakes or add to baked goods.

Popcorn
This is a separate strain of corn that is grown specifically to make the popular snack food. The kernel's hard outer casing explodes when heated.

Quinoa

Popcorn can easily be made at home and flavored sweet or non-sweet according to taste. The store-bought types are often high in salt or sugar.

Health Benefits: In American folk medicine, corn is considered a diuretic and a mild stimulant. Corn is said to prevent cancer of the colon, breast, and prostate and to lower the risk of heart disease. It is believed to be the only grain that contains vitamin A as well as some of the B vitamins and iron.

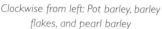

Clockwise from left: Pot barley, barley flakes, and pearl barley

BARLEY
Believed to be the oldest cultivated grain, barley is still a fundamental part of the everyday diet in Eastern Europe, the Middle East, and Asia.

Pearl barley, the most usual form, is husked, steamed, and then polished to give it its characteristic ivory-colored appearance. It has a mild, sweet flavor and chewy texture, and can be added to soups, stews, and bakes. It is also used to make old-fashioned barley water.

Pot barley is the whole grain with just the inedible outer husk removed. It takes much longer to cook than pearl barley.

Barley flakes, which make a satisfying breakfast dish, and barley flour are also available.

Health Benefits: Pot barley is more nutritious than pearl barley because it contains extra fiber, calcium, phosphorus, iron, magnesium, and B vitamins. Barley was once used to increase potency and boost physical strength. More recently, studies have shown that its fiber content may help to prevent constipation and other digestive problems, as well as heart disease and certain cancers. In addition, the protease inhibitors in barley have been found to suppress cancer of the intestines, and eating barley regularly may also reduce the amount of harmful cholesterol produced by the liver.

Lemon Barley Water

INGREDIENTS
1 cup pearl barley (8 ounces)
7 1/2 cups water
grated rind of 1 lemon
1/4 cup golden superfine sugar (2 ounces)
juice of 2 lemons

1 Rinse the barley, then place in a large saucepan and cover with the water. Bring to a boil, then reduce the heat and simmer gently for 20 minutes, skimming off any scum from time to time. Remove the pan from the heat.

2 Add the lemon rind and sugar to the pan, stir well, and let cool. Strain and add the lemon juice.

3 Taste the lemon barley water and add more sugar, if necessary. Serve chilled with ice and slices of lemon.

QUINOA

Hailed as the supergrain of the future, quinoa (pronounced "keen-wa") is a grain of the past. It was called "the mother grain" by the Incas, who cultivated it for hundreds of years, high in the Andes, solely for their own use.

Nowadays, quinoa is widely available. The tiny, bead-shaped grains have a mild, slightly bitter taste and firm texture. It is cooked in the same way as rice, but the grains quadruple in size, becoming translucent with an unusual white outer ring. Quinoa is useful for making stuffings, pilaffs, bakes, and breakfast cereals.

Health Benefits: Quinoa's supergrain status hails from its rich nutritional value. Unlike other grains, quinoa is a complete protein because it contains all eight essential amino acids. It is an excellent source of calcium, potassium, and zinc as well as iron, magnesium, and B vitamins. It is particularly valuable for people with celiac disease as it is gluten-free.

MILLET

Although millet is usually associated with bird food, it is a highly nutritious grain. It once rivaled barley as the main food of Europe and remains a staple ingredient in many parts of the world, including Africa, China, and India. Its mild flavor makes it an ideal accompaniment to spicy stews and curries, and it can be used as a base for pilaffs or milk puddings. The tiny, firm grains can also be flaked or ground into flour. Millet is gluten-free, so it is a useful food for people with celiac disease. The flour can be used for baking, but needs to be combined with high-gluten flours to make leavened bread.

Health Benefits: Millet is an easily digestible grain. It contains more iron than other grains and is a good source of zinc, calcium, manganese, and B vitamins. It is believed to be beneficial to those suffering from candidiasis, a fungal infection caused by the yeast *Candida albicans*.

Millet

Amaranth

There are several other grains that deserve a mention, as they are not only becoming more popular, but also are often far richer in nutrients than their better-known counterparts.

Amaranth

This plant, which is native to Mexico, is unusual in that it can be eaten as both a vegetable and a grain. Amaranth is considered a supergrain owing to its excellent nutritional content. The tiny pale seed or "grain" has a strong and distinctive, peppery flavor. It is best used in stews and soups, or it can be ground into flour to make bread, turnovers, and cookies. The flour is gluten-free and has to be mixed with wheat or another flour that contains gluten to make leavened bread. Amaranth leaves are similar to spinach and can be cooked or eaten raw in salads.

Health Benefits: Although its taste may take some getting used to, the nutritional qualities of amaranth more than make up for it. It has more protein than pulses and is rich in amino acids, particularly lysine. Amaranth is also high in iron and calcium.

Kamut

An ancient relative of wheat, this grain has long, slender, brown kernels with a creamy, nutty flavor. It is as versatile as wheat and, when ground into flour, can be used to make pasta, breads, cakes, and pastry. Puffed kamut cereals and kamut crackers are available in health-food stores.

BUCKWHEAT

In spite of its name, buckwheat is not a type of wheat, but is actually related to the rhubarb family. Available plain or toasted, it has a nutty, earthy flavor. It is a staple food in Eastern Europe, as well as Russia, where the triangular grain is milled into a speckled-gray flour and used to make blini. The flour is also used in Japan for soba noodles and in Italy for pasta. Buckwheat pancakes are popular in parts of the United States and France. The whole grain, which is also known as kasha, makes a creamy dessert.

Health Benefits: Like quinoa, buckwheat is a complete protein. It contains all eight essential amino acids, as well as rutin, which aids circulation and helps treat high blood pressure. It is an excellent, sustaining cereal, rich in both iron and some of the B complex vitamins. It is also reputed to be good for the lungs, the kidneys, and the bladder. Buckwheat is gluten-free, and so is useful for people who suffer from celiac disease.

Above, from left: Plain buckwheat, buckwheat flour, and toasted buckwheat

Health Benefits: Kamut has a higher nutritional value than wheat and is easier to digest. Although it contains gluten, people suffering from celiac disease have found that they can tolerate the grain if eaten in moderation.

Sorghum

This grain is best known for its thick sweet syrup, which is used in cakes and desserts. The grain is similar to millet and is an important, extremely nutritious staple food in Africa and India. It can be used much like rice, and when ground into flour is used to make unleavened bread.

Health Benefits: Sorghum is a useful source of calcium, iron, and B vitamins.

Spelt

This is one of the most ancient cultivated wheats and, because of its high nutritional value, is becoming more widely available. Spelt grain looks very similar to wheat and the flour can be substituted for wheat flour in bread.

Health Benefits: Spelt is richer in vitamins and minerals than wheat, and they are in a more readily digestible form. Although spelt contains gluten, it usually can be tolerated in moderate amounts by people suffering from celiac disease.

Triticale

A hybrid of wheat and rye, triticale was created by Swedish researchers in 1875. It has a sweet, nutty taste and chewy texture, and can be used in the

Spelt grain and flour

same way as rice, and is ground into flour. It contains more protein than wheat but has less gluten and may need to be mixed with other flours when baking. Triticale flakes can be used in breakfast cereals and crumbles.

Health Benefits: Triticale contains significant amounts of calcium, iron, and B vitamins. It is particularly rich in lysine.

Buying and Storing: To ensure freshness, buy grains in small quantities from a store with a high turnover of stock. Grains can be affected by heat and moisture, and easily become rancid. Store in a dry, cool, dark place.

Kamut

How to Cook Grains

Grains can be simply boiled in water but, to enhance their flavor, first cook them in a little oil for a few minutes. When they are well coated in oil, add two or three times their volume of water or stock. Bring to a boil, then simmer, covered, until the water is absorbed and the grains are tender. Do not disturb the grains while they are cooking. Other flavorings, such as chopped herbs and whole or ground spices, can be added to the cooking liquid.

Fabulous Fiber

Whole grains are one of the few food groups to contain both soluble and insoluble fiber. The former is prevalent in oats and rye, while wheat, rice, and corn contain insoluble fiber. Both are fundamental to good health and may prevent constipation, ulcers, colitis, colon and rectal cancer, heart disease, diverticulitis, and irritable bowel syndrome. Soluble fiber slows down the absorption of energy from the gut, which means there are no sudden demands on insulin, making it especially important for diabetics.

Legumes

Lentils, peas, and pulses provide the cook with a diverse range of flavors and textures. They have long been a staple food in the Middle East, South America, India, and the Mediterranean, but there is hardly a country that does not have its own favorite legume-based dish, from Boston baked beans in the United States to lentil dahl in India. In Mexico, they are spiced and used to make refried beans, while in China they are fermented for black bean and yellow bean sauces. Low in fat and high in complex carbohydrates, vitamins, and minerals, legumes are also an important source of protein for vegetarians and, when eaten with cereals, easily match animal-based sources.

Lentils and Peas

The humble lentil is one of our oldest foods. It originated in Asia and North Africa and continues to be cultivated in those regions, as well as in France and Italy. Lentils are hard even when fresh, so they are always sold dried. Unlike most other pulses, they do not need soaking.

Red lentils

Puy lentils

GREEN AND BROWN LENTILS

Sometimes referred to as continental lentils, these disk-shaped pulses retain their shape when cooked. They take longer to cook than split lentils—about 40–45 minutes—and are ideal for adding to warm salads, casseroles, and stuffings.

Alternatively, green and brown lentils can be cooked and blended with herbs or spices to make a nutritious pâté.

PUY LENTILS

These tiny, dark, blue-green, marbled lentils grow in the Auvergne region in central France. They are considered to be far superior in taste and texture to other varieties, and they retain their bead-like shape during cooking, which takes 25–30 minutes. Puy lentils are a delicious addition to simple dishes such as warm salads, and are also good braised in wine and flavored with fresh herbs.

RED LENTILS

Orange-colored red split lentils, sometimes known as Egyptian lentils, are the most familiar variety. They cook in just 20 minutes, eventually disintegrating into a thick purée. They are ideal for thickening soups and casseroles and, when cooked with spices, make a delicious dahl. In the Middle East, red or yellow lentils are cooked and mixed with spices and vegetables to form balls known as *kofte*.

YELLOW LENTILS

Less well-known, yellow lentils taste very similar to the red variety and are used in much the same way.

PEAS

Dried peas come from the field pea not the garden pea, which is eaten fresh. Unlike lentils, peas are soft when young and require drying. They are available whole or split; the latter have a sweeter flavor and cook more quickly. Like split lentils, split peas do not hold their shape when cooked, making them perfect for dahls, purées, casseroles, and soups.

Green and brown lentils

Cooking Lentils

Lentils are easy to cook and don't need to be soaked. Split red and green lentils cook down to a soft consistency, while whole lentils hold their shape when cooked.

Green, Brown, and Puy Lentils

1 Place generous 1 cup whole lentils in a strainer and rinse under cold running water. Transfer to a saucepan.

2 Cover with water and bring to a boil. Simmer for 25–30 minutes, until tender, replenishing the water if necessary. Drain and season with salt and freshly ground black pepper.

Split Red and Yellow Lentils

1 Place generous 1 cup split lentils in a strainer and rinse under cold running water. Transfer to a saucepan.

2 Cover with 2½ cups water and bring to a boil. Simmer for 20–25 minutes, stirring occasionally, until the water is absorbed and the lentils are tender. Season to taste.

They take about 45 minutes to cook. Marrow fat peas are larger in size and are used to make the traditional British dish "mushy" peas. Like other whole peas, they require soaking overnight before use.

Buying and Storing: Although lentils and peas can be kept for up to a year, they toughen with time. Buy from stores with a fast turnover of stock and store in airtight containers in a cool, dark place. Look for bright, unwrinkled pulses that are not dusty. Rinse well before use.

Health Benefits: Lentils and peas share an impressive range of nutrients including iron, selenium, folate, manganese, zinc, phosphorus, and some B vitamins. Extremely low in fat and richer in protein than most pulses, lentils and peas are reputed to be important in fighting heart disease by reducing harmful LDL cholesterol in the body. They are high in fiber, which aids the functioning of the bowels and colon. Fiber also slows down the rate at which sugar enters the bloodstream, providing a steady supply of energy, which can help control diabetes.

Marrow fat peas (above) and yellow and green split peas

COOK'S TIP

Avoid adding salt to the water when cooking lentils and peas as this prevents them softening. Season when cooked.

Pulses

The edible seeds from plants belonging to the legume family, pulses, which include black-eyed peas and a vast range of beans, are packed with protein, vitamins, minerals, and fiber, and are extremely low in fat. For the cook, their ability to absorb the flavors of other foods means that pulses can be used as the base for an infinite number of dishes. Most pulses require soaking overnight in cold water before use, so it is wise to plan ahead if using the dried type.

Adzuki beans

BLACK BEANS

These shiny, black, kidney-shaped beans are often used in Caribbean cooking. They have a sweetish flavor, and their distinctive color adds a dramatic touch to soups, mixed bean salads, or casseroles.

ADZUKI BEANS

Also known as aduki beans, these tiny, deep-red beans have a sweet, nutty flavor and are popular in Asian dishes. In Chinese cooking, they form the base of red bean paste. Known as the "king of beans" in Japan, the adzuki bean is reputed to be good for the liver and kidneys. They cook quickly and can be used in casseroles and bakes. They are also ground into flour for use in cakes, breads, and pastries.

BLACK-EYED PEAS

Also known as black-eye beans or cow peas, black-eyed peas are an essential ingredient in Creole cooking and some spicy Indian curries. The small, creamy-colored bean is characterized by the black spot on its side where it was once attached to the pod. Good in soups and salads, they can also be added to non-sweet bakes and casseroles, and can be used in place of navy or cannellini beans in a wide variety of dishes.

Black beans (left), black-eyed peas (center), and borlotti beans

---

Cannellini Bean Purée

Cooked cannellini beans make a delicious herb- and garlic-flavored purée. Serve spread on toasted pita bread or to use as a dip with chunky raw vegetable crudités.

INGREDIENTS

2½ cups canned or 1¼ cups
    dried cannellini beans
2 tablespoons olive oil
1 large garlic clove, finely chopped
2 shallots, finely chopped
5 tablespoons vegetable stock
2 tablespoons chopped fresh flat
    leaf parsley
1 tablespoon snipped fresh chives
salt and freshly ground black pepper

SERVES 4

1 If using dried beans, soak them overnight in cold water, then drain, and rinse. Place in a saucepan and cover with cold water, then bring to a boil and boil rapidly for 10 minutes. Reduce the heat and simmer for about 1 hour, or until tender. If using canned beans, rinse and drain well.

2 Heat the oil in a saucepan and sauté the garlic and shallots for about 5 minutes, stirring occasionally, until soft. Add the beans, stock, parsley, and seasoning, then cook for a few minutes, until heated through.

3 To make a coarse purée, mash the beans with a potato masher. Alternatively, place in a food processor and process until thick and smooth. Serve sprinkled with snipped chives.

Butter beans

The F Word

Many people are put off eating beans due to their unfortunate side effects. The propensity of beans to cause flatulence stems from the gases they produce in the gut. This can be reduced by following these guidelines:
• Never cook pulses in their soaking water, as it contains indigestible sugars.
• Skim off any scum that forms on the surface of the water during cooking.
• Add "digestive" spices, such as dill, asafetida, ginger, and caraway, to the cooking water.

BORLOTTI BEANS

These oval beans have red-streaked, pinkish-brown skin and a bitter-sweet flavor. When cooked, they have a tender, moist texture, which is good in Italian bean and pasta soups, as well as hearty vegetable stews. In most recipes, they are interchangeable with red kidney beans.

FAVA BEANS

These large beans were first cultivated by the ancient Egyptians. Usually eaten in their fresh form, fava beans change in color from green to brown when dried, making them difficult to recognize in their dried state. The outer skin can be very tough and chewy, and some people prefer to remove it after cooking. They can also be bought ready-skinned.

Cannellini beans

Fava beans

LIMA AND BUTTER BEANS

Similar in flavor and appearance, both lima beans and butter beans are characterized by their flattish, kidney shape and soft, mealy texture. Cream-colored butter beans are familiar in Britain and Greece, while lima beans are popular in the United States. In Greek cooking, butter beans are oven-baked with tomato, garlic, and olive oil until tender and creamy. The pale-green lima bean is the main ingredient in succotash, a traditional dish that also includes corn kernels. Lima and butter beans are also good with creamy herb sauces. Care should be taken not to overcook both lima and butter beans as they become pulpy and mushy in texture.

CANNELLINI BEANS

These small, white, kidney-shaped beans have a soft, creamy texture when cooked and are popular in Italian cooking. They can be used in place of navy beans and, when dressed with olive oil, lemon juice, crushed garlic, and chopped fresh parsley, make an excellent warm salad.

82 •

GARBANZO BEANS

Also known as chick-peas, robust and hearty garbanzo beans resemble shelled hazelnuts and have a delicious nutty flavor and creamy texture. They need lengthy cooking and are much used in Mediterranean and Middle Eastern cooking. In India, they are known as gram and are ground into flour to make fritters and flat breads. Gram flour, also called besan, can be found in health-food stores and Asian grocery stores.

Garbanzo beans

FLAGEOLET BEANS

These young navy beans are removed from the pod before they are fully ripe, hence their fresh delicate flavor. A pretty, mint-green color, they are the most expensive bean to buy and are best treated simply. Cook them until they are tender, then season, and drizzle with a little olive oil and lemon juice.

PINTO BEANS

A smaller, paler version of the borlotti bean, the savory-tasting pinto has an attractive speckled skin—it is aptly called the painted bean. One of the many relatives of the kidney bean, pinto beans feature extensively in Mexican cooking,

NAVY BEANS

Most commonly used for canned baked beans, these versatile, ivory-colored beans are small and oval in shape. Also called haricot or Boston beans, they suit slow-cooked dishes, such as casseroles and bakes.

Above, clockwise from left: Navy beans, red kidney beans, flageolet beans and pinto beans

most familiarly in refried beans, when they are cooked until tender and fried with garlic, chile, and tomatoes. The beans are then mashed, resulting in a wonderful, spicy, rough purée that is usually served with warm tortillas. Sour cream and garlic-flavored guacamole are good accompaniments.

RED KIDNEY BEANS

Glossy, mahogany-red kidney beans retain their color and shape when cooked. They have a soft, mealy texture and are much used in South American cooking. An essential ingredient in spicy chiles, they can also be used to make refried beans (although this dish is traditionally made from pinto beans). Cooked kidney beans can be used to make a variety of salads, but they are especially good combined with red onion and chopped flat leaf parsley and mint, then tossed in an olive oil dressing.

It is essential to follow the cooking instructions when preparing kidney beans, as they contain a substance that causes severe poisoning if they are not boiled vigorously for 10–15 minutes.

Cooking Kidney Beans

Most types of beans, with the exception of adzuki beans and mung beans, require soaking for 5–6 hours or overnight and then boiling rapidly for 10–15 minutes to remove any harmful toxins. This is particularly important for kidney beans, which can cause serious poisoning if not treated in this way.

1 Wash the beans well, then place in a bowl that allows plenty of room for expansion. Cover with cold water and let soak overnight or for 8–12 hours, then drain and rinse.

2 Place the beans in a large saucepan and cover with fresh cold water. Bring to a boil and boil rapidly for 10–15 minutes, then reduce the heat and simmer for 1–1½ hours until tender. Drain and serve.

The Flatulence-free Bean

The American space program NASA is involved in research into flatulence-free foods. One such food is the manteca bean, discovered by Dr Colin Leakey in Chile. This small, yellow bean is flatulence-free and easy to digest. It is now being grown both in Cambridgeshire, England and the Channel Islands, and should become more widely available, called either manteca beans or Jersey yellow beans.

FUL MEDAMES

A member of the fava bean family, these small Egyptian beans form the base of the national dish of the same name, in which they are flavored with ground cumin and then baked with olive oil, garlic, and lemon, and

Ful medames

served topped with hard-cooked egg. They have a strong, nutty flavor and tough, light brown outer skin. Ful medames need to be soaked overnight in cold water, then cooked slowly for about 1 hour until soft.

SOYBEANS

These small, oval beans vary in color from creamy-yellow through brown to black. In China, they are known as "meat of the earth" and were once considered sacred. Soybeans contain all the nutritional properties of animal products but without the disadvantages. They are extremely dense and need to be soaked for 12 hours before cooking. They combine well with robust ingredients such as garlic, herbs, and spices, and they make a healthy addition to soups, casseroles, bakes, and salads.

They are also used to make bean curd, tempeh, textured vegetable protein, flour and soy sauce.

White and black soybeans

How to Prepare and Cook Pulses

There is much debate as to whether soaking pulses before cooking is necessary, but it certainly reduces cooking times, and can enhance flavor by starting the germination process. First, wash pulses under cold running water, then place in a bowl of fresh cold water, and let soak overnight. Discard any pulses that float to the surface, drain, and rinse again. Put in a large saucepan and cover with fresh cold water. Boil rapidly for 10–15 minutes, then reduce the heat, cover, and simmer until tender.

Cooking Times for Pulses

As cooking times can vary depending on the age of the pulses, this table should be used as a general guide.

Adzuki beans	30–45 minutes
Black beans	1 hour
Black-eyed peas	1–1¼ hours
Borlotti beans	1–1½ hours
Cannellini beans	1 hour
Fava beans	1½ hours
Flageolet beans	1½ hours
Ful medames	1 hour
Garbanzo beans	1½–2½ hours
Kidney beans	1–1½ hours
Lima/butter beans	1–1¼ hours
Mung beans	25–40 minutes
Navy beans	1–1½ hours
Pinto beans	1–1¼ hours
Soybeans	2 hours

MUNG BEANS

Instantly recognizable in their sprouted form as bean sprouts, mung or moong beans are small, olive-colored beans native to India. They are soft and sweet when cooked, and are used in the spicy curry, moong dahl. Soaking is not essential, but if they are soaked overnight, this will reduce the usual 40 minutes cooking time by about half.

Mung beans

Using Canned Beans

Canned beans are convenient storecupboard stand-bys, because they require no soaking or lengthy cooking. Choose canned beans that do not have added sugar or salt, and rinse well and drain before use. The canning process reduces the levels of vitamins and minerals, but canned beans still contain reputable amounts.

Canned beans tend to be softer than cooked, dried beans so they are easy to mash, which makes them good for pâtés, stuffings, croquettes, and rissoles, but they can also be used to make quick salads. They can, in fact, be used for any dish that calls for cooked, dried beans: a drained 15-ounce can is roughly the equivalent of ¾ cup dried beans. Firmer canned beans, such as kidney beans, can be added to stews and re-cooked, but softer beans, such as navy beans, should be just heated through.

Buying and Storing: Look for plump, shiny beans with unbroken skin. Beans toughen with age so, although they will keep for up to a year in a cool, dry place, it is best to buy them in small quantities from stores with a regular turnover of stock. Avoid beans that look dusty or dirty and store them in an airtight container in a cool, dark, dry place.

Health Benefits: The health attributes of beans are plentiful. They are packed with protein, soluble and insoluble fiber, iron, potassium, phosphorus, manganese, magnesium, folate, and most B vitamins.

Soybeans are the most nutritious of all beans. Rich in high-quality protein, this wonder-pulse contains all eight essential amino acids that cannot be synthesized by the body but are vital for the renewal of cells and tissues.

Insoluble fiber ensures regular bowel movements, while soluble fiber has been found to lower blood cholesterol, thereby reducing the risk of heart disease and stroke. Studies show that eating dried beans on a regular basis can lower cholesterol levels by almost 20 percent. Beans contain a concentration of lignins, also known as phytoestrogens, which protect against cancer of the breast, prostate, and colon. Lignins may also help to balance hormone levels in the body.

COOK'S TIPS

• If you are short of time, the long soaking process can be speeded up: first, cook the beans in boiling water for 2 minutes, then remove the pan from the heat. Cover and leave for about 2 hours. Drain, rinse, and cover with plenty of fresh cold water before cooking.

• Cooking beans in a pressure cooker will reduce the cooking time by around three-quarters.

• Do not add salt to beans while they are cooking as this will cause them to toughen. Cook the beans first, then season with salt and pepper. Acid foods, such as tomatoes, lemons, or vinegar will also toughen beans, so only add these ingredients once the beans are soft.

Quick Cooking and Serving Ideas for Pulses

• To flavor beans, add an onion, garlic, herbs, or spices before cooking. Remove whole flavorings before serving.

• Spoon spicy, red lentil dahl and some crisp, fried onions on top of a warm tortilla, then roll up, and eat.

• Dress cooked beans with extra virgin olive oil, lemon juice, crushed garlic, diced tomato, and fresh basil.

• Mix cooked garbanzo beans, scallions, olives, and chopped parsley, then drizzle with olive oil and lemon juice.

• Mash cooked beans with olive oil, garlic, and cilantro and pile onto toasted bread. Top with a poached egg.

• Fry cooked red kidney beans in olive oil with chopped onion, chile, garlic, and fresh cilantro leaves.

• Sauté a little chopped garlic in olive oil, add cooked or canned flageolet beans, canned tomatoes, and chopped fresh chile, then cook for a few minutes, until the sauce has thickened slightly and the beans are heated through.

• Roast cooked garbanzo beans, which have been drizzled with olive oil and garlic, for 20 minutes at 400°F, then toss in a little ground cumin and sprinkle with chile flakes. Serve with chunks of feta cheese and nan bread.

Soybean Products

Soybeans are incredibly versatile and are used to make an extensive array of by-products that are used in cooking— bean curd, tempeh, textured vegetable protein, flour, miso, and a variety of sauces. The soybean is the most nutritious of all beans. Rich in high-quality protein, it is one of the few vegetarian foods that contains all eight essential amino acids that cannot be synthesized in the body and are vital for the renewal of cells and tissues.

BEAN CURD

Also known as tofu, bean curd is made in a similar way to soft cheese. The beans are boiled, mashed, and strained to make soy "milk," and the "milk" is then curdled using a coagulant. The resulting curds are drained and pressed to make bean curd, and there are several different types to choose from.

Firm bean curd

This type of bean curd is sold in blocks and can be cubed or sliced, and used in vegetable stir-fries, kebabs, salads, soups, and casseroles. Alternatively, firm bean curd can be mashed and used in bakes and burgers. The bland flavor of firm bean curd is improved by marinating, because its porous texture readily absorbs flavors and seasonings.

Silken bean curd

Soft with a silky, smooth texture, this type of bean curd is ideal for use in sauces, dressings, dips, and soups. It is a useful dairy-free alternative to cream, soft cheese, or yogurt, and can be used to make creamy desserts.

Other forms of bean curd

Smoked, marinated, and deep-fried tofu are all readily available in health-food stores and Asian stores, as well as in some supermarkets.

Deep-fried bean curd is fairly tasteless, but it has an interesting texture. It puffs up during cooking and under the golden, crisp coating the bean curd is white and soft, and easily absorbs the flavor of other ingredients. It can be used in the same way as firm bean curd and, as it has been fried in vegetable oil, it is suitable for vegetarians.

Buying and Storing: All types of fresh bean curd can be kept in the fridge for up to 1 week. Firm bean curd should be kept covered in water, which must be changed regularly. Freezing bean curd is not recommended because it alters the texture. Silken bean curd is often available in long-life vacuum packs, which do not have to be kept in the fridge and have a much longer shelf-life.

TEMPEH

This Indonesian specialty is made by fermenting cooked soybeans with a cultured starter. Tempeh is similar to bean curd, but has a nuttier, more savory flavor. It can be used in the same way as firm bean curd and also benefits from marinating. While some types of bean curd are regarded as a dairy replacement, the firmer texture of tempeh means that it can be used instead of meat in pies and casseroles dishes.

Buying and Storing: Tempeh is available chilled or frozen in health-food stores and Asian stores. Chilled tempeh can be stored in the fridge for up to a week. Frozen tempeh can be left in the freezer for 1 month; thaw before use.

BEAN CURD SKINS AND STICKS

Made from soy "milk," dried bean curd skins and sticks, like fresh bean curd, have neither aroma nor flavor until they are cooked, when they will rapidly absorb the flavor of seasonings and other ingredients. They are used in Chinese cooking and

Above, clockwise from left: Silken bean curd, bean curd skins, firm bean curd, and marinated bean curd

TVP

Textured vegetable protein, or TVP, is a useful meat replacement and is usually bought in dry chunks or ground. Made from processed soybeans, TVP is very versatile and readily absorbs the strong flavors of ingredients such as herbs, spices, and vegetable stock. It is inexpensive and is a convenient storecupboard item. TVP needs to be rehydrated in boiling water or vegetable stock, and can be used in stews and curries, or as a filling for pies.

Tempeh

need to be soaked until pliable before use. Bean curd skins should be soaked for an hour or two and can be used to wrap a variety of fillings.

Bean curd sticks need to be soaked for several hours or overnight. They can be chopped and added to soups, stir-fries, and casseroles.

Bean Curd Fruit Fool

1 Place a packet of silken bean curd in the bowl of a food processor. Add some soft fruit or berries—for example, strawberries, raspberries, or blackberries.

2 Process the mixture to form a smooth purée, then sweeten to taste with a little honey, maple syrup, or corn malt syrup.

Marinated Bean Curd Kebabs

Bean curd is relatively tasteless, but readily takes on other flavors. It is at its best when marinated in aromatic oils, soy sauce, spices, and herbs.

1 Cut a block of bean curd into ½-inch cubes and marinate in a mixture of peanut oil, sesame oil, soy sauce, crushed garlic, grated fresh ginger root, and honey for at least 1 hour.

2 Thread the cubes of bean curd onto skewers with chunks of zucchini, onions, and mushrooms. Brush with the marinade and broil or grill until golden, turning occasionally.

Soy flour

SOY FLOUR

This is a finely ground, high-protein flour, which is also gluten-free. It is often mixed with other flours in bread and pastries, adding a pleasant nuttiness, or it can be used as a thickener in sauces.

Buying and Storing: Store TVP and soy flour in an airtight container in a cool, dry, dark place.

SOY SAUCE

This soy by-product originated over 2,000 years ago and the recipe has changed little since then. It is made by combining crushed soybeans with wheat, salt, water, and a yeast-based culture called *koji*, and the mixture is left to ferment for between 6 months and 3 years.

There are two basic types of soy sauce: light and dark. Light soy sauce is slightly thinner in consistency and saltier. It is used in dressings and soups. Dark soy sauce is heavier and sweeter, with a more rounded flavor, and is used in marinades, stir-fries, and sauces. Try to buy naturally brewed soy sauce as many other kinds are now chemically prepared to hasten the fermentation process, and may contain flavorings and colorings.

SHOYU

Made in Japan, shoyu is aged for 1–2 years to produce a full-flavored sauce that can be used in the same way as dark soy sauce. You can buy it in health-food stores and Asian foodstores.

TAMARI

This form of soy sauce is a natural by-product of making miso, although it is often produced in the same way as soy sauce. Most tamari is made without wheat, which means that it is gluten-free. It has a rich, dark, robust flavor and is used in cooking or as a condiment.

Buying and Storing: Keep soy sauce, shoyu, and tamari in a cool, dark place.

MISO

This thick paste is made from a mixture of cooked soybeans, rice, wheat or barley, salt, and water, and is left to ferment for up to 3 years. Miso can be used to add a savory flavor to soups, stocks, stir-fries, and noodle dishes, and is a staple food in Asia. There are three main types: kome, or white miso, which is the lightest and sweetest; medium-strength mugi miso, which has a mellow flavor and is preferred for everyday use; and hacho miso, which is a dark chocolate color, and has a thick texture and a strong flavor.

Soybean Sauces

Black bean sauce Made from fermented black soybeans, this has a rich, thick consistency and a salty, full flavor. It should always be heated before use to bring out the flavor. Fermented black beans, which Chinese cooks use to make homemade black bean sauce, can be bought in vacuum-packs or cans from Asian stores.

Yellow bean sauce Produced from fermented yellow soybeans, this sauce has an intense flavor.

Hoisin sauce A thick red-brown sauce made from soybeans, flour, garlic, chile, sesame oil, and vinegar. Mainly intended as a marinade, it can be used as a dipping sauce.

Kecap manis An Indonesian-style dark, sweet soy sauce, which can be found in Asian stores.

Ground and cubed textured vegetable protein (TVP)

Buying and Storing: Miso keeps well and can be stored for several months, but should be kept in the fridge once it has been opened.

Health Benefits: Soy is one of today's healthiest foods. Rich in minerals, particularly iron and calcium, it is also low in saturated fats and is cholesterol-free. It has the ability to help reduce osteoporosis, blood pressure, and blood cholesterol, and there is evidence to suggest that it can help reduce the risk of cancer.

Japanese women (whose diets are rich in soy) have a lower incidence of breast cancer than women who consume a typical Western diet. Likewise, Japanese men have a lower incidence of prostate cancer than Western men. This is thought to be because soy contains hormone-like substances called phytoestrogens.

Studies have also shown that eating miso on a regular basis can increase the body's natural resistance to radiation. Additionally, miso is said to prevent cancer of the liver, and it can also help to expel toxins from the body.

Light soy sauce (below) and dark soy sauce

Watch Point

Although soybeans and products are nutritionally beneficial, they are also common allergens and can provoke reactions such as headaches and digestive problems. Avoid eating excessive amounts of soy, and always cook sprouted soybeans before use.

Mugi miso (left) and hacha miso

Tamari (left) and shoyu

Dairy Foods and Alternatives

Some people may question the inclusion of dairy products in a whole food cookbook, and while it would be foolish to advocate the consumption of vast quantities of high-fat milk, cream, and cheese, a diet that includes moderate amounts of dairy products does provide valuable vitamins and minerals. There is little reason to reject dairy products as they can enrich vegetarian cooking. However, for those who choose to avoid dairy foods, there are plenty of alternatives.

Milk, Cream, and Yogurt

This wide group of ingredients includes milk, cream, and yogurt made from cow, goat, and sheep milk, as well as non-dairy products, such as soy "milk" and "cream" and other non-dairy "milks," which are made from nuts and grains. They are used in a huge range of sweet and non-sweet dishes, from sauces and soups to drinks and desserts.

MILK

Often referred to as a complete food, milk is one of our most widely used ingredients. Cow's milk remains the most popular type although, with the growing concern about saturated fat and cholesterol, low-fat and skim milks now outsell the full-fat version. Skim milk contains half the calories of full-fat milk and only a fraction of the fat, but nutritionally it is on a par, retaining its vitamins, calcium, and other minerals.

Buy organic milk if you can, because it comes from cows that have been fed on a pesticide-free diet, and are not routinely treated with hormones, antibiotics, or BST (bovine somatotrophin), which is used in some countries to boost the milk yield from cows.

Sour cream and crème fraîche

Goat and sheep milk

These milks make useful alternatives for people who are intolerant to cow milk. The lactose in cow milk can cause severe indigestion, and an intolerance to dairy products often manifests itself in eczema or sinus congestion. Goat and sheep milk are nutritionally similar to cow milk, but are easier to digest.

Goat milk has a distinctive, musky flavor, while sheep milk is a little creamier and has a less assuming flavor.

CREAM

The high fat content of cream means that it is not an ingredient to be eaten lavishly on a daily basis. Used with discretion, however, cream lends a richness to soups, sauces, bakes, and desserts.

The fat content of cream ranges enormously: half-cream contains about 12 percent, light cream 18 percent, heavy 48 percent, and clotted cream, which is the highest, contains about 55 percent.

From left: Goat, cow, and sheep milk, and soy "milk"

Smetana

SOUR CREAM

This thick-textured cream is treated with lactic acid, which gives it its characteristic tang. Full-fat sour cream contains about 20 percent fat, although low- and non-fat versions are available. It can be used in the same way as cream. Care should be taken when cooking, as it can curdle if heated to too high a temperature.

CREME FRAICHE

This rich, cultured cream is similar to sour cream, but its high fat content, at around 35 percent, means that it does not curdle

when cooked. Crème fraîche is delicious served with fresh fruit, such as ripe summer berries, puréed mangoes, or sliced bananas.

BUTTERMILK

Traditionally made from the milky liquid left over after butter making, buttermilk is now more likely to be made from skim milk, mixed with milk solids and then cultured with lactic acid. It has a creamy, mild, sour taste and makes a tangy and distinctive addition to desserts. Used in baking, buttermilk gives cakes and soda bread a moist texture. It is low in fat, containing only 0.1 percent.

SMETANA

Originally made in Russia, this rich version of buttermilk is made from skim milk and single cream with an added culture. It has a similar fat content to strained yogurt (about 10 percent), and should be treated in the same way. Smetana can curdle if it is overheated.

Buying and Storing: When buying milk, cream, and cream-related products, don't forget to check the label. Manufacturers and retailers are obliged to give a "best before" or "sell-by" date on the packet. The fat content, nutritional information, and list of ingredients will also be

Buttermilk

detailed. Try to avoid products that contain unnecessary additives or flavorings. For instance, low-fat crème fraîche, yogurts, and cream may contain animal-based gelatin, which acts as a thickener. Store dairy products in the fridge and consume within a few days of opening. Long-life cartons will keep indefinitely but once opened, must be treated as fresh and kept in the fridge.

Health Benefits: Milk is an important source of calcium and phosphorus, both of which are essential for healthy teeth and bones, and are said to prevent osteoporosis. Milk also contains significant amounts of zinc and the B vitamins, including B_{12}, along with a small amount of vitamin D. Numerous studies have revealed that, due to its high calcium content, milk fortified with vitamin D may have a role in preventing colon cancer. The antibodies found in milk may boost the immune system and help gastrointestinal problems, and skim milk may reduce the amount of cholesterol produced by the liver.

Above, clockwise from bottom left: Whipping cream, light cream, and whipped heavy cream

Other Non-dairy "Milks"

Apart from soy "milk", non-dairy "milks" or drinks are usually either nut- or grain-based. They can be used as a substitute for regular milk in a wide variety of sweet and non-sweet dishes, such as milk puddings, custards, hot and cold milk drinks, and sauces, but shouldn't be overheated or cooked for too long or they may curdle.

Oat "milk" Made from oat kernels and either vegetable or sunflower oil, this nutritious drink is high in fiber.

Rice "milk" With a similar consistency to soy "milk", rice "milk" is also non-mucous forming. Rice "milk" is easily digested and almost non-allergenic.

Nut "milk" Crushed and ground almonds or cashew nuts are mixed with water to form this mild-tasting non-dairy "milk".

Clockwise from left: "Milks" made from rice, almonds, and oats

Making Yogurt

It is easy to make yogurt at home—simply make sure that you use live yogurt as a starter and that it is as fresh as possible. Once you have made the first batch, you can reserve some of the yogurt as a starter for the next. Don't use too much starter or the yogurt may become sour and grainy. Yogurt can be flavored with fresh or dried fruit, or honey, or to make a more substantial dish, stir in soaked oats, chopped nuts, and toasted seeds.

1 Pour 2½ cups whole, low-fat, or skim milk into a saucepan and bring to a boil. Remove the pan from the heat and let the milk cool to 113°F.

2 If you don't have a thermometer, you can use your finger—the milk should feel slightly hotter than is comfortable. Pour the warm milk into a medium-size, sterilized bowl.

3 Whisk in 1–2 tablespoons live yogurt—this acts as a starter. Leave in the bowl or transfer it to a large jar.

4 Cover the bowl or jar with plastic wrap, then insulate the bowl or jar with several layers of dish cloths, and place in a warm airing cupboard. Alternatively, the yogurt can be transferred to a vacuum flask to keep it warm. Leave for 10–12 hours until set. Transfer to the fridge.

SOY SUBSTITUTES

Soy "milk"

This is the most widely used alternative to milk. Made from pulverized soybeans, it is suitable for both cooking and drinking and is used to make yogurt, cream, and cheese. Soy "milk" is interchangeable with cow milk, although it has a slightly thicker consistency and a nutty flavor. Fruit- and chocolate-flavored soy "milk", and versions fortified with extra vitamins, are widely available in heath food stores and larger supermarkets.

Soy "cream"

This is made from a higher proportion of beans than that in soy "milk", which gives it a richer flavor and thicker texture. It has a similar consistency to light cream and can be used in the same ways.

Buying and Storing: Most soy "milks" and "creams" are sold in long-life cartons, which extends their shelf-life and means that they do not require refrigeration until opened. Buy soy "milk" that is fortified with extra vitamins and calcium and, depending on how you intend to use it, choose the sweetened or unsweetened variety. Some retailers stock fresh soy "milk" and this should be treated in the same way as cow milk.

Health Benefits: Soy "milk" and "cream" are a valuable source of protein, calcium, iron, magnesium, phosphorus, and vitamin E. The "milk" is low in calories and contains no cholesterol. Numerous studies have shown that soy can reduce the risk of certain cancers, heart disease, kidney disease, and osteoporosis.

YOGURT

Praised for its health-giving qualities, yogurt has earned a reputation as one of the most valuable health foods. The fat content ranges from 0.5 grams per 100 grams for very low-fat or virtually fat-free yogurts to 4 grams per 100 grams for wholemilk yogurt. The consistency may be thin or thick. Greek-style yogurt, which is made from cow or sheep milk, contains about 10 grams of fat per 100 grams— just enough to prevent it from curdling during cooking. However, although it is higher in fat than other types of yogurt, it contains less fat than cream and makes a healthier alternative. Lower-fat yogurts can also be used instead of cream, but are best used in uncooked dishes. Strained yogurt has its watery whey removed to

make it thicker and richer, and has a similar fat content to Greek-style yogurts. When buying yogurt, look for "live" on the label. This signifies that it has been fermented with a starter culture bacteria (usually *Lactobacillus bulgaricus* or *Streptococcus thermophilous*), which is beneficial to health. Bio yogurts, which contain extra bacteria (often *Lactobacillus acidophilus* or *Bifidobacterium bifidum*), have a milder flavor than other yogurts, and may have wider healing benefits.

Buying and Storing: Yogurt has a limited shelf-life, so it is important to check the "best before" or "sell-by" date on the label. Although yogurt making is essentially a natural process, many manufacturers add unnecessary amounts of sugar, colorings, flavorings, and other additives, such as thickeners and stabilizers. Some yogurts, especially low-fat varieties, may contain gelatin, an animal by-product. Low-calorie yogurts usually contain artificial sweeteners. Fruit yogurts may contain a high amount of sugar, as well as colorings and flavorings; check the label before buying, and choose varieties that have a high fruit content—those with the highest amount will mention fruit first in the list of ingredients. More expensive, specialty yogurts may be the least adulterated.

Health Benefits: Yogurt is rich in calcium, phosphorus, and B vitamins. The bacteria present in live yogurt ensure that it is easily digestible: it may stimulate the friendly bacteria in the gut and suppress harmful bacteria, so aiding digestion and relieving gastrointestinal problems. Evidence suggests that yogurt can help protect against vaginal thrush and may be applied externally.

Live and bio yogurts have extra health benefits, although their levels of good bacteria can vary. The bacteria in bio yogurt may help boost natural resistance to food poisoning and tummy bugs and, if eaten after a course of antibiotics, may restore the internal flora of the intestines. There is also evidence to suggest that bio yogurt that contains the *acidophilus* culture could prevent cancer of the colon.

Cooking with Yogurt

Yogurt is a useful culinary ingredient, but does not respond well to heating. It is best added at the end of cooking, just before serving, to prevent it from curdling and to retain its vital bacteria. High-fat yogurts are more stable, but it is possible to stabilize and thicken low-fat yogurt by stirring in a little blended cornstarch before cooking. Unsweetened yogurt can be used in a wide range of sweet and non-sweet dishes, and it makes a calming addition to hot curries.

Clockwise from top left: Thick cow milk yogurt, thin cow milk yogurt, Greek-style yogurt, soy yogurt, goat milk yogurt, and sheep milk yogurt

Soft and Hard Cheeses

The selection of cheeses in this section is a mere fraction of the extensive range that is available in good cheese stores and supermarkets. Some, like mozzarella and feta, are more often cooked in pies or on pizzas, or used in salads, while others, like the soft, white, Camembert-type goat cheeses, make a good addition to a cheese board.

MOZZARELLA

This delicate, silky-white cheese is usually made from cow milk, although authentically it should be made from buffalo milk. The sweet milky balls of cheese have excellent melting qualities, hence its use on pizzas and in bakes, but it is equally delicious served in salads. When combined with avocado and tomato it makes the classic Italian three-color salad.

FETA

Believed to be one of the first cheeses, feta is curdled naturally without the addition of rennet. Although it was once made with goat or sheep milk, it is now more often made with milk from cows. It is preserved in brine, hence its saltiness, and has a firm, crumbly texture. It is used in the classic Greek salad with cucumber, tomatoes, and olives. To reduce the salty taste of feta, rinse it in water, then let soak in cold water for 10 minutes.

Feta, which is packed in brine, can be bought as small rounds or larger blocks

GOAT CHEESE

Indispensable for those intolerant or allergic to cow milk, goat cheese varieties range from soft, mild and creamy through a Camembert-type, which has a soft center and downy rind, to the firm Cheddar alternative. Similarly, the flavor of goat cheese spans from fresh, creamy and mild to sharp and pungent.

HALLOUMI

This ancient cheese was first made by nomadic Bedouin tribes. It is commonly sold in small blocks, and is often sprinkled with mint. Halloumi has a firm, rubbery texture and retains its shape when broiled or fried. Some people consider it to be the vegetarian alternative to bacon.

CHEDDAR

Unfortunately, much of the Cheddar sold today is made in factories. Avoid these fairly tasteless, rubbery blocks and look for traditional farmhouse Cheddar, which is matured for between nine and 24 months, and has a rich, strong, savory flavor.

Mozzarella

Goat cheese comes in a multitude of different forms

Halloumi

Non-dairy Cheeses

Soy cheese is the most common non-dairy variety. It can lack the depth of flavor of cheese made from cow, goat, or sheep milk, but it is nevertheless a valuable alternative for people who prefer not to buy dairy products or who are lactose intolerant. Soy cheese is made from a blend of processed soybeans and vegetable fats and may be flavored with herbs and spices. Other non-dairy cheeses include a Parmesan-type cheese made from rice and a spice-flavored cheese produced from nuts.

PARMESAN

...allowed to mature for at least 18 months and up to four years, this richly flavored cheese may be high in fat—although not as high as Cheddar—but a little goes a long way. Avoid ready-grated Parmesan and opt for a chunk freshly cut off the block. Parmesan keeps for a long time in the fridge and is excellent grated and added to pasta, risottos, and bakes, or shaved over salads.

Buying and Storing: Hard cheeses are best stored in a cool pantry but, if kept in the fridge, the cheese should be left at room temperature for at least an hour before eating. Cheese starts to dry out as soon as it is cut, so keep it loosely wrapped in foil or waxed paper.

Health Benefits: Semisoft cheeses, such as mozzarella, and hard cheeses, such as Parmesan and Cheddar, contain valuable amounts of calcium, protein, vitamins, and minerals. Hard cheeses are also high in saturated fat. When buying hard cheeses, choose a sharp, good-quality type, as the strong flavor means that relatively small quantities are needed to add flavor to a dish. Saturated fat is known to increase blood cholesterol, which can lead to heart disease and stroke, so always eat cheese in moderation. On the plus side, research shows that cheese—particularly a waxy, hard cheese like Cheddar—eaten after a meal, may reduce the likelihood of tooth decay by as much as 50 percent.

Parmesan

Fresh Unripened Cheeses

As their name suggests, fresh unripened cheeses are young and immature. They have a light, mild taste that readily accepts stronger flavored ingredients, such as herbs and spices. Their high moisture content means that they are lower in fat and are less likely to induce migraines. Fresh cheeses can be used in both non-sweet dishes and desserts.

FROMAGE FRAIS

This smooth, fresh cheese has the same consistency as thick yogurt, but is less acidic. It can be used in the same way as yogurt: mixed with fruit purée to make fools; combined with dried fruit, nuts, and grains; or in sweet and non-sweet tarts. The fat content varies from almost nothing to about 8 percent. Full-fat fromage frais is the best choice for cooking, as it is less likely to separate.

RICOTTA

A soft, low-fat unsalted cheese, which can be made from sheep, goat, or cow milk, ricotta has a slightly granular texture and is widely used in Italian cooking. Its mild, clean flavor means that it is incredibly versatile. It makes a neutral base for crêpe fillings, and can be used as a stuffing for pasta, when it is often combined with spinach. Ricotta is also good in tarts, cakes, and cheesecakes, or it can be served simply on its own with fruit. Mixed with herbs and garlic, it make a tasty sandwich filling.

Below, clockwise from left: Ricotta, fromage frais, quark, cream cheese, and cottage cheese

QUARK

This low-fat cheese is usually made with low-fat or skim milk. Its mild, slightly tangy flavor and light, creamy texture make it perfect in cheesecakes and desserts, or it can be diluted with milk to make an alternative to cream. In northern European countries, it is used as a spread instead of butter.

COTTAGE CHEESE

Lower in fat than most other cheeses (between 2 and 5 percent), cottage cheese is not usually used for cooking, but is good in salads and dips. It makes a fine accompaniment to soft fruits and is best eaten as fresh as possible.

CREAM CHEESE

Commonly used in cheesecakes, dips, and spreads, this cheese has a rich, velvety consistency, mild flavor, and a high fat content—about 35 percent—although it is possible to buy lower-fat alternatives made from skim milk.

NON-DAIRY SOFT CHEESES

A wide range of soft, soy-based cheeses is available from health-food stores. They are a valuable alternative for people who prefer not to buy dairy products.

Buying and Storing: Fresh unripened cheeses do not keep for very long and are best bought in small quantities and eaten soon after purchase. Store in an airtight container in the fridge.

Health Benefits: Fresh unripened cheeses generally have a lower fat content than hard cheeses and are less likely to trigger migraines. They also provide plenty of protein, calcium, and vitamin B_{12}.

Always Read the Label

Check the labels on low-fat yogurts and soft cheeses as these products sometimes contain animal-derived gelatin, which is used as a setting agent. Until relatively recently, the rennet use for cheese-making was obtained from animals. Nowadays, however, vegetarian rennet is more widely used, although this may not be mentioned on the pack. If in doubt, check with the manufacturer.

Making Fresh Soft Cheese

Fresh soft cheese can be made using sour milk (made from milk mixed with yogurt) or sour cream. Use unsweetened or sweeten with honey, orange flower water, or soft fruit. Alternatively, mix with chopped fresh herbs and garlic.

1 Place 4 cups low-fat milk and ½ cup live yogurt or sour cream in a heavy-based saucepan and mix thoroughly. Bring to a boil, lower the heat, then simmer for 5 minutes, or until the milk curdles, stirring continuously.

2 Line a metal strainer or colander with cheesecloth and place over a large bowl. Pour the milk mixture into it and let drain for 1 hour, or until it stops dripping. Alternatively, gather together the edges of the cheesecloth, tie with string, and suspend over the bowl for about 1 hour, until it stops dripping.

3 The residue in the cheesecloth is the soft cheese. Store in a covered bowl in the fridge for 3–4 days.

Butter Versus Margarine

Whether butter is better than margarine has been the focus of much debate. The taste, especially of good-quality, farmhouse butter, is certainly superior to margarine. However, butter, which contains 80 percent saturated fat, has the ability to raise cholesterol levels in the body.

Vegetable margarine contains the same amount of fat as butter, but the fat is polyunsaturated, which was once considered to give margarine greater health benefits. Unfortunately, margarine manufacturing processes change the fats into trans fats, or hydrogenated fats. Studies have shown that trans fats may be more likely than the saturated fat in butter to damage the heart and blood vessels. In addition, cooking removes many of the health benefits of polyunsaturated fats.

SPREADS

Lower-fat margarines are known as spreads. They contain less than 80 percent fat and those that are under 65 percent fat can be classified as reduced-fat. When the fat content falls below 41 percent, a spread can be called low-fat or half-fat. Very low-fat spreads may contain gelatin, and their high water content means they are not suitable for cooking. Olive-oil based spreads are rich in monounsaturated fats and are said to reduce cholesterol levels. They can be used for cooking.

Buying and Storing: When buying margarine and spreads always choose good-quality brands that contain no hydrogenated fats. Butter, margarines, and spreads absorb other flavors, so they need to be kept well-wrapped. Always store these products in the fridge; unsalted butters will keep for up to 2 weeks, other butters for up to a month, and margarines and spreads will keep for about 2 months.

Below: There is a wide variety of different butters, margarines, and spreads available. Whichever you choose to use, don't consume too much of these high-fat foods.

Eggs

An inexpensive, self-contained source of nourishment, hen eggs offer the cook tremendous scope, whether served simply solo or as part of a dish. There are several different types, but the best are organic, free-range eggs from a small producer.

ORGANIC FREE-RANGE EGGS

These eggs are from hens that are fed on a natural pesticide-free diet, which has not had hormones or artificial colorants added. The hens are able to roam on land that has not been treated with chemical fertilizers and is certified organic. Free-range hens have the same indoor conditions as barn hens, but also have daytime access to the open air.

It is important to note that eggs can be either free-range or organic, without being both. Check the labeling carefully, or ask the seller to confirm the details.

SIZE

Several factors influence the size of an egg. The major factor is the size of the hen. As the hen ages, her eggs increase in size. Egg sizes are Jumbo, Extra Large, Medium, Small and Peewee. Medium, Large and Extra Large are most commonly available.

FRESHNESS

How recently an egg was laid has a bearing on freshness, but the temperature at which it is held, the humidity and handling, also play their part. An egg one week old, held under ideal conditions, can be fresher than an egg left at room temperature for a day.

Organic free-range eggs

CARTON DATES

Egg cartons for USDA-inspected plants must display a Julian date — the date the eggs were packed. Although not required, they may also carry an expiration date beyond which the eggs should not be sold. In USDA-inspected plants, this date cannot exceed 30 days after the pack date. Plants not under USDA inspection are governed by the laws of their states.

Cooking with Eggs: Eggs can be cooked in myriad ways. Simply boiled, fried, or poached, they make a wonderful breakfast dish. Lightly cooked poached eggs are also delicious served as a lunch dish with high-fiber lentils or beans. Eggs are delicious baked, either on their own, with a drizzle of cream, or broken into a nest of lightly cooked bell peppers or leeks. They make delicious omelets, whether cooked undisturbed until just softly set, combined with tomatoes and bell peppers to make an Italian frittata, or cooked with diced potato and onions to make the classic Spanish omelet. They are also often used as a filling for pies, savory tarts, and quiches.

Eggs are not only used in savory dishes. They are essential to many sweet dishes, too. They are added to cake, crêpe and popover batter, are crucial to meringues, mousses, and hot and cold soufflés, and are used in all kinds of desserts, from ice creams and custards to rice pudding.

When separated, egg yolks are used to thicken sauces and soups, giving them a rich, smooth consistency, while egg whites can be whisked to make meringues and soufflés. Use eggs at room temperature and remove them from the refrigerator about 30 minutes before cooking.

Misleading Labels

Eggs are often described with phrases such as "farm fresh", "natural," or "country-fresh," which conjure up images of hens roaming around in the open, but they may well refer to eggs that are laid by birds reared in indoor systems. Organic or free-range eggs will always be labeled as such.

Buying and Storing: Freshness is paramount when buying eggs. Buy from a store that has a high turnover of stock. You should reject any eggs that have a broken, dirty, or damaged shell. Most eggs are date stamped, but you can easily check if an egg is fresh by placing it in a bowl of cold water: if the egg sinks and lays flat it is fresh. The older the egg, the more it will stand on its end. A really old egg will actually float and shouldn't be eaten. Store eggs in a box in the main part of the fridge and not in a rack in the door as this can expose them to odors and damage. The shells are extremely porous, so eggs can be tainted by strong smells. Eggs should be stored large-end up for no longer than 3 weeks.

Health Benefits: Eggs have received much adverse publicity owing to their high cholesterol levels. However, attention has moved away from dietary cholesterol to cholesterol that is produced in the body from saturated fats. Saturated fats are now claimed to play a bigger role in raising cholesterol levels, and as eggs are low in saturated fat, they have been somewhat reprieved. They should, however, be eaten in moderation, and people with raised cholesterol levels should take particular care. Nutritionists recommend that we eat no more than four eggs a week. Eggs provide B vitamins, especially B_{12}, vitamins A and D, iron, choline, and phosphorus, and cooking does not significantly alter their nutritional content.

Quick Ideas for Eggs

• Brush beaten egg onto pastries and bread before baking to give them a golden glaze.
• For a protein boost, top Thai- or Chinese-flavored rice or noodle dishes with strips of thin omelet.
• Turn mixed salad greens into a light supper dish by adding a soft-cooked egg and some half-fat mayonnaise.
• For a simple dessert, make a soufflé omelet. Separate 2 eggs and whisk the whites and yolks separately. Fold together and add a little sugar. Cook in the same way as a non-sweet omelet and serve plain or fill with fruit conserve or lemon curd.

Herb Omelet

A simple, herb-flavored omelet is quick to cook and, served with a salad and a chunk of crusty bread, makes a nutritious, light meal. Even if you are going to serve more than one, it is better to cook individual omelets and eat them as soon as they are ready.

INGREDIENTS

2 eggs
1 tablespoon chopped fresh herbs, such as tarragon, parsley, or chives
1 teaspoon butter
salt and freshly ground black pepper

SERVES 1

1 Lightly beat the eggs in a bowl, add the fresh herbs, and season to taste.

2 Melt the butter in a heavy-based, non-stick skillet and swirl it around to coat the base evenly.

3 Pour in the egg mixture and, as the egg sets, push the edges toward the center using a spoon, allowing the raw egg to run on to the hot skillet.

4 Cook for about 2 minutes, without stirring, until the egg is just lightly set. Quickly fold over the omelet and serve at once.

The Pantry

The following section features a diverse range of foods that can enrich and add variety to a vegetarian diet. Some ingredients may be familiar, others less so, but all are useful to keep in the pantry. Each of the mentioned foods comes with notes on choosing, storage, and preparation, when necessary, as well as nutritional or medicinal properties.

Nuts

With the exception of peanuts, nuts are the fruits of trees. The quality and availability of fresh nuts varies with the seasons, although most types are sold dried, either whole or prepared ready for use. Shelled nuts come in many forms: they may be whole, blanched, halved, sliced, shredded, chopped, ground, or toasted.

Chestnuts

ALMONDS

There are two types of almond: sweet and bitter. The best sweet varieties are the flat and slender Jordan almonds from Spain. Heart-shaped Valencia almonds from Portugal and Spain, and the flatter Californian almonds are also widely available. For the best flavor, buy shelled almonds in their skins and blanch them yourself: cover with boiling water, leave for a few minutes, then drain, and the skins will peel off easily. Almonds are available ready-blanched, slivered, and ground. The latter adds a richness to cakes, tarts, pastry, and sauces. Bitter almonds are much smaller and are used in almond oil and essence. They should not be eaten raw as they contain traces of the lethal prussic acid.

BRAZIL NUTS

These are, in fact, seeds, and are grown mainly in the Amazon regions of Brazil and other neighboring countries. Between 12 and 20 Brazil nuts grow, packed snugly together, in a large brown husk, hence their three-cornered wedge shape. Brazil nuts have a sweet, milky taste and are used mainly as dessert nuts. They have a high fat content, so go rancid very quickly.

CASHEW NUTS

These are the seeds of the "cashew apple"—an evergreen tree with bright-orange fruit. Cashew nuts have a sweet flavor and crumbly texture. They make delicious nut butters, or can be sprinkled into stir-fries or over salads. They are never sold in the shell and undergo an extensive heating process that removes the seed from its outer casing.

CHESTNUTS

Raw chestnuts are not recommended as they are not only unpleasant to eat but also contain tannic acid, which inhibits the absorption of iron. Most chestnuts are imported from France and Spain and they are excellent after roasting, which complements their soft, mealy texture. Unlike other nuts, they contain very little fat. Out of season, chestnuts can be bought dried, canned, or puréed.

Blanched, whole and shelled almonds; shelled cashew nuts (in bowl); shelled and whole Brazil nuts

Add whole chestnuts to winter stews, soups, stuffings, or pies. The sweetened purée is delicious in desserts.

COCONUTS

This versatile nut grows all over the tropics. The white dense meat, or flesh, is made into shredded coconut, blocks of creamed coconut, and a thick and creamy milk. A popular ingredient in Asian, African, and South American cuisines, coconut lends a sweet, creamy flavor to desserts,

curries, soups, and casseroles. Use coconut in moderation, as it is particularly high in fat.

HAZELNUTS

Grown in the United States, Britain, Turkey, Italy, and Spain, hazelnuts are usually sold dried, and can be bought whole, shelled, and ground. They can be eaten raw, and the shelled nuts are especially good toasted. Hazelnuts can be grated or chopped for use in cakes and desserts, but they are also tasty in savory dishes and can be added to salads, stir-fries and pasta.

Hazelnuts

Macadamia nuts

Peeling Chestnuts

Peeling chestnuts can be awkward and time-consuming but this is one of the simplest and quickest methods.

1 Place the chestnuts in a saucepan of boiling water, turn off the heat. and let stand for 5 minutes.

2 Remove the nuts with a slotted spoon, then leave until cool enough to handle. Peel with a sharp knife.

MACADAMIA NUTS

This round nut, about the size of a large hazelnut, is native to Australia, but is now grown in California and South America. Macadamia nuts are commonly sold shelled (the shell is extremely hard to crack). They have a crisp texture, a rich, buttery flavor and a high fat content.

Coconut Milk

Coconut milk or cream can be bought in cans or long-life cartons, but it is easy to make at home: put 2⅔ cups shredded coconut into a food processor, add scant 2 cups boiling water, and process for 30 seconds. Let cool slightly, then transfer to a cheesecloth-lined strainer placed over a bowl, and gather the ends of the cloth. Twist the cloth to extract the liquid, then discard the spent coconut. Store any unused coconut milk in the fridge for 1–2 days, or freeze.

Thick coconut cream, coconut milk, and shredded coconut

PEANUTS

Not strictly a nut but a member of the pulse family, peanuts bury themselves just below the earth after flowering—hence their alternative name, groundnuts. They are a staple food in many countries, and are widely used in Southeast Asia, notably for satay sauce, and in African cuisines, where they are used as an ingredient in stews. In the West, peanuts are a popular snack food; the shelled nuts are frequently sold roasted and salted, and they are used to make peanut butter. Peanuts are particularly high in fat and should be eaten in moderation.

PECAN NUTS

A glossy, reddish-brown, oval-shaped shell encloses the pecan kernel, which looks like an elongated walnut, but has a sweeter, milder flavor. This native American nut is a favorite in sweet pies, especially the classic pecan pie, but is also good eaten on its own, or added to salads. However, pecan

Pecan nuts

nuts should be eaten only as an occasional treat because they have the highest fat content of any nut, with a calorie content to match.

PINE NUTS

These tiny, cream-colored nuts are the fruit of the Mediterranean stone pine tree. They have a rich, aromatic flavor, which lends itself to toasting. Buy in small quantities as their high oil content quickly turns them rancid. Pine nuts are a key

ingredient in Italian pesto sauce, where they are pounded with garlic, olive oil, and basil, and in the Middle Eastern sauce, tarator, in which toasted pine nuts are combined with bread, garlic, milk, and olive oil to make a creamy paste that has a similar consistency to hummus.

PISTACHIO NUTS

Incredibly irresistible when served as a snack, pistachio nuts have pale green flesh and thin, reddish-purple skin. Sold shelled or in a split shell, these mild nuts are often used chopped as a colorful garnish, sprinkled over both sweet and non-sweet foods. Pistachio nuts have a wonderful flavor, they are good in all manner of desserts and can be made into

Making Nut Butter

Store-bought nut butters often contain unwanted hydrogenated oil and can be loaded with sugar. To avoid additives, make your own butter using a combination of peanuts, hazelnuts, and cashew nuts.

1 Place ½ cup shelled nuts in a food processor or blender and process until finely and evenly ground.

2 Pour 1–2 tablespoons sunflower oil into the processor or blender and process to a coarse paste. Store in an airtight jar.

Peanuts

Pine nuts

Walnuts

Nut Allergy

Any food has the potential to cause an allergic reaction, but peanuts, as well as walnuts, Brazil nuts, hazelnuts, and almonds are known to be common allergens. In cases of extreme allergy, nuts can trigger a life-threatening reaction known as anaphylaxis. Symptoms include facial swelling, shortness of breath, dizziness, and loss of consciousness, so it is essential that sufferers take every precaution to avoid nuts.

a delicious ice cream. They are widely used in Turkish and Arabic candies, notably nougat and Turkish Delight. Check before buying pistachio nuts for cooking, as they are often sold salted.

WALNUTS

Most walnuts are grown in France, Italy, and California, but they are also grown in the Middle East, Britain, and China. This versatile nut has been around for hundreds of years. When picked young, walnuts are referred to as "wet" and have fresh, milky-white kernels, which can be eaten raw, but are often pickled.

Dried walnuts have a delicious bitter-sweet flavor and can be bought shelled, chopped, or ground. They can be used to make excellent cakes and cookies, as well as rich pie fillings, but are also good added to non-sweet dishes, such as stir-fries and salads—the classic Waldorf salad combines whole kernels with sliced celery and apples in a mayonnaise dressing.

Buying and Storing:
Always buy nuts in small quantities from a store with a high turnover of stock, because if kept for too long, they can turn rancid. Nuts in their shells should feel heavy for their size. Store nuts in airtight containers in a cool, dark place or in the fridge and they should keep fresh for at least 3 months. When buying a coconut, make sure that there is no sign of mold or a rancid smell. Give it a shake—it should be full of liquid. Keep coconut milk in the fridge or freezer once opened. Shredded coconut can be stored in an airtight container, but don't keep it too long, as its high fat content means that it is prone to rancidity.

Health Benefits: Rich in B complex vitamins, vitamin E, potassium, magnesium, calcium, phosphorus, and iron, nuts offer the vegetarian an abundance of nutrients, although they contain a hefty number of calories. Most nuts are rich in monounsaturated and polyunsaturated fats, with the exception of Brazil nuts and coconuts, which are high in saturated fat, but do not contain cholesterol. Numerous studies highlight the substantial health benefits of walnuts. According to one study, the essential fatty acids found in walnuts can decrease cholesterol levels and may reduce the risk of heart disease by 50 percent. Almonds and hazelnuts have similar properties.

Of all foods, Brazil nuts are the richest in selenium, which is a known mood enhancer. Apparently, a single Brazil nut each day will ensure that you are never deficient in this vital mineral.

Nuts are one of the richest vegetable sources of the antioxidant vitamin E, which has been associated with a lower risk of heart disease, stroke, and certain cancers.

Roasting and Skinning Nuts

The flavor of most nuts, particularly hazelnuts and peanuts, is improved by roasting. It also enables the thin outer skin to be removed more easily.

1 Place the nuts in a single layer on a cookie sheet. Bake in a preheated oven at 350°F for 10–20 minutes, or until the skins begin to split and the nuts are golden.

2 Put the nuts on to a dish cloth and rub to loosen and remove the skins.

Pistachio nuts

Seeds

They may look very small and unassuming, but seeds are nutritional powerhouses, packed with vitamins and minerals, as well as beneficial oils and protein. They can be used in a huge array of sweet and non-sweet dishes, and will add an instant, healthy boost, pleasant crunch, and nutty flavor when added to rice and pasta dishes, salads, stir-fries, soups, and yogurt.

Tahini (left) and black and white sesame seeds

SESAME SEEDS

These tiny, white or black seeds are a feature of Middle Eastern and Asian cooking. In the Middle East they are ground into tahini, a thick paste that is a key component of hummus. Sesame seeds are also ground to make halvah, a sweet confection from Greece, Israel, and Turkey. Gomassio, or gomashio, is the name of a crushed sesame seed condiment used in Japan. It can easily be made at home: toast the seeds, then crush with a little sea salt in a mortar using a pestle. Try a ratio of one part salt to five parts sesame seeds.

The flavor of sesame seeds is improved by roasting them in a dry skillet; it gives them a distinctive nuttiness. The toasted seeds make a good addition to salads and noodle dishes. Unroasted seeds can be used as a topping for breads, rolls, cakes, and cookies, and they can be added to pie dough.

When buying sesame seeds, try to find seeds that have been mechanically rolled—the tell-tale sign is a flat appearance. Seeds subjected to other methods of processing, such as salt-brining or a chemical bath, are usually glossy. Salt brining can affect the flavor of the seeds, as can chemical processing, which also damages their nutritional value.

SUNFLOWER SEEDS

These are the seeds of the sunflower, a symbol of summer and an important crop throughout the world. The impressive, golden-yellow flowers are grown for their seeds and oil; the leaves are used to treat malaria, and the stalks are made into fertilizer. Rich in vitamin E, the pale-green, tear-drop-shaped seeds have a semi-crunchy texture and an oily taste that is much improved by dry-roasting. Sprinkle sunflower seeds over salads, rice pilaffs, and couscous, or use in bread dough, muffins, casseroles, and baked dishes.

POPPY SEEDS

These are the seeds of the opium poppy, but without any of the habit-forming alkaloids. Poppy seeds can be blue (usually described as black) or white. The black variety looks good sprinkled over cakes and breads, adding a pleasant crunch.

Sunflower seeds

Black and white poppy seeds

Black poppy seeds can be used to make delicious seed cakes and sweet breads, and they are used in German and Eastern European pastries, strudels, and tarts. In India, the ground white seeds are used to thicken sauces, adding a nutty flavor.

PUMPKIN SEEDS

Richer in iron than any other seed and an excellent source of zinc, pumpkin seeds make a nutritious snack eaten on their own. They are also delicious lightly toasted, tossed in a little toasted sesame seed oil or soy sauce, and stirred into mixed salad greens or rice salad. Pumpkin seeds are widely used in South American cooking, where they are generally roasted and ground to make into sauces.

Quick Ideas for Seeds

• Sprinkle over breads, cakes, and cookies just before baking.
• Combine with dried or fresh fruit, chopped nuts and unsweetened yogurt to make a nutritious breakfast.
• Add to flapjacks, whole wheat biscuits, and pastry to give them a nutty flavor.
• Add a spoonful of seeds to rissoles, vegetable burgers, or casseroles.
• Mix with rolled oats, flour, butter or margarine, and sugar to make a sweet crumble topping. Omit the sugar to make a non-sweet topping and combine with chopped fresh herbs.
• Use sunflower or pumpkin seeds in place of pine nuts to make pesto.
• Scatter over mixed salad greens.
• Add a nutritional boost to stir-fries or noodle dishes, by scattering seeds over them.

Pumpkin seeds

HEMP SEEDS

The cultivation of hemp has a long history, but for various reasons it fell out of fashion. Today, hemp is making a comeback as a food. Hemp seeds are best roasted as this enhances their nutty flavor, and they can be used in a variety of sweet and non-sweet dishes.

LINSEEDS

Linseed oil has long been used to embellish wooden furniture. However, the golden seed, also known as flaxseed, is a rich source of polyunsaturated fat, including the essential fatty acid, linoleic acid. Linseeds can be added to muesli and other breakfast cereals, mixed into bread dough, or sprinkled over salads.

Buying and Storing: Seeds are best bought in small quantities from stores with a high turnover of stock. Purchase whole seeds, rather than ground, and store them in a cool, dark place as they are prone to turning rancid. After opening the packet, transfer the seeds to an airtight container.

Linseeds (left) and hemp seeds

Health Benefits: Seeds contain valuable amounts of the antioxidant vitamin E, which enhances the immune system and protects cells from oxidation. Vitamin E also improves blood circulation, and promotes healing and normal blood clotting, as well as reducing infections associated with aging. Numerous studies show that the vitamin works in tandem with beta carotene and vitamin C to fight off certain cancers and heart disease as well as slowing the progression of Alzheimer's disease.

Seeds, particularly sunflower seeds, may help to reduce blood cholesterol levels in the body because they contain plentiful amounts of linoleic acid, which is also known as omega-6 fatty acid.

For their size, seeds contain a huge amount of iron. Sesame seeds are particularly rich—2–3 tablespoons provide nearly half the daily requirement of iron, and ½ cup pumpkin seeds provides almost three-quarters of the iron we need each day. Sunflower seeds are often prescribed by natural medicine practitioners for their restorative qualities.

Roasting Seeds

The flavor of seeds is much improved by "roasting" them in a dry skillet. Black poppy seeds won't turn golden brown, so watch them carefully to make sure that they don't scorch.

1 Spread out a spoonful or two of seeds in a thin layer in a large, non-stick skillet and heat gently.

2 Cook over medium heat for 2–3 minutes, tossing the seeds frequently, until they are golden brown.

Spices

Highly revered for thousands of years, spices—the seeds, fruit, pods, bark, and buds of plants—have been the reason for wars and were sometimes traded as a currency. In addition to their ability to add flavor and interest to the most unassuming of ingredients, the evocative aroma of spices stimulates the appetite. Today, spices are still prized for their medicinal properties and culinary uses, and they play a vital role in healthy and appetizing vegetarian cooking.

Caraway seeds

Ground allspice

ALLSPICE

These small, dried berries of a tropical, South American tree have a sweet, warming flavor reminiscent of a blend of cloves, cinnamon, and nutmeg. Although allspice is available ready-ground, it is best to buy the spice whole to retain its flavor, and grind just before use in cakes and cookies. The whole berries can be added to marinades or mulled wine. Allspice is used to relieve digestive problems, including flatulence.

CARAWAY

An important flavoring in Eastern European, Austrian, and German cooking, caraway seeds are sprinkled over rye bread, cakes, and cookies. They have a distinctive, sweet, aniseed flavor, which is also a welcome addition to potato- and cheese-based dishes, steamed carrots, or cabbage. Caraway is recommended for colicky babies and has a similar effect in adults, relieving gas and aiding digestion. It can also be used to relieve menstrual pain.

CARDAMOM

Often used in Middle Eastern and Indian cooking, cardamom is best bought whole in its pod as it soon loses its aromatic flavor when ground. The pod can be used whole, slightly crushed, or for a more intense flavor, the seeds can be

Cardamom pods

ground. Cardamom is superb in both sweet and non-sweet dishes. It can be infused in milk used to flavor rice pudding or ice cream, and is often added to curries and other Indian dishes. The seeds can be chewed whole to freshen the breath and calm indigestion. Colds and coughs are also said to be relieved by eating cardamom.

CAYENNE

This fiery, reddish-brown powder adds color and heat, rather than flavor, to curries, soups, and stews. It comes from the ground pod and seeds of a very pungent variety of chile pepper, *Capsicum frutescens*, and is sometimes referred to as red pepper. Cayenne possesses stimulant, antiseptic, and digestive properties. It can improve blood circulation, but if eaten in large quantities may aggravate the stomach. A more unusual use of cayenne is to sprinkle it in your shoes to warm up cold feet!

Cayenne, celery seeds, chile powder, and chile flakes.

Above, clockwise from left: Cinnamon sticks, coriander seeds, cloves, and ground cinnamon

CELERY SEEDS

These tiny brown seeds have a similar flavor to celery, but are more highly aromatic. It is important to grind or crush them before use to avoid any bitterness. Celery seeds can be used in almost any dish that calls for celery, and they add a pungent flavor to vegetarian bakes, stews, soups, sauces, and egg dishes. Celery salt is a mixture of ground celery seeds, salt, and other herbs. Celery seeds are carminative, relieving both flatulence and indigestion.

CHILE

Fresh chile peppers are covered in the vegetable section, but this versatile spice is also sold in dried, powdered, and flaked form. Dried chiles tend to be hotter than fresh, and this is certainly true of chile flakes, which contain both the seeds and the flesh. The best pure chile powders do not contain added ingredients, such as onion and garlic. A powerful stimulant and expectorant, chile also has a reputation as an aphrodisiac.

CINNAMON

This warm, comforting spice is available in sticks (quills) and ground. As the bark is difficult to grind, it is useful to keep both forms in the pantry. Cinnamon can enhance both sweet and non-sweet dishes. Use the sticks to flavor pilaffs, curries, couscous, and dried fruit compotes, but remove before serving. Ground cinnamon adds a pleasing fragrance to cakes, cookies, and fruit. Cinnamon is an effective detoxifier and cleanser, containing substances that kill bacteria and other microorganisms.

CLOVES

The unopened bud of an evergreen tree from Southeast Asia, this spice is often used in combination with cinnamon to flavor desserts, cakes, and cookies. Cloves are often used to flavor the syrup when poaching oranges, but they are also delicious with cooked apples.

Clove oil has long been used as a cure for toothache, and both its antiseptic and anesthetic qualities can relieve other pains.

CORIANDER

Alongside cumin, ground coriander is a key ingredient in Indian curry powders and garam masala, and in northern Europe the ivory-colored seeds are used as a pickling spice. Coriander seeds have a sweet, earthy, burnt-orange flavor that is more pronounced than the fresh leaves. The ready-ground powder rapidly loses its flavor and aroma, so it is best to buy whole seeds, which are easily ground in a mortar using a pestle, or in a coffee grinder. Before grinding, lightly dry-roast the seeds in a skillet to enhance their flavor. Coriander has been prescribed as a digestive for thousands of years, relieving indigestion, diarrhea, and nausea. It also has antibacterial properties.

Cumin seeds, ground cumin, and (front) fenugreek

CUMIN

Extensively used in Indian curries, cumin is also a familiar component of Mexican, North African, and Middle Eastern cooking. The seeds have a robust aroma and slightly bitter taste, which is tempered by dry-roasting. Black cumin seeds, which are also known as nigella, are milder and sweeter. Ground cumin can be harsh, so it is best to buy the whole seeds and grind them just before use to ensure a fresh flavor. Cumin is good in tomato- or grain-based dishes, and its digestive properties mean that it is also ideal with beans.

FENUGREEK

This spice is commonly used in commercial curry powders, along with cumin and coriander. On its own though, fenugreek should be used in moderation because its bitter-sweet flavor, which is mellowed by dry-frying, can be quite overpowering. The seeds have a hard shell and are difficult to grind, but they can be sprouted and make a good addition to mixed salad greens and bean salads, as well as sandwich fillings. Fenugreek has long been prescribed to treat stomach and intestinal disorders, and its ability to cleanse the body may help in the release of toxins.

Fresh ginger root

GINGER

This spice is probably one of the oldest and most popular herbal medicines. The fresh root, which is spicy, peppery, and fragrant, is good in both sweet and non-sweet dishes, adding a hot, yet refreshing, flavor to marinades, stir-fries, soups, curries, grains, and fresh vegetables. It also adds warmth to poached fruit, pastries, and cakes.

Ground ginger is the usual choice for flavoring cakes, cookies, and other baked goods, but finely grated fresh ginger can also be used and is equally good.

Ground ginger

Ginger tea, made by steeping a few slices of fresh ginger root in hot water for a few minutes, can calm and soothe the stomach after a bout of food poisoning, as well as ward off colds and flu.

Pink pickled ginger

This pretty, finely sliced ginger pickle is served as an accompaniment to Japanese food and is used to flavor sushi rice.

Crystallized ginger

Preserved in a thick sugar syrup and sold in jars, this sweet ginger can be chopped and used in desserts, or added to cake mixtures, steamed puddings, cookies, shortbread, and muffins.

Buying and Storing: Fresh ginger root should look firm, thin-skinned, and unblemished. Avoid withered, woody-looking roots as these are likely to be dry and fibrous. Store in the fridge. Ground ginger should smell aromatic; keep in a cool, dark place.

Preparing Fresh Ginger

1 Fresh ginger root is most easily peeled using a vegetable peeler or a small, sharp paring knife.

3 Grate ginger finely—special graters can be found in Asian stores, but a box grater will do the job equally well.

2 Chop ginger, using a sharp knife, to the size specified in the recipe.

4 Freshly grated ginger can be squeezed to release the juice.

using a pestle. Bottled, chopped lemongrass and lemongrass purée are also available. Lemongrass is reputed to benefit rheumatism.

Galangal

Pink pickled ginger

GALANGAL

Closely related to ginger, fresh galangal looks similar but has a reddish-brown or cream-colored skin. It was popular in England during the Middle Ages, but fell out of favor. With the increased interest in Southeast Asian cooking, this knobby root is again widely available and can be found in Asian stores. Its fragrant, slightly peppery taste can be overpowering if used in excess. Avoid the powdered version, as it is nothing like the fresh. Prepare the root in the same way as ginger: peel, then slice,

grate, or pound in a mortar using a pestle. Galangal has similar medicinal properties to ginger, relieving nausea and stomach problems.

Health Benefits: The health benefits of ginger have been well documented for centuries. Recent studies confirm that ginger can successfully prevent nausea and may be more effective than prescribed drugs. Research also shows ginger to be effective in the treatment of pain and gastrointestinal disorders, and it may even halt certain cancers.

MUSTARD

There are three different types of mustard seed: white, brown, and black, which is the most pungent. The flavor and aroma is only apparent when the seeds are

LEMONGRASS

This long fibrous stalk has a fragrant citrus aroma and flavor when cut and is a familiar part of Southeast Asian and particularly Thai cooking, where it is used in coconut-flavored curries. If you have difficulty finding lemongrass, lemon rind is a suitable alternative, but it lacks the distinctive flavor of the fresh stalks.

To use, remove the tough, woody outer layers, trim the root, then cut off the lower 2 inches, and slice into thin rounds or pound in a mortar

crushed or mixed with liquid. If fried in a little oil before use, the flavor of the seeds is improved. As the intensity of mustard diminishes with both time and cooking; it is best added to dishes toward the end of cooking, or just before the dish is served.

Like many hot spices, mustard is traditionally used as a stimulant, cleansing the body of toxins and helping to ward off colds and flu.

Above: American mustard, Dijon mustard, wholegrain mustard, mustard powder, and black and white mustard seeds

Lemongrass

NUTMEG AND MACE

When it is picked, the nutmeg seed is surrounded by a lacy membrane called mace. Both are dried and used as spices. Nutmeg and mace taste similar, and their warm, sweet flavor enlivens white sauces, cheese-based dishes, and vegetables, as well as custards, cakes, and cookies. Freshly grated nutmeg is far superior to the ready-ground variety, which loses its flavor and aroma with time. Although it is a hallucinogen if eaten in excess, when consumed in the small quantities that are needed in recipes, nutmeg improves both appetite and digestion.

Ground saffron and saffron threads

White, black, and pink peppercorns

Green peppercorns

These unripened berries have a milder flavor than black or white peppercorns and may be dried or preserved in brine. They are sometimes used to make a spicy peppercorn sauce.

Pink peppercorns

These pretty, pink berries are not a true pepper. They are the processed berry of a type of poison ivy and should be used in small amounts as they are mildly toxic.

PAPRIKA

Paprika is a milder relative of cayenne and can be used more liberally, adding flavor as well as heat. Like cayenne, it is a digestive stimulant and has antiseptic properties. Paprika can also improve blood circulation, but if eaten in large quantities may aggravate the stomach.

SAFFRON

The world's most expensive spice is made from the dried stigmas of *Crocus salivus*. Only a tiny amount of this bright-orange spice is needed to add a wonderful color and delicate bitter-sweet flavor to rice, stews, soups, and milky puddings. Saffron has the ability to calm and balance the body and is believed to be an aphrodisiac.

ground in a peppermill when you need them because they quickly lose their aroma.

White pepper

This has a less aromatic flavor than black pepper and is generally used in white sauces and other dishes to avoid dark specks of black pepper.

PEPPER

Undoubtedly the oldest, most widely used spice in the world, pepper was as precious as gold and silver in medieval Europe. It is a very useful seasoning, because it not only adds flavor of its own to a dish, but also brings out the flavor of the other ingredients. Pepper is a digestive stimulant, as well as a decongestant and antioxidant.

Black peppercorns

These are the dried green berries of the vine pepper and they are relatively mild. Black peppercorns are best when freshly

Right, clockwise from top left: Pumpkin pie spice, ground and whole nutmegs, and paprika

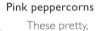

Ground and fresh turmeric

used more than once; simply rinse and dry before storing in an airtight jar. Buy natural vanilla extract or essence, which is made by infusing the beans in alcohol: artificial vanilla flavoring is nowhere near so good. Vanilla is considered to be an aphrodisiac and a tonic for the brain.

Buying and Storing: Buy spices in small quantities from a store with a regular turnover of stock. Aroma is the best indication of freshness, as this diminishes when the spice is stale. Store in airtight jars in a cool place away from direct light.

Grinding Spices

Whole spices ground by hand provide the best flavor and aroma. Grind as you need them and do not be tempted to grind too much, as they tend to lose their potency and flavor. Some spices, such as mace, fenugreek, cloves, turmeric, and cinnamon, are difficult to grind at home and are better bought ready-ground.

Grind whole spices in a mortar using a pestle—or use an electric coffee grinder if desired.

Toasting Spices

This process enhances the flavor and aroma of spices and is thought to make them more digestible.

Put the spices in a dry skillet and cook over low heat, shaking the skillet frequently, for 1 minute, or until the spices release their aroma.

TURMERIC

Sometimes used as an alternative to saffron, turmeric delivers a similar yellow color but has a very different flavor. It adds an earthy, peppery flavor to curries and stews. Turmeric is valued for its antibacterial and antifungal qualities. It can aid digestion and in Asia it is believed to be a remedy for liver problems.

VANILLA

These slender, chocolate-brown beans have a fragrant, exotic aroma and luscious, almost creamy flavor. They can be

Natural vanilla extract and vanilla pods

Salt

Moderate amounts of salt are needed by the body, but it is easy to consume too much, as salt is added to many processed foods. Too much salt can lead to high blood pressure, hypertension, water retention and may increase the risk of heart disease. Used in small amounts, salt can enhance the flavor of food. Use rock or sea salt rather than refined table salt.

Table salt (top), rock salt (right), and sea salt

Pasta

Once considered a fattening food, pasta is now recognized as an important part of a healthy diet. The variety of shapes is almost endless, from the myriad tiny soup pastas to huge shells used for stuffing. Pasta can be plain, made with egg, or flavored with ingredients such as tomato or spinach. Low in fat and high in complex carbohydrates, it provides plenty of long-term energy. Corn and buckwheat varieties are also available, as is whole wheat pasta, which is high in fiber.

Pasta is one of our simplest, yet most versatile foods. A combination of wheat flour and water produces the basic dough, which can then be formed into an infinite number of shape variations. Alter the type of flour, add fresh eggs or a vegetable purée, and the options are even greater. Although pasta is itself a low-fat food, it is important to take care when choosing the accompanying sauce, as overloading on cheese or cream can soon transform pasta into a high-fat food.

DURUM WHEAT PASTA

This is the most readily available type of pasta and can be made with or without egg. Plain wheat pasta is used for straight long shapes, such as spaghetti, while long shapes made with egg pasta, because it is more delicate, are traditionally packed in nests or compressed into waves. Lasagne can be made with either plain or egg pasta. At one time, almost all short pasta

Spaghetti, linguine, and tagliatelle

shapes were made from plain pasta, but shapes made with egg pasta are becoming increasingly available. Pasta made with egg has several advantages over plain pasta: it is more nutritious, many people consider it to have a superior flavor, and it is more difficult to overcook.

COLORED AND FLAVORED PASTA

A variety of ingredients can be added to the pasta dough to give it both flavor and color. The most common additions are tomato and spinach, but beet, saffron, fresh herbs, such as basil, and even chocolate are used. Mixed bags of pasta are also available—the traditional combination of plain and spinach-flavored

Buckwheat pasta spirals and short-cut pizzoccheri

Right: Corn or maize pasta can be bought in a wide variety of shapes, from simple elbow macaroni to fusilli and three-colored radiatori

CORN PASTA

This pasta is made with corn or maize flour, is gluten-free, and is a good alternative pasta for people who cannot tolerate gluten or wheat. It is made in a wide range of shapes, including spaghetti,

pasta is called paglia e fieno, which means straw and hay. However, there are many other mixtures, some having as many as seven different flavors and colors of pasta.

WHOLE WHEAT PASTA

This substantial pasta is made from whole wheat flour and contains more fiber than plain durum wheat pasta. It has a slightly chewy texture and nutty flavor and takes longer to cook. Whole wheat spaghetti (bigoli), a traditional Italian variety that comes from the area around Venice known as the Veneto, can be found in good Italian delicatessens, and in health-food stores and supermarkets. There is an increasing range of wholewheat shapes, from tiny soup pastas to rotelle (wheels) and lasagne.

BUCKWHEAT PASTA

Pasta made from buckwheat flour has a nutty taste and is darker in color than whole wheat pasta. Pizzoccheri from Lombardy is the classic shape. These thin, flat noodles are traditionally sold in nests like tagliatelle (although pizzoccheri are about half the length), but they are also available cut into short strips.

fusilli (spirals), and conchiglie (shells), as well as more unusual varieties. Plain corn pasta is a sunshine-yellow color, and may be flavored with spinach or tomato. It is cooked and used in the same way as wheat pasta and is available from many health-food stores and supermarkets.

PASTA SHAPES

Long pasta
Dried long pasta in the form of spaghetti is probably the best known, but there are many other varieties, from fine vermicelli to pappardelle—broad ribbon noodles. Tagliatelle, the most common form of ribbon noodles, is usually sold coiled into nests. Long pasta is best served with a thin sauce, made with olive oil, butter, cream, eggs, grated cheese, or chopped fresh herbs. When vegetables are added to the sauce, they should be finely chopped.
Fresh spaghetti, tagliatelle, and fettuccine are widely available.

Above: Pasta can be colored and flavored in a variety of ways, but plain, spinach, and tomato varieties are the most popular

Other buckwheat pasta shapes are available in health-food stores and supermarkets. Buckwheat pasta is gluten-free and suitable for people who are intolerant to gluten or wheat. It is also very nutritious, containing all eight amino acids, calcium, zinc, and B vitamins.

Short pasta
There are hundreds of different short dried pasta shapes, which may be made with plain pasta dough or the more nutritious yellow, egg pasta. Short pasta isn't often sold fresh because most shapes

are difficult to produce, but you may find one or two in some Italian delicatessens, and a few fresh shapes are also available from larger supermarkets.

Conchiglie (shells) are one of the most useful shapes because they are concave and trap virtually any sauce. Fusilli (spirals) are good with thick tomato-based sauces and farfalle (butterflies) can be served with creamy sauces, but are very versatile and work equally well with tomato- or olive oil-based sauces. Macaroni used to be the most common short shape, and being hollow, it is good for most sauces and baked dishes. However, penne (quills) have become more popular, perhaps because the hollow tubes with diagonally cut ends

Spinach and whole wheat lasagne and plain cannelloni

go well with virtually any sauce. They are particularly good with chunky vegetable sauces or baked with cheese sauce.

Flat pasta

Lasagne is designed to be baked between layers of sauce, or cooked in boiling water, then layered, or rolled around a filling to make cannelloni. Lasagne is made from plain or egg pasta and both fresh and dried versions are available. The pasta sheets may be flavored with tomato or spinach, or made with whole wheat flour.

Stuffed pasta

The most common stuffed pasta shapes are ravioli, tortellini (little pies), and cappelletti (little hats), although there are other lesser-known shapes available from Italian delicatessens. Plain, spinach, and tomato doughs are the most usual, and there is a wide range of vegetarian fillings.

Pasta for soup

These tiny shapes are mostly made from plain durum wheat pasta, although you may find them with egg. There are hundreds of different ones, from tiny risi, which look like grains of rice, to alfabeti (alphabet shapes), which are popular with children. Slightly larger shapes, such as farfalline (little bows) and tubetti (little tubes), are used in thicker soups.

Buying and Storing: The quality of pasta varies tremendously—choose good-quality Italian brands of pasta made from 100 percent durum wheat, and visit your local Italian delicatessen to buy fresh pasta, rather than buying pre-packed pasta from the supermarket. Dried pasta will keep almost indefinitely, but if you transfer the pasta to a storage jar, it is a good idea to use up the remaining pasta before adding any from a new packet. Fresh pasta from a delicatessen is usually sold loose

Large and small conchiglie (shells)

Quick Ideas for Pasta

• To make a simple, but richly flavored tomato sauce: place some plum or cherry tomatoes in an ovenproof dish and drizzle with a little olive oil. Roast in a hot oven for 15 minutes, then add one or two peeled garlic cloves, and continue roasting for about 15 minutes more. Transfer to a food processor and blend with basil leaves. Season and stir into cooked pasta.

• Toss cooked pasta in a little chile oil, scatter with arugula leaves and pine nuts, and serve with finely grated Parmesan cheese.

• Stir a spoonful of black olive tapenade into cooked pasta, then scatter a few lightly toasted walnuts on top before serving.

• Roast a head of garlic, then squeeze out the puréed cloves, and mix with olive oil. Toss with cooked pasta and sprinkle with plenty of fresh, chopped flat leaf parsley.

• Olives, mushrooms, eggplant, and artichokes bottled in olive oil make quick and delicious additions to pasta.

• Combine cooked pasta with small chunks of mozzarella cheese, sliced sun-dried tomatoes, chopped fresh mint, and a splash of olive oil.

Choosing the Right Shape

While it is unnecessary to stick rigidly to hard-and-fast rules, some pasta shapes definitely work better than others with particular sauces.

• Long pasta shapes, such as spaghetti, linguine, tagliatelle, and fettuccine, suit smooth cream- or olive oil-based sauces, or vegetable sauces where the ingredients are very finely chopped.

• Hollow shapes, such as penne (quills), fusilli (spirals), and macaroni, all work well with more robust sauces, such as cheese, tomato, and vegetable.

• Stuffed pasta shapes, such as ravioli and cappelletti, are good with simple sauces made with butter, extra virgin olive oil, or tomatoes.

• In soups, the delicate small shapes, risi (rice), orzi (barley), and quadrucci (squares), suit lighter broths, while the more substantial conchigliette (little shells) and farfalline (little butterflies) go well in heartier vegetable soups.

and is best cooked the same day, but can be kept in the fridge for a day or two. Fresh pasta from a supermarket is likely to be packed in plastic packs and bags, and these will keep for 3–4 days in the fridge. Fresh pasta freezes well and should be cooked from frozen. Packs and bags of supermarket pasta have the advantage of being easy to store in the freezer.

Fresh tortellini

Health Benefits: Pasta provides the body with fuel for all kinds of physical activity, from running a marathon to walking to the bus stop. High in complex carbohydrates, pasta is broken down slowly, providing energy over a long period of time. Whole wheat pasta is the most nutritious, containing a richer concentration of vitamins, minerals, and fiber. Nevertheless, all pasta is a useful source of protein, as well as being low in fat. Buckwheat is very nutritious; it contains all eight essential amino acids, making it a complete protein. It is also particularly high in fiber.

Cooking Pasta

Pasta should be cooked in a large pan of boiling salted water to allow the strands or shapes to expand, and stirred occasionally to prevent them from sticking together. Do not add oil to the cooking water, as it makes the pasta slippery and prevents it from absorbing the sauce. Cooking instructions are given on the packaging, but always taste just before the end of the given time to prevent overcooking. Dried pasta should be *al dente*, or firm to the bite, while fresh pasta should be just tender.

Bring a large pan of salted water to a boil. For shapes, add the pasta and cover the pan. Bring quickly back to a boil and remove the lid. Reduce the heat slightly, then stir the pasta, and cook according to the packet instructions. For long straight pasta, such as spaghetti, coil the pasta into the water as it softens.

Above: Tiny soup pasta is available in hundreds of different shapes

Noodles

The fast food of the East, noodles can be made from wheat flour, rice, buckwheat flour, or mung bean flour. Both fresh and dried noodles are readily available in health-food stores and Asian stores as well as supermarkets. Like pasta, noodles are low in fat and high in complex carbohydrates, so provide long-term energy.

Rice noodles

WHEAT NOODLES

There are two main types of noodle: plain and egg. Plain noodles are made from strong flour and water. They can be flat or round and come in various thicknesses.

Udon noodles

These thick Japanese noodles can be round or flat and are available fresh, pre-cooked, or dried. Whole wheat udon noodles have a more robust flavor.

Somen noodles

Usually sold in bundles held together by a paper band, these thin, white noodles are available from Asian stores.

Egg noodles

Far more common than the plain wheat variety, egg noodles are sold both fresh and dried. The Chinese type come in various thicknesses. Very fine egg noodles, which resemble vermicelli, are usually sold in coils. Whole wheat egg noodles are widely available from larger supermarkets.

Ramen noodles

These Japanese egg noodles are also sold in coils and are often cooked and served with an accompanying broth.

RICE NOODLES

These fine, delicate noodles are made from rice and are opaque-white in color. Like wheat noodles, they come in various widths, from the very thin strands known as rice vermicelli, which are popular in Thailand and southern China, to the thicker rice sticks, which are used more in Vietnam and Malaysia. A huge range of rice noodles is available dried in Asian grocers, and fresh ones are occasionally found in the chiller cabinets. Since all rice noodles are pre-cooked, they need only to be soaked in hot water for a few minutes to soften them before use in stir-fries and salads.

Udon noodles (above) and cellophane noodles

CELLOPHANE VERMICELLI AND NOODLES

Made from mung bean starch, these translucent noodles, also known as bean thread vermicelli and glass noodles, come in a variety of thicknesses and are only available dried. Although very fine, the strands are firm and fairly tough. Cellophane noodles don't need to be boiled, and are simply soaked in boiling water for 10–15 minutes. They have a fantastic texture, which they retain when cooked, never becoming soggy. Cellophane noodles are almost tasteless unless combined with other strongly flavored foods and seasonings. They are never eaten on their own, but used as an ingredient. They are good in vegetarian dishes, and as an ingredient in spring rolls.

BUCKWHEAT NOODLES

Soba are the best-known type of buckwheat noodles. They are a much darker color than wheat noodles—almost brownish gray. In Japan, soba noodles are traditionally served in soups or stir-fries with a variety of sauces.

Dried and fresh egg noodles

Quick Ideas for Noodles

• To make a simple broth, dissolve mugi miso in hot water, add cooked soba noodles; sprinkle with chile flakes, and sliced scallions.

• Cook ramen noodles in vegetable stock, then add a splash of dark soy sauce, shredded spinach, and grated ginger (above). Serve sprinkled with sesame seeds and fresh cilantro.

• Stir-fry sliced shiitake and oyster mushrooms in garlic and ginger, then toss with rice or egg noodles (above). Scatter with fresh chives and a little toasted sesame oil.
• In a food processor, blend together some lemon grass, chile pepper, garlic, ginger, kaffir lime leaves, and fresh cilantro. Fry the paste in a little sunflower oil and combine with cooked ribbon noodles. Sprinkle fresh basil and chopped scallions on top before serving.

Buying and Storing: Packets of fresh noodles are found in the chiller cabinets of Asian stores. They usually carry a "use-by" date and must be stored in the fridge. Dried noodles will keep for many months if stored in an airtight container in a cool, dry place.

Health Benefits: Noodles are high in complex carbohydrates, which are broken down slowly, providing energy over a long period of time. Whole wheat noodles are the most nutritious, containing a richer concentration of vitamins, minerals, and fiber. Nevertheless, all noodles are a useful source of protein, as well as being low in fat. Buckwheat noodles are made from buckwheat flour, which contains all eight essential amino acids, making it a complete protein. It is also particularly high in fiber. Cellophane noodles are made from mung bean starch, which is reputed to be one of the most powerful detoxifiers.

Cooking Wheat Noodles

Wheat noodles are very easy to cook. Both dried and fresh noodles are cooked in a large pan of boiling water; how long depends on the type of noodle and the thickness of the strips. Dried noodles need about 3 minutes cooking time, while fresh ones will often be ready in less than a minute. Fresh noodles may need to be rinsed quickly in cold water to prevent them from overcooking.

Whole wheat egg noodles

Oils

There is a wide variety of cooking oils and they are produced from a number of different sources: from cereals such as corn; from fruits such as olives; from nuts such as walnuts, almonds, and hazelnuts; and from seeds such as canola, safflower, and sunflower. They can be extracted by simple mechanical means such as pressing or crushing, or by further processing, usually heating. Virgin oils, which are obtained from the first cold pressing of the olives, nuts, or seeds, are sold unrefined, and have the most characteristic flavor. They are also the most expensive.

OLIVE OIL

Indisputably the king of oils, olive oil varies in flavor and color, depending on how it is made and where it comes from. Climate, soil, harvesting, and pressing all influence the end result—generally, the hotter the climate, the more robust the oil. Thus oils from southern Italy, Greece, and Spain have a stronger flavor and a darker color than those from the rest of Italy and France. Olive oil is rich in monounsaturated fat, which has been found to reduce cholesterol, thereby reducing the risk of heart disease. There are different grades to choose from.

Extra virgin olive oil

This premium olive oil has a superior flavor. It comes from the first cold pressing of the olives and has a low acidity—less than 1 percent. Extra virgin olive oil is not recommended for frying, as heat impairs its flavor, but it is good in salad dressings, especially when combined with lighter oils. It is delicious as a sauce on its own, stirred into pasta with chopped garlic and black pepper, or drizzled onto steamed vegetables.

Virgin olive oil

Also a pure first-pressed oil, this has a slightly higher level of acidity than extra virgin olive oil, and can be used in much the same way.

Extra virgin olive oil (left), sunflower oil (right), and safflower oil (far right)

Essential Fats

We all need some fat in our diet. It keeps us warm, adds flavor to our food, carries essential vitamins A, D, E, and K around the body, and provides essential fatty acids, which cannot be produced in the body, but are vital for growth and development, and may reduce the risk of heart attacks.

What is more important is the type and amount of fat that we eat. Some fats are better for us than others, and we should adjust our intake accordingly. It is recommended that fat should make up no more than 35 percent of our diet.

Peanut oil (left) and almond oil

Pure olive oil

Refined and blended to remove impurities, this type of olive oil has a much lighter flavor than virgin or extra virgin olive oil and is suitable for all types of cooking. It can be used for shallow frying.

OTHER OILS

There is a wide range of light, processed oils on the market, which are all relatively taste-free and have a variety of uses in the kitchen.

Corn oil

One of the most economical and widely used vegetable oils, corn oil has a deep golden color and a fairly strong flavor. It is suitable for cooking and frying, but should not be used for salad dressings. Corn is rich in omega-6 (linoleic) fatty acids, which are believed to reduce harmful cholesterol in the body.

Safflower oil

This is a light, all-purpose oil, which comes from the seeds of the safflower. It can be used in place of sunflower and peanut oils, but is a little thicker and has a slightly stronger flavor. It is suitable for deep-frying, but is best used with other more strongly flavored ingredients, and is ideal for cooking spicy foods. Safflower oil contains more polyunsaturated fat than any other type of oil and it is low in saturated fat.

Sunflower oil

Perhaps the best all-purpose oil, sunflower oil is very light and almost tasteless. It is very versatile, and can be used for frying and in cooking, or to make salad dressings, when it can be combined with a stronger flavored oil, such as olive oil or walnut oil. Sunflower oil is extracted from the seeds of the sunflower. It is very high in polyunsaturated fat and low in saturated fat.

Soy oil

This neutral flavored, all-purpose oil, which is extracted from soybeans, is probably the most widely used oil in the world. It is useful for frying because it has a high smoking point, and remains stable at high temperatures. It is also widely used in margarines. It is rich in polyunsaturated and monounsaturated fats and low in saturates. Find a brand that is not made from genetically modified soybeans.

Peanut oil

Also known as groundnut oil, this relatively tasteless oil is useful for frying, cooking, and dressing salads. Chinese peanut oil is darker in color than other types and has a

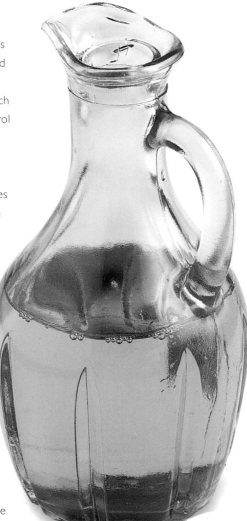

Soy oil

Quick Ideas for Marinades

• Mix olive oil with chopped fresh herbs, such as parsley, chives, oregano, chervil, and basil. Add a splash or two of lemon juice and season with salt and pepper.

• Combine peanut oil, toasted sesame oil, dark soy sauce, sweet sherry, rice vinegar, and crushed garlic. Use as a marinade for bean curd or tempeh.

• Mix together olive oil, lemon juice, sherry, honey, and crushed garlic and use as a marinade for vegetable and halloumi kebabs.

more distinctive nutty flavor. It is good in Asian salads and stir-fries. Peanut oil has a higher percentage of monounsaturated fat than soy oil, but also contains polyunsaturated fat.

Canola oil

This bland-tasting, all-purpose oil, also known as rapeseed, can be used for frying, cooking, and in salad dressings. It contains a higher percentage of monounsaturated fat than any other oil, with the exception of olive oil.

Grapeseed oil

A delicate, mild-flavored oil, which does not impose on other ingredients, grapeseed oil is pressed from grape seeds left over from wine-making. It is good in cooking and for frying, and can be used to make salad dressings, especially when combined with a stronger flavored nut or olive oil. Grapeseed oil is high in poly-unsaturated fat.

Canola oil

SPECIALTY OILS

As well as the light, all-purpose oils that are used for everyday cooking, there are several richly flavored oils that are used in small quantities, often as a flavoring ingredient in salad dressings and marinades, rather than for cooking.

Sesame oil

There are two types of sesame oil—the pale and light version that is pressed from untoasted seeds, and the rich, dark, toasted oil that is used in Asian cuisines. The lighter oil, popular in India and the Middle East, has a mild flavor and a high smoking point, and is useful for cooking. Dark sesame oil, which has a wonderfully nutty aroma and taste, is useful for flavoring marinades and stir-fries. It has a much stronger taste than either walnut oil or olive oil and is too overpowering to use in large quantities. However, it can be mixed with milder oils, such as peanut or soy. Heating helps to intensify the aroma of toasted sesame oil, but it should never be heated for too long. Both types of sesame oil are high in polyunsaturated fat.

Walnut oil

This is an intensely flavored oil that is delicious in salad dressings and marinades, but shouldn't be used for frying as heat diminishes its rich taste (it is also far too expensive to use in any great quantity). Instead, drizzle a little of the oil onto roasted or steamed vegetables, use it to make a simple sauce for pasta, or stir into freshly cooked noodles just before serving. It can be used in small quantities, in place of some of the fat or oil in a recipe, to add flavor to cakes and cookies, especially those that contain walnuts. Walnut oil does not keep for long and, after opening, should be kept in a cool, dark place to prevent it from becoming rancid. It can be stored in

Quick Ideas for Dressings and Salads

A good dressing should enhance rather than overpower the salad.

• To make a simple vinaigrette dressing, whisk together 4 tablespoons extra virgin olive oil with 1 tablespoon red or white wine vinegar or balsamic vinegar in a small pitcher. Add a pinch of sugar and 1 teaspoon Dijon mustard. Season to taste.

• To make a walnut oil dressing, whisk together 4 tablespoons walnut oil with 1 tablespoon sherry vinegar, then season to taste. This dressing is good with strong flavored leaves, such as arugula, watercress, or radicchio.

• Combine walnut oil and low-fat fromage frais or yogurt with chopped fresh flat leaf parsley. Season, then spoon the dressing over new potatoes, and garnish with snipped chives and toasted chopped walnuts.

• Mix together grated fresh ginger, fresh cilantro, lime juice, and toasted sesame oil and pour onto grated carrot. Sprinkle toasted sesame seeds on top of the carrot mixture.

• Mix together extra virgin olive oil and lemon juice, and spoon over warm flageolet and cannellini beans. Add chopped tomatoes and chopped fresh flat leaf parsley.

• Toss steamed broccoli flowerets or sugar snap peas in a dressing made from hazelnut oil, olive oil, white wine vinegar, and Dijon mustard.

the fridge, but this may cause it to solidify. Walnut oil is rich in polyunsaturated fats and contains vitamin E.

Hazelnut oil

This fine, fragrant oil is rich brown in color and has a delicious, roasted hazelnut flavor. It is quite expensive to buy but, because it has such a strong flavor, only a little is needed. It is good, combined with less strongly flavored oils, for salad dressings and sauces, and can be used to add a nutty flavor to sweet breads, cakes, cookies, and pastry. Hazelnut oil is rich in monounsaturated fat.

Almond oil

This pale, delicate oil is mainly used in confectionery and desserts. It has a subtle, sweet flavor of almonds, although it is not strong enough to give an almond flavor to baked goods, such as cakes and cookies. Almond oil is rich in monounsaturated fat as well as vitamins A and E. It is reputed to

Walnut, sesame, and hazelnut oils

be very good for the skin and is often used as a massage oil.

Buying and Storing: Cooking oils, such as sunflower, soy, and safflower, are more stable than nut or seed oils, and have longer keeping properties. To keep them at their peak, store in a cool, dark place away from direct sunlight. Nut and seed oils are more volatile and turn rancid quickly and should be kept in the fridge after opening.

Health Benefits: Oils are undeniably high in calories and should always be used in moderation, but they also have a number of health benefits. Monounsaturated fats, found particularly in olive oil and canola oil, either stabilize or raise the level of the beneficial high density lipoproteins (HDLs), while lowering harmful low density lipoproteins (LDLs), thus keeping down blood cholesterol levels in the body. A high level of LDLs in the blood is usually an indication of increased cholesterol levels, as the LDLs

carry the fatty substance (cholesterol) around the body; HDLs, however, carry much less fat.

Olive oil also contains vitamin E, a natural antioxidant that can help fight off free radicals, which damage cells in the body and have the potential to cause cancer. Polyunsaturated fats provide essential fatty acids known as omega-3 (alpha-linolenic) and omega-6 (linolenic acid), which must be included in the diet. Omega-3, which is found in walnut, canola, and soy oil, has been found to reduce the likelihood of heart disease and blood clots, while omega 6, provided by safflower, sunflower, and walnut oil, reduces harmful cholesterol levels. Polyunsaturated fats are more unstable than monounsaturated fats and are prone to oxidation, which can lead to the build-up of free radicals. Although polyunsaturates do contain vitamin E, it appears in varying amounts and so it is advisable to eat other foods that are rich in vitamin E to protect the fatty acids and the body from damage due to oxidation.

Vinegars

One of our oldest condiments, vinegar is made by acetic fermentation, a process that occurs when a liquid containing less than 18 percent alcohol is exposed to the air. Most countries produce their own type of vinegar, usually based on their most popular alcoholic drink—wine in France and Italy, sherry in Spain, rice wine in Asia, and beer and cider in Great Britain. Commonly used as a preservative in pickles and chutneys, it is also an ingredient in marinades and salad dressings. A spoonful or two of a good-quality vinegar can add flavor to cooked dishes and sauces.

WINE VINEGARS

These can be made from white, red, or rosé wine, and the quality of the vinegar will depend on the quality of the original ingredient. The finest wine vinegars are made by the slow and costly Orleans method. Cheaper and faster methods of fermentation involve heating, which produces a harsher vinegar that lacks the complexities of the original wine. Use in dressings, mayonnaise, sauces or to add flavor to stews and soups.

BALSAMIC VINEGAR

This is a rich, dark, mellow vinegar, which has become hugely popular. Made in Modena in northern Italy, balsamic vinegar

Balsamic vinegar

Sherry vinegar

is made from grape juice (predominantly from Trebbiano grapes), which is fermented in vast wooden barrels for a minimum of four to five years and up to 40 or more years, resulting in an intensely rich vinegar with a concentrated flavor. Balsamic vinegar is delicious in dressings or sprinkled over roasted vegetables. It is even good with strawberries.

SHERRY VINEGAR

This vinegar can be just as costly as balsamic vinegar and, if left to mature in wooden barrels, can be equally good. Sweet and mellow in flavor, sherry vinegar is caramel in color and can be used in the same way as balsamic vinegar—in dressings, sprinkled over roasted vegetables, or added to sauces and stews.

RASPBERRY VINEGAR

Any soft fruit can be used to enhance the flavor of white wine vinegar, but raspberries are the most popular. Raspberry vinegar can be made at home by macerating fresh raspberries in good-quality wine vinegar for 2–3 weeks. Once the mixture is strained, the vinegar is delicious as part of a salad dressing, or in sauces. It can be mixed with sparkling mineral water to make a refreshing drink.

MALT VINEGAR

Made from sour beer, malt vinegar is used in Britain and other northern European countries for pickling onions and other vegetables, or for sprinkling over french fries. It can be clear, but is often sold colored with caramel. Malt vinegar has a robust, harsh flavor and it is not suitable for salad dressings.

Red and white wine vinegars

Raspberry vinegar

RICE VINEGAR

There are two kinds of rice vinegar: the type from Japan is mellow and sweet and is most often used to flavor sushi rice, but it can also be added to dressings, stir-fries, and sauces; Chinese rice vinegar is much sharper in taste. Rice vinegar is usually a clear, pale brown color, but it can also be inky-black, red or white.

CIDER VINEGAR

Made from cider and praised for its health-giving properties, cider vinegar is made in the same way as wine vinegar. It is a clear, pale-brown color and has a slight apple flavor, but it is too strong and sharp to use in the same ways as wine vinegar. It can be used for salad dressings, but it is perhaps best kept for pickling fruits such as pears. Cider vinegar can be served as a soothing drink, mixed with honey, lemon juice, and hot water, as a remedy for colds and flu.

Health Benefits: Hippocrates prescribed vinegar as a cure for respiratory problems, and it may also be beneficial in cases of food poisoning. Cider vinegar is said to have many therapeutic benefits, which were highlighted in a book written in the 1960s by Dr DeForest Clinton Jarvis, entitled *Folk Medicine*. He attributed cider as a cure for everything, from arthritis and headaches, to obesity and hiccups.

Above: Cider vinegar

Fragrant Spiced Vinegar

This aromatic vinegar is good in dressings and marinades. Any type of vinegar can be used as a base but, to achieve the best results, ensure that it is good quality. If the vinegar develops an unpleasant appearance or aroma, it should be discarded straight away.

Different flavorings, including herb sprigs such as tarragon or rosemary, or whole spices such as cinnamon, star anise, or black, white, or green peppercorns can be used, and will impart a distinctive flavor.

1 Put a few red chile peppers, 1–2 garlic cloves, and some thick strips of lemon rind in a bottle of rice vinegar. Leave on a sunny window ledge or in a warm place for 3–4 weeks.

2 Strain the vinegar into a clean bottle and seal tightly with a cork. Store in a cool, dark place.

Rice vinegar (left) and brown malt vinegar

Teas & Tisanes

Tea has been a popular reviving drink for centuries and comes in many different forms, from traditional teas such as green tea, oolong tea, and black tea, to fragrant fruit infusions and healing herbal tisanes.

GREEN TEA

This tea is popular with the Chinese and Japanese who prefer its light, slightly bitter but nevertheless refreshing flavor. It is produced from leaves that are steamed and dried, but not fermented, a process that retains their green color.

OOLONG TEA

Partially fermented to produce a tea that falls between the green and black varieties in strength and color, oolong tea is particularly fragrant.

BLACK TEA

This is the most widely available tea and is made by fermenting withered tea leaves, then drying them. It produces a dark brown brew that has a more assertive taste than green tea. Darjeeling and English breakfast tea are two examples.

Health Benefits: The latest research shows that drinking about five cups of tea a day may help to prevent heart disease, stroke and certain cancers. These benefits have been attributed to a group of antioxidants found in tea, which are called polyphenols or flavonoids. Flavonoids have antiviral, antibacterial, and anti-inflammatory properties. Green tea contains the highest amount of flavonoids and black tea the lowest. Antioxidants help to mop up harmful free radicals, which cause damage to the body's cells and may cause cancer. Tea also contains fluoride, which can protect the teeth against decay. On the down side, tea can reduce the absorption of iron if drunk after a meal and it contains caffeine (although less than coffee), which is a well-known stimulant.

FRUIT TEAS

These are made from a blend of fruit flavors, such as rosehip, strawberry, orange, raspberry, and lemon, along with fruit pieces and sometimes herbs or real tea. It is a good idea to check the packaging to make sure the "tea" is naturally, rather than artificially, flavored. Fruit teas make refreshing caffeine-free drinks, which are almost calorie-free. They are an ideal drink for pregnant women and, because of their low-sugar content, are suitable for diabetics.

Black tea (left) and green tea

Oolong tea

Coffee

Although coffee is generally viewed as unhealthy, largely due to its high level of caffeine, studies have shown that it can enhance concentration and elevate mood. However, drinking more than six cups a day can increase the risk of heart disease and high blood pressure.

HERBAL TISANES

Although herbal tisanes are of little nutritional value, herbalists have prescribed them for centuries for a multitude of ailments and diseases. These teas (made from the leaves, seeds, and flowers of herbs) are a convenient and simple way of taking medicinal herbs. They do, however, vary in strength and effectiveness. Store-bought teas are generally mild in their medicinal properties, but are good, healthy, caffeine-free drinks. Even so, some varieties are not recommended for young children and pregnant women and so it is advisable to check the packaging. Teas that are prescribed by herbalists can be incredibly powerful and should be taken with care.

The most popular types of herbal teas are listed below.

Peppermint tea is recommended as a digestive to be drunk after a meal. It is also effective in settling other stomach problems and for treating colds. **Camomile tea** soothes and calms the nerves and can induce sleep. **Raspberry leaf tea** prepares the

Below: Naturally flavored fruit teas are caffeine-free and contain hardly any calories

Elderflower and dandelion herbal tisanes

uterus for birth and is said to reduce labor pains, but it is not recommended in early pregnancy. It can also relieve period pains. **Rosehip tea** is high in Vitamin C and may help to ward off colds and flu. **Dandelion and lemon verbena** teas are effective diuretics. **Rosemary tea** can stimulate the brain and improve concentration. **Thyme tea** can boost the immune system and fight viral, bacterial, and fungal infections. **Elderflower** tea can ease painful sinuses and bronchial conditions.

Flavored Teas

These could not be easier to make: simply steep your chosen herb, spice, or fruit in boiling water and leave to infuse before straining. Ginger tea is effective against nausea, colds and flu. and stomach upsets.

1 To make ginger tea, roughly chop a 1-inch piece of fresh ginger root. Place in a cup and pour in boiling water.

2 Cover and leave for 7–10 minutes. Strain or drink as it is—the ginger will stay in the bottom of the cup.

Sweeteners

Nutritionists have wide-ranging—and often extreme—opinions on sugar and sugar alternatives. Some maintain that these products cause hyperactivity in children, while others believe that sugars can induce relaxation and sleep. Many recipes from breads and cakes to desserts and puddings contain different types of sugar and/or sugar substitutes, such as molasses, honey, malt, and grain syrups, as well as dried fruit, and wouldn't be palatable without them. So, as long as a diet is well-balanced and varied, it is considered that moderate amounts of sugar are nutritionally acceptable.

Black molasses

MOLASSES

This rich, syrupy liquid is a by-product of sugar refining and ranges in quality and color. The most nutritionally valuable type is thick and very dark blackstrap molasses, which contains less sugar than lighter alternatives and is richer in iron, calcium, copper, magnesium, phosphorus, potassium, and zinc. However, it may be better to choose organically produced molasses, which doesn't contain the chemicals and additives that are used in the sugar-refining process.

Honey

HONEY

One of the oldest sweeteners used by man, honey was highly valued by the ancient Egyptians for its medicinal and healing properties. The color, flavor, consistency, and quality of honey depends on the source of nectar as well as the method of production. In general the darker the color, the stronger the flavor. Many commercial brands of honey are pasteurized and blended to give a uniform taste and texture, but from the point of view of both flavor and health, it is best to buy raw unfiltered honey from a single flower source.

Nutritionally, honey offers negligible benefits, but as it is much sweeter than sugar, less is needed; it is also lower in calories. Today, honey still retains its reputation as an antiseptic, and recent studies show that it is effective in healing and disinfecting wounds if applied externally. Mixed with lemon and hot water, it can relieve sore throats and is also thought to be helpful in treating diarrhea and asthma.

Carob and carob powder

CAROB

This caffeine-free alternative to chocolate is made from the aromatic, fleshy bean of a Mediterranean tree. Carob flour

Dried fruit

Malt extract

looks and tastes similar to unsweetened cocoa and can be used to replace it in hot drinks, confectionery, and baked goods. It is naturally sweeter and lower in fat than unsweetened cocoa, as well as being more nutritious, providing iron, calcium, vitamin B_6, riboflavin, and potassium.

MAPLE SYRUP

This is made from the sap of the maple tree. Look for pure varieties rather than maple-flavored syrup, which contains additives. Maple syrup has a rich, distinctive flavor and is sweeter than sugar, so less is required in cooking.

GRAIN SYRUPS

Corn, barley, wheat, and rice can be transformed into syrups that are used in place of sugar in baked goods and sauces. Grain syrups tend to be easier to digest and enter the bloodstream more slowly than other forms of refined sugar, which cause swings in blood-

sugar levels. Grain syrups are not as sweet as sugar and have a mild, subtle flavor. Malt extract, a by-product of barley, has a more intense flavor and is good in breads and other baked goods.

FRUIT JUICE

Freshly squeezed fruit juice is a useful alternative to sugar in baked goods, sauces, pies, and ice cream. Fruit juice concentrates, such as apple, pear, and grape, which have no added sugar or preservatives, are available from health-food stores. They can be diluted or used in concentrated form in cakes, pies, and desserts.

Clockwise from left: Date syrup, barley malt syrup and brown rice syrup

DRIED FRUIT

Dates are made into a syrup with a rich flavor that can be used to sweeten cakes. Puréed dried fruits, such as prunes, figs, dates, and apricots, can replace sugar in pies and cakes. Dried fruit can be added to both sweet and non-sweet foods.

Spiced Apricot Purée

This richly spiced purée is delicious stirred into thick unsweetened yogurt or can be used to sweeten cakes, crumbles, and pies.

1 Place 1½ cups dried apricots in a saucepan with enough water to cover. Add 1 cinnamon stick, 2 cloves, and ½ teaspoon freshly grated nutmeg. Bring to a boil, then simmer for 20 minutes, until the apricots are plump.

2 Let cool, then process in a food processor until smooth. Add more water if the mixture seems a little thick.

Vegetarian Recipes

If you've worked your way through the first section of this book, you'll be a
mine of information about a wide range of whole foods. However, it's one thing
to have a working knowledge of nutrition; quite another to put it into practice,
so the pages that follow are packed with exciting and inspirational recipes.
Each is designed to help you introduce more nutritious ingredients
into your diet with minimum fuss but maximum flavor.
Beginning with breakfast, the most important meal of the
day, this section takes a lingering look at brunches,
soups and light meals, main courses, pastries, salads
and side dishes, then moves on to delicious
desserts and baked goods. Many of the step-by-step
recipes include information boxes that highlight the
health benefits of key ingredients when used as part
of a balanced diet, and there are also valuable
variations and cook's tips.

BREAKFASTS and BRUNCHES

Start the day with a nutritious, low fat meal. The selection presented here will boost your energy levels through the morning, keeping you alert and awake, ready to face the day. The delicious yogurts, juices and cereals, omelets, and brunches are all quick and easy to prepare.

Banana and Strawberry Smoothie

FULL OF ENERGY-GIVING oats and fruits, this tasty drink makes a brilliant breakfast.

INGREDIENTS

2 bananas, quartered
2 cups strawberries
2 tablespoons oatmeal
2¹/2 cups plain live
    yogurt
Serves 2

COOK'S TIP

Prepare fruit drinks just before serving to gain maximum benefit from the nutrients.

Place the bananas, strawberries, oatmeal and yogurt in a food processor or blender and process for a few minutes until combined and creamy. Pour into tall glasses and serve.

Citrus Shake

PACKED WITH VITAMIN C, this refreshing juice is a great way to start the day.

INGREDIENTS

1 pineapple
6 oranges, peeled and chopped
juice of 1 lemon
1 pink grapefruit, peeled and
    quartered
Serves 4

1 To prepare the pineapple, cut the bottom and the spiky top off the fruit. Stand the pineapple upright and cut off the skin, removing all the spikes and as little of the flesh as possible. Lay the pineapple on its side and cut into bite-size chunks.

2 Place the pineapple, oranges, lemon juice and grapefruit in a food processor or blender and process for a few minutes until combined.

3 Press the juice through a strainer to remove any pith or membranes. Serve chilled.

Cranberry and Apple Juice

THIS GINGER-FLAVORED, cleansing juice offers a fine balance of sweet and sour flavors.

INGREDIENTS

4 eating apples
2¹/2 cups cranberry juice
1-inch piece fresh ginger root,
    peeled and sliced
Serves 4

HEALTH BENEFITS

Brightly colored fruits, such as cranberries, contain valuable amounts of antioxidant vitamins, which are believed to have cancer-fighting properties.

1 Peel the apples, if you wish, then core and chop.

2 Pour the cranberry juice into a food processor or blender. Add the chopped apples and sliced ginger and process for a few minutes until combined and fairly smooth. Serve chilled.

Zingy Vegetable Juice

GINGER PACKS A POWERFUL punch and certainly gets you going in the morning, even if you're feeling groggy.

INGREDIENTS

1 cooked beet in natural juice,
    sliced
1 large carrot, sliced
1¹/2-inch piece fresh ginger root,
    peeled and finely grated
2 apples, peeled if liked,
    chopped and cored
1¹/4 cups seedless white
    grapes
1¹/4 cups fresh orange
    juice
Serves 2

1 Place the beet, carrot, ginger, apples, grapes and orange juice in a food processor or blender and process for a few minutes until combined and fairly smooth. Serve immediately or chill until ready to serve.

Right: Clockwise from top right, Cranberry and Apple Juice, Citrus Shake, Banana and Strawberry Smoothie, Zingy Vegetable Juice.

Date, Banana and Walnut Yogurt

DATES AND bananas give a high fiber boost to this breakfast dish. Both fruits are also high in natural sugars.

INGREDIENTS

2/3 cup dried dates, pitted and chopped

1 1/4 cups low-fat plain yogurt

2 bananas

1/2 cup chopped walnuts

Serves 4

COOK'S TIP

Use standard dried dates and not those which have been sugared. Bananas are probably the best and most convenient instant-energy food there is. If you haven't got time for breakfast, just unzip a banana!

1 Stir the dates into the yogurt in a mixing bowl. Cover and leave overnight in the fridge, to allow the fruit to soften.

2 Peel, then slice the bananas into the yogurt mixture. Spoon into dishes and top with the walnuts.

VARIATION

In place of walnuts you can use hazelnuts or toasted pecan nuts. Figs, mangoes or pawpaw can replace dates.

Mixed Berry Yogurt Shake

BLEND THIS in a blender or food processor for a quick, low-fat and high vitality breakfast in a glass. Rosewater adds an exotic touch. You could also experiment with other fruits to create your own flavor shake, such as banana with vanilla extract, or apricot with a few drops of almond extract.

INGREDIENTS

1 cup low-fat milk, chilled

1 cup low-fat plain yogurt

4 ounces mixed summer fruits

1 teaspoon rosewater

a little honey, to taste

Serves 2

1 Blend the milk, yogurt, fruits and rosewater in a food processor.

2 Add honey to taste if necessary, depending on the sweetness of the fruits. Pour into two glasses.

COOK'S TIP

Any combination of soft red fruits can be used, such as strawberries, raspberries, bilberries, blackberries, red cherries and red currants.

Melon, Pineapple and Grape Cocktail

A LIGHT fresh fruit salad, with no added sugar, makes a refreshing start to the day, and can easily be prepared the night before.

INGREDIENTS

1/2 melon

8 ounces fresh pineapple, or 8-ounce can pineapple chunks in own juice

8 ounces seedless white grapes, halved

1/2 cup white grape juice

fresh mint leaves, to decorate (optional)

Serves 4

1 | Remove the seeds from the melon half and use a melon baller to scoop out even-size balls.

2 Using a sharp knife, cut the skin from the pineapple and discard. Cut the fruit into bite-size chunks.

3 Combine all the fruits in a glass serving dish and pour over the juice. If you are using canned pineapple, measure the drained juice and make it up to the required quantity with the grape juice.

4 If not serving immediately, cover and chill. Serve decorated with mint leaves, if liked.

VARIATION

You can also use a variety of different melons such as Canteloupe, Galia or Ogen, and watermelon, to add color to the cocktail.

Three Fruit Compôtes

INGREDIENTS

Orange and Prune Compôte

1 juicy orange, peeled

1/3 cup dried prunes

5 tablespoons orange juice

Pear and Kiwi Fruit Compôte

1 ripe eating pear, cored

1 kiwi fruit

4 tablespoons apple or pineapple juice

***Grapefruit and Strawberry
  Compôte***

1 grapefruit, peeled

4 ounces strawberries

4 tablespoons orange juice

plain yogurt and toasted hazelnuts, to serve

Each compôte serves 1

1 For the orange and prune compôte, segment the orange and place in a bowl with the prunes.

2 For the pear and kiwi fruit compôte, slice the pear. Peel and cut the kiwi fruit into wedges.

3 For the grapefruit and strawberry compôte, segment the grapefruit and halve the strawberries.

4 Place your selected fruits together in a bowl and pour over the juice. Choose "fresh squeezed" juices rather than those made from concentrates, or squeeze your own juice using a blender or food processor.

5 Serve the chosen compôte topped with a spoonful of low-fat plain yogurt together with a sprinkling of chopped toasted hazelnuts.

Fruity Sesame Porridge

HOT CEREAL made with skim milk makes a wonderfully nourishing breakfast. Dried fruit and toasted sesame seeds make it even better, providing useful amounts of iron and magnesium.

INGREDIENTS

$^1/_2$ cup rolled oats

2 cups skim milk

$^1/_2$ cup mixed dried fruits, chopped

2 tablespoons sesame seeds, toasted

Serves 2

1 Put the oats, milk and chopped dried fruit in a nonstick saucepan.

COOK'S TIP

If you use so-called "old-fashioned" or "original" oats, the porridge will be quite thick and coarse textured. You could also use "jumbo" oats. If you prefer a smoother porridge, try ordinary rolled oats (sometimes called oatflakes).

2 Bring to a boil, then lower the heat and simmer gently for 3 minutes, stirring occasionally, until thickened. Serve in individual bowls, sprinkled with sesame seeds.

VARIATION

If you prefer sweeter porridge, try using a teaspoonful of maple syrup instead of sugar.

Trail Mix

EAT THIS nutritious snack on the run, or sprinkle it on top of yogurt or stewed fruit. It makes an excellent nibble between meals, but is quite high in calories, so don't get too carried away with it!

INGREDIENTS

$^1/_3$ cup dried apricots or figs, quartered

$^1/_3$ cup raisins or golden raisins

$^1/_2$ cup hazelnuts

scant $^1/_2$ cup sunflower seeds

scant $^1/_2$ cup pumpkin seeds

Makes about 2 cups

1 Cut the apricots or figs into quarters and place in a large bowl.

2 Add all the remaining ingredients and toss everything together. Store in an airtight container and use within 2–3 weeks.

COOK'S TIP

Other dried fruits or nuts may be added or substituted for those already present in the mix. Both nuts and seeds have a high oil content so will turn rancid quite quickly. To keep longer, store in the fridge.

Crunchy Fruit Layer

ALL THE INGREDIENTS for a delicious and vitamin-rich breakfast are here, served in an attractive parfait glass. This would make an ideal brunch dish when you're having guests, but is so easy to make that you could simply treat yourself.

INGREDIENTS

1 peach or nectarine

1 cup crunchy toasted
 oat cereal

²/₃ cup low-fat plain yogurt

1 tablespoon pure fruit jam

1 tablespoon unsweetened fruit juice

Serves 2

1 Remove the pit from the peach or nectarine and cut the fruit into bite-size pieces with a sharp knife.

2 Divide the chopped fruit between two tall glasses, reserving a few pieces for decoration.

3 Sprinkle the oat cereal over the fruit in an even layer, then top with the yogurt.

4 Stir the jam and fruit juice together in a cup, then drizzle the mixture over the yogurt. Decorate with the reserved peach or nectarine and serve at once.

COOK'S TIP

If you prefer to use a flavored toasted oat cereal (raisin and almond, perhaps, or tropical fruits) be sure to check the nutritional information on the label and choose the variety with the lowest amount of added sugar. Any fruit jam and juice that complement each other and the chosen fruit can be used.

Apricot and Almond Muesli

THERE IS no added sugar in this whole wheat fruit and nut muesli, which is packed with fiber, vitamins and minerals. It makes a delicious change from store bought varieties because you can choose your own favorite ingredients.

INGREDIENTS

$1/2$ cup whole blanched almonds

$2/3$ cup dried apricots

2 cups whole rolled oats

2 cups whole wheat flakes or
 oat bran flakes

$1/3$ cup raisins or golden raisins

$1/3$ cup pumpkin seeds

$1/3$ cup sunflower seeds

skim milk or low-fat plain yogurt or fresh
 fruit juice, and fresh fruit, to serve

Serves 8

1 Using a sharp knife, carefully cut the almonds into slivers.

2 Cut the dried apricots into small even-size pieces.

3 Stir all the ingredients together in a large bowl. Store in an airtight container and use within 6 weeks.

4 Serve with skim milk, low-fat plain yogurt or fruit juice and top with fresh fruit, such as peach, banana or strawberry slices.

COOK'S TIP

This recipe is easy to change by adding other dried fruits, such as chopped dates, figs, peaches, pear, pineapple or apple chunks. Walnuts, brazil nuts or hazelnuts could be substituted for the almonds.

VARIATION

You can toast the seeds and nuts if you buy the raw variety. Watch them carefully when toasting so they don't burn.

Luxury Muesli

COMMERCIALLY MADE muesli really can't compete with this homemade version. This combination of seeds, grains, nuts and dried fruits works particularly well, but you can alter the balance of ingredients, or substitute others, if you like.

INGREDIENTS

$^1/_2$ cup sunflower seeds

$^1/_4$ cup pumpkin seeds

1 cup rolled oats

heaped 1 cup wheat flakes

heaped 1 cup barley flakes

1 cup raisins

1 cup chopped hazelnuts, roasted

$^1/_2$ cup unsulfured dried apricots, chopped

2 cups dried apple slices, halved

$^1/_3$ cup shredded coconut

Serves 4

1 Put the sunflower and pumpkin seeds in a dry frying pan and cook over medium heat for 3 minutes until golden, tossing the seeds regularly to prevent them burning.

VARIATION

Serve the muesli in a long glass layered with fresh raspberries and mascarpone or thick yogurt. Soak the muesli first in a little water or fruit juice in order to soften it slightly.

2 Mix the toasted seeds with remaining ingredients and leave to cool. Store in an airtight container.

HEALTH BENEFITS

• Sunflower seeds are rich in vitamin E, which is thought to reduce the risk of heart disease.

• Apricots are high on the list of fruits that are considered likely to help prevent certain cancers, notably that of the lung.

Granola

HONEY-COATED NUTS, seeds and oats, combined with sweet dried fruits, make an excellent and nutritious start to the day – without the additives often found in pre-packed cereals. Serve the granola with low-fat milk or plain live yogurt and fresh fruit.

INGREDIENTS

1 cup rolled oats

1 cup jumbo oats

$^1/_2$ cup sunflower seeds

2 tablespoons sesame seeds

$^1/_2$ cup hazelnuts, roasted

$^1/_4$ cup almonds, roughly chopped

$^1/_4$ cup sunflower oil

$^1/_4$ cup clear honey

$^1/_2$ cup raisins

$^1/_2$ cup dried sweetened cranberries

Serves 4

1 Preheat the oven to 275°F. Mix together the oats, seeds and nuts in a bowl.

HEALTH BENEFITS

Oats have been the focus of much publicity in recent years; numerous studies have shown that their soluble fiber content can significantly lower blood cholesterol levels. They also supply vitamins B and E and iron.

2 Heat the oil and honey in a large saucepan until melted, then remove the pan from the heat. Add the oat mixture and stir well. Spread out on one or two baking sheets.

3 Bake for about 50 minutes until crisp, stirring occasionally to prevent the mixture sticking. Remove from the oven and mix in the raisins and cranberries. Leave to cool, then store in an airtight container.

Porridge with Date Puree and Pistachio Nuts

FULL OF VALUABLE fiber and nutrients, dates give a natural sweet flavor to this warming winter breakfast dish.

INGREDIENTS

scant 2 cups fresh dates

2 cups rolled oats

2 cups low-fat milk

pinch of salt

$^1/_2$ cup shelled, unsalted pistachio nuts,
   roughly chopped

Serves 4

HEALTH BENEFITS

Oats have a reputation for being warming foods due to their fat and protein content, which is greater than that of most other grains. As well as providing energy and endurance, oats are one of the most nutritious cereals.

1 First make the date purée. Halve the dates and remove the stones and stems. Cover the dates with boiling water and leave to soak for about 30 minutes, until softened. Strain, reserving 6 tablespoons of soaking water.

2 Remove the skin from the dates and place them in a food processor with the reserved soaking water. Process to a smooth purée.

3 Place the oats in a saucepan with the milk, $1^1/_4$ cups water and salt. Bring to a boil, then reduce heat and simmer for 4–5 minutes until cooked and creamy, stirring frequently.

4 Serve the porridge in warm serving bowls, topped with a spoonful of the date purée and sprinkled with chopped pistachio nuts.

Apricot and Ginger Compote

FRESH GINGER adds warmth to this stimulating breakfast dish and complements the flavor of the plump, juicy apricots.

INGREDIENTS

$1^1/_2$ cups dried unsulfured
   apricots

$1^1/_2$-inch piece fresh ginger root,
   finely chopped

scant 1 cup plain live yogurt or low-fat
   cream cheese

Serves 4

COOK'S TIP

Fresh ginger freezes well. Peel the root and store it in a plastic bag in the freezer. You can grate it from frozen, then return the root to the freezer until the next time you need it for a recipe.

1 Cover the apricots with boiling water, then leave to soak overnight.

2 Place the apricots and their soaking water in a saucepan, add the ginger and bring to a boil. Reduce heat and simmer for 10 minutes until the fruit is soft and plump and the water becomes syrupy. Strain the apricots, reserving the syrup, and discard the ginger.

3 Serve the apricots warm with the reserved syrup and a spoonful of yogurt or cream cheese.

HEALTH BENEFITS

• *In Chinese medicine, ginger is revered for its health-giving properties. It is antispasmodic, aids digestion and can help treat colds and flu.*

• *Of all the dried fruits, apricots are the richest source of iron. They also provide calcium, phosphorus and vitamins A and C.*

• *Live yogurt can relieve gastrointestinal disorders by replacing valuable bacteria in the gut. The lactic acids, which yogurt contains, can help to regulate bowel function and they have anti-bacterial properties that can prevent infection. Yogurt also boosts our immune system.*

Griddled Pineapple and Mango on Toasted Panettone with Vanilla Yogurt

GRIDDLING CONCENTRATES the sweetness of the pineapple and mango, giving a caramel flavor that is complemented by the vanilla yogurt.

INGREDIENTS

1 large pineapple

1 large mango

2 tablespoons (1/4 stick) unsalted butter, melted

4 thick slices panettone

For the vanilla yogurt

generous 1 cup thick yogurt

2 tablespoons clear honey

1 1/2 teaspoons ground cinnamon

a few drops natural vanilla extract, to taste

Serves 4

To prepare the pineapple, cut the bottom and the spiky top off the fruit. Stand the pineapple upright and cut off the skin, removing all the spikes, but as little of the flesh as possible. Lay the pineapple on its side and cut into quarters; remove the core if it is hard. Cut the pineapple into thick wedges.

HEALTH BENEFITS

Pineapple contains the powerful enzyme bromelain, which improves the digestion. It contains compounds that have an anti-inflammatory effect, so is good for people who suffer from arthritis. Pineapple has also been shown to reduce the incidence of blood clots and to ease bronchitis.

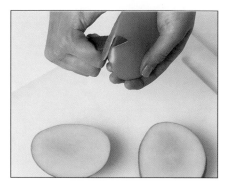

2 To prepare the mangoes, cut away the two thick sides of the mangoes as close to the stone as possible. Peel the mangoes, then cut the remaining flesh from the stone. Slice the fruit and discard the stone.

3 Heat a griddle pan over medium heat. Add the pineapple and mango (you may need to do this in batches). Brush with melted butter and cook for 8 minutes, turning once, until soft and slightly golden. Alternatively, heat the broiler to high and line the rack with foil. Place the pineapple and mango on the foil and grill for 4 minutes on each side.

4 Meanwhile, make the vanilla yogurt. Place the yogurt in a bowl with the honey, cinnamon and vanilla and stir well.

5 Lightly toast the panettone, then serve, topped with the pineapple and mango and accompanied by the vanilla yogurt.

Warm Bagels with Poached Apricots

TURN SWEET cinnamon and raisin bagels into an exotic dish.

INGREDIENTS

a few strips of orange peel

1 1/3 cups dried apricots

1 cup fresh orange juice

1/2 teaspoon orange flower water

2 cinnamon and raisin bagels

4 teaspoons pure fruit orange marmalade

4 tablespoons fat-free sour cream

2 tablespoons chopped pistachio nuts, to decorate

Serves 4

1 Cut the strips of orange peel into fine shreds. Place them in boiling water until softened, then drain and place in cold water.

2 Preheat the oven to 325°F. Combine the apricots and orange juice in a small saucepan. Heat gently for about 10 minutes, until the juice has reduced and looks syrupy. Allow to cool, then stir in the orange flower water. Meanwhile, place the bagels on a baking sheet and warm in the oven for 5 – 10 minutes.

3 Split the bagels in half horizontally. Lay one half, inside uppermost, on each serving plate. Spread 1 teaspoon orange marmalade on each bagel.

4 Spoon 1 tablespoon fat-free sour cream into the center of each bagel and place a quarter of the apricot compôte at the side. Sprinkle orange peel and pistachio nuts over the top to decorate. Serve immediately.

COOK'S TIP

Vary the bagels you use for the base: whole wheat or pumpernickel also taste good with this orangey topping.

Spiced Lentils and Rice

THIS TASTY brunch is a delicious variation of a traditional Indian dish, *kitchiri*. You can serve it as it is, or topped with quartered hard-cooked eggs if you'd like to add more protein. It is also delicious served on broiled, large portabello mushrooms.

INGREDIENTS

1/4 cup dried red lentils, rinsed

1 bay leaf

1 cup basmati rice, rinsed

4 cloves

4 tablespoons (1/2 stick) butter

1 teaspoon curry powder

1/2 teaspoon mild chili powder

2 tablespoons chopped Italian parsley

salt and freshly ground black pepper

4 hard-cooked eggs, quartered, to serve
   (optional)

Serves 4

1 Put the lentils in a saucepan, add the bay leaf and cover with cold water. Bring to a boil, skim off any foam, then reduce heat. Cover and simmer for 25–30 minutes, until tender. Drain, then discard the bay leaf.

2 Meanwhile, place the rice in a saucepan and cover with 2 cups boiling water. Add the cloves and a generous pinch of salt. Cook, covered, for 10–15 minutes, until all the water is absorbed and the rice is tender. Discard the cloves.

3 Melt the butter over gentle heat in a large frying pan, then add the curry and chili powders and cook for 1 minute.

4 Stir in the lentils and rice and mix well until they are coated in the spiced butter. Season and cook for 1–2 minutes until heated through. Stir in the parsley and serve with the hard-cooked eggs, if using.

HEALTH BENEFITS

• *Lentils are especially good for the heart, because of their ability to lower cholesterol levels in the body. They also contain chemicals that inhibit cancer and can regulate blood sugar levels.*
• *Rice is high-carbohydrate food that provides sustained amounts of energy, making it a perfect food to start the day. Rice can also help to ease diarrhea and stomach upsets.*

Griddled Tomatoes on Soda Bread

NOTHING COULD be simpler than this breakfast or brunch dish, yet a drizzle of olive oil and balsamic vinegar and shavings of Parmesan transform it into something really special.

INGREDIENTS

olive oil, for brushing and drizzling

6 tomatoes, thickly sliced

4 thick slices soda bread

balsamic vinegar, for drizzling

salt and freshly ground black pepper

shavings of Parmesan cheese, to serve

Serves 4

COOK'S TIP

Using a griddle pan reduces the amount of oil required for cooking the tomatoes and gives them a barbecued flavor.

1 Brush a griddle pan with olive oil and heat. Add the tomato slices and cook for 4–6 minutes, turning once, until softened and slightly blackened. Alternatively, heat a broiler to high and line the rack with foil. Broil the tomato slices for 4–6 minutes, turning once, until softened.

2 Meanwhile, lightly toast the soda bread. Place the tomatoes on top of the toast and drizzle each portion with a little olive oil and vinegar. Season to taste and serve immediately with thin shavings of Parmesan.

HEALTH BENEFITS

Numerous studies have shown that tomatoes are effective in preventing many forms of cancer, including lung, stomach and prostate cancer. This is probably explained by their antioxidant content, notably beta carotene and vitamins C and E. Antioxidants are also believed to prevent appendicitis.

Cheese and Banana Toasties

WHOLE WHEAT toast topped with low-fat soft cheese and sliced banana makes the perfect high-fiber breakfast and is especially delicious when drizzled with honey and broiled. It's easy to make, and provides a delicious start to any day.

INGREDIENTS

4 thick slices of whole wheat bread

$^{1}/_{2}$ cup low-fat soft cream cheese

$^{1}/_{4}$ teaspoon cardamom seeds, crushed (optional)

4 small bananas, peeled

4 teaspoons honey

Serves 4

1 Place the bread on a rack in a broiler pan and toast on one side only.

2 Turn the bread over, and spread the untoasted side of each slice with soft cheese. Sprinkle over the crushed cardamom seeds, if using.

3 Slice the bananas and arrange the slices on top of the cheese. Then drizzle each slice with 1 teaspoon of the honey. Slide the pan back under the moderately hot broiler and leave for a few minutes until bubbling. Serve immediately.

COOK'S TIP

For a delicious variation, use whole wheat bread with fruit or sesame or caraway seeds. Omit the cardamom seeds and sprinkle ground cinnamon on the bananas before adding the honey.

Mixed Pepper Pipérade

INGREDIENTS

2 tablespoons olive oil

I onion, chopped

I red bell pepper

I green bell pepper

4 tomatoes, peeled and chopped

I garlic clove, crushed

4 large eggs, beaten with I tablespoon water

ground black pepper

4 large, thick slices of whole wheat toast, to serve

Serves 4

1 Heat the oil in a large frying pan and sauté the onion gently until it becomes softened.

2 Remove the seeds from the red and green peppers and slice them thinly. Stir the pepper slices into the onion and cook together gently for 5 minutes. Add the tomatoes and garlic, season with black pepper, and cook for another 5 minutes.

3 Pour the egg mixture over the vegetables in the frying pan and cook over a moderate heat for 2–3 minutes, stirring now and then, until the pipérade has thickened to the consistency of lightly scrambled eggs.

4 Serve the pipérade immediately with warm whole wheat toast. A glass of orange juice or other fruit juice makes a perfect accompaniment.

COOK'S TIP

Choose eggs that have been date-stamped for freshness. Do not stir the pipérade too much or the eggs may become rubbery.

Chive Scrambled Eggs in Brioches

AN INDULGENT, but delicious, breakfast that should be reserved for Sundays or special occasions.

INGREDIENTS

8 tablespoons (1 stick) unsalted butter
generous 1 cup brown cap mushrooms, finely sliced
4 individual brioches
8 eggs
1 tablespoon snipped fresh chives, plus extra to garnish
salt and freshly ground black pepper
Serves 4

1 Preheat the oven to 350°F. Place a quarter of the butter in a frying pan and heat until melted. Fry the mushrooms for 3 minutes or until soft, then set aside and keep warm.

COOK'S TIP

Timing and temperature are crucial for perfect scrambled eggs. When cooked for too long over too high a heat, eggs become dry and crumbly; vice versa, and they are sloppy and unappealing.

HEALTH BENEFITS

Eggs are a good source of protein, selenium (which is an efficient antioxidant), iron, zinc and the complete range of B vitamins. However, although they are low in saturated fat, they are high in cholesterol, so should be eaten in moderation.

2 Slice the tops off the brioches, then scoop out the centres and discard. Put the brioches and lids on a baking sheet and bake for 5 minutes until hot and slightly crisp.

3 Meanwhile, beat the eggs lightly and season to taste. Heat the remaining butter in a heavy-based saucepan over gentle heat. When the butter has melted and is foaming slightly, add the eggs. Stir constantly using a wooden spoon to ensure the egg does not stick.

4 Continue to stir until about three-quarters of the egg is semi-solid and creamy – this should take 2–3 minutes. Remove the pan from the heat – the egg will continue to cook in the heat from the pan – then stir in the snipped chives.

5 To serve, spoon a little of the mushrooms into the bottom of each brioche and top with the scrambled eggs. Sprinkle with extra chives, balance the brioche lids on top and serve immediately.

Mushroom Hunter's Omelet

PERFECT FOR Sunday brunch, this omelet is simplicity itself to make. Use whatever mushrooms are in season at the time for the filling.

INGREDIENTS

2 tablespoons (1/4 stick) unsalted butter, plus extra for cooking

4 ounces assorted wild and cultivated mushrooms, such as young cèpes, chanterelles, cremini, portobellos, and oyster mushrooms, trimmed and sliced

3 eggs, at room temperature

salt and freshly ground black pepper

Serves 1

1 Melt the butter in a small omelet pan, add the mushrooms and cook until the juices run. Season with salt and pepper, remove the mushrooms from pan and set aside while you prepare the omelet. Wipe the pan.

2 Break the eggs into a bowl, season and beat with a fork. Heat the pan over high heat, add a pat of butter and let it begin to brown. Pour in the beaten egg and stir briskly with the back of a fork.

3 When the eggs are two-thirds set, add the cooked mushrooms and let the omelet finish cooking for 10–15 seconds.

4 Tap the handle of the omelet pan sharply with your fist to loosen the omelet from the pan, then fold and turn out onto a plate. Serve with warm crusty bread and a simple green salad.

SOUPS and APPETIZERS

Serve light flavorsome soups as appetizers or make a thick, nourishing soup as a meal in its own right for an ideal lunchtime choice. Many traditional favorites are included here along with a selection of dips and pâtés to be served with seasonal vegetables.

Gazpacho with Avocado Salsa

TOMATOES, CUCUMBER and peppers form the basis of this classic, chilled soup. Add a spoonful of chunky, fresh avocado salsa and a scattering of croûtons, and serve for a light lunch on a warm summer day.

INGREDIENTS

2 slices day-old bread
2¼ pounds tomatoes
1 cucumber
1 red bell pepper, seeded
  and chopped
1 green chile, seeded and chopped
2 garlic cloves, chopped
2 tablespoons extra virgin olive oil
juice of 1 lime and 1 lemon
a few drops Tabasco sauce
salt and freshly ground black pepper
a handful of basil leaves, to garnish
8 ice cubes, to serve

For the croûtons
2 slices day-old bread, crusts removed
1 garlic clove, halved
1 tablespoon olive oil

For the avocado salsa
1 ripe avocado
1 teaspoon lemon juice
1-inch piece cucumber, diced
½ red chile, finely chopped
Serves 4

1 Soak the bread in ⅔ cup of water for 5 minutes.

2 Meanwhile, place the tomatoes in a bowl and cover with boiling water. Leave for 30 seconds, then peel, seed, and chop the flesh.

HEALTH BENEFITS

The powerful combination of fresh raw vegetables, garlic, lemon and lime juice, olive oil and chile boosts the immune system and the circulation, and helps to cleanse the body.

3 Peel the cucumber, cut in half lengthways and scoop out the seeds with a teaspoon. Discard the seeds and chop the flesh.

4 Place the bread, tomatoes, cucumber, red pepper, chile, garlic, olive oil, citrus juices, and Tabasco in a food processor or blender with scant 2 cups chilled water, and blend until well combined but still chunky. Season to taste and chill for 2–3 hours.

5 To make the croûtons, rub the slices of bread with the garlic clove. Cut the bread into cubes and place in a plastic bag with the olive oil. Seal the bag and shake until the bread cubes are coated with the oil. Heat a large non-stick frying pan and fry the croûtons over medium heat until crisp and golden.

6 Just before serving, make the avocado salsa. Halve the avocado, remove the stone, then peel and dice. Toss the avocado in the lemon juice to prevent it browning, then mix with the cucumber and chile.

7 Ladle the soup into bowls, add the ice cubes, and top with a spoonful of avocado salsa. Garnish with the basil and hand round the croûtons separately.

Carrot and Cilantro Soup

NEARLY ALL root vegetables make excellent soups, as they purée and have an earthy flavor that complements the sharper flavors of herbs and spices. Carrots are particularly versatile. This simple soup is elegant in both flavor and appearance.

INGREDIENTS

1 pound carrots, preferably young
   and tender
1 tablespoon sunflower oil
3 tablespoons (1/6 stick) butter
1 onion, chopped
1 celery rib, plus 2–3 pale leafy
   celery tops
2 small potatoes, peeled
4 cups vegetable stock
2–3 teaspoons ground coriander
1 tablespoon chopped cilantro
1 cup milk
salt and freshly ground black pepper
Serves 4–6

1 Trim and peel the carrots and cut into chunks. Heat the oil and 2 tablespoons butter in a large flameproof casserole or heavy saucepan and sauté the onion over gentle heat for 3–4 minutes, until slightly softened.

2 Slice the celery and chop the potatoes. Add them to the onion in the pan, cook for a few minutes and then add the carrots. Cook over gentle heat for 3–4 minutes, stirring, and then cover.

3 Reduce the heat even further and sweat for about 10 minutes. Shake the pan or stir occasionally so the vegetables do not stick to the bottom.

4 Add the stock and bring to a boil. Half-cover the pan and simmer for another 8–10 minutes, until the carrots and potatoes are tender.

5 Remove 6–8 tiny celery leaves for garnish and finely chop the remaining celery tops (about 1 tablespoon once chopped). Melt the remaining butter in a small saucepan and sauté the ground coriander for about 1 minute, stirring constantly.

6 Reduce the heat, add the chopped celery tops and cilantro and sauté for about 1 minute. Set aside until required.

7 Process the soup in a food processor or blender and pour into a clean saucepan. Stir in the milk and the cilantro mixture. Season, heat gently, taste and adjust the seasoning. Serve garnished with the reserved celery leaves.

COOK'S TIP

For a more piquant flavor, add a little lemon juice just before serving.

Fresh Pea Soup

THIS HEARTY soup is known in France as *Potage Saint-Germain*, a name that comes from a suburb of Paris where peas used to be cultivated in market gardens. If fresh peas are not available, use frozen peas instead, but thaw and rinse them before use.

INGREDIENTS

2 tablespoons (¹/₄ stick) butter

2 or 3 shallots, finely chopped

3 cups shelled fresh peas (from about
   3 pounds garden peas) or thawed
   frozen peas

3–4 tablespoons whipping cream (optional)

salt and freshly ground black pepper

croutons, to garnish

Serves 2–3

1 Melt the butter in a heavy saucepan or flameproof casserole. Add the shallots and cook for about 3 minutes over a moderate heat, stirring occasionally.

2 Add 2 cups water and the peas, and season with salt and pepper.

3 Cover and simmer for 12 minutes for young or frozen peas and up to 18 minutes for large or older peas, stirring occasionally.

4 When the peas are tender, ladle them into a food processor or blender with a little of the cooking liquid and process until smooth.

5 Strain the soup into the saucepan or casserole, stir in the cream, if using, and heat through without boiling. Season with salt and pepper and serve hot, garnished with croutons.

Minestrone with Pesto

MINESTRONE IS a thick, mixed vegetable soup using almost any combination of seasonal vegetables. Short cuts of pasta or rice may also be added. This version includes pesto sauce.

INGREDIENTS

3 tablespoons olive oil
1 large onion, finely chopped
1 leek, sliced
2 carrots, finely chopped
1 celery rib, finely chopped
2 cloves garlic, finely chopped
2 potatoes, peeled and cut into small dice
6 1/4 cups hot vegetable stock or water, or a combination of both
1 bay leaf
1 sprig of fresh thyme, or 1/4 teaspoon dried thyme
3/4 cup peas, fresh or frozen
2–3 zucchini, finely chopped
3 medium tomatoes, peeled and finely chopped
2 cups cooked or canned beans, such as cannellini
3 tablespoons pesto sauce
salt and freshly ground black pepper
Parmesan cheese, freshly grated, to serve

Serves 6

1 Heat the oil in a saucepan. Stir in the onion and leek, and cook for 5–6 minutes. Add the carrots, celery and garlic, and cook over moderate heat for 5 minutes. Add the potatoes and cook for 2–3 minutes more.

2 Pour in the hot stock or water and stir well. Add the herbs and season with salt and pepper. Bring to a boil, reduce the heat and cook for 10–12 minutes.

3 Stir in the peas, if fresh, and the zucchini. Simmer for 5 minutes. Add the frozen peas, if using, and the tomatoes. Cover the pan and simmer for 5–8 minutes.

4 About 10 minutes before serving, uncover the pan and stir in the beans. Simmer for 10 minutes. Stir in the pesto sauce. Simmer for another 5 minutes. Remove from the heat and let stand for a few minutes. Serve with the grated Parmesan cheese.

Pumpkin Soup

THIS BEAUTIFULLY flavored, golden-colored soup would be perfect for an autumn dinner.

INGREDIENTS

1-lb piece of peeled pumpkin
4 tablespoons (1/2 stick) butter
1 medium onion, finely chopped
3 cups vegetable stock or water
2 cups milk
pinch of grated nutmeg
1 1/2 ounces spaghetti, broken into small pieces
6 tablespoons Parmesan cheese, freshly grated
salt and freshly ground black pepper

Serves 4

1 Chop the piece of pumpkin into 1-inch cubes.

2 Heat the butter in a saucepan. Add the onion and cook over moderate heat until it softens, about 6–8 minutes. Stir in the pumpkin pieces and cook for 2–3 minutes more.

3 Add the stock or water and cook until the pumpkin is soft, about 15 minutes. Remove from the heat.

4 Process the soup in a blender or food processor. Return it to the pan. Stir in the milk and nutmeg. Season with salt and pepper. Bring the soup back to a boil.

5 Stir the broken spaghetti into the soup. Cook until the pasta is done. Stir in the Parmesan, sprinkle with nutmeg, and serve at once.

Jerusalem Artichoke Soup with Gruyère Toasts

SMALL, KNOBBLY jerusalem artichokes have a delicious, mild, nutty flavor. They make a remarkably good, creamy soup, which is best served with crunchy, grilled Gruyère and French bread toasts.

INGREDIENTS

2 tablespoons olive oil

1 large onion, chopped

1 garlic clove, chopped

1 celery stalk, chopped

1 1/2 pounds jerusalem artichokes, peeled and chopped

5 cups vegetable stock

1 1/4 cups low-fat milk

salt and freshly ground black pepper

To serve

8 slices French bread

1 cup Gruyère cheese, grated

Serves 4–6

1 Heat the butter and oil in a large saucepan. Add the onion, garlic and celery, and cook over medium heat for about 5 minutes or until softened, stirring occasionally. Add the prepared jerusalem artichokes and cook for a further 5 minutes.

2 Add the stock and seasoning, and bring the soup to a boil. Reduce heat and simmer for 20–25 minutes, stirring occasionally, until the artichokes are tender.

3 Transfer the soup to a food processor or blender (or use a hand blender) and process for a few minutes until smooth. Return the soup to the pan, stir in the milk and heat through gently for 2 minutes.

4 To make the Gruyère toasts, heat the broiler to high. Lightly toast the bread on one side, then sprinkle the untoasted side with the Gruyère. Broil until the cheese melts and is golden. Ladle the soup into bowls and top with the Gruyère toasts.

COOK'S TIP

To preserve soluble nutrients, scrub the jerusalem artichokes rather than peel them.

HEALTH BENEFITS

High in fiber and low in fat, jerusalem artichokes also contain valuable amounts of vitamin C.

Garlic, Chickpea and Spinach Soup

THIS DELICIOUS, thick and creamy soup is richly flavored and makes a great one-pot meal.

INGREDIENTS

2 tablespoons olive oil
4 garlic cloves, crushed
1 onion, roughly chopped
2 teaspoons ground cumin
2 teaspoons ground coriander
5 cups vegetable stock
12 ounces potatoes, peeled and
    finely chopped
15-ounce can chickpeas, drained
1 tablespoon cornstarch
2/3 cup heavy cream
2 tablespoons light tahini
7 ounces spinach, shredded
cayenne pepper
salt and freshly ground black pepper
Serves 4

1 Heat the oil in a large saucepan and cook the garlic and onion for 5 minutes, or until they are softened and golden brown.

2 Stir in the cumin and coriander and cook for another minute.

3 Pour in the stock and add the chopped potatoes to the pan. Bring to a boil and simmer for 10 minutes. Add the chickpeas and simmer for 5 minutes more, or until the potatoes and chickpeas are just tender when pierced.

4 Blend together the cornstarch, cream, tahini and plenty of seasoning. Stir into the soup with the spinach. Bring to a boil, stirring, and simmer for another 2 minutes. Season with cayenne pepper, salt and black pepper. Serve immediately, sprinkled with a little cayenne pepper.

Classic French Onion Soup

WHEN FRENCH onion soup is made slowly and carefully, the onions caramelize to a deep mahogany color. The soup has a superb flavor and is a perfect winter supper dish.

INGREDIENTS

4 large onions

2 tablespoons sunflower or olive oil, or 1 tablespoon of each

2 tablespoons (1/4 stick) butter

3 3/4 cups vegetable stock

4 slices French bread

1 1/2–2 ounces Gruyère or Cheddar cheese, grated

salt and freshly ground black pepper

Serves 4

1 Peel and quarter the onions and slice or chop them into 1/4-inch pieces. Heat the oil and butter in a deep, medium-size saucepan, so that the onions form a thick layer on the bottom of the saucepan.

2 Sauté the onions briskly for a few minutes, stirring constantly.

3 Reduce the heat and cook the onions gently for 45–60 minutes. At first the onions need to be stirred only occasionally, but as they begin to color, stir frequently. The color of the onions gradually turns golden and then more rapidly turns very brown, so take care to stir constantly at this stage so that they do not burn or stick on the bottom of the pan.

4 When the onions are a rich mahogany brown, add the vegetable stock and a little seasoning. Simmer, partially covered, for 30 minutes, then season the mixture with salt and pepper.

5 Preheat the broiler and toast the French bread. Spoon the soup into four ovenproof serving dishes and place a piece of bread in each. Sprinkle with the cheese and broil for a few minutes, until golden. Season with plenty of freshly ground black pepper.

White Bean Soup

A THICK puree of cooked dried beans is at the heart of this substantial country soup from Tuscany. It makes a warming lunch or supper dish.

INGREDIENTS

1 1/2 cups dried cannellini or other
   white beans
1 bay leaf
5 tablespoons olive oil
1 medium onion, finely chopped
1 carrot, finely chopped
1 celery rib, finely chopped
3 medium tomatoes, peeled and finely
   chopped
2 cloves garlic, finely chopped
1 teaspoon fresh thyme leaves or
   1/2 teaspoon dried thyme
3 cups boiling water
salt and freshly ground black pepper
olive oil, to serve

Serves 6

1 Pick over the beans carefully, discarding any stones or other particles. Rinse thoroughly in cold water. Then soak in a large bowl of cold water overnight.

2 Drain the beans and place them in a large saucepan of water, bring to a boil and cook for 20 minutes. Drain. Return the beans to the pan, cover with cold water and bring to a boil again. Add the bay leaf and cook for 1–2 hours, until the beans are tender. Drain again. Remove the bay leaf.

3 Puree about three-quarters of the beans in a food processor or pass them through a food mill, adding a little water if necessary, to create a smooth paste.

4 Heat the oil in a large saucepan. Stir in the onion and cook until it softens. Add the carrot and celery, and cook for 5 minutes more, until they are soft but not mushy.

5 Stir in the tomatoes, garlic and thyme. Cook for 6–8 minutes more, stirring often.

6 Pour in the boiling water. Stir in the beans and the bean purée. Season with salt and pepper. Simmer for 10–15 minutes. Serve the soup in individual soup bowls, sprinkled with a little olive oil.

COOK'S TIP

Canned cooked beans, such as cannellini or borlotti, may be substituted in this recipe. Simply drain the beans and omit Steps 1 and 2.

Hot-and-sour Soup

THIS LIGHT and invigorating soup originates from Thailand. It is best served at the beginning of a Thai meal to stimulate the appetite.

INGREDIENTS

2 carrots

3³/4 cups vegetable stock

2 Thai chiles, seeded and finely sliced

2 lemongrass stalks, outer leaves removed and each stalk cut into 3 pieces

4 kaffir lime leaves

2 garlic cloves, finely chopped

4 scallions, finely sliced

1 teaspoon sugar

juice of 1 lime

3 tablespoons cilantro, chopped

salt

1 cup Japanese tofu, sliced

Serves 4

1 To make carrot flowers, cut each carrot in half crossways, then, using a sharp knife, cut four v-shaped channels lengthways. Slice the carrots into thin rounds and set aside.

COOK'S TIP

Kaffir lime leaves have a distinctive citrus flavor. The fresh leaves can be bought from Asian markets, and some supermarkets now sell them dried.

2 Pour the stock into a large saucepan. Reserve ¹/2 teaspoon of the chiles and add the rest to the pan with the lemongrass, lime leaves, garlic and half the scallions. Bring to a boil, then reduce heat and simmer for 20 minutes. Strain the stock and discard the flavorings.

3 Return the stock to the pan, add the reserved chiles and scallions, the sugar, lime juice, cilantro and salt to taste.

4 Simmer for 5 minutes, then add the carrot flowers and tofu, and cook for a further 2 minutes until the carrot is just tender. Serve hot.

HEALTH BENEFITS

Hot spices, including chiles, are good for the respiratory system. They help to relieve congestion and may, as a result, soothe the symptoms of colds, flu and hayfever. Chiles encourage the brain to release endorphins, which increase the sensation of pleasure, and so they have been described as aphrodisiacs.

Fresh Tomato, Lentil and Onion Soup

THIS DELICIOUS, wholesome soup is ideal served with thick slices of whole wheat bread.

INGREDIENTS

2 teaspoons sunflower oil
1 large onion, chopped
2 celery ribs, chopped
3/4 cup split red lentils
2 large tomatoes, peeled and roughly chopped
3 3/4 cups vegetable stock
2 teaspoons dried herbes de Provence
salt and freshly ground black pepper
chopped parsley, to garnish

Serves 4–6

1 Heat the oil in a large saucepan. Add the chopped onion and celery and cook for 5 minutes, stirring occasionally. Add the split red lentils and cook the mixture for 1 minute.

2 Stir in the tomatoes, stock, dried herbs, salt and pepper. Cover, bring to a boil and simmer for about 20 minutes, stirring occasionally.

3 When the lentils are cooked and tender, set the soup aside to cool slightly before pureeing it.

4 Puree in a blender or food processor until smooth. Season with salt and pepper, return to the saucepan and reheat gently until piping hot. Ladle into soup bowls to serve and garnish each with chopped parsley.

Italian Pea and Basil Soup

PLENTY OF crusty country bread is a must with this fresh-tasting soup.

INGREDIENTS

5 tablespoons olive oil

2 large onions, chopped

1 celery rib, chopped

1 carrot, chopped

1 garlic clove, finely chopped

3 1/2 cups frozen peas

3 3/4 cups vegetable stock

1 cup fresh basil leaves, roughly torn, plus extra to garnish

salt and freshly ground black pepper

Parmesan cheese, freshly grated, to serve

Serves 4

VARIATION

Use mint or a mixture of parsley, mint and chives in place of the basil.

1 Heat the oil in a large saucepan and add the onions, celery, carrot and garlic. Cover the pan and cook over a low heat for 45 minutes or until the vegetables are soft, stirring occasionally to prevent the vegetables sticking.

2 Add the peas and stock to the pan and bring to a boil. Reduce the heat, add the basil and seasoning, then simmer for 10 minutes.

3 Spoon the soup into a food processor or blender and process until the soup is smooth. Ladle into warm bowls, sprinkle with grated Parmesan and garnish with basil.

HEALTH BENEFITS

As freezing usually takes place soon after picking, frozen peas may have a higher vitamin C content than fresh.

Spiced Red Lentil and Coconut Soup

HOT, SPICY and richly flavored, this substantial soup is almost a meal in itself. If you are really hungry, serve with chunks of warmed naan bread or thick slices of toast.

INGREDIENTS

2 tablespoons sunflower oil

2 red onions, finely chopped

1 bird's eye chile, seeded and finely sliced

2 garlic cloves, chopped

1-inch piece fresh lemongrass, outer leaves removed and inside finely sliced

scant 1 cup red lentils, rinsed

1 teaspoon ground coriander

1 teaspoon paprika

1 2/3 cups coconut milk

juice of 1 lime

3 scallions, chopped

scant 1 cup cilantro, finely chopped

salt and freshly ground black pepper

Serves 4

1 Heat the oil in a large, deep frying pan and add the onions, chile, garlic and lemongrass. Cook for 5 minutes or until the onions have softened, stirring occasionally.

HEALTH BENEFITS

Lentils provide a rich supply of minerals, including iron and calcium, as well as folic acid. The latter is recommended for pregnant women as it can lower the risk of spina bifida in the unborn child.

2 Add the lentils and spices. Pour in the coconut milk and 3 3/4 cups water, and stir. Bring to a boil, stir, then reduce the heat and simmer for 40–45 minutes or until the lentils are soft and mushy.

3 Pour in the lime juice and add the scallions and cilantro, reserving a little of each for the garnish. Season, then ladle into bowls. Garnish with the reserved scallions and cilantro.

Guacamole

THIS IS quite a fiery version, although nowhere near as hot as you would be served in Mexico!

INGREDIENTS

2 ripe avocados, peeled and pitted

2 tomatoes, peeled, seeded and finely
    chopped

6 scallions, finely chopped

1–2 fresh chiles, seeded and finely
    chopped

2 tablespoons fresh lime or lemon juice

1 tablespoon cilantro, chopped

salt and freshly ground black pepper

cilantro sprigs, to garnish

Serves 4

1 Put the avocado halves in a large bowl and mash them roughly with a large fork.

2 Add the remaining ingredients. Mix well and season with salt and pepper. Serve garnished with a few cilantro sprigs.

Chickpea Falafel with Cilantro Dip

LITTLE BALLS of spicy chickpea puree, deep-fried until crisp, are served with a zesty cilantro-flavored mayonnaise.

INGREDIENTS

14-ounce can chickpeas, drained

6 scallions, finely chopped

1 egg

1/2 teaspoon ground turmeric

1 garlic clove, crushed

1 teaspoon ground cumin

4 tablespoons cilantro, chopped

oil for deep-frying

1 small fresh red chile, seeded and
   finely chopped

3 tablespoons mayonnaise

salt and freshly ground black pepper

sprig of cilantro, to garnish

Serves 4

1 Put the chickpeas in a food processor or blender. Add the scallions and process to a smooth puree. Add the egg, ground turmeric, garlic, cumin and about 1 tablespoon of the chopped cilantro. Process briefly to mix, then season with salt and pepper.

2 Working with clean, wet hands, shape the chickpea mixture into about 16 small balls.

3 Heat the oil for deep-frying to 350°F, or until a cube of bread added to the oil browns in 30–45 seconds. Deep-fry the falafel in batches for 2–3 minutes, or until golden. Drain the falafel on paper towels. Place in a serving bowl and keep warm.

4 Stir the remaining chopped cilantro and the chile into the mayonnaise. Garnish with the cilantro sprig and serve alongside the falafel.

Crisp Spring Rolls with Sweet Chile Dip

DAINTY, MINIATURE spring rolls make delicious appetizers or perfect party finger food. Here they are served with a tangy dip.

INGREDIENTS

1 ounce rice vermicelli noodles
peanut oil
1 teaspoon fresh ginger root, finely grated
2 scallions, finely shredded
2 ounces carrot, finely shredded
2 ounces snow peas, shredded
1 ounce young spinach leaves
2 ounces fresh bean sprouts
1 tablespoon fresh mint, finely chopped
1 tablespoon cilantro, finely chopped
2 tablespoons light soy sauce
20–24 spring roll wrappers, each
  5 inches square
1 egg white, lightly beaten

For the dipping sauce
¹/4 cup sugar
¹/4 cup rice vinegar
2 fresh red chiles, seeded and
  finely chopped

Makes 20–24

1 First make the dipping sauce. Place the sugar and vinegar in a small saucepan with 2 tablespoons water. Heat gently, stirring until the sugar dissolves, then boil rapidly until it forms a light syrup. Stir in the chiles and let cool thoroughly.

2 Soak the noodles according to the package instructions. Rinse and drain well. Using scissors, snip the noodles into short lengths.

3 Heat a wok until hot. Add 1 tablespoon oil. Add the ginger and scallions and stir-fry for 15 seconds. Add the carrot and snow peas and stir-fry for 2–3 minutes. Add the spinach, bean sprouts, mint, cilantro, soy sauce and noodles and stir-fry the whole mixture for another minute. Set aside to cool.

4 Place a spring roll wrapper on the work surface. Put a spoonful of filling in the middle. Fold the wrapper to encase the filling.

5 Fold in each side, then roll up tightly. Brush the end with beaten egg white to seal. Repeat until all the filling has been used.

6 Half-fill a wok with oil and heat to 350°F. Deep-fry the spring rolls in batches for 3–4 minutes, until golden and crisp. Drain on paper towels. Serve hot, with the sweet chile dipping sauce.

COOK'S TIP

You can cook the spring rolls 2–3 hours in advance. Then all you have to do is reheat them on a foil-lined baking sheet at 400°F for about 10 minutes, until they are piping hot.

Marinated Vegetable Antipasto

THIS COLORFUL selection of fresh vegetables and herbs makes a great appetizer when served with fresh crusty bread.

INGREDIENTS

For the peppers
3 red bell peppers
3 yellow bell peppers
4 garlic cloves, sliced
handful of fresh basil
1/2 cup olive oil
salt and freshly ground black pepper

For the mushrooms
1 pound portobello mushrooms, thickly sliced
1/4 cup olive oil
1 large garlic clove, crushed
1 tablespoon fresh rosemary, chopped
1 cup dry white wine
fresh rosemary sprigs, to garnish

For the olives
1 dried red chile, crushed
grated zest of 1 lemon
1/2 cup olive oil
8 ounces Italian black olives
2 tablespoons fresh flat-leaf parsley, chopped
basil leaves, to garnish
1 lemon wedge, to serve

Serves 4

1 Place the peppers under a hot broiler. Cook until they are black and blistered all over. Remove from the heat and place them in a large plastic bag to cool.

2 When the peppers are cool, remove their skins, halve the flesh and remove the seeds. Cut into strips lengthwise and place them in a bowl with the sliced garlic and basil leaves. Season, then cover with oil and marinate for 3–4 hours, tossing occasionally. Garnish with basil leaves.

3 Place the mushrooms in a bowl. Heat the oil in a pan and add the garlic, rosemary and wine. Bring to a boil, then simmer for 3 minutes. Season. Pour over the mushrooms.

4 Mix well and let cool, stirring occasionally. Cover and marinate overnight. Serve at room temperature, garnished with rosemary sprigs.

5 Place the chile and lemon zest in a small pan with the oil. Heat gently for about 3 minutes. Add the olives and heat for 1 minute more. Pour the olive mixture into a bowl and let cool. Marinate overnight. Before serving, sprinkle with parsley and garnish with basil leaves. Serve with the lemon wedge and good Italian bread to mop up the juices, if desired.

Mushroom Croustades

Scoop out the bread dough to keep this starter light with a crispy texture and appetizing flavor.

INGREDIENTS

1 short French bread, about 10 inches

2 teaspoons olive oil

9 ounces portobello mushrooms, quartered

2 teaspoons tomato ketchup

2 teaspoons lemon juice

2 tablespoons skim milk

2 tablespoons fresh chives, snipped, plus extra to garnish

salt and freshly ground black pepper

Serves 2–4

2 Place the mushrooms in a small saucepan with the tomato ketchup, lemon juice and milk. Simmer for about 5 minutes, or until most of the liquid is evaporated but before it becomes dry.

3 Remove from the heat, then add the snipped fresh chives and season with salt and pepper. Spoon the mushroom into the bread croustades and serve hot, garnished with more snipped chives.

1 Preheat the oven to 400°F. Cut the French bread in half lengthways. Cut a scoop out of the middle of each half, leaving a thick border. Brush the bread with oil, place on a baking sheet and bake for 6–8 minutes, until golden.

COOK'S TIP

If portabello mushrooms are not available, any other variety of flavorful mushrooms will do.

Fried Mozzarella

THESE CRISPY cheese slices make an unusual and tasty appetizer. They must be cooked just before serving.

INGREDIENTS

12 ounces mozzarella cheese

oil, for deep-frying

2 eggs

flour seasoned with salt and freshly ground black pepper

plain dry bread crumbs

flat-leaf parsley, to garnish

Serves 2–3

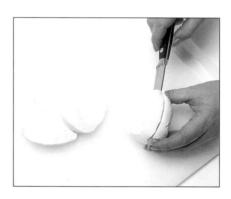

1 Cut the mozzarella into slices about ½ inch thick. Gently pat off any excess moisture with paper towels. Reserve while you make the breading.

2 Heat the oil to 360°F, or until a small piece of bread sizzles as soon as it is dropped in. While the oil is heating, beat the eggs in a shallow bowl. Spread some seasoned flour on one plate and some bread crumbs on another plate.

3 Press the cheese slices into the flour, coating them evenly with a thin layer of flour. Shake off any excess. Dip them into the egg, then into the bread crumbs. Dip them once more into the egg, then again into the bread crumbs, covering the whole slice.

4 Fry immediately in the hot oil until golden brown. (You may have to do this in two batches, but do not let the breaded cheese wait for too long, or the bread crumb coating will separate from the cheese while it is being fried.) Drain on paper towels and serve hot, garnished with parsley.

Greek Cheese and Potato Patties

DELICIOUS LITTLE fried morsels of potato and feta cheese, flavored with dill and lemon juice.

INGREDIENTS

1 ¼ pounds potatoes

4 ounces feta cheese

4 scallions, chopped

3 tablespoons fresh dill, chopped

1 tablespoon lemon juice

1 egg, beaten

flour, for dredging

3 tablespoons olive oil

salt and freshly ground black pepper

Serves 4

COOK'S TIP

Whip the cooked potatoes using an electric beater for lump-free mash.

1 Boil the potatoes in their skins in lightly salted water until soft. Drain and cool slightly, then peel while still warm. Place the cooked potatoes in a bowl and mash. Crumble the feta cheese into the potatoes and add the scallions, dill, lemon juice and egg. Season the mixture with salt and pepper (the cheese is salty, so taste before you add salt). Stir well.

2 Cover the mixture and chill until firm. Divide the mixture into walnut-size balls, then flatten them slightly. Dredge in the flour. Heat the oil in a frying pan and fry the patties until golden brown on each side. Drain on paper towels and serve at once. These potato patties taste delicious with a spinach and tomato salad, the classic Greek accompaniment.

Cheese-Stuffed Pears

THESE PEARS, with their scrumptious creamy topping, make a sublime dish when served with a simple salad.

INGREDIENTS

1/4 cup ricotta cheese
1/4 cup dolcelatte cheese
1 tablespoon honey
1/2 celery rib, finely sliced
8 green olives, pitted and roughly chopped
4 dates, pitted and cut into thin strips
pinch of paprika
4 ripe pears
2/3 cup apple juice

Serves 4

1 Preheat the oven to 400°F. Place the ricotta in a bowl and crumble in the dolcelatte. Add the rest of the ingredients except for the pears and apple juice and mix well. Set aside while you prepare the pears.

2 Halve the pears lengthwise and use a melon baller to remove the cores. Place in an ovenproof dish and divide the filling equally among the eight halves.

3 Pour the apple juice carefully into the dish and cover completely with foil. Bake for 20 minutes, or until the pears are tender.

4 Remove the foil and place the dish under a hot broiler for 3 minutes. Serve immediately.

COOK'S TIP

Choose ripe pears in season such as Bosc, Bartlett or Comice.

Roquefort Tartlets

THESE CAN be made in shallow muffin pans to serve hot as a first course. You could also make them in tiny tart pans, to serve warm as appetizing bite-size snacks with a drink before a meal.

INGREDIENTS

1 1/2 cups all-purpose flour
large pinch of salt
8 tablespoons (1 stick) butter
1 egg yolk
2 tablespoons cold water

For the filling

1 tablespoon (1/8 stick) butter
2 tablespoons flour
2/3 cup milk
4 ounces Roquefort cheese, crumbled
2/3 cup heavy cream
1/2 teaspoon dried mixed herbs, such as tarragon, thyme, or savory
3 egg yolks
salt and freshly ground black pepper
Makes 12

1 To make the pastry, sift the flour and salt into a bowl and rub the butter into the flour until it resembles bread crumbs. Mix the egg yolk with the water and stir into the flour to make a soft dough. Knead until smooth, wrap in plastic wrap and chill for 30 minutes. (You can also make the dough in a food processor.)

2 In a saucepan, melt the butter and stir in the flour and then the milk. Boil to thicken, stirring constantly. Off the heat, beat in the cheese and season with salt and pepper. Let cool. In another saucepan, bring the cream and herbs to a boil and cook until the liquid has reduced to 2 tablespoons. Beat into the cheese sauce with the eggs.

3 Preheat the oven to 375°F. On a lightly floured work surface, roll out the pastry to 1/8 inch thick. Stamp out rounds with a fluted cutter and use to line your chosen pans.

4 Divide the filling among the tartlets; they should be filled or two-thirds full. Stamp out smaller fluted rounds or star shapes for the tops and lay on top of each tartlet. Bake for 20–25 minutes, or until golden brown.

Buckwheat Blinis with Mushroom Caviar

THESE LITTLE Russian pancakes are
traditionally served with fish roe
caviar and sour cream. The term
caviar is also given to fine vegetable
mixtures called *ikry*. This wild
mushroom caviar has a rich and
silky texture.

INGREDIENTS

1 cup white bread flour

1/3 cup buckwheat flour

1/2 teaspoon salt

1 1/4 cups milk

1 teaspoon active dry yeast

2 eggs, separated

1 cup sour cream or crème fraîche,
     to serve

For the caviar

12 ounces assorted wild mushrooms, such
     as cremini, porcini, oyster or
     portobello mushrooms

1 teaspoon celery salt

2 tablespoons walnut oil

1 tablespoon lemon juice

3 tablespoons fresh parsley, chopped

freshly ground black pepper

Serves 4

1 To make the caviar, trim and chop the
mushrooms and place them in a glass
bowl. Toss with the celery salt and
cover with a weighted plate.

2 Let the mushrooms sit for
2 hours, until the juices have run
out into the bottom of the bowl. Rinse
them thoroughly to remove the salt.

3 Drain the mushrooms and press
out as much liquid as you can
with the back of a spoon. Return them
to the bowl and toss with the walnut
oil, lemon juice and parsley. Season
with pepper and chill the mixture until
ready to serve.

4 For the blinis, sift the two flours
together with the salt in a large
mixing bowl. Warm the milk to
lukewarm. Add the yeast to the milk,
stirring until dissolved, then pour into
the flour. Add the egg yolks and stir to
make a smooth batter. Cover with a
damp cloth and let sit in a warm place
to rise for about 30 minutes.

5 Beat the egg whites in a clean
bowl until stiff, then fold into the
risen batter.

6 Heat a cast-iron pan to moderate.
Moisten with oil, then drop
spoonfuls of the batter onto the
surface, turn them over and cook
briefly on the other side. Spoon the
mushroom caviar on top and serve
with the sour cream.

Broccoli Timbales

THIS ELEGANT but easy-to-make dish can be made with almost any pureed vegetable, such as carrot or celeriac. To avoid last-minute fuss, make the timbales a few hours ahead and cook while the first course is being eaten. Or serve them on their own as an appetizer with a little white wine butter sauce.

INGREDIENTS

1 tablespoon (1/8 stick) butter

12 ounces broccoli florets

3 tablespoons crème fraîche or
*   whipping cream*

1 egg, plus one egg yolk

1 tablespoon scallion, chopped

pinch of freshly grated nutmeg

salt and freshly ground black pepper

white wine butter sauce, to serve (optional)

fresh chives, to garnish (optional)

Serves 4

3 Put the broccoli in a food processor fitted with the metal blade and process with the cream, egg and egg yolk until smooth.

4 Add the scallion and season with salt, pepper and nutmeg. Pulse to mix. The texture should be very fine but with a slight crunch.

5 Spoon the purée into the ramekins and place in a roasting pan. Add boiling water to come halfway up the sides. Bake for 25 minutes, until just set. Invert onto warmed plates and peel off the paper. If serving as an appetizer, pour sauce around each timbale and garnish the top with chives.

1 Preheat the oven to 375°F. Lightly butter four 3/4-cup ramekins. Line the bottoms with waxed paper and butter the paper.

2 Steam the broccoli in the top of a covered steamer over boiling water for 8–10 minutes, until very tender but not mushy.

Garlic Mushrooms with a Parsley Crust

THESE GARLIC mushrooms are perfect for dinner parties, or you could serve them in larger portions as a light supper dish with a green salad.

INGREDIENTS

12 ounces large mushrooms, stems removed

3 garlic cloves, crushed

12 tablespoons (1 1/2 sticks) butter, softened

1 cup fresh white bread crumbs

1 cup fresh parsley, chopped

1 egg, beaten

salt and cayenne pepper

8 cherry tomatoes, to garnish

Serves 4

1 Preheat the oven to 375°F. Arrange the mushrooms, cup side up, on a baking sheet. Mix together the garlic and butter in a small bowl and divide 8 tablespoons of the butter among the mushrooms.

2 Heat the remaining butter in a small frying pan and lightly sauté the bread crumbs until golden brown. Place the chopped parsley in a bowl, add the bread crumbs, season the mixture with salt and cayenne pepper and mix well.

3 Stir in the egg and use the mixture to fill the mushroom caps. Bake for 10–15 minutes, until the topping has browned and the mushrooms have softened. Garnish with quartered cherry tomatoes.

COOK'S TIP

If you are planning ahead, stuffed mushrooms can be prepared up to 12 hours in advance and kept in the refrigerator before baking.

Asparagus Rolls with Herb Butter Sauce

FOR A taste sensation, try tender asparagus spears wrapped in crisp phyllo pastry. The buttery herb sauce makes the perfect accompaniment.

INGREDIENTS

4 sheets of phyllo pastry
4 tablespoons (1/2 stick) butter, melted
16 young asparagus spears, trimmed

For the sauce

2 shallots, finely chopped
1 bay leaf
2/3 cup dry white wine
12 tablespoons (1 1/2 sticks) butter, softened
1 tablespoon fresh herbs, chopped
salt and freshly ground black pepper
chopped chives, to garnish
Serves 2

1 Preheat the oven to 400°F. Cut the phyllo sheets in half. Brush a half sheet with melted butter. Fold one corner of the sheet down to the bottom edge to give a wedge shape.

2 Lay 4 asparagus spears on top at the longest edge, and roll up toward the shortest edge. Using the remaining phyllo and asparagus spears, make three more rolls in the same way. The tops of the asparagus should protrude from the parcel.

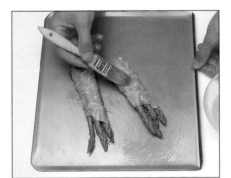

3 Lay the rolls on a greased baking sheet. Brush with the remaining melted butter. Bake for 8 minutes, until golden brown.

4 Meanwhile, put the shallots, bay leaf and wine in a pan. Cover and cook over high heat until the wine is reduced to 3–4 tablespoons.

5 Strain the wine mixture into a medium bowl. Whisk in the butter a little at a time until the sauce is smooth and glossy.

6 Stir in the herbs and add salt and pepper to taste. Return to the pan and keep the sauce warm. Serve the rolls on individual plates with a salad garnish, if desired. Serve the sauce separately, sprinkled with the chopped chives.

Curried Eggs

HARD-BOILED EGGS are served on a bed of mild, creamy sauce with a hint of curry.

INGREDIENTS

4 eggs
1 tablespoon sunflower oil
1 small onion, finely chopped
1-inch piece of fresh ginger root, peeled and grated
1/2 teaspoon ground cumin
1/2 teaspoon garam masala
1 1/2 teaspoons tomato paste
2 teaspoons tandoori paste
2 teaspoons lemon juice
1/4 cup light cream
1 tablespoon chopped cilantro
salt and freshly ground black pepper
cilantro sprigs, to garnish

Serves 2

1 Put the eggs in a pan of water. Bring to a boil, lower the heat and simmer for 10 minutes.

2 Meanwhile, heat the oil in a frying pan. Cook the onion for 2–3 minutes. Add the ginger and cook for 1 minute more.

3 Stir in the ground cumin, garam masala, tomato paste, tandoori paste, lemon juice and cream. Cook for 1–2 minutes, then stir in the cilantro. Season with salt and pepper. Set aside while you prepare the eggs.

4 Drain the eggs, remove the shells and cut each egg in half. Spoon the sauce into a serving bowl, top with the eggs, yolk side up, and garnish with cilantro sprigs. Serve at once.

LIGHT MEALS

Summer brings warmer days and the inclination to
spend less time preparing food. Meals need to be light
and quick to prepare, yet nutritious and appetizing.
Pasta and noodles, omelets and tortillas all provide a
good base for serving the myriad of fresh vegetables in
season at this time of year.

Summer Tomato Pasta

THIS IS a deliciously light pasta dish, full of fresh flavors. Use buffalo-milk mozzarella if you can—the flavor is noticeably better.

INGREDIENTS

2^1/4 cups dried penne

1 pound plum tomatoes

10 ounces mozzarella, drained

^{1}/4 cup olive oil

1 tablespoon balsamic vinegar

zest, grated and juice of 1 lemon

15 fresh basil leaves, shredded

salt and freshly ground black pepper

fresh basil leaves, to garnish

Serves 4

3 Mix together the olive oil, balsamic vinegar, grated lemon zest, 1 tablespoon of the lemon juice and the basil. Season with salt and pepper. Add the tomatoes and mozzarella and let stand until the pasta is cooked.

4 Drain the pasta and toss with the tomato mixture. Serve immediately, garnished with fresh basil leaves. Serve with crusty bread to mop any leftover sauce, if desired.

1 Cook the pasta in boiling salted water, according to the package instructions, until just tender.

2 Quarter the tomatoes and remove the seeds, then chop the flesh into small cubes. Slice the mozzarella into similar-size pieces.

Stir-Fried Vegetables with Cashew Nuts

STIR-FRYING IS the perfect way to make a delicious, colorful and very speedy meal.

INGREDIENTS

2 pounds mixed vegetables (see Cook's Tip)

2–4 tablespoons sunflower or olive oil

2 garlic cloves, crushed

1 tablespoon fresh ginger root, grated

1/2 cup cashew nuts or 4 tablespoons sunflower seeds, pumpkin seeds or sesame seeds

soy sauce

salt and freshly ground black pepper

Serves 4

1 Prepare the vegetables according to type. Carrots and cucumber should be cut into very fine matchsticks.

COOK'S TIP

Use a package of stir-fry vegetables or make up your own mixture. Choose from carrots, snow peas, baby corn, bok choy, cucumber, bean sprouts, mushrooms, bell peppers and scallions. Drained canned bamboo shoots and water chestnuts are delicious additions.

2 Heat a frying pan, then trickle the oil around the rim so that it runs down to coat the surface. When the oil is hot, add the garlic and ginger and cook for 2–3 minutes, stirring. Add the harder vegetables and toss over the heat for another 5 minutes, until they start to soften.

3 Add the softer vegetables and stir-fry everything over high heat for 3–4 minutes.

4 Stir in the cashew nuts or seeds. Season with soy sauce, salt and pepper. Serve at once.

Tofu Stir-Fry with Egg Noodles

SWEET AND delicately flavored, this is the perfect supper for lovers of Chinese food.

INGREDIENTS

8 ounces firm smoked tofu
2 tablespoons sherry or vermouth
3 tablespoons dark soy sauce
3 leeks, thinly sliced
1-inch piece fresh ginger root, peeled and
    finely grated
1–2 fresh red chiles, seeded and sliced in
    rings
1 small red bell pepper, seeded and
    thinly sliced
2/3 cup vegetable stock
2 teaspoons honey
2 teaspoons cornstarch
8 ounces medium Chinese egg noodles
salt and freshly ground black pepper

Serves 4

1 Cut the tofu into 3/4-inch cubes. Put it in a bowl with the sherry or vermouth and the soy sauce. Toss to coat each piece and then let marinate for about 30 minutes.

2 Put the leeks, ginger, chiles, pepper and stock in a frying pan. Bring to a boil and cook quickly over high heat for 2–3 minutes, until all the ingredients are just soft. The vegetables will be limp if they are overcooked.

3 Strain the tofu, reserving the marinade, and set the tofu aside. Mix the honey and cornstarch into the marinade. Set aside.

4 Put the egg noodles into a large pan of boiling water. Remove from the heat and let stand for about 6 minutes, until cooked (or follow the package instructions).

5 Heat a nonstick frying pan and quickly sauté the tofu until lightly golden brown on all sides.

6 Place the vegetable mixture and the tofu in a saucepan with the marinade and stir well until the liquid is thick and glossy. Spoon onto the egg noodles and serve at once.

VARIATION

Tofu absorbs flavors readily when marinated. If you are not a great fan of tofu, you could substitute any type of firm smoked cheese and omit step 5.

Sun-Dried Tomato and Parmesan Carbonara

THE INGREDIENTS for this recipe can easily be doubled to serve four. When unexpected guests arrive why not try it with homemade garlic bread and a big green salad?

INGREDIENTS

6 ounces tagliatelle

10 sun-dried tomatoes in olive oil, drained

2 eggs, beaten

2/3 cup heavy cream

1 tablespoon whole-grain mustard

2/3 cup Parmesan cheese, freshly grated

12 fresh basil leaves, shredded

salt and pepper

fresh basil leaves, to garnish

crusty bread, to serve

Serves 2

1 Cook the pasta in boiling salted water until it is just tender but still retains a little bite (*al dente*). Test a piece just before cooking time is up.

2 Meanwhile, cut the sun-dried tomatoes into small pieces.

3 Beat together the eggs, cream and mustard in a bowl, adding plenty of salt and pepper, until they are well combined and smooth. Do not allow the mixture to become frothy.

4 Drain the pasta and immediately return to the hot saucepan with the cream mixture, sun-dried tomatoes, Parmesan cheese and shredded fresh basil. Return to very low heat for 1 minute, stirring gently, until the mixture thickens slightly. Adjust the seasoning and serve immediately, garnished with basil leaves. Serve with plenty of crusty bread.

Sliced Frittata with Tomato Sauce

THIS DISH—cold frittata with a tomato sauce—is ideal for a light summer lunch.

INGREDIENTS

6 eggs

2 tablespoons fresh mixed herbs such as basil, parsley, thyme and tarragon, finely chopped

1/4 cup Parmesan cheese, freshly grated

3 tablespoons olive oil

salt and freshly ground black pepper

For the tomato sauce

2 tablespoons olive oil

1 small onion, finely chopped

12 ounces fresh tomatoes, chopped, or 14-ounce can chopped tomatoes

1 garlic clove, chopped

salt and freshly ground black pepper

Serves 3–4

1 To make the frittata, break the eggs into a bowl and beat them lightly with a fork. Beat in the herbs and grated Parmesan. Season with salt and pepper.

2 Heat the oil in a large nonstick frying pan until hot.

3 Pour in the seasoned egg mixture. Cook, without stirring, for a short time until the frittata is puffed and golden brown underneath.

4 Take a large plate, place it upside down over the pan and, holding it firmly with oven mitts, turn the pan and the frittata over onto it. Slide the frittata back into the pan and continue cooking for 3–4 minutes more, until it is golden brown on the second side. Remove from the heat and let cool completely.

5 To make the tomato sauce, heat the oil in a medium-heavy saucepan. Add the onion and cook slowly until it is soft. Add the tomatoes, garlic and 1/4 cup water and season with salt and pepper. Cover the pan and cook over moderate heat for about 15 minutes.

6 Remove from the heat and let cool slightly before pressing the sauce through a food mill or sieve. Let cool completely.

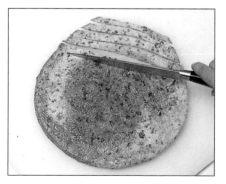

7 To assemble the salad, cut the frittata into thin slices. Place them in a serving bowl and toss lightly with the sauce. Serve at room temperature or chilled.

Spicy Bean and Lentil Loaf

AN APPETIZING, high-fiber savory loaf, ideal for brown-bag lunches. Serve this colorful dish with a large salad.

INGREDIENTS

2 teaspoons olive oil

1 onion, finely chopped

1 garlic clove, crushed

2 celery ribs, finely chopped

14-ounce can red kidney beans

14-ounce can lentils

1 egg

1 carrot, coarsely grated

1/2 cup aged Cheddar cheese, finely grated

1 cup fresh whole wheat bread crumbs

1 tablespoon tomato paste

1 tablespoon ketchup

1 teaspoon each ground cumin, ground
    coriander and hot chili powder

salt and freshly ground black pepper

salad, to serve

Serves 12

1 Preheat the oven to 350°F. Lightly grease a 9 x 5 x 3-inch (8-cup) loaf pan. Meanwhile, heat the oil in a large saucepan.

2 When the oil sizzles, add the onion, garlic and celery and cook gently for 5 minutes, stirring occasionally. Remove the pan from

the heat and cool slightly.

3 Rinse and drain the beans and lentils. Place in a blender or food processor with the onion mixture and egg and process until smooth.

4 Transfer the mixture to a bowl, add all the remaining ingredients and mix well. Season the mixture with salt and pepper.

5 Spoon the mixture into the prepared pan and level the surface. Bake for about 1 hour, then remove from the pan and serve hot or cold in slices, accompanied by a salad.

Savory Nut Loaf

THIS DELICIOUS nut loaf makes perfect picnic food or serve as a light supper with new potatoes and a salad.

INGREDIENTS

1 tablespoon olive oil, plus extra
  for greasing
1 onion, chopped
1 leek, chopped
2 celery ribs, finely chopped
8 ounces mushrooms, chopped
2 garlic cloves, crushed
14-ounce can lentils, rinsed and drained
1 cup mixed nuts, such as hazelnuts,
  cashews and almonds, finely chopped
1/2 cup all-purpose flour
1/2 cup aged Cheddar cheese, grated
1 medium egg, beaten
3–4 tablespoons fresh mixed herbs,
  chopped
salt and freshly ground black pepper
chives and sprigs of flat-leaf parsley,
  to garnish
Serves 4

1 Preheat the oven to 375°F. Lightly grease the bottom and sides of a 9 x 5 x 3-inch (8-cup) loaf pan and line with waxed paper.

2 Heat the oil in a large saucepan, add the chopped onion, leek, celery ribs, mushrooms and the crushed garlic, then cook gently for 10 minutes, until the vegetables have softened, stirring occasionally.

3 Add the lentils, mixed nuts, flour, grated cheese, egg and herbs. Season the ingredients with salt and pepper and mix thoroughly.

4 Spoon the nut, vegetable and lentil mixture into the prepared loaf pan, making sure that it is pressed into the corners, and level the surface. Bake, uncovered, for 50–60 minutes, or until the nut loaf is lightly browned on top and firm to the touch.

5 Cool the loaf slightly in the pan, then turn out onto a serving plate. Serve the loaf hot or cold, cut into slices and garnished with chives and flat-leaf parsley.

Omelet with Beans

EVERY GOOD cook should have a few omelets in his or her repertoire. This version includes soft white beans and is finished with a layer of toasted sesame seeds.

INGREDIENTS

2 tablespoons olive oil

1 teaspoon sesame oil

1 Spanish onion, chopped

1 small red bell pepper, seeded and diced

2 celery ribs, chopped

14-ounce can soft white beans,
   such as cannellini, drained

8 eggs

3 tablespoons sesame seeds

salt and freshly ground black pepper

green salad, to serve

Serves 4

3 In a medium bowl, beat the eggs with a fork and season with salt and pepper, then pour over the ingredients in the pan.

4 Stir the egg mixture with a flat wooden spoon until it begins to stiffen, then allow to firm over low heat for 6–8 minutes.

5 Preheat the broiler to moderate. Sprinkle the omelet with sesame seeds and brown evenly under the broiler.

6 Cut the omelet into thick wedges and serve warm with a green salad. Accompany with crusty bread, if desired.

1 Heat the olive and sesame oils in a 12-inch flameproof frying pan. Add the onion, pepper and celery and cook to soften without coloring.

2 Add the beans and continue to cook the mixture for several minutes to heat through.

VARIATION

You can also use sliced cooked potatoes, any seasonal vegetables, baby artichoke hearts and chickpeas in this omelet.

Cilantro Omelet Packages with Oriental Vegetables

STIR-FRIED VEGETABLES in black bean sauce make a remarkably good filling for these omelet parcels, which are quick and easy to prepare.

INGREDIENTS

5 ounces broccoli, cut into small florets
2 tablespoons peanut oil
1/2-inch piece fresh root ginger, finely grated
1 large garlic clove, crushed
2 red chiles, seeded and finely sliced
4 scallions, sliced diagonally
3 cups pak choi, shredded
2 cups fresh cilantro leaves, plus extra to garnish
1/2 cup beansprouts
3 tablespoons black bean sauce
4 eggs
salt and freshly ground black pepper

Serves 4

1 Blanch the broccoli in boiling salted water for 2 minutes, drain, then refresh under cold running water.

2 Meanwhile, heat 1 tablespoon of the oil in a frying pan or wok. Add the ginger, garlic and half the chile and stir-fry for 1 minute. Add the scallions, broccoli and pak choi, and stir-fry for 2 minutes more, tossing the vegetables continuously to prevent sticking and to cook them evenly.

3 Chop three-quarters of the cilantro and add to the frying pan or wok. Add the beansprouts and stir-fry for 1 minute, then add the black bean sauce and heat through for 1 minute more. Remove the pan from the heat and keep warm.

HEALTH BENEFITS

Pak choi is a member of the brassica family. People who regularly eat this type of green leafy vegetable have a lower risk of developing certain cancers. These vegetables also assist in the treatment of asthma, gout and constipation.

4 Mix the eggs lightly with a fork and season well. Heat a little of the remaining oil in a small frying pan and add a quarter of the beaten egg. Swirl the egg until it covers the base of the pan, then scatter over a quarter of the reserved cilantro leaves. Cook until set, then turn out the omelet on to a plate and keep warm while you make three more omelets, adding more oil when necessary.

5 Spoon the vegetable stir-fry on to the omelets and roll up. Cut in half crossways and serve garnished with cilantro leaves and chile.

Spicy Baked Potatoes

Simple baked potatoes take on an exciting new character with the addition of a few herbs and spices.

INGREDIENTS

2 large baking potatoes
1 teaspoon sunflower oil
1 small onion, finely chopped
1-inch piece fresh ginger root, grated
1 teaspoon ground cumin
1 teaspoon ground cilantro
1/2 teaspoon ground turmeric
garlic salt
plain yogurt and sprigs of cilantro,
    to serve

Serves 2–4

1 Preheat the oven to 375°F. Prick the potatoes with a fork. Bake for 1 hour, or until soft. To save time, you may like to part cook the potatoes in the microwave.

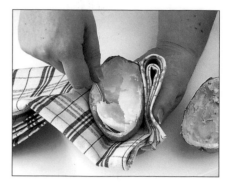

2 Cut the potatoes in half, scoop out the flesh and set aside. Heat the oil in a nonstick frying pan and fry the onion for a few minutes to soften. Stir in the ginger, cumin, cilantro and turmeric.

3 Stir over low heat for about 2 minutes, then add the potato flesh and garlic salt to taste.

4 Cook the potato mixture for another 2 minutes, stirring occasionally. Spoon the mixture back into the potato shells and top each with a spoonful of plain yogurt and a sprig or two of cilantro. Serve hot.

Baked Leeks with Cheese and Yogurt

LIKE ALL vegetables, the fresher leeks are, the better their flavor. Use the freshest leeks available for this dish. Small, young leeks are in the stores at the beginning of the season and are perfect to use here.

INGREDIENTS

2 tablespoons (^{1}/4 stick) butter

8 small leeks, about 1 ^{1}/2 pounds

2 small eggs or 1 large one, beaten

5 ounces fresh goat cheese

^{1}/3 cup plain yogurt

^{1}/2 cup Parmesan cheese, grated

^{1}/2 cup fresh white or brown bread crumbs

salt and freshly ground black pepper

Serves 4

1 Preheat the oven to 350°F. Butter a shallow ovenproof dish. Trim the leeks, cut a slit from top to bottom and rinse well under cold water. Place the leeks in a saucepan of water and bring to a boil.

2 Simmer the leeks gently for 6–8 minutes, until just tender. Remove from the pan and drain well using a slotted spoon. Arrange in a straight row in the prepared dish.

3 Beat the eggs with the goat cheese, yogurt and half the Parmesan cheese. Season well with salt and pepper.

4 Pour the cheese and yogurt mixture over the leeks. Mix the bread crumbs and remaining Parmesan cheese together and sprinkle over the sauce. Bake for 35–40 minutes, until the top is crisp and golden brown.

Vegetable Fajitas

THIS IS a colorful medley of mushrooms and bell peppers in a spicy sauce, wrapped in tortillas and served with creamy guacamole.

INGREDIENTS

1 onion
1 red bell pepper
1 green bell pepper
1 yellow bell pepper
1 garlic clove, crushed
8 ounces mushrooms
6 tablespoons vegetable oil
2 tablespoons medium chili powder
salt and freshly ground black pepper

For the guacamole
1 ripe avocado
1 shallot, coarsely chopped
*1 fresh green chile, seeded and
   coarsely chopped*
juice of 1 lime

To serve
4–6 flour tortillas, warmed
1 lime, cut into wedges
sprigs of cilantro
Serves 2

1 Slice the onion. Cut the peppers in half, remove the seeds, and cut the flesh into strips. Combine the onion and peppers in a bowl. Add the crushed garlic and mix lightly.

2 Remove the mushroom stalks. Save for making stock, or discard. Slice the mushroom caps and add to the pepper mixture in the bowl. Mix the oil and chili powder in a cup, pour over the vegetable mixture and stir well. Set aside.

3 Make the guacamole. Cut the avocado in half and remove the pit and the peel. Put the flesh into a food processor or blender with the shallot, green chile and lime juice. (Blend it by hand with a fork for a chunkier texture.)

4 Process for 1 minute, until smooth. Scrape into a small bowl, cover tightly and put in the refrigerator to chill until required.

5 Heat a frying pan or wok until very hot. Add the marinated vegetables and stir-fry over high heat for 5–6 minutes, until the mushrooms and peppers are just tender. Season with salt and pepper. Spoon the filling onto each tortilla and roll up, leaving the ends open. Garnish with cilantro and serve with the guacamole and lime wedges.

Baked Eggs with Creamy Leeks

THIS IS a traditional French way of enjoying eggs. You can vary the dish quite easily by experimenting with other vegetables, such as pureed spinach or ratatouille, as a base.

INGREDIENTS

1 tablespoon (1/8 stick) butter, plus extra
*   for greasing*
8 ounces small leeks, thinly sliced
5–6 tablespoons whipping cream
freshly grated nutmeg
4 eggs
salt and freshly ground black pepper
Serves 4

1 Preheat the oven to 375°F. Generously butter the bottoms and sides of four ramekins or individual soufflé dishes. Set aside in a cool place while you make the eggs.

3 Add 3 tablespoons of the cream and cook gently, lowering the heat slightly for about 5 minutes, until the leeks are very soft and the cream has thickened a little. Season with salt, pepper and nutmeg.

4 Arrange the ramekins in a small roasting pan and divide the leeks among them. Break an egg into each, spoon 1–2 teaspoons of the remaining cream over each egg and season lightly with salt and pepper.

5 Pour boiling water into the roasting pan to come halfway up the side of the ramekins or soufflé dishes. Bake for about 10 minutes, until the egg whites are set and the yolks are still soft, or a little longer if you prefer them to be cooked through. Serve with warm, crusty bread, if desired.

2 Melt the butter in a small frying pan and cook the leeks over medium heat, stirring frequently, until softened but not browned.

VARIATION

Put 1 tablespoon of cream in each dish with some chopped herbs. Break in the eggs, add 1 tablespoon cream and a little grated cheese, then bake.

Baked Onions Stuffed with Feta

SERVE THESE cheesy, nutty onions with warm olive bread for a fabulous light lunch.

INGREDIENTS

4 large red onions

1 tablespoon olive oil

1/4 cup pine nuts

4 ounces feta cheese, crumbled

1/2 cup fresh white bread crumbs

1 tablespoon cilantro, chopped

salt and freshly ground black pepper

Serves 4

1 Preheat the oven to 350°F. Lightly grease a shallow ovenproof dish. Peel the onions and cut a thin slice from the top and bottom of each. Place the onions in a large saucepan of boiling water and cook for 10–12 minutes.

2 Remove the onions with a slotted spoon. Lay them out to drain on a sheet of paper towel and let them cool slightly.

3 Using a small knife or your fingers, remove the inner sections of the onions, leaving about two or three outer rings. Finely chop the inner sections and place the outer shells in an ovenproof dish.

4 Heat the oil in a medium-size frying pan and sauté the chopped onions for 4–5 minutes, until golden, then add the pine nuts and stir-fry for a few minutes.

5 Place the feta cheese in a small bowl and stir in the onions, pine nuts, bread crumbs and cilantro. Season with a little salt and pepper.

6 Spoon the mixture into the onion shells. Cover loosely with foil and bake for about 30 minutes, removing the foil for the last 10 minutes to allow them to brown slightly. Serve hot.

Onion Tarts with Goat Cheese

A VARIATION of the classic French *Tarte à l'Oignon*, this recipe uses young goat cheese as well as cream. The goat cheese is mild and creamy and complements the flavor of the onions.

INGREDIENTS

1 1/2 cups all purpose flour

5 tablespoons (5/8 stick) butter

1 ounce goat cheese or Cheddar cheese, grated

For the filling

1–1 1/2 tablespoons olive or sunflower oil

3 onions, finely sliced

6 ounces young goat cheese

2 eggs, beaten

1 tablespoon light cream

2 ounces firm goat cheese or Cheddar cheese, grated

1 tablespoon fresh tarragon, chopped

salt and freshly ground black pepper

Serves 8

1 To make the pastry, sift the flour into a bowl and rub in the butter until the mixture resembles fine bread crumbs. Stir in the cheese and enough cold water to make a dough. Knead lightly, put in a plastic bag and chill. Preheat the oven to 375°F.

2 Roll out the dough on a lightly floured surface, then cut into eight rounds using a 4 1/2-inch pastry cutter, and line eight 4-inch tart pans. Prick the bottoms with a fork and bake for 10–15 minutes. Reduce the heat to 350°F. Set aside.

3 Heat the oil in a large frying pan and cook the onions over low heat for 20–25 minutes, until they are a deep golden brown. Stir to prevent them from burning.

4 Beat the goat cheese with the eggs, cream, firm goat cheese or Cheddar and tarragon. Season with salt and pepper and stir in the onions.

5 Pour the mixture into the partially baked pastry shells and bake for 20–25 minutes, until golden. Serve warm or cold with a green salad.

Ratatouille

A CLASSIC vegetable stew, packed full of fresh vegetables and herbs and absolutely bursting with wonderful flavor.

INGREDIENTS

2 large eggplants, roughly chopped
4 zucchini, roughly chopped
2/3 cup olive oil
2 onions, sliced
2 garlic cloves, chopped
1 large red bell pepper, seeded and roughly chopped
2 large yellow bell peppers, seeded and roughly chopped
sprig of fresh rosemary
sprig of fresh thyme
1 teaspoon coriander seeds, crushed
3 plum tomatoes, peeled, seeded and chopped
8 basil leaves, torn
salt and freshly ground black pepper
sprigs of fresh parsley or basil, to garnish
Serves 4

1 Sprinkle the eggplant and zucchini with salt, then put them in a colander with a plate and a weight on top to extract the bitter juices. Let sit for about 30 minutes.

2 Heat the olive oil in a large saucepan. Add the onions and cook gently for 6–7 minutes, until just softened. Add the garlic and cook for another 2 minutes.

3 Rinse the eggplant and zucchini and pat dry with a clean dish towel. Add to the pan with the peppers, increase the heat and sauté the mixture until the peppers are just turning brown.

4 Add the herbs and coriander seeds, then cover the pan and cook gently for about 40 minutes.

5 Add the tomatoes and season with salt and pepper. Cook gently for another 10 minutes, until the vegetables are soft but not too mushy. Remove the sprigs of herbs. Stir in the torn basil leaves and check the seasoning. Let cool slightly and serve warm or cold, garnished with sprigs of parsley or basil.

Mushroom and Fennel Hot-pot

MARVELLOUS FLAVORS permeate this unusual dish, which makes a light meal or accompaniment. Mushrooms provide useful amounts of vitamins, minerals and fiber.

INGREDIENTS

1 ounce dried shiitake mushrooms

1 small head of fennel or 4 celery stalks

2 tablespoons olive oil   *1 tbsp oil*

12 shallots, peeled

2 cups button mushrooms, trimmed
   and halved

1 1/4 cups dry cider   *wine*

1 ounce sun-dried tomatoes

2 tablespoons sun-dried tomato paste

1 bay leaf

fresh parsley, chopped, to garnish

Serves 4

COOK'S TIP

Dried mushrooms swell up a great deal after soaking, so a little goes a long way both in terms of flavor and quantity.

1 Place the dried mushrooms in a bowl. Pour over boiling water *broth* to cover and set aside for 10 minutes.

2 Coarsely chop the fennel or celery stalks and heat the oil in a flameproof casserole. Add the shallots and fennel or celery and sauté for about 10 minutes over moderate heat until the mixture is softened and lightly browned. Add the button mushrooms and fry for 2 – 3 minutes.

3 Drain the dried mushrooms, strain, and reserve the liquid. Cut up any large pieces and add to the pan.

VARIATION

Replace the shiitake mushrooms with other flavorful varieties if necessary and add more cider or water if more liquid is needed.

4 Pour in the cider and stir in the sun-dried tomatoes and the paste. Add the bay leaf. Bring to a boil, then lower the heat, cover the casserole and simmer gently for about 30 minutes.

5 If the mixture seems dry, stir in the reserved liquid from the soaked mushrooms. Reheat briefly, then remove the bay leaf and serve, sprinkled with plenty of chopped parsley.

Rice Noodles with Vegetable Chile Sauce

VIBRANT COLORS and the flavor kick of fresh chile make this vegetable dish a real treat.

INGREDIENTS

1 tablespoon sunflower oil
1 onion, chopped
2 garlic cloves, crushed
1 fresh red chile, seeded and finely chopped
1 red bell pepper, seeded and diced
2 carrots, finely chopped
6 ounces baby corn, halved
8-ounce can sliced bamboo shoots, rinsed
    and drained
14-ounce can red kidney beans, rinsed and
    drained
1¼ cups passata or tomato sauce
1 tablespoon soy sauce
1 teaspoon ground coriander
9 ounces rice noodles
2 tablespoons cilantro, chopped
salt and freshly ground black pepper
fresh parsley sprigs, to garnish

Serves 4

3 Meanwhile, place the noodles in a bowl and cover with boiling water. Stir with a fork and let stand for 3–4 minutes, or according to the package instructions. Rinse and drain. Keep warm.

4 Stir the chopped cilantro into the sauce. Adjust the seasoning and add more liquid if necessary. Spoon the noodles onto warmed serving plates, top with the sauce, garnish with parsley and serve.

1 Heat the oil in a saucepan, add the onion, garlic, chile and pepper and cook gently for 5 minutes, stirring. Add the carrots, corn, bamboo shoots, kidney beans, passata, soy sauce and ground coriander and stir to mix.

2 Bring to a boil, then cover and simmer gently for 30 minutes, stirring occasionally, until the vegetables are tender. Season with salt and pepper.

Frittata with Sun-Dried Tomatoes

ADDING JUST a few sun-dried tomatoes gives this frittata a distinctly Mediterranean flavor. Serve it with salad and a bottle of good wine.

INGREDIENTS

6 sun-dried tomatoes, dry or packed in
  oil and drained
¹/4 cup olive oil
1 small onion, finely chopped
pinch of fresh thyme leaves
6 eggs
¹/2 cup Parmesan cheese, freshly grated
salt and freshly ground black pepper

Serves 3–4

1 Place the tomatoes in a small bowl and pour on enough hot water to just cover them. Soak for about 15 minutes. Lift the tomatoes out of the water and slice them into thin strips. Reserve the soaking water.

2 Heat the oil in a large nonstick or heavy frying pan. Stir in the onion and cook for 5–6 minutes, or until soft and golden. Add the tomatoes and thyme and continue to stir over moderate heat for 2–3 minutes. Season with salt and pepper.

3 Break the eggs into a bowl and beat lightly with a fork. Stir in 3–4 tablespoons of the tomato soaking water and then add the grated Parmesan cheese.

4 Raise the heat under the pan. When the oil is sizzling, pour in the eggs. Mix them quickly into the other ingredients and stop stirring. Lower the heat to moderate and cook for 4–5 minutes on the first side, or until the frittata is puffed and golden brown underneath.

5 Take a large plate, place it upside down over the pan and, holding it firmly with oven mitts, turn the pan and the frittata over onto it. Slide the frittata back into the pan and continue cooking until golden brown on the second side, 3–4 minutes more. Remove from the heat. The frittata can be served hot, at room temperature or cold. Cut it into wedges to serve.

Thai Tempeh Cakes with Sweet Dipping Sauce

MADE FROM soybeans, tempeh is similar to tofu but has a nuttier taste. Here, it is combined with a fragrant blend of lemongrass, cilantro and ginger and then formed into small patties.

INGREDIENTS

1 lemongrass stalk, outer leaves removed and inside finely chopped
2 garlic cloves, chopped
2 scallions, finely chopped
2 shallots, finely chopped
2 chiles, seeded and finely chopped
1-inch piece fresh root ginger, finely chopped
4 tablespoons fresh cilantro, chopped, plus extra to garnish
2¼ cups tempeh, defrosted if frozen, sliced
1 tablespoon lime juice
1 teaspoon sugar
3 tablespoons all-purpose flour
1 large egg, lightly beaten
vegetable oil, for frying
salt and freshly ground black pepper

For the dipping sauce
3 tablespoons mirin
3 tablespoons white wine vinegar
2 scallions, finely sliced
1 tablespoon sugar
2 chiles, finely chopped
2 tablespoons cilantro, chopped
large pinch of salt
Makes 8 Cakes

HEALTH BENEFITS

Although tempeh does not contain quite the same levels of calcium, iron and B vitamins as tofu, in many ways it is healthier. It is made from fermented whole soybeans and the mold used in the fermentation process is said to boost the immune system and free the body of harmful toxins.

To make the dipping sauce, mix together the mirin, vinegar, scallions, sugar, chiles, cilantro and salt in a small bowl and set aside.

2 Place the lemongrass, garlic, scallions, shallots, chiles, ginger and cilantro in a food processor or blender, then process to a coarse paste. Add the tempeh, lime juice and sugar, then blend until combined. Add the seasoning, flour and egg. Process again until the mixture forms a coarse, sticky paste.

3 Take 1 heaped serving-spoonful of the tempeh mixture at a time and form into rounds with your hands —the mixture will be quite sticky.

4 Heat enough oil to cover the base of a large frying pan. Fry the tempeh cakes for 5–6 minutes, turning once, until golden. Drain on paper towels and serve warm with the dipping sauce, garnished with the reserved cilantro.

Sesame Seed-coated Falafel with Tahini Yogurt Dip

SESAME SEEDS are used to give a crunchy coating to these spicy bean patties. Serve with the tahini yogurt dip and warm pita bread as a light lunch or supper dish.

INGREDIENTS

1 1/3 cups dried chickpeas
2 garlic cloves, crushed
1 red chile, seeded and finely sliced
1 teaspoon ground coriander
1 teaspoon ground cumin
1 tablespoon fresh mint, chopped
1 tablespoon fresh parsley, chopped
2 scallions, finely chopped
1 large egg, beaten
sesame seeds, for coating
sunflower oil, for frying
salt and freshly ground black pepper

For the tahini yogurt dip

2 tablespoons light tahini
scant 1 cup plain live yogurt
1 teaspoon cayenne pepper, plus extra
   for sprinkling
1 tablespoon fresh mint, chopped
1 scallion, finely sliced

Serves 4

1 Place the chickpeas in a bowl, cover with cold water and leave to soak overnight. Drain and rinse the chickpeas, then place in a saucepan and cover with cold water. Bring to a boil and boil rapidly for 10 minutes, then reduce the heat and simmer for 1 1/2–2 hours until tender.

2 Meanwhile, make the tahini yogurt dip. Mix together the tahini, yogurt, cayenne pepper and mint in a small bowl. Sprinkle the scallion and extra cayenne pepper on top and chill until required.

3 Combine the chickpeas with the garlic, chile, ground spices, herbs, scallions and seasoning, then mix in the egg. Place in a food processor and blend until the mixture forms a coarse paste. If the paste seems too soft, chill it for 30 minutes.

4 Form the chilled chickpea paste into 12 patties with your hands, then roll each one in the sesame seeds to coat thoroughly.

5 Heat enough oil to cover the base of a large frying pan. Fry the falafel, in batches if necessary, for 6 minutes, turning once.

HEALTH BENEFITS

Chickpeas are a good source of iron, manganese, folate, zinc and vitamin E.

Tortilla Wrap with Tabbouleh and Guacamole

TO BE SUCCESSFUL this classic Middle Eastern salad needs scallions, lemon juice, plenty of fresh herbs and lots of freshly ground black pepper. It is best served at room temperature and goes surprisingly well with the Mexican-style dip.

INGREDIENTS

1 cup bulgur
2 tablespoons fresh mint, chopped
2 tablespoons fresh Italian parsley, chopped
1 bunch scallions (about 6), sliced
1/2 cucumber, diced
1/4 cup extra virgin olive oil
juice of 1 large lemon
salt and freshly ground black pepper
4 wheat tortillas, to serve
Italian parsley, to garnish (optional)

For the guacamole
1 ripe avocado, stoned, peeled and diced
juice of 1/2 lemon
1/2 red chile, seeded and sliced
1 garlic clove, crushed
1/2 red pepper, seeded and finely diced

Serves 4–6

1 To make the tabbouleh, place the bulgur in a large heatproof bowl and pour over enough boiling water to cover. Leave for 30 minutes until the grains are tender but still retain a little resistance to the bite. Drain thoroughly in a strainer, then tip back into the bowl.

2 Add the mint, parsley, scallions and cucumber to the wheat and mix thoroughly. Blend together the olive oil and lemon juice and pour over the tabbouleh, season to taste and toss well to mix. Chill for 30 minutes to allow the flavors to mingle.

COOK'S TIP

The soaking time for bulgur can vary. For the best results, follow the instructions on the package and taste the grain every now and again to check whether it is tender enough.

3 To make the guacamole, place the avocado in a bowl and add the lemon juice, chile and garlic. Season to taste and mash with a fork to form a smooth puree. Stir in the red pepper.

4 Warm the tortillas in a dry frying pan and serve either flat, folded or rolled up with the tabbouleh and guacamole. Garnish with parsley, if using.

HEALTH BENEFITS

- *Bulgur is a useful source of dietary fiber and B complex vitamins.*
- *Parsley and mint are good digestives.*

Tomato and Lentil Dahl with Toasted Almonds

RICHLY FLAVORED with spices, coconut milk and tomatoes, this lentil dish makes a filling supper. Warm naan bread and plain yogurt are all that are needed as accompaniments. Split red lentils give the dish a vibrant color, but you could use larger yellow split peas instead, if you wish.

INGREDIENTS

2 tablespoons vegetable oil

1 large onion, finely chopped

3 garlic cloves, chopped

1 carrot, diced

2 teaspoons cumin seeds

2 teaspoons yellow mustard seeds

1-inch piece fresh root ginger, grated

2 teaspoons ground turmeric

1 teaspoon mild chili powder

1 teaspoon garam masala

1 cup split red lentils

1 2/3 cups water

1 2/3 cups coconut milk

5 tomatoes, peeled, seeded and chopped

juice of 2 limes

4 tablespoons cilantro, chopped

salt and freshly ground black pepper

1/4 cup slivered almonds, toasted,
   to serve

Serves 4

HEALTH BENEFITS

• Spices have long been recognized for their medicinal qualities, from curing flatulence (useful when added to a lentil dish) to warding off colds and flu.

• Lentils are a useful source of low-fat protein. They contain good amounts of B vitamins and provide a rich source of zinc and iron.

• You need to eat foods rich in vitamin C at the same meal to improve absorption of iron. Limes are a good source, but you could also serve a fresh fruit dessert containing apples, kiwi fruit and oranges.

1 Heat the oil in a large heavy-based saucepan. Sauté the onion for 5 minutes until softened, stirring occasionally. Add the garlic, carrot, cumin and mustard seeds, and ginger. Cook for 5 minutes, stirring, until the seeds begin to pop and the carrot softens slightly.

2 Stir in the ground turmeric, chili powder and garam masala, and cook for 1 minute or until the flavors begin to mingle, stirring to prevent the spices burning.

3 Add the lentils, water, coconut milk and tomatoes, and season well. Bring to a boil, then reduce the heat and simmer, covered, for about 45 minutes, stirring occasionally to prevent the lentils sticking.

4 Stir in the lime juice and 3 tablespoons of the cilantro, then check the seasoning. Cook for 15 minutes more until the lentils soften and become tender. To serve, sprinkle with the remaining cilantro and the slivered almonds.

Baked Squash with Parmesan

SPAGHETTI SQUASH is an unusual vegetable—the flesh separates into long strands when baked. One squash makes an excellent supper dish for two.

INGREDIENTS

1 medium spaghetti squash

8 tablespoons (1 stick) butter

3 tablespoons mixed herbs such as parsley, chives and oregano, chopped

1 garlic clove, crushed

1 shallot, chopped

1 teaspoon lemon juice

1/2 cup Parmesan cheese, freshly grated

salt and black pepper

Serves 2

1 Preheat the oven to 350°F. Cut the squash in half lengthwise. Place the halves, cut side down, in a roasting pan. Pour a little water around them, and then bake for about 40 minutes until tender. Do not allow to burn—cover with foil if necessary.

2 Meanwhile, put the butter, herbs, garlic, shallot and lemon juice in a food processor and process until thoroughly blended and creamy in consistency. Season to taste.

3 When the squash is tender, scrape out any seeds and cut a thin slice from the base of each half, so that they will sit level. Place the squash halves on warmed serving plates.

4 Using a fork, pull out a few of the spaghetti-like strands in the centre of each to make room for filling. Add a dollop of herb butter, then sprinkle with a little of the grated Parmesan. Serve the remaining herb butter and Parmesan separately, adding them as you pull out more strands.

Beans with Mushrooms

A MIXTURE of wild and cultivated mushrooms helps to give this dish a rich and nutty flavor.

INGREDIENTS

2 tablespoons olive oil
4 tablespoons butter
2 shallots, chopped
2–3 garlic cloves, crushed
1 1/2 pounds mixed mushrooms, sliced
4 pieces sun-dried tomatoes in oil, drained and chopped
6 tablespoons dry white wine
15oz can red kidney, pinto or borlotti beans, drained
3 tablespoons Parmesan cheese, grated
2 tablespoons fresh parsley, chopped
salt and black pepper
freshly cooked pappardelle pasta, to serve

Serves 4

1 Heat the oil and butter in a frying pan and fry the shallots until soft.

2 Add the garlic and mushrooms to the pan and fry for 3–4 minutes. Stir in the sun-dried tomatoes, wine and seasoning to taste.

3 Stir in the beans and cook for about 5–6 minutes, until most of the liquid has evaporated and the beans are warmed through.

4 Stir in the grated Parmesan cheese. Sprinkle with parsley and serve immediately with pappardelle.

Beet, Wild Mushroom and Potato Casserole

THIS INEXPENSIVE dish captures the spirit of some traditional Polish autumn menus.

INGREDIENTS

2 tablespoons vegetable oil
1 medium onion, chopped
3 tablespoons all-purpose flour
1 1/4 cups vegetable stock
1 1/2 pounds cooked beets, peeled
   and chopped
5 tablespoons light cream
2 tablespoons creamed horseradish
1 teaspoon hot mustard
1 tablespoon wine vinegar
1 teaspoon caraway seeds
2 tablespoons (1/4 stick) butter
1 shallot, chopped
8 ounces assorted wild and cultivated
   mushrooms, trimmed and sliced
3 tablespoons fresh parsley, chopped

For the potato border
2 pounds floury potatoes, peeled
2/3 cup milk
1 tablespoon fresh dill, chopped (optional)
salt and freshly ground black pepper
Serves 4

1 Preheat the oven to 375°F. Lightly oil a 9-inch round baking dish. Heat the oil in a large saucepan, add the onion and cook until soft, without coloring. Stir in the flour, remove from the heat and gradually add the stock, stirring until well blended.

2 Return to the heat, stir and simmer to thicken, then add the beets, cream, creamed horseradish, mustard, vinegar and caraway seeds. Stir to mix.

3 To make the potato border, bring the potatoes to a boil in salted water and cook for 20 minutes. Drain well and mash with the milk. Add the dill, if using, and season with salt and black pepper.

4 Spoon the potatoes into the prepared dish and make a well in the center. Spoon the beet mixture into the well and set aside.

5 Melt the butter in a large nonstick frying pan and cook the shallot until soft, without browning. Add the mushrooms and cook over moderate heat until their juices begin to run. Increase the heat and boil off the moisture. When quite dry, season with salt and pepper and stir in most of the chopped parsley.

6 Spread the mushrooms over the beet mixture, cover the dish and bake for about 30 minutes. Serve immediately, garnished with the reserved parsley.

COOK'S TIP

If you are planning ahead, this entire dish can be made in advance and heated when needed. Allow 50 minutes baking time from room temperature.

Potato Gnocchi

GNOCCHI ARE little dumplings made either with mashed potato and flour, as here, or with semolina. They should be light in texture, and must not be overworked while being made.

INGREDIENTS

2¼ pounds waxy potatoes, scrubbed
1 tablespoon salt
2–2½ cups all-purpose flour
1 egg
pinch of grated nutmeg
2 tablespoons (¼ stick) butter
freshly grated Parmesan cheese, to serve

Serves 4–6

1 Place the unpeeled potatoes in a large pan of salted water. Bring to a boil and cook until the potatoes are tender but not falling apart. Drain. Peel as soon as possible, while the potatoes are still hot but cool enough to handle.

VARIATION

Green gnocchi are made in exactly the same way as potato gnocchi, with the addition of fresh or frozen spinach. Use 1½ pounds fresh spinach or 14 ounces frozen leaf spinach. Mix with the potato and the flour in step 2. Almost any pasta sauce is suitable for serving with gnocchi; they are particularly good with a creamy Gorgonzola sauce, or simply drizzled with olive oil. Gnocchi can also be served in clear soup.

2 On a work surface, spread out a layer of flour. Mash the hot potatoes with a food mill, dropping them directly onto the flour layer. Sprinkle with about half of the remaining flour and mix very lightly into the potatoes.

3 Break the egg into the mixture, add the nutmeg, and knead lightly with your hands, drawing in more flour as necessary. When the dough is light to the touch and no longer moist or sticky, it is ready to be rolled. Do not overwork the dough or the gnocchi will be heavy.

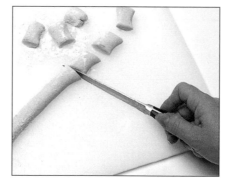

4 Divide the dough into four parts. On a lightly floured board form each part into a roll about ¾ inch in diameter, taking care not to overhandle the dough. Cut the rolls crossways into pieces about ¾ inch long.

5 Hold an ordinary table fork with long tines sideways, leaning on the board. One by one, press and roll the gnocchi lightly along the tines of the fork toward the points, making ridges on one side and a depression with your thumb on the other.

6 Bring a large saucepan of water to a hard boil. Add salt and drop in about half the gnocchi. The gnocchi will sink.

7 When the gnocchi rise to the surface, after 3–4 minutes, they are done. Scoop them out, drain and place in a warmed serving bowl. Dot with butter. Keep warm while the remaining gnocchi are boiling. As soon as they are cooked, toss the gnocchi with the butter or a heated sauce, sprinkle with grated Parmesan cheese and serve.

Red Cabbage and Apple Casserole

THE BRILLIANT color and pungent flavor make this an excellent winter dish. Serve it with plenty of rye bread.

INGREDIENTS

1 ½ pounds red cabbage

3 onions, chopped

2 fennel bulbs, roughly chopped

2 tablespoons caraway seeds

3 large, tart eating apples or 1 large
   cooking apple

1 ¼ cups plain yogurt

1 tablespoon creamed horseradish

salt and freshly ground black pepper

crusty rye bread, to serve

Serves 6

1 Preheat the oven to 300°F. Shred the cabbage finely, discarding any tough stalks. Mix with the onions, fennel and caraway seeds in a large bowl. Peel, core and chop the apples, then stir them into the cabbage mixture. Transfer the mixture to a casserole dish. Set aside.

2 Mix the yogurt with the creamed horseradish. Stir the yogurt and horseradish mixture into the casserole, season with salt and pepper and cover tightly.

3 Bake for 1 ½ hours, stirring once or twice during cooking. Serve hot, with rye bread.

Mixed Vegetables with Artichokes

BAKING A vegetable medley in the oven is a wonderfully easy way of producing a quick and simple, wholesome midweek meal.

INGREDIENTS

2 tablespoons olive oil

1 ½ pounds frozen fava or lima beans

4 turnips, peeled and sliced

4 leeks, sliced

1 red bell pepper, seeded and sliced

7 ounces fresh spinach leaves or
   4 ounces frozen spinach

2 x 14-ounce cans artichoke
   hearts, drained

¼ cup pumpkin seeds

soy sauce

salt and freshly ground black pepper

Serves 4

1 Preheat the oven to 350°F. Pour the olive oil into a casserole. Cook the beans in a saucepan of boiling lightly salted water for about 10 minutes. Drain the beans and place them in the casserole with the turnips, leeks, red pepper, spinach and canned artichoke hearts.

2 Cover the casserole and bake the vegetables for 30–40 minutes, or until the turnips are slightly soft and the rest of the vegetables are tender.

3 Stir in the pumpkin seeds and soy sauce to taste. Season with salt and pepper to taste, and serve immediately.

Sweet and Sour Mixed Bean Hot Pot

AN APPETIZING mixture of beans and
vegetables in a tasty sweet and sour
sauce, topped with potato.

INGREDIENTS

1 pound unpeeled potatoes
1 tablespoon olive oil
3 tablespoons (³/8 stick) butter
¹/3 cup whole wheat flour
1 ¹/4 cups passata or tomato sauce
²/3 cup unsweetened apple juice
¹/4 cup each light brown sugar,
    ketchup, dry sherry, cider vinegar and
    light soy sauce
14-ounce can lima beans
14-ounce can flageolet beans
14-ounce can chickpeas
6 ounces green beans, chopped
    and blanched
8 ounces shallots, sliced and blanched
8 ounces mushrooms, sliced
1 tablespoon each fresh thyme and
    marjoram, chopped
salt and freshly ground black pepper
sprigs of fresh herbs, to garnish
Serves 6

1 Preheat the oven to 400°F. Thinly
slice the potatoes and part-boil them
for 4 minutes. Drain the potatoes
thoroughly, toss them in the oil so they
are lightly coated all over and set aside.

2 Place the butter, flour, passata,
apple juice, sugar, ketchup, sherry,
vinegar and soy sauce in a saucepan.
Heat gently, whisking constantly, until
the sauce comes to a boil and thickens.
Simmer gently for 3 minutes, stirring
occasionally. Keep warm while you add
the beans.

3 Rinse and drain the lima beans,
flageolet beans and chickpeas and
add to the sauce with all the remaining
ingredients except the herb garnish.
Mix well.

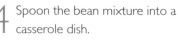

4 Spoon the bean mixture into a
casserole dish.

5 Arrange the potato slices over the
top of the dish, overlapping them
slightly and completely covering the
bean mixture.

6 Cover the casserole with foil and
bake for about 1 hour, until the
potatoes are cooked and tender.
Remove the foil for the last 20 minutes
of the cooking time, to lightly brown
the potatoes. Serve garnished with
fresh herb sprigs.

COOK'S TIP

Vary the proportions of beans used in
this recipe, depending on what
ingredients you have in your pantry.

Jamaican Black Bean Pot

MOLASSES IMPARTS a rich treacly flavor to the spicy sauce, which incorporates a stunning mix of black beans, vibrant red and yellow bell peppers and orange butternut squash. This dish is delicious served with cornbread or plain rice.

INGREDIENTS

1¼ cups dried black beans

1 bay leaf

2 tablespoons vegetable oil

1 large onion, chopped

1 garlic clove, chopped

1 teaspoon mustard powder

1 tablespoon blackstrap molasses

2 tablespoons dark brown sugar

1 teaspoon dried thyme

½ teaspoon dried chili flakes

1 teaspoon vegetable broth powder

1 red bell pepper, seeded and diced

1 yellow bell pepper, seeded and diced

5¼ cups butternut squash or
　pumpkin, seeded and cut into
　½-inch dice

salt and freshly ground black pepper

sprigs of thyme, to garnish

Serves 4

2 Heat the oil in the saucepan and sauté the onion and garlic for about 5 minutes until softened, stirring occasionally. Add the mustard powder, molasses, sugar, thyme and chili and cook for 1 minute, stirring. Stir in the black beans and spoon the mixture into a flameproof casserole.

3 Add enough water to the reserved cooking liquid to make 1⅔ cups, then mix in the broth powder and pour into the casserole. Bake for 25 minutes.

4 Add the bell peppers and squash or pumpkin and mix well. Cover, then bake for 45 minutes until the vegetables are tender. Serve garnished with thyme.

HEALTH BENEFITS

Blackstrap molasses is a by-product of sugar processing and contains less sugar than treacle. It is a good source of iron, calcium, zinc, copper and chromium. Eating molasses regularly is said to help acne, arthritis, angina, constipation and anemia.

1 Soak the beans overnight in plenty of water, then drain and rinse well. Place in a large saucepan, cover with fresh water and add the bay leaf.
Bring to a boil, then boil rapidly for 10 minutes. Reduce the heat, cover, and simmer for 30 minutes until tender. Drain, reserving the cooking water. Preheat the oven to 350°F.

Parsnip, Eggplant and Cashew Biryani

FULL OF the flavors of India, this hearty supper dish is great for chilly winter evenings.

INGREDIENTS

1 small eggplant, sliced
10 ounces basmati rice
3 parsnips
3 onions
2 garlic cloves
1-inch piece of fresh ginger root, peeled
about 4 tablespoons vegetable oil
6 ounces unsalted cashew nuts
1/4 cup golden raisins
1 red bell pepper, seeded and sliced
1 teaspoon ground cumin
1 teaspoon ground coriander
1/2 teaspoon chili powder
1/2 cup plain yogurt
1 1/4 cups vegetable stock
2 tablespoons (1/4 stick) butter
salt and freshly ground black pepper
2 hard-boiled eggs, quartered, and sprigs of
    cilantro, to garnish

Serves 4–6

1 Sprinkle the eggplant with salt and set aside for 30 minutes. Rinse, pat dry and cut into bite-size pieces.

2 Soak the rice in a bowl of cold water for 40 minutes. Peel and core the parsnips. Cut into 1/2-inch pieces. Process 1 onion, the garlic and ginger in a food processor. Add 2–3 tablespoons water and process to a paste.

3 Finely slice the remaining onions. Heat 3 tablespoons of the oil in a large flameproof casserole and sauté the onions gently for 10–15 minutes, until they are soft and deep golden brown. Remove and drain.

4 Add 1/4 cup of the cashew nuts to the pan and stir-fry on moderate heat for 2 minutes, checking that they do not burn. Add the raisins and cook gently until they swell. Remove and drain on paper towels until all the oil is drained off.

5 Add the eggplant and sliced pepper to the pan and stir-fry for 4–5 minutes. Drain on paper towels. Cook the parsnips for 4–5 minutes. Stir in the remaining cashew nuts and cook for 1 minute. Transfer to the plate with the eggplant and set aside.

6 Add the remaining 1 tablespoon of oil to the pan. Add the onion paste. Cook, stirring, over moderate heat for 4–5 minutes, until the mixture turns golden. Stir in the cumin, coriander and chili powder. Cook, stirring, for 1 minute, then reduce the heat and add the yogurt.

7 Bring the mixture slowly to a boil and stir in the stock, parsnips, eggplant and bell pepper. Season with salt and pepper, cover and simmer for 30–40 minutes, until the parsnips are tender. Transfer to an ovenproof casserole.

8 Preheat the oven to 300°F. Drain the rice and add to 1 1/4 cups salted boiling water. Cook gently for 5–6 minutes, until the rice is tender but slightly undercooked.

9 Drain the rice and pile it in a mound on top of the parsnip mixture. Make a hole from the top to the bottom using the handle of a wooden spoon. Sprinkle the reserved fried onions, cashew nuts and raisins over the rice and dot with butter. Cover with a double layer of foil and secure it in place with a lid.

10 Bake for 35–40 minutes. To serve, spoon the mixture onto a warmed serving dish and garnish with quartered eggs and sprigs of cilantro.

Zucchini Fritters with Chile Jam

CHILE JAM is hot, sweet and sticky—
rather like a thick chutney. It adds
a piquancy to these light zucchini
fritters but is also delicious with pies
or a chunk of cheese.

INGREDIENTS

3 1/2 cups zucchini, coarsely grated
2/3 cup Parmesan cheese, freshly grated
  2 eggs, beaten
4 tablespoons unbleached
  all-purpose flour
vegetable oil, for frying
salt and freshly ground black pepper

For the chile jam

5 tablespoons olive oil
4 large onions, diced
4 garlic cloves, chopped
1–2 Thai chiles, seeded and sliced
2 tablespoons dark brown sugar
Makes 12 Fritters

2 Leave the onion mixture to cool,
then transfer to a food processor
or blender. Add the chiles and sugar
and blend until smooth, then return
the mixture to the saucepan. Cook for
10 minutes, stirring frequently, until the
liquid evaporates and the mixture has
the consistency of jam. Cool slightly.

3 To make the fritters, squeeze
the zucchini in a dish towel to
remove any excess water, then
combine with the Parmesan, eggs,
flour and salt and pepper.

4 Heat enough oil to cover the base
of a large frying pan. Add
2 tablespoons of the mixture for each
fritter and cook three fritters at a time.
Cook for 2–3 minutes on each side
until golden, then keep warm while you
cook the remaining fritters. Drain on
paper towels and serve warm with a
spoonful of the chile jam.

COOK'S TIP

Stored in an airtight jar in the refrigerator,
the jam will keep for up to 1 week.

1 First make the chile jam. Heat the oil
in a frying pan until hot, then add the
onions and garlic. Reduce heat
to low, then cook for 20 minutes,
stirring frequently, until the onions
are very soft.

HEALTH BENEFITS

• Parmesan provides valuable amounts
of vitamin B_{12}, protein and calcium but
its high saturated fat content means it
should be eaten in moderation.
• Vitamin C and beta carotene are both
found in zucchini.

Vegetable Moussaka

THIS IS a really flavorful main-course dish. It can be served with warm fresh bread for a hearty, satisfying meal.

INGREDIENTS

1 pound eggplant, sliced
4 ounces whole green lentils
2¹/₂ cups vegetable stock
1 bay leaf
3 tablespoons olive oil
1 onion, sliced
1 garlic clove, crushed
8 ounces mushrooms, sliced
14-ounce can chickpeas, rinsed
   and drained
14-ounce can chopped tomatoes
2 tablespoons tomato paste
2 teaspoons dried herbes de Provence
1¹/₄ cups plain yogurt
3 eggs
¹/₂ cup aged Cheddar cheese, grated
salt and freshly ground black pepper
sprigs of fresh flat-leaf parsley,
   to garnish

Serves 6

1 Sprinkle the eggplant slices with salt and place in a colander. Cover and place a weight on top. Let sit for at least 30 minutes, to allow the bitter juices to be extracted.

2 Meanwhile, place the green lentils, stock and bay leaf in a saucepan. Cover, bring to a boil and simmer for about 20 minutes, until the lentils are just tender but not mushy. Drain thoroughly and keep the mixture warm, stirring occasionally.

3 Heat 1 tablespoon of the oil in a large saucepan, add the onion and garlic and cook, stirring, for 5 minutes. Stir in the lentils, mushrooms, chickpeas, tomatoes, tomato paste, herbs and 3 tablespoons water. Bring to a boil, cover and simmer gently for 10 minutes, stirring occasionally. Keep the sauce warm.

4 Preheat the oven to 350°F. Rinse the eggplant slices, drain and pat dry. Heat the remaining oil in a frying pan and cook the slices in batches for 3–4 minutes, turning once so both sides are browned.

5 Season the lentil mixture with salt and pepper. Arrange a layer of eggplant slices in the bottom of a large, shallow, ovenproof dish or roasting pan, then spoon a generous layer of the lentil mixture on top. Repeat the eggplant and lentil layers until all the eggplant slices and lentil mixture are used up.

6 Beat the yogurt, eggs and salt and pepper together and pour the mixture over the vegetables. Sprinkle generously with the grated Cheddar cheese and bake for about 45 minutes, until the topping is golden brown and bubbling. Serve immediately, garnished with the flat-leaf parsley.

VARIATION

Sliced and sautéed zucchini or potatoes can be used instead of the eggplant in this dish.

Broccoli and Ricotta Cannelloni

A FABULOUS pasta dish that looks very impressive but is actually quite quick and simple to prepare and tastes wonderful.

INGREDIENTS

2 teaspoons olive oil

12 dried cannelloni tubes, 3 inches long

4 cups broccoli florets

1 1/2 cups fresh bread crumbs

2/3 cup milk

4 tablespoons olive oil, plus extra for brushing

1 cup ricotta cheese

pinch of grated nutmeg

6 tablespoons Parmesan or Pecorino cheese, grated

2 tablespoons pine nuts

salt and freshly ground black pepper

For the tomato sauce

2 tablespoons olive oil

1 onion, finely chopped

1 garlic clove, crushed

2 x 14-ounce cans chopped tomatoes

1 tablespoon tomato paste

4 black olives, pitted and chopped

1 teaspoon dried thyme

Serves 4

1 Preheat the oven to 375°F. Lightly grease four ovenproof dishes with olive oil.

2 Bring a large saucepan of water to a boil, add the olive oil to the water to prevent the pasta from sticking together and simmer the cannelloni, uncovered, for 6–7 minutes, or until it is nearly cooked.

3 Meanwhile, steam or boil the broccoli for 10 minutes, until tender but not mushy. Drain the pasta, rinse under cold water to keep it from sticking, and set aside. Drain the broccoli and let it cool, then place in a food processor or blender and process until smooth. Set aside.

4 Place the bread crumbs in a bowl, add the milk and oil and stir until softened. Add the ricotta, broccoli puree, nutmeg and 4 tablespoons of the grated Parmesan or Pecorino cheese. Season with salt and pepper, then set aside.

5 To make the sauce, heat the oil in a frying pan and add the onions and garlic. Cook for 5–6 minutes, until softened, then stir in the tomatoes, tomato paste, black olives and thyme. Season with salt and pepper. Boil rapidly for 2–3 minutes, then pour into the four ovenproof dishes.

6 Spoon the cheese mixture into a pastry bag fitted with a 1/2-inch nozzle. Carefully open the cannelloni tubes. Standing each one upright on a board, pipe the filling into each tube, taking care not to overfill with the mixture. Divide the tubes equally among the four dishes and lay them in rows on the tomato sauce.

7 Brush the tops of the cannelloni with a little olive oil and sprinkle with the remaining Parmesan or Pecorino cheese and pine nuts. Bake for 25–30 minutes, until golden.

COOK'S TIP

If you don't have cannelloni tubes, you can cook lasagne sheets until al dente, spoon the mixture along one short edge of the sheet and roll it up to encase the filling. Cook seam side down.

Whole Wheat Pasta with Caraway Cabbage

CRUNCHY CABBAGE and Brussels sprouts are the perfect partners for pasta in this healthy dish.

INGREDIENTS

6 tablespoons olive oil or sunflower oil

3 onions, roughly chopped

12-ounce round white cabbage, roughly chopped

12 ounces Brussels sprouts, trimmed and halved

2 teaspoons caraway seeds

1 tablespoon fresh dill, chopped

1²/₃ cups vegetable stock

7 ounces fresh or dried whole wheat pasta spirals

salt and freshly ground black pepper

fresh dill sprigs, to garnish

Serves 6

1 Heat the oil in a large saucepan and sauté the onions over low heat for 10 minutes, until softened.

2 Add the cabbage and Brussels sprouts and cook for 2–3 minutes, then stir in the caraway seeds and dill. Pour in the stock and season with salt **and pepper. Cover** and simmer for 5–10 minutes, until the cabbage and sprouts are crisp-tender.

3 Meanwhile, cook the pasta in a pan of lightly salted boiling water, following the package instructions, until just tender (al dente).

4 Drain the pasta, pour it into a bowl and add the cabbage mixture. Toss lightly, adjust the seasoning, garnish with dill and serve immediately.

Cauliflower and Broccoli with Tomato Sauce

THE ADDITION of broccoli to the cauliflower gives an extra color dimension to this dish.

INGREDIENTS

1 onion, finely chopped

14-ounce can chopped tomatoes

3 tablespoons tomato paste

3 tablespoons whole wheat flour

1¹/₄ cups skim milk

1¹/₄ cups water

2¹/₂ pounds mixed cauliflower and broccoli florets

salt and freshly ground black pepper

Serves 6

1 Mix the onion, chopped tomatoes and tomato paste in a small saucepan. Bring to a boil, lower the heat and simmer gently for 15–20 minutes, stirring occasionally.

2 Mix the flour to a paste with a little of the milk. Stir the paste into the tomato mixture, then gradually add the remaining milk and water.

3 Stir the mixture constantly until it boils and thickens. Season with salt and pepper. Keep the sauce hot.

4 Steam the cauliflower and broccoli over boiling water for 5–7 minutes, or until the florets are just tender. Transfer the vegetables to a dish, pour the tomato sauce over them and serve with extra pepper sprinkled over the top, if you like.

Ravioli with Ricotta and Spinach

HOMEMADE RAVIOLI are fun to make, and can be stuffed with different cheese or vegetable fillings. This filling is particularly easy to make.

INGREDIENTS

14 ounces fresh spinach or 6 ounces frozen
  spinach
3/4 cup ricotta cheese
1 egg
1/2 cup Parmesan cheese, grated
pinch of grated nutmeg
salt and freshly ground black pepper

For the pasta
1 1/2 cups flour
3 eggs

For the sauce
6 tablespoons (3/4 stick) butter
5–6 sprigs of fresh sage
Serves 4

1 Wash the fresh spinach well in several changes of water. Place in a saucepan, cover and cook until tender, about 5 minutes. Drain. If you are using frozen spinach, cook according to the package instructions. When cool, squeeze out as much moisture as possible. Chop finely. Transfer into a large bowl.

2 Combine the chopped spinach with the ricotta, egg, Parmesan and nutmeg. Season with salt and pepper. Cover and set aside.

3 To make the pasta, place the flour in the center of a clean smooth work surface. Make a well in the middle. Break the eggs into the well. Add a pinch of salt.

4 Start beating the eggs with a fork, gradually drawing the flour from the inside walls of the well. As the paste thickens, continue mixing with your hands.

5 Incorporate as much flour as possible until the mixture forms a mass. It will still be lumpy. If it still sticks to your hands, add a little more flour. Set the dough aside. Scrape off the dough from the work surface until it is smooth and fairly clean.

6 Lightly flour the work surface. Knead the dough. Work for about 10 minutes, or until the dough is smooth and elastic.

7 Divide the dough in half. Flour the rolling pin and the work surface. Pat the dough into a disk and begin rolling out into a flat circle. Roll until it is about 1/8 inch thick. Do the same with the second half of the dough, making it the same size.

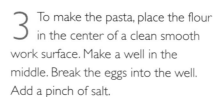

8 Cut the dough into sheets. Place small teaspoons of filling along the pasta in rows 2 inches apart. Cover with another sheet of pasta, pressing down gently to expel any air pockets.

9 Use a fluted pastry wheel to cut between the rows to form small squares with filling in the center of each. If the edges do not stick well, moisten with milk or water and press together.

10 Place the ravioli on a lightly floured surface and allow to dry for at least 30 minutes. Turn occasionally so they are completely dry on both sides. Bring a large pan of salted water to a boil.

11 Heat the butter and sage together over very low heat, taking care that the butter melts but does not darken.

12 Drop the ravioli into the boiling water. Stir gently to prevent them from sticking together. They will be cooked in very little time, 4–5 minutes. Drain carefully and arrange in individual serving dishes. Spoon on the sauce and serve at once.

Spinach and Ricotta Conchiglie

LARGE PASTA shells are designed to hold a variety of delicious stuffings. Few are more pleasing than this classic mixture of chopped spinach and ricotta cheese which is rich and creamy with just a hint of nutmeg.

INGREDIENTS

12 ounces large conchiglie

scant 2 cups passata or tomato pulp

10 ounces frozen chopped spinach, thawed

2 slices crustless white bread, crumbled

1/2 cup milk

1/4 cup olive oil

2 1/4 cups ricotta cheese

pinch of grated nutmeg

1 garlic clove, crushed

1/2 teaspoon black olive paste (optional)

1/4 cup Parmesan cheese, freshly grated

2 tablespoons pine nuts

salt and freshly ground black pepper

Serves 4

1 Preheat the oven to 350°F. Bring a large saucepan of salted water to a boil. Add the pasta and cook according to the package instructions. Refresh under cold water, drain and reserve until needed.

2 Pour the passata or tomato pulp into a nylon sieve over a bowl and strain to thicken. Place the spinach in another sieve and press out any excess liquid with the back of a spoon. Set aside the two ingredients.

3 Place the bread, milk and 3 tablespoons of the oil in a food processor and process. Add the spinach and ricotta and season with salt, pepper and nutmeg. Process briefly to combine.

4 Mix together the sieved passata or tomato pulp, garlic, remaining oil and olive paste, if using. Spread the sauce evenly over the bottom of a flameproof dish.

5 Spoon the spinach mixture into a pastry bag fitted with a large plain nozzle and fill the pasta shells (alternatively, fill with a spoon). Arrange the pasta shells over the sauce leaving very small gaps between them.

6 Heat the pasta in the oven for 15 minutes. Preheat the broiler to moderate. Sprinkle pasta with Parmesan cheese and pine nuts and replace under the broiler to brown the cheese and toast the pine nuts.

COOK'S TIP

Choose a large saucepan when cooking pasta, and give an occasional stir to prevent the shapes from sticking together. If passata is not available, use a can of chopped tomatoes, sieved and pureed.

Risotto alla Milanese

THIS TRADITIONAL Italian risotto is rich and creamy, and deliciously flavored with garlic, shavings of Parmesan and fresh parsley.

INGREDIENTS

2 garlic cloves, crushed
4 tablespoons fresh parsley, chopped
finely grated zest of 1 lemon

For the risotto
1 teaspoon saffron strands
2 tablespoons (1/4 stick) butter
1 large onion, finely chopped
1 1/2 cups arborio rice
2/3 cup dry white wine
4 cups vegetable stock
Parmesan cheese shavings, to serve
salt and freshly ground black pepper

Serves 4

1 Mix together the garlic, parsley and lemon zest in a bowl. Reserve and set aside.

2 Put the saffron in a small bowl with 1 tablespoon boiling water and let stand while the saffron is infused. Melt the butter in a heavy frying pan and gently cook the onion for 5 minutes, until softened and golden.

3 Stir in the rice and cook for about 2 minutes, until it becomes translucent. Add the wine and saffron mixture and cook for several minutes, until all the wine is absorbed.

4 Add 2 1/2 cups of the stock to the pan and simmer gently until the stock is absorbed, stirring frequently.

5 Gradually add more stock, a ladleful at a time, until the rice is tender. (The rice might be tender and creamy before you've added all the stock, so add it slowly toward the end of the cooking time.)

6 Season the risotto with salt and pepper and transfer to a serving dish. Sprinkle lavishly with shavings of Parmesan cheese and the garlic and parsley mixture.

Vegetable Pilaf

A POPULAR vegetable rice dish that makes a tasty light supper.

INGREDIENTS

1 cup basmati rice
2 tablespoons oil
$1/2$ teaspoon cumin seeds
2 bay leaves
4 green cardamom pods
4 cloves
1 onion, finely chopped
1 carrot, finely diced
$1/3$ cup thawed frozen peas
$1/3$ cup thawed frozen corn
$1/4$ cup cashew nuts, lightly fried
$1/4$ teaspoon ground cumin
salt

Serves 4–6

1 Wash the rice in several changes of cold water. Put in a bowl and cover with water. Let soak for about 30 minutes.

2 Heat the oil in a large frying pan and sauté the cumin seeds for 2 minutes. Do not let the seeds burn. Add the bay leaves, cardamom and cloves and sauté for another 2 minutes.

3 Add the onion and cook for 5 minutes, until softened and lightly browned.

4 Stir in the carrot and cook for 3–4 minutes.

5 Drain the rice and add to the pan together with the peas, corn and cashew nuts. Cook for 4–5 minutes over medium heat.

6 Add 2 cups water, ground cumin and salt. Bring to a boil, cover and simmer for 15 minutes over low heat, until all the water is absorbed. Let stand, covered, for 10 minutes before serving. Turn out onto a platter and fluff up before serving.

Spinach and Wild Mushroom Soufflé

WILD MUSHROOMS combine especially well with eggs and spinach in this sensational soufflé. Almost any combination of mushrooms can be used for this recipe, although the firmer varieties provide the best texture for the dish.

INGREDIENTS

8 ounces fresh spinach, washed, or
    4 ounces frozen chopped spinach
4 tablespoons (¹/₂ stick) unsalted butter,
    plus extra for greasing
1 garlic clove, crushed
6 ounces assorted wild mushrooms, such as
    porcini, cremini, oyster and
    portobello mushrooms
1 cup milk
3 tablespoons all-purpose flour
6 eggs, separated
pinch of grated nutmeg
¹/₄ cup Parmesan cheese, grated
salt and freshly ground black pepper
Serves 4

1 Preheat the oven to 375°F. Steam the spinach over moderate heat for 3–4 minutes. Cool under running water, then drain. Press out as much liquid as you can with the back of a large spoon and chop finely. If using frozen spinach, defrost and prepare following the package instructions. Squeeze dry in the same way.

2 Melt the butter in a saucepan and cook the garlic and mushrooms over low heat until softened. Turn up the heat until the juices evaporate. When dry, add the spinach and transfer to a bowl. Cover and keep warm.

3 Measure 3 tablespoons of the milk into a bowl. Bring the remainder to a boil. Stir the flour and egg yolks into the cold milk in the bowl and blend well. Stir the boiling milk into the egg and flour mixture, return to the pan and simmer to thicken. Add the spinach mixture to the pan. Season with salt, pepper and nutmeg. Remove from the heat and set aside.

4 Butter a 4-cup soufflé dish, paying particular attention to the sides. Sprinkle with a little of the Parmesan cheese. Set aside.

5 Beat the egg whites until stiff. Bring the spinach mixture back to a boil. Stir in a spoonful of beaten egg white, then fold the mixture into the remaining egg white.

6 Turn the mixture into the soufflé dish, spread the top level, sprinkle with the remaining cheese and bake in the oven for about 25 minutes, until puffed and golden brown. Serve immediately, before the soufflé has a chance to deflate.

COOK'S TIP

The soufflé base can be prepared up to 12 hours in advance and reheated before the beaten egg whites are folded in.

Potato, Red Onion and Feta Frittata

THIS ITALIAN omelet is cooked with vegetables and cheese, and is served flat, like a Spanish tortilla. Cut it into wedges and serve with crusty bread and a tomato salad for a light supper.

INGREDIENTS

1 1/2 tablespoons olive oil

1 red onion, sliced

12 ounces cooked new potatoes, halved or quartered, if large

6 eggs, lightly beaten

1 cup feta cheese, diced

salt and freshly ground black pepper

Serves 2–4

3 Preheat the broiler to high. Season the beaten eggs, then pour the mixture over the onion and potatoes. Sprinkle the cheese on top and cook over a moderate heat for 5–6 minutes until the eggs are just set and the base of the frittata is lightly golden.

4 Place the pan under the broiler and cook the top for 3 minutes until set and lightly golden. Serve the frittata warm or cold, cut into wedges.

1 Heat the oil in a large heavy-based, flameproof frying pan. Add the onion and sauté for 5 minutes until softened, stirring occasionally.

2 Add the potatoes and cook for 5 minutes or more until golden, stirring to prevent them sticking. Spread the mixture evenly over the base of the pan.

HEALTH BENEFITS

Eggs are an important source of vitamin B_{12}, which is vital for the nervous system and the development of red blood cells. They also supply other B vitamins, zinc and selenium and a useful amount of iron. It is beneficial to eat a food rich in vitamin C at the same time in order to help the absorption of iron. Do not eat too many eggs, though—no more than three per week.

Layered Polenta Bake

POLENTA, TOMATOES, spinach and
beans make a tasty supper dish.

INGREDIENTS
1 teaspoon salt
3 cups fine polenta
olive oil, for greasing and brushing
1/3 cup Parmesan cheese, freshly grated
salt and freshly ground black pepper

For the tomato sauce
1 tablespoon olive oil
2 garlic cloves, chopped
3 cups chopped tomatoes
1 tablespoon chopped fresh sage
1/2 teaspoon brown sugar
*1 1/2 cups canned cannellini beans, rinsed
  and drained*

For the spinach sauce
9 ounces spinach, tough stems removed
2/3 cup light cream
1 cup Gorgonzola cheese, cubed
large pinch of ground nutmeg
Serves 6

1 Make the polenta. Bring 8 cups water to a boil in a large heavy-based saucepan and add the salt. Remove the pan from the heat. Gradually pour in the polenta, whisking continuously as you do so.

2 Return the pan to the heat and stir constantly for 15–20 minutes until the polenta is thick and comes away from the side of the pan. Remove the pan from the heat.

3 Season well with pepper, then spoon the polenta on to a wet work surface or piece of marble. Using a wet spatula, spread out the polenta until it is 1/2 inch thick. Leave to cool for about 1 hour.

4 Preheat the oven to 375°F. To make the tomato sauce, heat the oil in a saucepan, then fry the garlic for 1 minute. Add tomatoes and sage and bring to a boil. Reduce the heat, add sugar, seasoning and simmer for 10 minutes until slightly reduced, stirring occasionally. Stir in the beans and cook for 2 minutes more.

5 Meanwhile, wash the spinach thoroughly and place in a large pan with only the water that clings to the leaves. Cover the pan tightly and cook over medium heat for about 3 minutes or until tender, stirring occasionally. Tip the spinach into a strainer and drain, then squeeze out as much excess water as possible with the back of a wooden spoon.

6 Heat the cream, cheese and nutmeg in a small heavy-based saucepan. Bring to a boil, then reduce the heat. Stir in the spinach and seasoning, then cook gently until slightly thickened, stirring frequently.

7 Cut the polenta into triangles, then place a layer of polenta in an oiled, deep baking dish. Spoon over the tomato sauce, then top with another layer of polenta. Top with spinach sauce and cover with the remaining polenta triangles. Brush with olive oil, sprinkle with Parmesan cheese and bake for 35–40 minutes. Heat the broiler to high and broil until the top is golden before serving.

SPECIAL OCCASIONS

Impress your dinner guests with one of these special meals, each of which has been chosen for its visual appeal, flavor and nutritional value. All are easy to make.

Sweet Potato Roulade

SWEET POTATO works particularly well as the base for this roulade. Cut it in thin slices and serve with a crisp green salad for a truly impressive dinner party dish.

INGREDIENTS

Serves 6

1 cup low-fat cream cheese

5 tablespoons plain yogurt

6–8 scallions, finely chopped

2 tablespoons Brazil nuts, chopped
   and roasted

1 pound sweet potatoes, peeled and cubed

12 allspice berries, crushed

4 eggs, separated

1/4 cup Edam cheese, finely grated

1 tablespoon sesame seeds

salt and freshly ground black pepper

green salad, to serve

1 Preheat the oven to 400°F. Grease and line a 13 x 10-inch jelly roll pan with baking parchment, snipping the corners with scissors to fit.

COOK'S TIP

Choose the orange-fleshed variety of sweet potato for the most striking color.

2 In a small bowl, mix together the cheese, yogurt, scallions and Brazil nuts. Set aside.

3 Boil or steam the sweet potatoes until tender when pierced. Drain well. Place in a food processor with the allspice and blend until smooth. Spoon into a bowl and stir in the egg yolks and Edam. Season with salt and pepper. Set aside.

4 Beat the egg whites until stiff but not dry. Fold one-third of the egg whites into the sweet potatoes to lighten the mixture before gently folding in the rest.

5 Pour the mixture into the prepared pan, tipping it to get the mixture into all the corners. Smooth gently with a spatula and bake for 10–15 minutes.

6 Meanwhile, lay a large sheet of waxed paper on a clean dish towel and sprinkle with the sesame seeds. When the roulade is cooked, turn it out onto the paper, trim the edges and roll it up. Let cool. When cool, carefully unroll, spread with the cheese filling and roll up again. Cut into slices and serve with a green salad.

Goat Cheese Soufflé

MAKE SURE everyone is seated before the soufflé comes out of the oven, because it will begin to deflate almost immediately. This recipe works equally well with strong blue cheeses, such as Roquefort.

INGREDIENTS

3 tablespoons (1/6 stick) butter
1/4 cup all-purpose flour
3/4 cup milk
1 bay leaf
freshly grated nutmeg
Parmesan cheese, grated, for sprinkling
1 1/2 ounces herb and garlic soft cheese
5 ounces firm goat cheese, diced
6 egg whites, at room temperature
1/4 teaspoon cream of tartar
salt and freshly ground black pepper

Serves 4–6

1 Melt 2 tablespoons butter in a heavy saucepan over medium heat. Add the flour and cook until golden, stirring occasionally.

2 Pour in half the milk, stirring vigorously until smooth. Stir in the remaining milk and add the bay leaf. Season with a pinch of salt and plenty of pepper and nutmeg. Reduce the heat to medium low, cover and simmer gently for about 5 minutes, stirring occasionally.

3 Preheat the oven to 375°F. Generously butter a 6 1/4-cup soufflé dish and sprinkle with Parmesan cheese.

4 Remove the sauce from the heat and discard the bay leaf. Stir in both cheeses.

5 In a medium, clean, grease-free bowl, using an electric mixer or balloon whisk, beat the egg whites slowly until they become frothy. Add the cream of tartar, increase the speed of the mixing and continue beating until the egg whites form soft peaks, then stiffer peaks that just flop over a little at the top.

6 Stir a spoonful of beaten egg whites into the cheese sauce to lighten it, then pour the cheese sauce over the remaining whites. Using a large metal spoon, gently fold the sauce into the whites until the mixtures are just combined.

7 Pour the soufflé mixture into the prepared dish and bake for 25–30 minutes, until puffed and golden brown. Serve at once.

Celeriac and Blue Cheese Roulade

CELERIAC ADDS a delicate and subtle flavor to this attractive dish.

INGREDIENTS

1 tablespoon (1/8 stick) butter
8 ounces cooked spinach, drained
   and chopped
2/3 cup light cream
4 large eggs, separated
2 tablespoons Parmesan cheese, grated
pinch of nutmeg
salt and freshly ground black pepper

For the filling

8 ounces celeriac
lemon juice
3 ounces Gorgonzola cheese
4 ounces fromage frais

Serves 6

1 Preheat the oven to 400°F. Line a 13 x 9-inch jelly roll pan with baking parchment.

2 Melt the butter in a large saucepan and add the cooked, chopped spinach. Cook until all the liquid has evaporated from the pan. Remove the pan from the heat. Stir in the cream, egg yolks, grated Parmesan and nutmeg. Season and set aside.

3 Beat the egg whites until stiff, fold them gently into the spinach mixture and then spoon into the prepared pan. Spread the mixture evenly and use an icing spatula to smooth the surface.

4 Bake for 10–15 minutes, until the roulade is firm to the touch. Turn out onto a sheet of waxed paper and peel away the lining paper. Roll up the roulade with the waxed paper inside and let cool slightly.

5 To make the filling, peel the celeriac and grate it into a bowl. Sprinkle with lemon juice to taste. Blend the Gorgonzola cheese and fromage frais together and mix with the celeriac and a little black pepper.

6 Unroll the roulade, spread with the filling and roll up again, this time without the paper. Serve at once or wrap loosely and chill.

Puree of Lentils with Baked Eggs

THIS UNUSUAL dish makes an
excellent supper. For a nutty flavor
you could add a 14-ounce can of
unsweetened chestnut purée to the
lentil mixture.

INGREDIENTS

2 cups brown lentils, washed

3 leeks, thinly sliced

2 teaspoons coriander seeds, crushed

1 tablespoon cilantro, chopped

2 tablespoons fresh mint, chopped

1 tablespoon red wine vinegar

4 cups vegetable stock

4 eggs

salt and freshly ground black pepper

generous handful of chopped
   parsley to garnish

Serves 4

1 Put the lentils in a deep saucepan.
Add the leeks, coriander seeds,
cilantro, mint, vinegar and stock. Bring
to a boil, then lower the heat and
simmer for 30–40 minutes, until the
lentils are cooked and have absorbed
all the liquid. Stir the mixture
occasionally to keep it from sticking
or burning.

2 Preheat the oven to 350°F.

3 Season the lentils with salt
and pepper and mix well. Spread
out in four lightly greased baking dishes
each about 6 inches in diameter and
2 inches deep.

4 Using the back of a spoon, make a
hollow in the lentil mixture in each
dish. Break an egg into each hollow.
Cover the dishes with foil and bake for
15–20 minutes, or until the whites are
set and the yolks are still soft. Sprinkle
with plenty of parsley and serve at once.
Serve with triangles of toast or thick
slices of crusty bread, if liked.

Leek Soufflé

SOUFFLÉS ARE a great way to impress guests at a dinner party. This one is simple to make but it looks very sophisticated.

INGREDIENTS

4 tablespoons (¹/2 stick) butter

1 tablespoon sunflower oil

2 leeks, thinly sliced

about 1 ¹/4 cups milk

¹/4 cup all-purpose flour

4 eggs, separated

3 ounces Gruyère or Emmenthal cheese, grated

salt and freshly ground black pepper

Serves 2–3

1 Preheat the oven to 350°F. Grease a large soufflé dish with 1 tablespoon of the butter. Heat the sunflower oil and 1 tablespoon butter in a small saucepan or flameproof casserole and cook the leeks over gentle heat for 4–5 minutes, until soft but not brown.

2 Stir in the milk and bring to a boil. Cover and simmer for 4–5 minutes, until the leeks are tender. Strain the liquid through a sieve into a measuring cup.

3 Melt the remaining butter, stir in the flour and cook for 1 minute. Remove from the heat.

4 Add enough milk to the reserved liquid to make 1 ¹/4 cups. Gradually stir the milk into the flour mixture to make a smooth sauce. Return to the heat and bring to a boil, stirring. When thickened, remove from the heat. Cool slightly and beat in the egg yolks, cheese and leeks.

5 Beat the egg whites until stiff and, using a large metal spoon, fold into the leek and egg mixture. Pour into the prepared soufflé dish and bake for about 30 minutes, until puffed and golden brown. Serve immediately.

Broccoli and Chestnut Terrine

Served hot or cold, this versatile terrine is equally suitable for a dinner party or for a picnic. A light salad makes an ideal accompaniment.

INGREDIENTS

1 pound broccoli, cut into small florets
8 ounces cooked chestnuts,
    roughly chopped
1 cup fresh whole wheat
    bread crumbs
1/4 cup plain yogurt
2 tablespoons Parmesan cheese,
    finely grated
    2 eggs, beaten
pinch of grated nutmeg
salt and freshly ground black pepper
new potatoes, to serve

For the salad and dressing (optional)

1/4 cup olive oil
1 tablespoon lemon juice
1/2 teaspoon sugar
salt and freshly ground black pepper
1 tablespoon fresh thyme or dill, chopped
9 ounces mixed salad greens

Serves 4–6

1 Preheat the oven to 350°F. Line a 9 × 5 × 3-inch (8-cup) loaf pan with baking parchment.

2 Blanch or steam the broccoli for 3–4 minutes, until just tender. Drain well. Reserve one-fourth of the smallest florets and chop the rest finely. Set aside.

3 In a large bowl, mix together the chestnuts, bread crumbs, yogurt and Parmesan. Season with salt, pepper and nutmeg.

4 Gradually fold in the chopped broccoli, reserved florets and the beaten eggs.

5 Spoon the broccoli mixture into the prepared pan.

6 Place in a roasting pan and pour in boiling water to come halfway up the sides of the loaf pan. Bake for 20–25 minutes.

7 Meanwhile, to make the salad dressing, if using, mix together the olive oil, lemon juice and sugar. Season with salt and pepper and stir in the thyme or dill. Arrange the salad greens on a plate. Pour the dressing over the salad.

8 Remove the roasting pan from the oven and turn the terrine out onto a plate. Cut into even slices and serve with new potatoes.

Broiled Vegetable Terrine

IMPRESS YOUR guests with a colorful layered terrine using a mixture of Mediterranean vegetables.

INGREDIENTS

2 large red bell peppers, quartered, cored
    and seeded
2 large yellow bell peppers, quartered, cored
    and seeded
1 large eggplant, sliced lengthwise
2 large zucchini, sliced lengthwise
6 tablespoons olive oil
1 large red onion, thinly sliced
1/2 cup raisins
1 tablespoon tomato paste
1 tablespoon red wine vinegar
1 2/3 cups tomato juice
2 tablespoons agar-agar
fresh basil leaves, to garnish

For the dressing
6 tablespoons olive oil
2 tablespoons red wine vinegar
salt and freshly ground black pepper
Serves 6

1 Place the peppers skin side up under a hot broiler until blackened. Put in a bowl. Cover.

2 Arrange the eggplant and zucchini slices on separate baking sheets. Brush them with oil and cook under the broiler.

3 Heat the remaining olive oil in a frying pan. Add the onion, raisins, tomato paste and red wine vinegar. Cook until soft.

4 Line the bottom and sides of a 7 1/2-cup terrine with plastic wrap.

5 Pour half the tomato juice into a saucepan. Sprinkle with the agar-agar. Dissolve over low heat.

6 Layer the red peppers in the terrine and cover with some of the tomato juice and agar-agar. Add the eggplant, zucchini, yellow peppers and onion mixture.

7 Pour tomato juice over each layer of vegetables and finish with another layer of red peppers.

8 Add the remaining tomato juice to any left in the pan and pour into the terrine. Give the terrine a sharp tap to disperse the juice. Cover and chill in the refrigerator until set.

9 To make the dressing, whisk together the oil and vinegar. Season with salt and pepper.

10 Turn out the terrine and remove the plastic wrap. Serve in thick slices, drizzled with dressing. Garnish with basil leaves.

Fonduta with Steamed Vegetables

FONDUTA IS a creamy cheese sauce from Italy. Traditionally, it is garnished with slices of white truffles and eaten with toasted bread rounds.

INGREDIENTS

assorted vegetables, such as fennel, broccoli,
   carrots, cauliflower and zucchini
8 tablespoons (1 stick) butter
12–16 rounds of Italian bread or French
   baguette

For the fonduta

11 ounces Fontina cheese
1 tablespoon all-purpose flour
milk, as required
4 tablespoons ($^{1}/_{2}$ stick) butter
$^{1}/_{2}$ cup Parmesan cheese, freshly grated
pinch of grated nutmeg
2 egg yolks, at room temperature
a few slivers of white truffle (optional)
salt and freshly ground black pepper

Serves 4

1 About 6 hours before you want to serve the fonduta, cut the Fontina into chunks and place in a bowl. Sprinkle with the flour. Pour in enough milk to barely cover the cheese and set aside in a cool place. The cheese should be at room temperature before being cooked.

2 Just before preparing the fonduta, steam the vegetables until tender. Cut into pieces. Place on a serving platter, dot with butter and keep warm.

3 Butter the bread and toast lightly in the oven or under the broiler. Pass the egg yolks through a sieve and set aside.

4 For the fonduta, melt the butter in a bowl set over a pan of simmering water, or in a double boiler. Strain the Fontina and add it with 3–4 tablespoons of its soaking milk. Cook, stirring, until the cheese melts. When it is hot and has formed a homogeneous mass, add the Parmesan and stir until melted. Season with nutmeg, salt and pepper.

5 Remove from the heat and immediately beat in the sieved egg yolks. Spoon into warmed individual serving bowls, garnish with white truffle slivers, if using, and serve with the vegetables and toasted bread.

Spring Vegetable Boxes with Pernod Sauce

PERNOD IS the perfect companion for the tender taste of early vegetables in crisp pastry shells. This is a very impressive dish for a dinner party, and it tastes as good as it looks.

INGREDIENTS

8 ounces puff pastry, thawed if frozen
1 tablespoon Parmesan cheese, freshly grated
1 tablespoon fresh parsley, chopped
beaten egg to glaze
6 ounces fava beans, shelled
4 ounces baby carrots, scraped
4 baby leeks, cleaned
generous 1/2 cup peas, thawed if frozen
2 ounces snow peas, trimmed
salt and freshly ground black pepper
sprigs of fresh dill, to garnish

For the sauce

7-ounce can chopped tomatoes
2 tablespoons (1/4 stick) butter
2 tablespoons all-purpose flour
pinch of sugar
3 tablespoons fresh dill, chopped
1 1/4 cups water
1 tablespoon Pernod

Serves 4

1 Preheat the oven to 425°F. Lightly grease a baking sheet.

2 Roll out the pastry very thinly. Sprinkle the grated cheese and parsley over the surface of the pastry sheets, fold and roll once more, so that the cheese and parsley are mixed into the pastry. Cut into four 3 x 4-inch rectangles.

3 Lift the rectangles onto the baking sheet. With a sharp knife, score an inner rectangle about 1/2 inch from the edge of each rectangle, cutting halfway through. (This inner rectangle will be removed once the boxes are cooked.) Score crisscross lines on the inner rectangles, brush with the beaten egg and bake for 12–15 minutes, until golden.

4 Meanwhile, make the sauce. Press the tomatoes through a sieve into a pan, add the remaining ingredients and bring to a boil, stirring all the time. Lower the heat and simmer until required. Season with salt and pepper.

5 Bring a large pan of lightly salted water to a boil. Cook the fava beans in the boiling water for about 8 minutes. Add the carrots, leeks and peas and cook for another 5 minutes. Add the snow peas and cook for 1 minute more. Drain all the vegetables thoroughly.

6 Using a knife, remove the notched inner rectangles from the pastry boxes. Set them aside to use as lids. Spoon the vegetables into the pastry boxes, pour the sauce over them, put the pastry lids on top and serve garnished with dill.

COOK'S TIP

If there is time, chill the pastry boxes for 20 minutes before baking.

Potato Rösti and Tofu with Fresh Tomato and Ginger Sauce

ALTHOUGH THIS dish features various components, it is not difficult to make and the finished result is well worth the effort. Make sure you marinate the tofu for at least an hour to allow it to absorb the flavors of the ginger, garlic and tamari. Serve with a mixed leaf salad, dressed with a splash each of toasted sesame oil and lime juice.

INGREDIENTS

3³/4 cups tofu, cut into ¹/2-inch cubes
4 large potatoes, about 2 pounds
    total weight
sunflower oil, for frying
salt and freshly ground black pepper
2 tablespoons sunflower seeds, toasted,
    to serve

For the marinade
2 tablespoons tamari or dark soy sauce
1 tablespoon clear honey
2 garlic cloves, crushed
1¹/2-inch piece fresh root ginger, grated
1 teaspoon toasted sesame oil

For the sauce
1 tablespoon olive oil
8 tomatoes, halved, seeded and chopped
Serves 4

1 Mix together all the marinade ingredients in a shallow dish and add the tofu. Spoon the marinade over the tofu and leave to marinate in the fridge for at least 1 hour. Turn the tofu occasionally in the marinade to allow the flavors to infuse.

HEALTH BENEFITS

Made from processed soybeans, tofu is a highly nutritious protein food and is the richest non-dairy source of calcium. Tofu also contains valuable B vitamins and iron.

2 To make the rösti, par-boil the potatoes for 10–15 minutes until almost tender. Leave to cool, then grate coarsely. Season well. Preheat the oven to 400°F.

3 Using a slotted spoon, remove the tofu from the marinade and reserve. Spread out the tofu on a baking tray and bake for 20 minutes, turning occasionally, until golden and crisp on all sides.

4 Take a quarter of the potato mixture in your hands at a time and form into rough cakes.

5 Heat a frying pan with just enough oil to cover the base. Place the cakes in the frying pan and flatten the mixture, using your hands or a spatula to form rounds about ¹/2-inch thick.

6 Cook for about 6 minutes until golden and crisp underneath. Carefully turn over the rösti and cook for a further 6 minutes until golden.

7 Meanwhile, make the sauce. Heat the oil in a saucepan, add the reserved marinade and the tomatoes and cook for 2 minutes, stirring. Reduce the heat and simmer, covered, for 10 minutes, stirring occasionally, until the tomatoes break down. Press through a strainer to make a thick, smooth sauce.

8 To serve, place a rösti on each of four warm serving plates. Scatter the tofu on top, spoon over the tomato sauce and sprinkle with sunflower seeds.

COOK'S TIP

Tamari is a thick, mellow-flavored Japanese soy sauce, which unlike conventional Chinese soy sauce is wheat-free, and so is suitable for people who are on wheat- or gluten-free diets. It is sold in Japanese food shops and some larger health food stores.

Cauliflower and Mushroom Gougère

THIS PUFFY, golden brown, cheese-flavored pastry shell filled with lovely fresh vegetables is a wonderful dinner party dish.

INGREDIENTS

8 tablespoons (1 stick) butter

1 1/4 cups all-purpose flour

4 eggs

4 ounces Gruyère or Cheddar cheese, finely diced

1 teaspoon Dijon mustard

salt and freshly ground black pepper

For the filling

1 small head cauliflower

7-ounce can tomatoes

1 tablespoon sunflower oil

1 tablespoon (1/8 stick) butter

1 onion, chopped

4 ounces button mushrooms, halved if large

sprig of fresh thyme

Serves 4–6

1 Preheat the oven to 400°F. Butter a large ovenproof dish. Place 1 1/4 cups water and the butter together in a large saucepan and heat until the butter has melted. Remove from the heat and add all the flour at once. Beat well with a wooden spoon for about 30 seconds, until smooth. Allow to cool slightly.

2 Beat in the eggs, one at a time, and continue beating until the mixture is thick and glossy. Stir in the cheese and mustard and season with salt and pepper. Spread the mixture around the sides of the ovenproof dish, leaving a hollow in the center for the filling.

3 To make the filling, cut the cauliflower into florets, discarding the woody, hard stalk.

4 Puree the tomatoes in a blender or food processor, then pour into a measuring cup. Add enough water to make 1 1/4 cups of liquid.

5 Heat the oil and butter in a nonstick frying pan. Sauté the onion for 3–4 minutes. Add the mushrooms and cook for 2–3 minutes. Add the cauliflower and stir-fry for 1 minute. Add the tomato liquid and thyme. Season. Cook over low heat for 5 minutes.

6 Spoon into the hollow in the ovenproof dish. Bake for 40 minutes, until the pastry has risen.

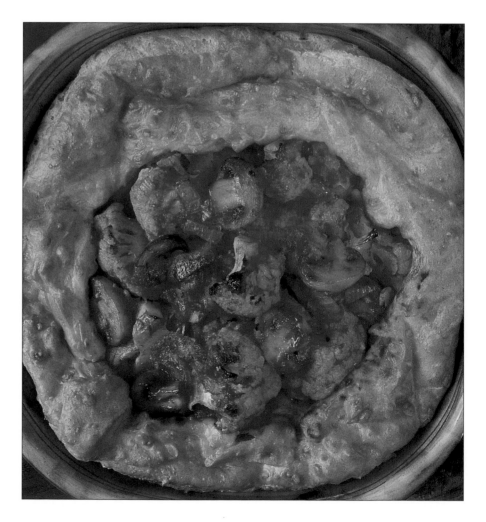

Potato, Spinach and Pine Nut Gratin

PINE NUTS add a satisfying crunch to this gratin of wafer-thin potato slices and spinach in a creamy cheese sauce. Serve with a simple lettuce and tomato salad for a special light lunch.

INGREDIENTS

1 pound potatoes
1 garlic clove, crushed
3 scallions, thinly sliced
2/3 cup light cream
1 cup milk
8 ounces frozen chopped spinach, thawed
1 cup Cheddar cheese, grated
scant 1/4 cup pine nuts
salt and freshly ground black pepper
lettuce and tomato salad, to serve

Serves 2

1 Peel the potatoes and cut them carefully into wafer-thin slices. Spread them out in a large, heavy nonstick frying pan.

2 Sprinkle the crushed garlic and sliced scallions evenly over the potatoes.

3 Pour the cream and milk over the potatoes. Place the pan over gentle heat, cover and cook for 8 minutes, or until the potatoes are tender when pricked with a fork.

4 Using your hands, squeeze the spinach dry. Add the spinach to the potatoes, mixing lightly. Cover the pan and cook for 2 minutes more.

5 Season the mixture with salt and pepper, then spoon the mixture into a shallow flameproof casserole. Preheat the broiler.

6 Sprinkle the grated cheese and pine nuts over the spinach mixture. Heat under the broiler for 2–3 minutes, until the topping begins to turn golden. Serve with a lettuce and tomato salad.

Red Pepper and Watercress Phyllo Parcels

PEPPERY WATERCRESS combines well with sweet red pepper in these crisp little parcels.

INGREDIENTS

3 red bell peppers
6 ounces watercress
1 cup ricotta cheese
1/4 cup blanched almonds, toasted
  and chopped
8 sheets phyllo pastry
2 tablespoons olive oil
salt and freshly ground black pepper
green salad, to serve

Makes 8

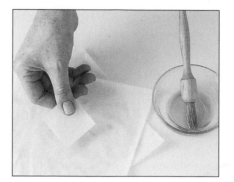

3 Gradually mix in the ricotta and almonds, and season with salt and black pepper.

5 Carefully place one of the squares in the center of the star shape. Brush the pastry square lightly with olive oil and top with the second phyllo square.

1 Preheat the oven to 375°F. Place the red peppers under a hot broiler until blistered and charred. Remove carefully and place in a paper bag. When the peppers are cool enough to handle, peel, seed and pat dry on paper towels.

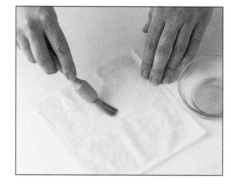

4 Working with 1 sheet of phyllo pastry at a time, cut out two rectangles 2 x 7-inch and two squares 2 x 2-inch from each sheet. Brush 1 of the large pieces with a little olive oil and place the second large piece at an angle of 90° to form a star shape.

6 Top with one-eighth of the red pepper mixture. Bring the edges of the pastry together to form a purse shape and twist to seal. Place on a lightly greased baking sheet and cook for 25–30 minutes, until crisp and golden. Serve with a green salad.

COOK'S TIP

Keep phyllo pastry refrigerated until you need to use it. When working with the pastry, try to handle it as little as possible, and keep the work area cool.

2 Place the peppers and watercress in a food processor and pulse until coarsely chopped. Spoon into a medium bowl.

Cilantro Ravioli with Pumpkin Filling

A STUNNING pasta that combines fresh herbs with a superb creamy pumpkin and roast garlic filling— homemade pasta at its best!

INGREDIENTS

scant 1 cup unbleached bread flour

2 eggs

pinch of salt

3 tablespoons cilantro, chopped

sprigs of cilantro, to garnish

For the filling

4 garlic cloves in their skins

1 pound pumpkin, peeled and
*   seeds removed*

1/2 cup ricotta cheese

4 sun-dried tomatoes in olive oil,
*   drained and finely chopped*
*   (reserve 2 tablespoons of the oil)*

freshly ground black pepper

Serves 4–6

1 Place the flour, eggs, salt and cilantro in a food processor. Pulse until the ingredients are combined.

2 Knead the dough on a lightly floured board until smooth.

3 Wrap the dough in plastic wrap and let rest in the refrigerator for 20–30 minutes.

4 Preheat the oven to 400°F. Place the garlic cloves on a baking sheet and bake for 10 minutes, until softened. Cut the pumpkin into pieces. Steam the pumpkin for 5–8 minutes in a steamer or double boiler, until tender, and drain well.

5 Peel the garlic cloves and mash them into the steamed pumpkin together with the ricotta and sun-dried tomatoes. Season with plenty of black pepper.

6 Divide the pasta into four pieces and flatten slightly. Using a pasta machine on its thinnest setting, roll out each piece. Lay the sheets of pasta on a clean dish towel until slightly dried.

7 Using a 3-inch crinkle-edged round cutter, stamp out 36 rounds.

8 Top 18 of the rounds with a teaspoonful of the pumpkin mixture, brush the edges with water and place another round of pasta on top. Press firmly around the edges to seal. Bring a large pan of water to a boil, add the ravioli and cook for 3–4 minutes. Drain well and toss with the reserved tomato oil. Add pepper and serve garnished with cilantro sprigs.

VARIATION

For an alternative filling you could replace the ricotta cheese with 1 ounce grated Parmesan cheese mixed with 4 ounces cottage cheese. Serve with shavings of Parmesan.

Rice and Beans with Avocado Salsa

MEXICAN-STYLE RICE and beans make a delicious supper dish. Spoon on to tortillas and serve with a tangy salsa and soured cream. Alternatively, serve as an accompaniment to a spicy stew.

INGREDIENTS

1/4 cup dried or 1/2 cup canned kidney
    beans, rinsed and drained
4 tomatoes, halved and seeded
2 garlic cloves, chopped
1 onion, sliced
3 tablespoons olive oil
generous 1 cup long grain brown
    rice, rinsed
2 1/2 cups vegetable stock
2 carrots, diced
3/4 cup green beans
salt and freshly ground black pepper
4 wheat tortillas and soured cream,
    to serve

For the avocado salsa
1 avocado
juice of 1 lime
1 small red onion, diced
1 small red chile, seeded and chopped
1 tablespoon fresh cilantro, chopped
Serves 4

1 If using dried kidney beans, place in a bowl, cover with cold water and leave to soak overnight, then drain and rinse well. Place in a saucepan with enough water to cover and bring to a boil. Boil rapidly for 10 minutes, then reduce the heat and simmer for 40 minutes until tender. Drain and set aside.

2 Heat the broiler to high. Place the tomatoes, garlic and onion on a cookie sheet. Pour over 1 tablespoon of the olive oil and toss to coat. Broil for 10 minutes or until the tomatoes and onions are softened, turning once. Set aside to cool.

3 Heat the remaining oil in a saucepan, add the rice and cook for 2 minutes, stirring, until light golden.

HEALTH BENEFITS

Brown rice contains a good, healthy combination of valuable nutrients, including vitamin E, minerals and fiber.

4 Puree the cooled tomatoes and onions in a food processor or blender, then add the mixture to the rice and cook for a further 2 minutes, stirring frequently. Pour in the stock, then cover and cook gently, for 20 minutes, stirring occasionally.

5 Reserve 2 tablespoons of the kidney beans for the salsa. Add the rest to the stock mixture with the carrots and green beans and cook for 15 minutes until the vegetables are tender. Season well. Remove the pan from the heat and leave to stand, covered, for 15 minutes.

6 To make the avocado salsa, cut the avocado in half and remove the pit. Peel and dice the flesh, then toss in the lime juice. Add the onion, chile, cilantro and reserved kidney beans, then season with salt.

7 To serve, spoon the hot rice and beans on to the tortillas. Hand round the salsa and soured cream.

Teriyaki Soba Noodles with Tofu and Asparagus

YOU CAN, of course, buy ready-made teriyaki sauce, but it is easy to prepare at home using ingredients that are now readily available in supermarkets and specialist shops. Japanese soba noodles are made from buckwheat flour, which gives them a unique texture and color.

INGREDIENTS

12 ounces soba noodles

2 tablespoons toasted sesame oil

1/2 bunch asparagus tips

2 tablespoons peanut or vegetable oil

8-ounce block of tofu

2 scallions, cut into thin strips

1 carrot, cut into matchsticks

1/2 teaspoon chili flakes

1 tablespoon sesame seeds

salt and freshly ground black pepper

For the teriyaki sauce

4 tablespoons dark soy sauce

4 tablespoons Japanese sake or dry sherry

4 tablespoons mirin

1 teaspoon sugar

Serves 4

1 Cook the noodles according to the instructions on the package, then drain and rinse under cold running water. Set aside.

2 Heat the sesame oil in a griddle pan or on a baking tray placed under the broiler until very hot. Turn down the heat to medium, then cook the asparagus for 8–10 minutes, turning frequently, until tender and browned. Set aside.

HEALTH BENEFITS

Sesame seeds are an excellent source of the antioxidant vitamin E, which acts as a natural preservative, preventing oxidation and strengthening the heart and nerves.

3 Meanwhile, heat the peanut or vegetable oil in a wok or large frying pan until very hot. Add the tofu and fry for 8–10 minutes until golden, turning it occasionally to crisp all sides. Carefully remove from the wok or pan and leave to drain on paper towels. Cut the tofu into 1/2-inch slices.

VARIATION

Use dried egg or rice noodles instead of soba noodles, if you wish.

4 To prepare the teriyaki sauce, mix the soy sauce, sake or dry sherry, mirin and sugar together, then heat the mixture in the wok or frying pan.

5 Toss in the noodles and stir to coat them in the sauce. Heat through for 1–2 minutes, then spoon into warmed individual serving bowls with the tofu and asparagus. Scatter the scallions and carrot on top and sprinkle with the chili flakes and sesame seeds. Serve immediately.

Lemon, Thyme and Aduki Bean-stuffed Mushrooms with Pine Nut Tarator

PORTABELLO MUSHROOMS have a rich flavor and a meaty texture that go well with this fragrant herb and lemon stuffing. The garlicky pine nut accompaniment is a traditional Middle Eastern dish with a smooth, creamy consistency similar to that of hummus. Green leafy vegetables, such as spinach or Swiss chard, and roast or baked potatoes are ideal side dishes.

INGREDIENTS

1 cup dried or 2 cups drained, canned
    aduki beans
3 tablespoons olive oil, plus extra
    for brushing
1 onion, finely chopped
2 garlic cloves, crushed
2 tablespoons fresh chopped thyme or
    1 teaspoon dried thyme
8 large portabello mushrooms, stalks
    finely chopped
1 cup fresh whole wheat bread crumbs
juice of 1 lemon
3/4 cup goat cheese, crumbled
salt and freshly ground black pepper

For the pine nut tarator
1/2 cup pine nuts toasted
1 cup cubed white bread
2 garlic cloves, chopped
scant 1 cup milk
3 tablespoons olive oil
1 tablespoon fresh parsley, chopped,
    to garnish (optional)
Serves 4–6

1 If using dried beans, soak them overnight, then drain and rinse well. Place in a saucepan, add enough water to cover and bring to a boil. Boil rapidly for 10 minutes, then reduce the heat, cook for 30 minutes until tender, then drain. If using canned beans, rinse, drain well, then set aside.

2 Preheat the oven to 400°F. Heat the oil in a large heavy-based frying pan, add the onion and garlic and sauté for 5 minutes until softened. Add the thyme and the mushroom stalks, cook for 3 minutes more, stirring occasionally until tender.

3 Stir in the beans, bread crumbs and lemon juice, season well, then cook for 2 minutes until heated through. Mash two-thirds of the beans with a fork or potato masher, leaving the remaining beans whole.

4 Brush a baking dish and the base and sides of the mushrooms with oil, then top each one with a spoonful of the bean mixture. Place the mushrooms in the dish, cover with foil and bake for 20 minutes. Remove the foil. Top each mushroom with some of the goat cheese and bake for 15 minutes more, or until the cheese is melted and bubbly and the mushrooms are tender.

5 To make the pine nut tarator, place all the ingredients in a food processor or blender and blend until smooth and creamy. Add more milk if the mixture appears too thick. Sprinkle with parsley, if using, and serve with the stuffed mushrooms.

HEALTH BENEFITS

Aduki beans are high in protein and fiber and low in fat. They also contain some B vitamins and iron.

Spiced Couscous with Halloumi and Zucchini Ribbons

A STAPLE FOOD in North Africa, couscous is commonly served with meat or vegetable stews. Here, it forms the foundation of the dish and is topped with griddled sliced zucchini and halloumi, a mild cheese from Cyprus.

INGREDIENTS

1²/3 cups couscous

1 bay leaf

1 cinnamon stick

2 tablespoons olive oil, plus extra
    for brushing

1 large red onion, chopped

2 garlic cloves, chopped

1 teaspoon mild chili powder

1 teaspoon ground cumin

1 teaspoon ground coriander

5 cardamom pods, bruised

¹/4 cup whole almonds, toasted

1 peach, pitted and diced

2 tablespoons butter

3 zucchini, sliced lengthways into ribbons

8 ounces halloumi cheese, sliced

salt and freshly ground black pepper

fresh Italian parsley, chopped, to garnish

Serves 4

1 Place the couscous in a bowl and pour over 2¹/4 cups boiling water. Add the bay leaf and cinnamon stick and season with salt. Leave the couscous for 10 minutes until the water is absorbed, then fluff up the grains with a fork.

HEALTH BENEFITS

Almonds have long been regarded as having special protective properties. Although they have a high fat content, the fat is monounsaturated and can help lower cholesterol levels. Best eaten whole, almonds are also a useful source of calcium and vitamin E.

2 Meanwhile, heat the oil in a large heavy-based saucepan, add the onion and garlic and sauté for about 7 minutes until the onion has softened, stirring occasionally.

3 Stir in the chili powder, cumin, coriander and cardamom pods, and cook for 3 minutes more to allow the flavors to mingle. Add the couscous, almonds, diced peach and butter, and heat through for 2 minutes.

4 Brush a griddle pan with olive oil and heat until very hot. Turn down heat to medium, then place the zucchini on the griddle and cook for 5 minutes until tender and slightly charred. Turn the zucchini over, add the halloumi and continue cooking for 5 minutes more, turning the halloumi halfway through.

5 Remove the cinnamon stick, bay leaf and cardamom pods from the couscous, then arrange it on a plate and season well. Top with the halloumi and zucchini. Sprinkle the parsley over the top and serve.

COOK'S TIP

If you don't own a griddle pan, cook the zucchini under a hot broiler, which will impart a similar smoky flavor.

Mushroom and Okra Curry

THIS SIMPLE but delicious curry with its fresh gingery mango relish is best served with plain basmati rice.

INGREDIENTS

4 garlic cloves, roughly chopped

1-inch piece of fresh ginger root, peeled and roughly chopped

1–2 fresh red chiles, seeded and chopped

3/4 cup cold water

1 tablespoon sunflower oil

1 teaspoon coriander seeds

1 teaspoon cumin seeds

1 teaspoon ground cumin

2 green cardamom pods, seeds removed and ground

pinch of ground turmeric

14-ounce can tomatoes, chopped

1 pound mushrooms, quartered if large

8 ounces okra, trimmed and cut into 1/2-inch slices

2 tablespoons cilantro, chopped

For the mango relish

1 large ripe mango, about 1 1/4 pounds

1 small garlic clove, crushed

1 onion, finely chopped

2 teaspoons fresh ginger root, grated

1 fresh red chile, seeded and finely chopped

pinch of salt and sugar

Serves 4

1 To make the mango relish, first peel the mango and cut off the flesh from the pit.

COOK'S TIP

When buying okra, choose firm, brightly colored pods that are less than 4 inches in length.

2 In a bowl, mash the mango flesh with a fork, or process in a food processor or blender. Mix in the rest of the relish ingredients. Season with salt and pepper. Set aside.

3 Place the garlic, ginger, chiles and 3 tablespoons of the water in a blender or food processor and process until smooth.

4 Heat the sunflower oil in a large saucepan. Add the whole coriander and cumin seeds and allow them to sizzle in the pan for a few seconds. Add the ground cumin, cardamom and turmeric and cook for about 1 minute more.

5 Add the garlic paste, tomatoes and remaining water. Stir to mix well, then add the mushrooms and okra. Stir again, then bring to a boil. Reduce the heat, cover and simmer for 5 minutes.

6 Remove the cover, turn up the heat slightly and cook for another 5–10 minutes, until the okra is tender but not too soft.

7 Stir in the chopped cilantro and serve with the mango relish and the rice.

Thai Vegetable Curry with Lemongrass Rice

FRAGRANT JASMINE rice, subtly flavored with lemongrass and cardamom, is the perfect accompaniment to this richly spiced vegetable curry. Don't be put off by the long list of ingredients—this curry is very simple to make.

INGREDIENTS

2 teaspoons vegetable oil

1 2/3 cups coconut milk

1 1/4 cups vegetable stock

8 ounces new potatoes, halved or
    quartered, if large

5 ounces baby corn

1 teaspoon golden sugar

7 ounces broccoli florets

1 red bell pepper, seeded and sliced
    lengthways

4 ounces spinach, tough stalks removed
    and shredded

2 tablespoons chopped cilantro

salt and freshly ground black pepper

For the spice paste

1 red chile, seeded and chopped

3 green chiles, seeded and chopped

1 lemongrass stalk, outer leaves removed
    and inside finely chopped

2 shallots, chopped

finely grated rind of 1 lime

2 garlic cloves, chopped

1 teaspoon ground coriander

1/2 teaspoon ground cumin

1/2-inch piece of fresh galangal, finely
    chopped or 1/2 teaspoon dried (optional)

2 tablespoons cilantro, chopped

1 tablespoon cilantro roots and stems,
    chopped (optional)

For the rice

generous 1 cup jasmine rice, rinsed

1 lemongrass stalk, outer leaves removed
    and cut into 3 pieces

6 cardamom pods, bruised

Serves 4

1 Make the spice paste. Place all the ingredients in a food processor or blender and blend to a coarse paste.

2 Heat the oil in a large heavy-based saucepan and fry the spice paste for 1–2 minutes, stirring constantly. Add the coconut milk and stock, and bring to a boil.

3 Reduce the heat, add the potatoes and simmer for 15 minutes. Add the baby corn and seasoning, then cook for 2 minutes. Stir in the sugar, broccoli and red pepper, and cook for 2 minutes more until the vegetables are tender. Stir in the shredded spinach and half the cilantro. Cook for 2 minutes.

HEALTH BENEFITS

Broccoli provides valuable amounts of calcium, vitamin C, folic acid, zinc and iron. The vitamin and mineral content of this dish is given a further boost by the addition of all the other vegetables.

4 Meanwhile, prepare the rice. Tip the rinsed rice into a saucepan and add the lemongrass and cardamom pods. Pour over 2 cups of water.

5 Bring to a boil, then reduce the heat, cover, and cook for 10–15 minutes until the water is absorbed and the rice is tender and slightly sticky. Season with salt to taste, leave to stand for 10 minutes, then fluff up the rice with a fork.

6 Remove the spices and serve the rice with the curry, sprinkled with the remaining cilantro.

Eggplant Curry

A SIMPLE and delicious way of cooking eggplant that retains their full flavors.

INGREDIENTS

2 large eggplants, about 1 pound each

3 tablespoons oil

1/2 teaspoon black mustard seeds

1 bunch scallions, finely chopped

4 ounces button mushrooms, halved

2 garlic cloves, crushed

1 fresh red chile, finely chopped

1/2 teaspoon chili powder

1 teaspoon ground cumin

1 teaspoon ground coriander

1/4 teaspoon ground turmeric

1 teaspoon salt

14-ounce can tomatoes, chopped

1 tablespoon cilantro, chopped

sprigs of cilantro, to garnish

Serves 4

1 Preheat the oven to 400°F. Brush the skin of both of the eggplant with 1 tablespoon of the oil and prick with a fork. Bake for 30–35 minutes, until soft.

2 Meanwhile, heat the remaining oil in a saucepan and sauté the mustard seeds for 2 minutes, until they begin to splutter. Take care not to get splashed by the hot oil.

3 Add the scallions, mushrooms, crushed garlic and chopped chile and cook for 5 minutes. Stir in the chili powder, cumin, coriander, turmeric and salt and cook for 3–4 minutes. Add the tomatoes and simmer for 5 minutes.

4 Cut each eggplant in half lengthwise and scoop out the soft flesh into a bowl. Mash the flesh briefly with a fork.

5 Add the mashed eggplant and chopped cilantro to the saucepan. Bring to a boil and simmer for 5 minutes, or until the sauce thickens. Serve garnished with cilantro sprigs.

COOK'S TIP

If you want to omit some of the oil, wrap the eggplants in foil and bake them for 1 hour.

Phyllo Vegetable Pie

THIS IS a memorable main course which is deceptively simple to make.

INGREDIENTS

8 ounces leeks
11 tablespoons (1 3/8 stick) butter
8 ounces carrots, cubed
8 ounces mushrooms, sliced
8 ounces Brussels sprouts, quartered
2 garlic cloves, crushed
4 ounces (1/2 cup) cream cheese
4 ounces Roquefort or Stilton cheese
2/3 cup heavy cream
2 eggs, beaten
8 ounces cooking apples
8 ounces cashew nuts or pine nuts, toasted
12 ounces frozen phyllo pastry, thawed
salt and freshly ground black pepper
Serves 6–8

3 Whisk the cream cheese, blue cheese, cream and eggs in a bowl. Season with salt and pepper. Pour over the vegetables.

4 Peel and core the apples and cut into 1/2-inch cubes. Add them to the vegetables with the toasted cashew or pine nuts.

5 Melt the remaining butter in a pan. Brush the inside of a 9-inch springform pan with melted butter. Brush two-thirds of the pastry sheets with butter, one at a time, and use them to line the bottom and sides of the pan, overlapping the layers so that there are no gaps.

6 Spoon in the vegetable mixture and fold the excess phyllo pastry over toward the center to cover all the filling.

7 Brush the remaining phyllo sheets with butter and cut them into 1-inch strips. Cover the surface of the pie with the strips, arranging them decoratively in a rough mound.

8 Bake for 35–40 minutes, until golden brown and crisp all over. Let stand for 5 minutes to cool, then carefully remove the pan and transfer the pie to a serving plate.

COOK'S TIP

For a firmer crust on the pastry, brush the top of the pie with beaten egg just before baking.

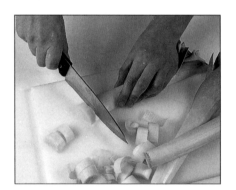

1 Preheat the oven to 350°F. Cut the leeks in half through the root and wash them to remove any soil, separating the layers slightly to check that they are clean. Slice into 1/2-inch pieces, drain and dry on paper towels.

2 Heat 3 tablespoons of the butter in a large pan and cook the leeks and carrots over medium heat for 5 minutes. Add the mushrooms, Brussels sprouts and garlic and cook for another 2 minutes. Turn the vegetables out into a bowl and let them cool.

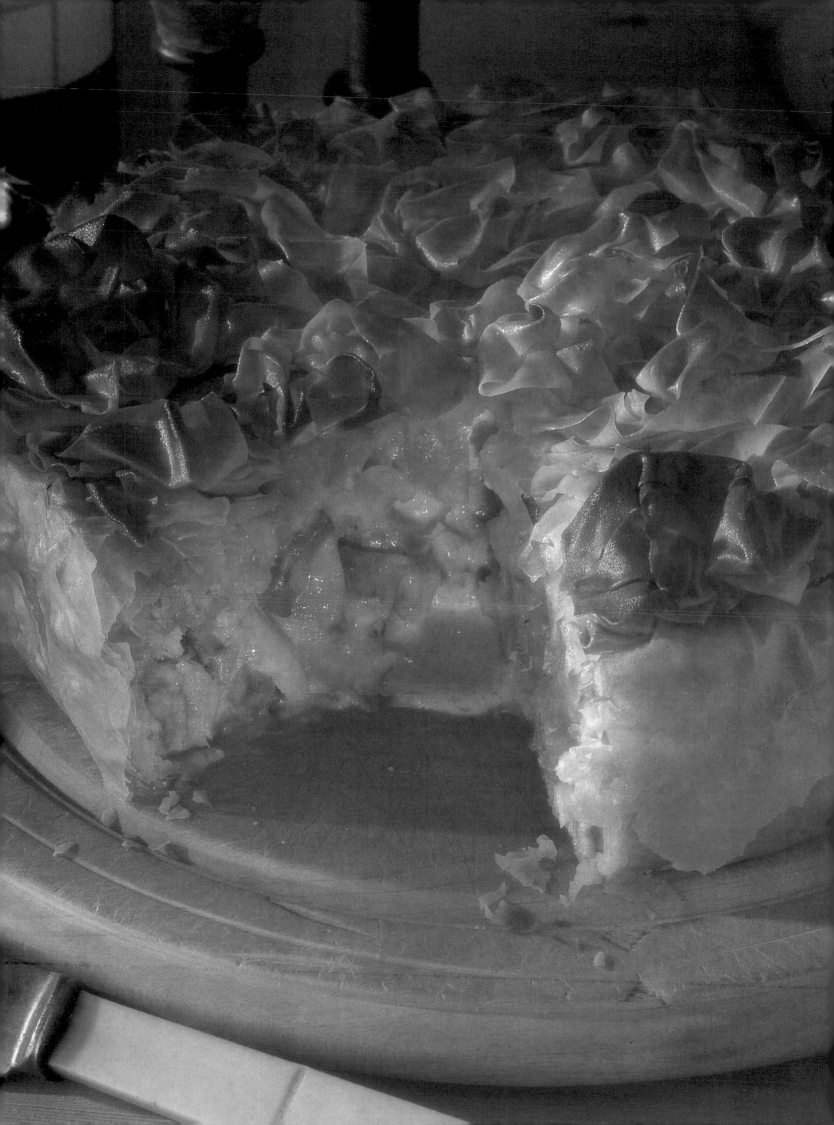

Corn and Bean Tamale Pie

INGREDIENTS

2 ears of fresh corn

2 tablespoons vegetable oil

1 onion, chopped

2 garlic cloves, crushed

1 red bell pepper, seeded and chopped

2 green chiles, seeded and chopped

2 teaspoons ground cumin

1 pound ripe tomatoes, peeled, seeded and chopped

1 tablespoon tomato paste

14-ounce can red kidney beans, drained and rinsed

1 tablespoon fresh oregano, chopped

oregano leaves, to garnish

For the topping

1 cup polenta

1 tablespoon flour

$1/2$ teaspoon salt

2 teaspoon baking powder

1 egg, lightly beaten

$1/2$ cup milk

1 tablespoon butter ($1/8$ stick), melted

2 ounces smoked Cheddar cheese, grated

Serves 4

1 Preheat the oven to 425°F. Remove the outer husks and silky threads from the ears of corn, then part-boil in boiling, but not salted, water for 8 minutes. Drain and leave until cool enough to handle, then run a sharp knife down the ears of corn to remove the kernels.

2 Heat the oil in a large pan and fry the onion, garlic and pepper for 5 minutes, until softened. Add the chiles and cumin and fry for 1 minute.

3 Stir in the tomatoes, tomato paste, beans, corn kernels and oregano. Season. Bring to a boil, then simmer, uncovered, for 10 minutes.

4 Meanwhile, make the topping. Mix together the polenta, flour, salt, baking powder, egg milk and butter in a bowl to form a smooth, thick batter.

5 Transfer the corn kernels and beans to an ovenproof dish, spoon the polenta mixture over the top and spread evenly. Bake for 30 minutes. Remove from the oven, sprinkle over the cheese, then return to the oven for a further 5–10 minutes, until golden.

Onion and Thyme Tart

INGREDIENTS

2 tablespoons butter or olive oil

2 onions, thinly sliced

1/2 teaspoon fresh or dried thyme

1 egg

1/2 cup sour cream or plain yogurt

2 teaspoons poppy seeds

1/4 teaspoon ground mace or nutmeg

salt and black pepper

For the base

1 cup flour

1 1/4 teaspoons baking powder

1/2 teaspoon salt

3 tablespoons (3/8 stick) cold butter

6 tablespoons milk

Serves 6

1 Heat the butter or oil in a medium-size frying pan. Add the onions and cook over low heat for 10–12 minutes, until soft and golden. Season with thyme, salt and pepper. Remove from the heat and let cool. Preheat the oven to 425°F.

2 For the base, sift the flour, baking powder, and salt into a bowl. Using a pastry blender or two knives, cut the butter into the dry ingredients until the mixture resembles bread crumbs. Add the milk and stir in lightly with a wooden spoon to make a dough.

3 Turn out the dough onto a floured surface and knead lightly.

4 Pat out the dough into an 8-in round. Transfer to a deep 8-in baking pan. Press the dough into an even layer, then cover with the onions.

5 Beat together the egg and sour cream or yogurt. Spread evenly over the onions. Sprinkle with the poppy seeds and mace or nutmeg. Bake for about 35–30 minutes, until the egg topping is puffed and golden.

6 Leave the tart to cool in the pan for 10 minutes. Slip a knife between the tart and the pan to loosen, then unmold onto a plate. Cut the tart into wedges and serve warm.

Corn and Cheese Beggar's Purses

THESE TASTY pastries are so simple to make, why not make double? They'll go like hot cakes.

INGREDIENTS

2 medium ears corn, or 9 ounces
    canned corn
4 ounces feta cheese
1 egg, beaten
2 tablespoons whipping cream
2 tablespoons fresh Parmesan, grated
3 scallions, chopped
8–10 small sheets phyllo pastry
8 tablespoons (1 stick) butter, melted
freshly ground black pepper
Makes 18–20

1 Preheat the oven to 375°F. Butter two muffin pans.

2 If using fresh corn, strip the kernels from the cob using a large sharp knife, cutting downward from top to bottom of the cob. Simmer in a little salted water for 3–5 minutes, until tender. For canned corn, drain and rinse well under cold running water.

COOK'S TIP

Any combination of vegetables, such as broccoli or courgettes, will go with the cheese in these purses.

3 Crumble the feta cheese into a bowl and stir in the corn. Add the egg, cream, Parmesan cheese, scallions and ground black pepper and stir well.

4 Take one sheet of phyllo pastry and cut it in half to make a square. (Keep the remaining pastry covered with a damp cloth to prevent it from drying out.) Using a pastry brush, brush the square with melted butter and then fold in four to make a smaller square (about 3 inches).

5 Place a heaped teaspoon of filling in the center of each pastry square and then squeeze the pastry together around the filling to make a "beggar's purse."

6 Continue making beggar's purses until all the filling is used up. Brush the outside of each purse with any remaining butter, put them in the prepared pans, and bake for about 15 minutes, until golden brown. Serve immediately, while hot.

Cheese and Spinach Tart

THIS TART freezes well and can be reheated. It makes an excellent addition to a festive buffet.

INGREDIENTS

8 tablespoons (1 stick) butter
2 cups all-purpose flour
1/2 teaspoon English mustard powder
1/2 teaspoon paprika
large pinch of salt
4 ounces Cheddar cheese, finely grated
1 egg, beaten, to glaze

For the filling

1 pound frozen spinach
1 onion, chopped
pinch of grated nutmeg
8 ounces cottage cheese
2 large eggs, beaten
1/2 cup Parmesan cheese, freshly grated
2/3 cup light cream
salt and freshly ground black pepper

Serves 8

1 Rub the butter into the flour until it resembles fine bread crumbs. Stir in the mustard powder, paprika, salt and cheese. Blend to a dough with 3–4 tablespoons cold water. Knead until smooth, wrap and chill in the refrigerator for 30 minutes.

2 Put the spinach and onion in a pan, cover and cook slowly. Season with salt, pepper and nutmeg. Turn the spinach out into a bowl and cool slightly. Add the remaining filling ingredients.

3 Roll out two-thirds of the pastry on a lightly floured surface and use it to line a 9-inch tart pan. Press it well into the edges, removing excess pastry with a rolling pin. Spoon the filling into the pastry shell.

4 Preheat the oven to 400°F. Put a baking sheet in the oven for a few minutes to preheat.

5 Roll out the remaining pastry and cut it with a lattice pastry cutter. With the help of a rolling pin, lay it over the tart. Brush the seams with egg glaze. Press the edges together and trim off the excess pastry. Brush the pastry lattice with egg glaze and bake on the hot baking sheet for 35–40 minutes, or until golden brown. Serve hot or cold. A salad of tomato, onion and basil complements this dish.

Caramelized Onion Tart

SERVED WARM with a mixed leaf salad, this classic and elegant French tart makes a perfect light summer lunch.

INGREDIENTS

1 tablespoon (1/8 stick) unsalted butter

1 tablespoon olive oil

1 1/4 pounds onions, sliced

large pinch of ground nutmeg

1 teaspoon dark brown sugar

2 eggs

2/3 cup light cream

1/2 cup Gruyère cheese, grated

salt and freshly ground black pepper

For the pastry

2/3 cup unbleached all-purpose flour

2/3 cup whole wheat flour

6 tablespoons (3/4 stick) unsalted butter

1 egg yolk

Serves 6

1 To make the pastry, rub together the two flours and butter until the mixture resembles fine bread crumbs. Mix in the egg yolk and enough cold water to form a dough.

2 Turn out the dough on to a lightly floured work surface and knead gently until smooth. Form into a ball, then wrap in plastic wrap and chill for about 30 minutes.

3 Meanwhile, make the filling. Heat the butter and oil in a large heavy-based frying pan. Cook the onions over low heat for 30 minutes until very soft and translucent, stirring often. Stir in the nutmeg, sugar and seasoning, and cook for 5 minutes more until the onions are golden and caramelized. Set aside and allow to cool slightly.

4 Preheat the oven to 425°F. Lightly grease a loose-based 14 x 4 1/2-inch fluted pie pan. Roll out the pastry and use to line the prepared pan. Trim the top, then chill for 20 minutes.

5 Prick the pastry base with a fork, then line with waxed paper and baking beans and bake blind for 10 minutes until lightly golden. Remove the paper and beans, then spoon the onions into the pastry shell.

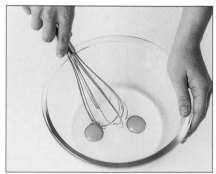

6 Beat the eggs with the cream, then add the cheese and season to taste. Pour the mixture over the onions and bake for 30 minutes until set and golden.

Mediterranean One-crust Pie

THIS FREE-FORM pie encases a rich tomato, eggplant and kidney bean filling. If your pastry cracks, just patch it up—it adds to the pie's rustic character.

INGREDIENTS

1 1/4 pounds eggplant, cubed

1 red bell pepper

2 tablespoons olive oil

1 large onion, finely chopped

1 zucchini, sliced

2 garlic cloves, crushed

1 tablespoon fresh oregano or
   1 teaspoon dried, plus extra fresh
   oregano to garnish

1 1/2 cups canned red kidney beans, drained
   and rinsed

1 cup pitted black olives, rinsed

2/3 cup passata

1 egg, beaten, or a little milk

2 tablespoons semolina

salt and freshly ground black pepper

For the pastry

2/3 cup unbleached all-purpose flour

2/3 cup whole wheat flour

6 tablespoons vegetable margarine

2/3 cup Parmesan cheese, freshly grated

Serves 4

1 Preheat the oven to 425°F. To make the pastry, sift the the two flours into a large bowl. Rub in the vegetable margarine until the mixture resembles fine bread crumbs, then stir in the grated Parmesan. Mix in enough cold water to form a firm dough.

2 Turn out the dough on to a lightly floured work surface and knead lightly for 1 minute until it forms a smooth dough. Wrap in plastic wrap and chill for 30 minutes.

3 To make the filling, place the eggplant in a strainer and sprinkle with salt, then leave for about 30 minutes. Rinse and pat dry with paper towels. Meanwhile, place the pepper on a baking tray and bake in the oven for 20 minutes. Put the pepper in a plastic bag and leave until cool. Peel and seed, then dice the flesh. Set aside.

4 Heat the oil in a large, heavy-based frying pan. Fry the onions for 5 minutes until softened, stirring occasionally. Add the eggplant and fry for 5 minutes until tender. Add the zucchini, garlic and oregano, and cook for 5 minutes more, stirring frequently. Add the kidney beans and olives, stir, then add the passata and pepper. Cook until heated through, and set aside to cool.

5 Roll out the pastry on a lightly floured board or work surface to form a rough 12-inch round. Place on a lightly oiled baking sheet. Brush with a little of the beaten egg, sprinkle over the semolina, leaving a 1 1/2-inch border, then spoon over the filling.

6 Gather up the edges of the pastry to partly cover the filling—it should be open in the middle. Brush with egg and bake for 30–35 minutes until golden.

Summer Herb Ricotta Tart

SIMPLE TO MAKE and infused with aromatic herbs, this delicate tart makes a delightful lunch dish.

INGREDIENTS

olive oil, for greasing and glazing

3 1/2 cups ricotta cheese

1 cup Parmesan cheese, finely grated

3 eggs, separated

4 tablespoons fresh basil leaves, torn, plus a few extra leaves to garnish

4 tablespoons fresh chives, snipped

3 tablespoons fresh oregano leaves

1/2 teaspoon salt

1/2 teaspoon paprika

freshly ground black pepper

For the tapenade

3 1/2 cups pitted black olives, rinsed and halved, plus a few whole to garnish (optional)

5 garlic cloves, crushed

1/3 cup olive oil

Serves 4

1 Preheat the oven to 350°F and lightly grease a 9-inch springform cake pan with oil. Mix together the ricotta, Parmesan and egg yolks in a food processor or blender. Add the herbs and seasoning, and blend until smooth and creamy.

2 Whisk the egg whites in a large bowl until they form soft peaks. Gently fold the egg whites into the ricotta mixture, taking care not to knock out too much air. Spoon the ricotta mixture into the pan and smooth the top.

3 Bake for 1 hour 20 minutes or until the tart is risen and the top golden. Remove from the oven and brush lightly with olive oil, then sprinkle with paprika. Leave the tart to cool before removing from the pan.

4 Make the tapenade. Place the olives and garlic in a food processor or blender and process until finely chopped. Gradually add the olive oil and blend to a coarse paste, then transfer to a serving bowl. Garnish the tart with the basil leaves and olives and serve with the tapenade.

Red Onion and Goat Cheese Pastries

THESE ATTRACTIVE little pastries couldn't be easier to make. Ring the changes by spreading the pastry base with pesto or tapenade before you add the filling.

INGREDIENTS

1 tablespoon olive oil

1 1/2 cups red onions, sliced

2 tablespoons fresh thyme or 2 teaspoons dried plus a few fresh thyme sprigs, to garnish (optional)

1 tablespoon balsamic vinegar

1-pound packet ready-rolled puff pastry

1/2 cup goat cheese, cubed

1 egg, beaten

salt and freshly ground black pepper

mixed green salad leaves, to serve

Serves 4

1 Heat the oil in a large heavy-based frying pan, add the onions and fry over gentle heat for 10 minutes or until softened, stirring occasionally to prevent them browning. Add the thyme, seasoning and balsamic vinegar, and cook for 5 minutes more. Remove the pan from the heat and leave to cool.

2 Preheat the oven to 425°F. Unroll the pastry and using a 6-inch plate as a guide, cut four rounds. Place the pastry rounds on a dampened baking sheet and, using the point of a knife, score a border, 3/4 inch inside the edge of each round.

3 Divide the onions among the pastry rounds and top with the goat cheese. Brush the edge of each round with beaten egg and bake for 25–30 minutes until golden. Garnish with thyme, if using, before serving with salad leaves.

Wild Mushroom and Fontina Tarts

ITALIAN FONTINA cheese gives these tarts a creamy, nutty flavor. Serve them warm with arugula leaves.

INGREDIENTS

1/2 cup dried wild mushrooms
2 tablespoons olive oil
1 red onion, chopped
2 garlic cloves, chopped
2 tablespoons medium-dry sherry
1 egg
1/2 cup light cream
1 ounce Fontina cheese, thinly sliced
salt and freshly ground black pepper
arugula leaves, to serve

For the pastry

1 cup whole wheat flour
4 tablespoons (1/2 stick) unsalted butter
1/4 cup shelled walnuts, roasted
   and ground
1 egg, lightly beaten

Serves 4

1 To make the pastry, rub the flour and butter together until the mixture resembles fine bread crumbs, then stir in the walnuts. Add the egg and mix to form a soft dough. Wrap the pastry in plastic wrap and chill for about 30 minutes.

COOK'S TIP

You can prepare the tart shells in advance, bake them blind for 10 minutes, then store in an airtight container for up to 2 days.

2 Meanwhile, soak the dried mushrooms in 1 1/4 cups boiling water for 30 minutes. Drain and reserve the liquid. Heat the oil in a frying pan. Add the onion and fry for 5 minutes, then add garlic and fry for 2 minutes, stirring.

3 Add the soaked mushrooms and cook for 7 minutes over high heat until the edges become crisp. Add the sherry and the reserved liquid. Cook over high heat for about 10 minutes until the liquid evaporates. Season and set aside to cool.

4 Preheat the oven to 400°F. Lightly grease four 4-inch tart pans. Roll out the pastry on a lightly floured work surface and use to line the tart pans.

5 Prick the pastry, line with waxed paper and baking beans and bake blind for 10 minutes. Remove the paper and beans.

6 Whisk the egg and cream to mix, add to the mushroom mixture, then season to taste. Spoon into the tart shells, top with cheese slices and bake for 18 minutes until the filling is set. Serve warm with arugula leaves.

Mushroom, Nut and Prune Jalousie

JALOUSIE, THE French word for shutter, refers to this pie's slatted top. The pie has a rich, nutty filling and, served with crisp roast potatoes and steamed vegetables, makes a great Sunday lunchtime meal for the family.

INGREDIENTS

$1/3$ cup green lentils, rinsed

I teaspoon vegetable broth powder

I tablespoon sunflower oil

2 large leeks, sliced

2 garlic cloves, chopped

3 cups portabello mushrooms,
    finely chopped

2 teaspoons dried mixed herbs

$3/4$ cup mixed nuts, chopped

I tablespoon pine nuts (optional)

$1/3$ cup ready-to-eat pitted prunes

$1/2$ cup fresh bread crumbs

2 eggs, beaten

2 sheets ready-rolled puff pastry, total
    weight about I pound

flour, for dusting

salt and freshly ground black pepper

Serves 6

I Put the lentils in a saucepan and cover with cold water. Bring to a boil, then reduce heat and add the vegetable broth powder. Partly cover the pan and simmer for 20 minutes or until the lentils are tender. Set aside.

2 Heat the oil in a large heavy-based frying pan, add the leeks and garlic and fry for 5 minutes or until softened. Add mushrooms and herbs and cook for 5 minutes more. Transfer the mushroom mixture to a bowl using a slotted spoon. Stir in the nuts, pine nuts, if using, prunes, bread crumbs and lentils.

COOK'S TIP

Try other combinations of vegetables, nuts and dried fruit.

3 Preheat the oven to 425°F. Add two-thirds of the beaten egg to the mushroom mixture and season well. Set aside and leave to cool.

4 Meanwhile, unroll one of the pastry sheets. Cut off 1 inch from its width and length, then lay it on a dampened cookie sheet. Unroll the second pastry sheet, dust lightly with flour, then fold in half lengthways. Make a series of cuts across the fold, $1/2$ inch apart, leaving a 1-inch border around the edge of the pastry.

5 Spoon the mushroom mixture evenly over the pastry base, leaving a 1-inch border. Dampen the edges of the pastry with water. Open out the folded piece of pastry and carefully lay it over the top of the filling. Trim the edges, if necessary, then press the edges of the pastry together to seal and crimp the edges.

6 Brush the top of the pastry with the remaining beaten egg and bake for 25–30 minutes until golden. Leave to cool slightly before serving.

Apple, Onion and Gruyère Tart

INGREDIENTS

2 cups flour

1/4 teaspoon dry mustard

6 tablespoons soft margarine

6 tablespoons Gruyère cheese, finely grated

For the filling

2 tablespoons (1/4 stick) butter

I large onion, finely chopped

I large or 2 small eating apples, peeled
  and grated

2 eggs

2/3 cup heavy cream

1/4 teaspoon dried mixed herbs

1/2 teaspoon dry mustard

4 ounces Gruyère cheese

salt and black pepper

Serves 4–6

1 To make the pastry, sift the flour, salt and dry mustard into a bowl. Rub in the margarine and cheese until the mixture forms soft bread crumbs. Add 2 tablespoons water and bring together into a ball. Chill, covered or wrapped for 30 minutes.

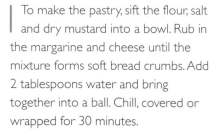

2 Meanwhile, make the filling. Melt the butter in a pan, add the onion and cook gently for 10 minutes, stirring occasionally, until softened but not browned. Stir in the apple and cook for 2–3 minutes. Leave to cool.

3 Roll out the pastry and use to line a lightly greased 8-in fluted quiche pan. Chill for 20 minutes. Preheat the oven to 400°F.

4 Line the pastry with wax paper and fill with baking beans. Bake the pie shell blind for 20 minutes.

5 Beat together the eggs, cream, herbs, seasoning and mustard. Grate three-quarters of the cheese and stir into the egg mixture, then slice the remaining cheese and set aside. When the pastry is cooked, remove the paper and beans and pour in the egg mixture.

6 Arrange the sliced cheese over the top. Reduce the oven temperature to 375°F. Return the tart to the oven and cook for a further 20 minutes, until the filling is golden and just firm. Serve hot or warm.

COOK'S TIP

You could substitute other hard cheeses, such as Cheddar, Provolone, or Emmenthaler for the Gruyère.

Chile, Tomato and Spinach Pizza

THIS RICHLY flavored topping with a hint of spice makes a colorful and satisfying pizza.

INGREDIENTS

1–2 fresh red chiles
3 tablespoons tomato oil (from jar of sun-dried tomatoes)
1 onion, chopped
2 garlic cloves, chopped
10 sun-dried tomatoes in oil, drained
14-ounce can tomatoes, chopped
1 tablespoon tomato paste
6 ounces fresh spinach
1 pizza crust, 10–12 inches in diameter
3 ounces firm smoked cheese, grated
3 ounces aged Cheddar cheese, grated
salt and freshly ground black pepper

Serves 3

| Seed and finely chop the chiles.

2 Heat 2 tablespoons of the tomato oil in a saucepan, add the chopped onion, garlic and chiles and cook gently for about 5 minutes, until they are soft but not brown.

3 Roughly chop the sun-dried tomatoes. Add to the pan with the chopped tomatoes and tomato paste. Season with salt and pepper. Simmer, uncovered, stirring occasionally, for 15 minutes.

4 Remove the stalks from the spinach and wash the leaves in plenty of cold water. Drain well and pat dry with paper towels. Roughly chop the spinach.

5 Stir the spinach into the sauce. Cook, stirring, for another 5–10 minutes, until the spinach has wilted and no excess moisture remains. Let cool.

6 Meanwhile, preheat the oven to 425°F. Brush the pizza crust with the remaining tomato oil, then spoon the sauce over it. Sprinkle with the grated cheeses and bake for 15–20 minutes, until crisp and golden. Serve immediately.

COOK'S TIP

The smoked cheese used in this pizza topping creates an unusual, rich flavor, that complements the hot, spicy chiles. If you want to heighten this taste, replace the Cheddar with another 3 ounces of the smoked cheese.

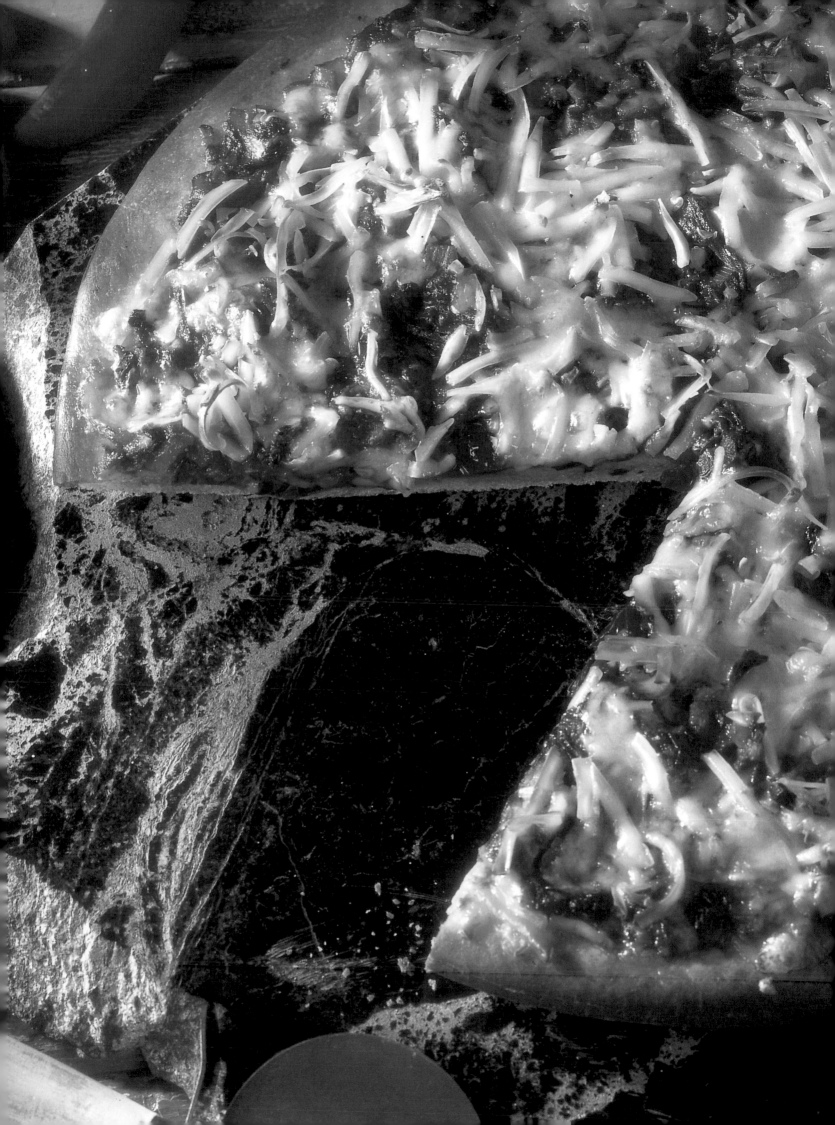

Eggplant, Shallot and Tomato Calzone

EGGPLANT, SHALLOTS and sun-dried tomatoes make an unusual filling for calzone. Add more or less crushed red pepper, depending on how fiery you like your food.

INGREDIENTS

1/4 teaspoon active dry yeast
pinch of sugar
2 cups white bread flour
1 teaspoon salt
1/4 cup olive oil
4 baby eggplant
3 shallots, chopped
1 garlic clove, chopped
10 sun-dried tomatoes in oil,
   drained and chopped
1/4 teaspoon crushed red pepper
2 teaspoons fresh thyme, chopped
3 ounces mozzarella cheese, cubed
salt and freshly ground black pepper
1–2 tablespoons Parmesan cheese,
   freshly grated, to serve

Serves 2

1 To make the dough, put 2/3 cup warm water in a measuring cup. Add the yeast and sugar and let sit for 5–10 minutes, until frothy.

2 Sift the flour and salt into a large bowl and make a well in the center. Gradually pour in the yeast mixture and 1 tablespoon oil. Mix to make a smooth dough. Knead the dough on a lightly floured surface for 10 minutes, until smooth. The dough should be springy and elastic.

3 Place the dough in a floured bowl, cover and let rise in a warm place for 1 1/2 hours. Preheat the oven to 425°F. Trim the eggplant, then cut into small cubes.

4 Heat 1 tablespoon of the oil in a frying pan and cook the shallots until soft. Add the whole baby eggplant, chopped garlic, sun-dried tomatoes, crushed red pepper, thyme and seasoning. Cook for 4–5 minutes over medium heat, stirring frequently, until the eggplant is beginning to soften. Set aside.

5 Divide the dough in half and roll out each piece on a lightly floured surface, reshaping and piecing if necessary, to a 7-inch round.

6 Spread the eggplant mixture over half of each round, leaving a 1-inch border, then sprinkle with the mozzarella cubes.

7 Dampen the edges with water, then fold over the other half of dough to enclose the filling. Press the edges firmly together to seal using your fingers or the tines of a fork. Place the calzones on two greased baking sheets.

8 Brush with half the remaining olive oil and make a small hole in the top of each to allow the steam to escape. Bake for 15–20 minutes, until golden. Remove from the oven and brush with the remaining oil. Sprinkle with the Parmesan cheese and serve immediately.

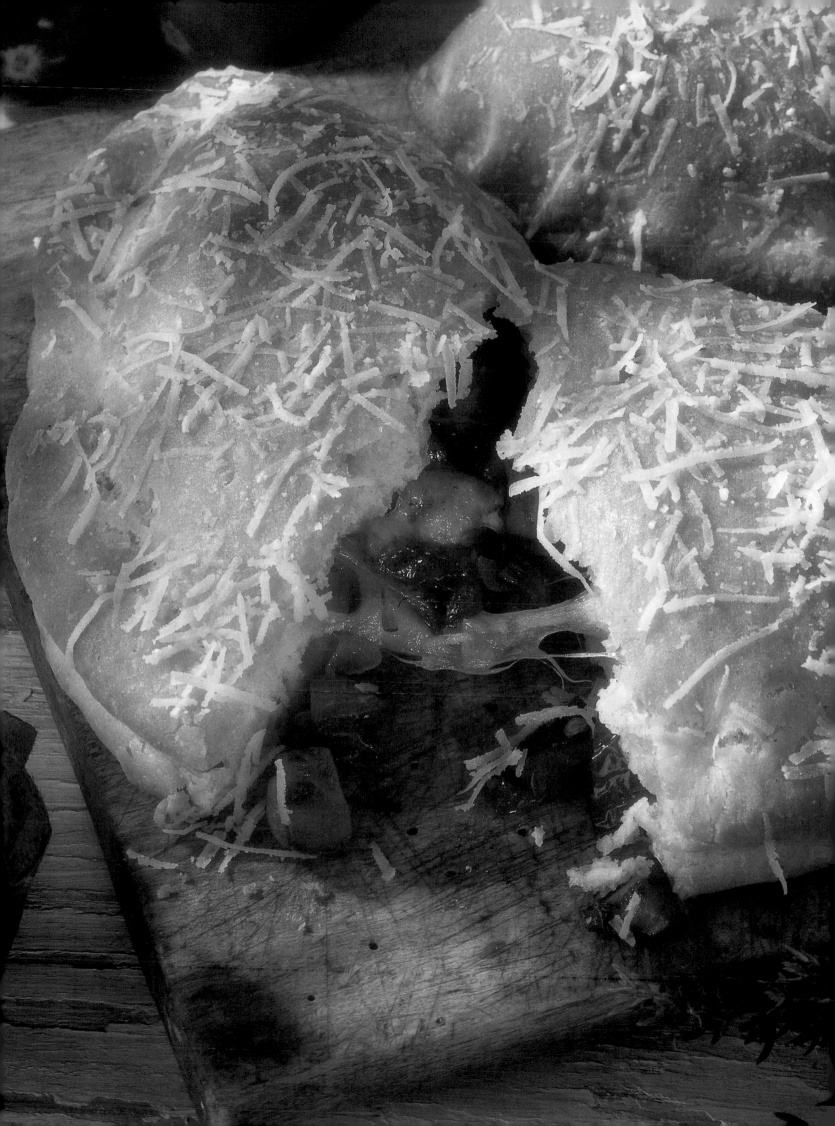

SALADS

Think of salads and you think of summer. The best salads are full of fresh tastes, textures and colors, appealing to the eye as well as the taste buds. Salads are not confined to summer; plenty of these recipes have year-round appeal, with warm selections for spring and fall.

Classic Greek Salad

IF YOU have ever visited Greece, you'll know that a Greek salad with a chunk of bread makes a delicious, filling meal.

INGREDIENTS

1 head romaine lettuce

1/2 cucumber, halved lengthwise

4 tomatoes

8 scallions

1/3 cup Greek black olives

4 ounces feta cheese

6 tablespoons white wine vinegar

1/2 cup olive oil

salt and freshly ground black pepper

olives and bread, to serve (optional)

Serves 4

3 Slice the scallions. Add them, with the olives, to the salad bowl and toss well.

4 Cut the feta cheese into cubes and add to the salad.

5 Put the vinegar, olive oil and salt and pepper into a small bowl and whisk well. Pour the dressing over the salad and toss to combine. Serve at once, with olives and chunks of bread, if desired.

1 Tear the lettuce into pieces and place them in a large mixing bowl. Slice the cucumber and add to the salad bowl.

2 Cut the tomatoes into wedges and put them in the bowl.

COOK'S TIP

The salad can be assembled in advance and chilled, but add the lettuce and dressing just before serving. Keep the dressing at room temperature, as chilling deadens its flavor.

Fresh Spinach and Avocado Salad

YOUNG, TENDER spinach leaves are
delicious served with avocado,
cherry tomatoes and radishes in a
tofu sauce.

INGREDIENTS

1 large avocado
juice of 1 lime
8 ounces fresh baby spinach leaves
4 ounces cherry tomatoes
4 scallions, sliced
1/2 cucumber
2 ounces radishes, sliced
radish roses and herb sprigs, to garnish

For the dressing

4 ounces soft, silken tofu
3 tablespoons milk
2 teaspoons prepared mustard
1/2 teaspoon white wine vinegar
pinch of cayenne, plus extra to serve
salt and freshly ground black pepper

Serves 2–3

1 Cut the avocado in half, remove the
pit, and strip off the skin. Cut the
flesh into even slices. Transfer to a
plate, drizzle with the lime juice and
set aside.

COOK'S TIP

Soft, silken tofu can be found in most
supermarkets in long-life cartons.

2 Wash and dry the spinach leaves.
Put them in a mixing bowl.

3 Cut the larger cherry tomatoes in
half and add all the tomatoes to
the mixing bowl, with the scallions. Cut
the cucumber into chunks and add to
the bowl with the sliced radishes.

4 Make the dressing. Put the tofu,
milk, mustard, wine vinegar and
cayenne in a food processor or
blender. Add salt and pepper to taste.
Process for 30 seconds, until smooth.
Scrape the dressing into a bowl and
add a little extra milk if you like a
thinner dressing. Sprinkle with a little
extra cayenne and garnish with radish
roses and herb sprigs.

Sweet and Sour Peppers with Pasta Bows

A ZESTY dressing makes this simple pasta salad really special.

INGREDIENTS

1 each red, yellow and orange bell pepper

1 garlic clove, crushed

2 tablespoons capers

2 tablespoons raisins

1 teaspoon whole-grain mustard

grated zest and juice of 1 lime

1 teaspoon honey

2 tablespoons cilantro, chopped

8 ounces pasta bows

salt and freshly ground black pepper

shavings of Parmesan cheese, to
   serve (optional)

Serves 4–6

1 Quarter the peppers and remove the stalks and seeds. Place in boiling water and cook for 10–15 minutes, until tender. Drain and rinse under cold water. Peel away the skins and seeds and slice the flesh lengthwise into thin strips.

2 Put the garlic, capers, raisins, mustard, lime zest and juice, honey and cilantro into a bowl. Season with salt and pepper and whisk the ingredients together.

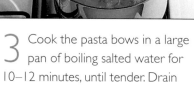

3 Cook the pasta bows in a large pan of boiling salted water for 10–12 minutes, until tender. Drain thoroughly.

4 Return the pasta to the pan and add the peppers and dressing. Heat gently and toss to mix. Transfer to a warm serving bowl. Serve with a few shavings of Parmesan cheese on top, if you like.

Bulgur and Fava Bean Salad

THIS APPETIZING salad is ideal served with fresh crusty whole wheat bread and homemade chutney or relish.

INGREDIENTS

2 cups bulgur
8 ounces frozen fava or lima beans
1 cup frozen petit pois
8 ounces cherry tomatoes, halved
1 Spanish onion, chopped
1 red bell pepper, seeded and chopped
2 ounces snow peas, chopped
2 ounces watercress
1 tablespoon fresh parsley, chopped
1 tablespoon fresh basil, chopped
1 tablespoon fresh thyme, chopped
French dressing
salt and freshly ground black pepper

Serves 6

3 Add the cherry tomatoes, onion, pepper, snow peas and watercress to the bulgur mixture. Toss the ingredients together in the bowl until all the ingredients are well combined but be careful not to allow them to get mushy.

4 Add the chopped fresh parsley, basil, thyme and French dressing to taste. Season with salt and pepper and toss the ingredients together. Serve immediately or cover and chill in the refrigerator before serving.

1 Soak and cook the bulgur according to the package instructions. Drain thoroughly and put into a serving bowl.

2 Meanwhile, cook the beans and petit pois in boiling water for 3 minutes. Drain and add to the prepared bulgur.

COOK'S TIP

Use cooked couscous, boiled brown rice or whole wheat pasta in place of the bulgur in the salad.

Sweet and Sour Artichoke Salad

AGRODOLCE IS a sweet and sour sauce that works perfectly in this salad.

INGREDIENTS

6 small globe artichokes
juice of 1 lemon
2 tablespoons olive oil
2 medium onions, roughly chopped
6 ounces fresh or frozen fava beans,
    about 1 cup
6 ounces fresh or frozen peas,
    about 1 1/2 cups
salt and freshly ground black pepper
fresh mint leaves, to garnish

For the salsa agrodolce

1/2 cup white wine vinegar
1 tablespoon sugar
handful of fresh mint leaves, roughly torn

Serves 4

1 Peel the outer leaves from the artichokes and cut into quarters. Place them in a bowl of water with the lemon juice.

2 Heat the oil in a large saucepan and cook the onions until golden. Add the beans and stir.

3 Drain the artichokes and add them to the pan. Pour in about 1 1/4 cups of water and cover. Simmer gently for 10–15 minutes.

4 Add the peas, season with salt and pepper and cook for another 5 minutes, stirring from time to time, until the vegetables are tender.

5 Drain the vegetables in a sieve and place them in a bowl. Allow them to cool, then cover and chill in the refrigerator until you are ready to use them. Meanwhile, prepare the salsa agrodolce.

6 To make the salsa, mix all the ingredients in a pan. Heat gently until the sugar has dissolved. Simmer for 5 minutes. Let cool. Drizzle the cool salso over the salad and garnish with mint leaves.

Tomato and Feta Cheese Salad

SWEET, SUN-RIPENED tomatoes are rarely more delicious than when served with feta cheese and olive oil. This salad, popular in Greece and Turkey, is enjoyed as a light meal with pieces of crisp bread.

INGREDIENTS

2 pounds tomatoes

7 ounces feta cheese

1/2 cup olive oil, preferably Greek

12 black olives

4 sprigs of fresh basil

freshly ground black pepper

Serves 4

| Remove the tough cores from the tomatoes with a small, sharp knife.

COOK'S TIP

Feta cheese has a strong flavor and can be salty. The least salty varieties are imported from Greece and Turkey and are available at good delicatessens.

2 Slice the tomatoes thickly and arrange in a shallow dish.

3 Crumble the cheese over the tomatoes, drizzle with olive oil, then sprinkle with olives and fresh basil. Season with black pepper and serve at room temperature.

Parmesan and Poached Egg Salad

Soft poached eggs, hot garlic croutons and cool, crisp salad greens make an unforgettable combination.

INGREDIENTS

1/2 small loaf sandwich bread

5 tablespoons olive oil

2 eggs

4 ounces mixed salad greens

2 garlic cloves, crushed

1/2 tablespoon white wine vinegar

1 ounce Parmesan cheese

freshly ground black pepper (optional)

Serves 2

1 Remove the crusts from the bread. Cut the bread into 1-inch cubes.

2 Heat 2 tablespoons of the olive oil in a frying pan. Sauté the bread for about 5 minutes, tossing the cubes occasionally, until they are golden brown.

3 Meanwhile, bring a pan of water to a boil. Carefully slide in the shelled eggs, one at a time. Gently poach the eggs for 4 minutes, until lightly cooked.

4 Divide the salad greens between two plates. Remove the croutons from the pan and arrange them over the leaves. Wipe the pan clean with paper towels.

5 Heat the remaining oil in the pan, add the crushed garlic and wine vinegar and cook over high heat for 1 minute. Pour the warm dressing over each salad.

6 Place a poached egg on each salad. Sprinkle with shavings of Parmesan and freshly ground black pepper, if using.

COOK'S TIP

Add a dash of vinegar to the water before poaching the eggs. This helps to keep the whites together. To make sure that a poached egg has a good shape, swirl the water with a spoon, whirlpool-fashion, before sliding in the egg.

VARIATION

As an alternative to the poached eggs, you could add 1 1/2 ounces of Greek black olives.

New Spring Vegetable Salad

This chunky salad makes a satisfying meal. Use other spring vegetables, if you like and experiment with color, texture and flavor.

INGREDIENTS

1 1/2 pounds small new potatoes, halved

14-ounce can fava beans, drained

4 ounces cherry tomatoes

1/2 cup walnut halves

2 tablespoons white wine vinegar

1 tablespoon whole-grain mustard

1/4 cup olive oil

pinch of sugar

8 ounces young asparagus spears, trimmed

6 scallions, trimmed

salt and freshly ground black pepper

baby spinach leaves, to serve

Serves 4

1 Put the potatoes in a saucepan. Cover with cold water and bring to a boil. Cook for 10–12 minutes, until tender. Meanwhile, put the fava beans in a bowl. Cut the tomatoes in half and add them to the bowl with the walnut halves.

2 Put the white wine vinegar, mustard, olive oil and sugar into a screw-top jar. Season with salt and pepper. Close the jar tightly and shake the ingredients well.

3 Add the asparagus to the potatoes and cook for 3 minutes more. Drain the cooked vegetables well. Cool under cold running water and drain again. Thickly slice the potatoes and cut the scallions in half.

4 Add the asparagus, potatoes and scallions to the bowl containing the fava bean mixture. Pour the dressing over the salad and toss well. Serve on a bed of baby spinach leaves.

Couscous Salad

THIS IS a spicy variation on a classic lemon-flavored tabbouleh, which is traditionally made with bulgur rather than couscous.

INGREDIENTS

3 tablespoons olive oil

5 scallions, chopped

1 garlic clove, crushed

1 teaspoon ground cumin

1 1/2 cups vegetable stock

1 cup couscous

2 tomatoes, peeled and chopped

1/4 cup fresh parsley, chopped

1/4 cup fresh mint, chopped

1 fresh green chile, seeded and
   finely chopped

2 tablespoons lemon juice

salt and freshly ground black pepper

pine nuts, toasted and lemon zest, grated
   to garnish

crisp lettuce leaves, to serve

Serves 4

1 Heat the oil in a saucepan. Add the scallions and garlic. Stir in the cumin and cook for 1 minute. Add the stock and bring to a boil.

2 Remove the pan from the heat, stir in the couscous, cover the pan and let it stand for 10 minutes, until the couscous has swelled and all the liquid has been absorbed. If you are using instant couscous, follow the package instructions.

3 Scrape the couscous into a bowl. Stir in the tomatoes, parsley, mint, chile and lemon juice. Season with salt and pepper. If possible, set aside for up to an hour, to allow the flavors to develop fully.

4 To serve, line a bowl with lettuce leaves and spoon the couscous salad over the top. Sprinkle the toasted pine nuts and grated lemon rind over the top, to garnish.

Brown Bean Salad

BROWN BEANS are a smaller variety of the fava bean, sometimes called "ful." They are used in a classic Egyptian dish called "ful madames" and are occasionally seen in health food stores. Dried fava beans, black or kidney beans make a good substitute.

INGREDIENTS

12 ounces dried brown beans
2 sprigs of fresh thyme
2 bay leaves
1 onion, halved
4 garlic cloves, crushed
1 1/2 teaspoons cumin seeds, crushed
3 scallions, finely chopped
6 tablespoons fresh parsley, chopped
4 teaspoons lemon juice
6 tablespoons olive oil
3 hard-boiled eggs, shelled and
   roughly chopped
1 pickled cucumber, roughly chopped
salt and freshly ground black pepper

Serves 6

1 Put the beans in a bowl with plenty of cold water and let soak overnight. Drain, transfer to a saucepan and cover with fresh water. Bring to a boil and boil rapidly for 10 minutes.

COOK'S TIP

The cooking time for dried beans can vary considerably. They may need only 45 minutes, or a lot longer.

2 Reduce the heat and add the thyme, bay leaves and onion. Simmer very gently for about 1 hour, until tender. Drain and discard the herbs and onion.

3 Mix together the garlic, cumin, scallions, parsley, lemon juice and oil. Season with salt and pepper. Pour over the beans and toss lightly together. Gently stir in the eggs and cucumber and serve at once.

Pepper and Wild Mushroom Pasta Salad

A COMBINATION of broiled peppers and wild mushrooms makes this pasta salad colorful as well as nutritious.

INGREDIENTS

1 red bell pepper, halved
1 yellow bell pepper, halved
1 green bell pepper, halved
12 ounces whole wheat pasta shells or twists
2 tablespoons olive oil
3 tablespoons balsamic vinegar
5 tablespoons tomato juice
2 tablespoons fresh basil, chopped
1 tablespoon fresh thyme, chopped
6 ounces shiitake mushrooms, sliced
6 ounces oyster mushrooms, sliced
14-ounce can black-eyed peas, rinsed and drained
2/3 cup golden raisins
2 bunches scallions, finely chopped
salt and freshly ground black pepper
Serves 6

1 Preheat the broiler. Put the peppers cut side down on a broiler rack and place under the hot broiler for 10–15 minutes, until the skins are charred on top. Cover the peppers with a clean, damp dish towel and set aside to cool.

2 Meanwhile, cook the pasta shells in lightly salted boiling water for 10–12 minutes, until tender, then drain thoroughly.

3 Mix together the oil, vinegar, tomato juice, fresh basil and thyme. Add to the warm pasta and toss together.

4 Remove and discard the skins from the bell peppers. Seed and slice the peppers and add to the pasta with the mushrooms, black-eyed peas, golden raisins and scallions. Season with salt and pepper. Toss to mix and serve immediately or cover and chill in the refrigerator before serving.

Tomato, Scallion and Cilantro Salad

KNOWN AS "cachumbar," this salad relish is most commonly served with Indian curries. There are many versions; this one will leave your mouth feeling cool and fresh after a spicy meal.

INGREDIENTS

3 ripe tomatoes

2 scallions, chopped

1/4 teaspoon sugar

3 tablespoons chopped cilantro

salt

Serves 4

2 Halve the tomatoes, remove the seeds and dice the tomato flesh finely.

3 Combine the tomatoes with the scallions, sugar, chopped cilantro and salt. Serve the relish at room temperature.

1 Remove the tough cores from the tomatoes with a small, sharp knife.

COOK'S TIP

This refreshing salad also makes a fine filler for pita bread with hummus.

Fresh Cèpes with a Parsley Dressing

To capture the just-picked flavor of mushrooms, try this delicious salad enriched with an egg yolk and walnut oil dressing. Choose small cèpes or portobellos for a firm texture and a fine flavor.

INGREDIENTS

12 ounces fresh cèpes or portobello mushrooms

6 ounces mixed salad greens, such as young spinach and frisée

1/2 cup broken walnut pieces, toasted

2 ounces Parmesan cheese

salt and freshly ground black pepper

For the dressing

2 egg yolks

1/2 teaspoon Dijon mustard

5 tablespoons peanut oil

3 tablespoons walnut oil

2 tablespoons lemon juice

2 tablespoons fresh parsley, chopped

pinch of sugar

Serves 4

1 For the dressing, place the egg yolks in a screw-top jar with the mustard, oils, lemon juice, parsley and sugar. Shake well.

COOK'S TIP

The dressing for this salad uses raw egg yolks. Be sure to use only the freshest eggs from a reputable supplier. Pregnant women, young children and the elderly are advised not to eat raw egg yolks. If this presents a problem, the dressing can be made without the egg yolks.

2 Slice the mushrooms thinly using a sharp knife.

3 Place the mushrooms in a large salad bowl and combine with the dressing. Let stand for 10–15 minutes for the flavors to mingle. Stir occasionally to distribute the juices.

4 Wash and spin the salad greens to remove excess water, then toss with the mushrooms.

5 Season with salt and pepper, then sprinkle with toasted walnut pieces and shavings of Parmesan cheese. Serve with crusty bread.

Gado Gado

THE PEANUT sauce on this traditional Indonesian vegetable dish owes its flavor to galangal, an aromatic rhizome that resembles ginger.

INGREDIENTS
9 ounces white cabbage, shredded
4 carrots, cut into matchsticks
4 celery ribs, cut into matchsticks
9 ounces bean sprouts
1/2 cucumber, cut into matchsticks
fried onion, salted peanuts and sliced fresh
     chile, to garnish

For the peanut sauce
1 tablespoon oil
1 small onion, finely chopped
1 garlic clove, crushed
1 small piece galangal, peeled and grated
1 teaspoon ground cumin
1/4 teaspoon chili powder
1 teaspoon tamarind paste or lime juice
4 tablespoons crunchy peanut butter
1 teaspoon light brown sugar
Serves 4

1 Steam the cabbage, carrots and celery for 3–4 minutes, until just tender. Let cool. Spread out the bean sprouts on a large serving dish. Arrange the cabbage, carrots, celery and cucumber on top.

2 To make the sauce, heat the oil in a saucepan, add the onion and garlic and cook gently for 5 minutes, until soft.

COOK'S TIP

As long as the sauce remains the same, the vegetables can be altered at the whim of the cook and to reflect the contents of the vegetable bin.

3 Stir in the galangal and spices and cook for 1 minute. Add the tamarind paste or lime juice, peanut butter and sugar. Mix well.

4 Heat the sauce gently, stirring occasionally and adding a little hot water if necessary, to make the sauce runny enough to coat the vegetables when poured.

5 Spoon a little of the sauce over the vegetables and toss lightly together. Garnish with fried onion, peanuts and sliced chile. Serve the rest of the sauce separately in a medium bowl.

Fruity Rice Salad

AN APPETIZING and colorful rice salad combining many different flavors. This recipe makes an ideal packed lunch for the office or school.

INGREDIENTS

1 cup mixed brown and wild rice
1 yellow bell pepper, seeded and diced
1 bunch scallions, chopped
3 celery ribs, chopped
1 large beefsteak tomato, chopped
2 green-skinned eating apples, chopped
6 ounces chopped dried apricots
4 ounces raisins
2 tablespoons unsweetened apple juice
2 tablespoons dry sherry
2 tablespoons light soy sauce
dash of Tabasco sauce
2 tablespoons fresh parsley, chopped
1 tablespoon fresh rosemary, chopped
salt and freshly ground black pepper

Serves 4–6

2 Place the pepper, scallions, celery, tomato, apples, apricots, raisins and the cooked rice in a serving bowl and mix well.

3 In a small bowl, mix together the apple juice, sherry, soy sauce, Tabasco sauce and herbs. Season with salt and pepper.

4 Pour the dressing over the rice mixture and toss the ingredients together to mix. Serve immediately or cover and chill in the refrigerator before serving.

1 Cook the rice in a large saucepan of lightly salted boiling water for about 30 minutes (or according to the package instructions), until tender. Rinse the cooked rice under cold running water to cool quickly, drain thoroughly and stir gently.

Marinated Cucumber Salad

SLICED CUCUMBER is given a tangy kick in this summer salad.

INGREDIENTS

2 medium cucumbers
1 tablespoon salt
$^1/_2$ cup sugar
$^3/_4$ cup dry cider
1 tablespoon cider vinegar
3 tablespoons fresh dill, chopped
pinch of freshly ground black pepper
sprig of dill, to garnish
Serves 4–6

1 Slice the cucumbers thinly and place them in a colander, sprinkling salt between each layer. Set the colander over a bowl large enough to catch the water and let drain for 1 hour.

2 Thoroughly rinse the cucumber slices under cold running water to remove excess salt, then pat dry on absorbent paper towels. (Sprinkling the cucumber with salt draws out some of the liquid.)

3 Gently heat the sugar, cider and vinegar in a saucepan until the sugar has dissolved. Remove from the heat and let cool. Put the cucumber slices in a bowl, pour the cider mixture over them and let marinate for 2 hours.

4 Drain the cucumber and sprinkle with the dill and pepper to taste. Mix well and transfer to a serving dish. Garnish with a sprig of dill. Chill until ready to serve.

Fennel, Orange and Arugula Salad

THIS LIGHT and refreshing salad is the ideal companion for spicy or rich foods.

INGREDIENTS

2 oranges

1 fennel bulb

4 ounces arugula leaves

1/3 cup black olives

For the dressing

2 tablespoons olive oil

1 tablespoon balsamic vinegar

1 small garlic clove, crushed

salt and freshly ground black pepper

Serves 4

1 With a vegetable peeler, cut strips of zest from the oranges, leaving the pith behind.

2 Cut the strips into thin julienne strips. Cook in boiling water for a few minutes. Drain.

3 Peel the oranges, removing all the white pith. Cut the orange flesh crossways into thin rounds and discard any seeds.

4 Cut the fennel bulb in half lengthwise and slice across the bulb as thinly as possible. It is easier to do this with a food processor fitted with a slicing disk or using a mandoline.

5 Combine the oranges and fennel in a serving bowl and toss with the arugula leaves.

6 Mix together the oil, vinegar, garlic and seasoning and pour over the salad. Toss well and let stand for a few minutes. Sprinkle with the black olives and julienne strips of orange zest.

Eggplant, Lemon and Caper Salad

THIS COOKED vegetable relish is delicious served with pasta or simply on its own with crusty bread.

INGREDIENTS

1 large eggplant, about 1 1/2 pounds

1 teaspoon salt

4 tablespoons olive oil

grated zest and juice of 1 lemon

2 tablespoons capers, rinsed

12 pitted green olives

1 small garlic clove, chopped

2 tablespoons fresh flat-leaf parsley, chopped

salt and freshly ground black pepper

Serves 4

1 Cut the eggplant into 1-inch cubes. Place the cubes in a colander and sprinkle with the salt. Set aside for 30 minutes, then rinse thoroughly under cold running water. Pat dry with paper towels.

2 Heat the olive oil in a large frying pan. Cook the eggplant cubes over medium heat for about 10 minutes, tossing regularly, until golden and softened. You may need to do this in two batches to ensure that all the eggplant cubes brown well. Drain the cubes on paper towels and season with a little salt.

COOK'S TIP

This salad will taste even better if you make it the day before you need it. It will keep, covered, in the refrigerator for up to 4 days. To enrich this dish to serve on its own as a main course, add toasted pine nuts and shavings of Parmesan cheese. Serve with crusty bread.

3 Place the eggplant cubes in a large serving bowl and toss with the lemon zest and juice, capers, olives, garlic and chopped parsley.

4 Season with salt and pepper. Serve at room temperature.

Warm Vegetable Salad with Peanut Sauce

BASED ON the classic Indonesian salad, *gado-gado*, this salad features raw red bell pepper and sprouted beans, which make a crunchy contrast to the warm steamed broccoli, green beans and carrots. Topped with slices of hard-cooked egg, this salad is substantial enough to serve as a main course.

INGREDIENTS

8 new potatoes

8 ounces broccoli, cut into small florets

1 1/2 cups fine green beans

2 carrots, cut into thin ribbons with a
    vegetable peeler

1 red bell pepper, seeded and cut into strips

1/2 cup sprouted beans

sprigs of watercress, to garnish

For the peanut sauce

1 tablespoon sunflower oil

1 bird's eye chile, seeded and sliced

1 garlic clove, crushed

1 teaspoon ground coriander

1 teaspoon ground cumin

4 tablespoons crunchy peanut butter

5 tablespoons water

1 tablespoon dark soy sauce

1/2-inch piece of fresh ginger root,
    finely grated

1 teaspoon dark brown sugar

1 tablespoon lime juice

4 tablespoons coconut milk

Serves 2–4

HEALTH BENEFITS

Sprouted beans, which are available from health food stores and some supermarkets, are easily digestible and packed with concentrated goodness. When fresh, their vitamin and enzyme content is at its peak and they are believed to stimulate the body's ability to cleanse itself. They provide valuable amounts of vitamin E, which is said to improve fertility.

1 First make the peanut sauce. Heat the oil in a saucepan, add the chile and garlic, and cook for 1 minute or until softened. Add the spices and cook for 1 minute. Stir in peanut butter and water, then cook for 2 minutes until combined, stirring constantly.

2 Add the soy sauce, ginger, sugar, lime juice and coconut milk, then cook over low heat until smooth and heated through, stirring frequently. Transfer to a bowl.

3 Bring a saucepan of lightly salted water to a boil, add the potatoes and cook for 10–15 minutes, until tender. Drain, then halve or thickly slice the potatoes, depending on their size.

4 Meanwhile, steam the broccoli and green beans for 4–5 minutes until tender but still crisp. Add the carrots 2 minutes before the end of the cooking time.

5 Arrange the cooked vegetables on a serving platter with the red bell pepper and sprouted beans. Garnish with watercress and serve with the peanut sauce.

Avocado, Red Onion and Spinach Salad with Polenta Croûtons

THE SIMPLE lemon dressing gives a sharp tang to creamy avocado, sweet red onions and crisp spinach. Golden polenta croutons, with their crunchy golden exterior and soft center, add a delicious contrast.

INGREDIENTS

1 large red onion, cut into wedges
12 ounces ready-made polenta, cut into
   $^1/_2$-inch cubes
olive oil, for brushing
$^1/_2$ pound baby spinach leaves
1 avocado, peeled, pitted and sliced
1 teaspoon lemon juice

For the dressing

4 tablespoons extra virgin olive oil
juice of $^1/_2$ lemon
salt and freshly ground black pepper

Serves 4

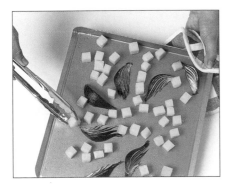

1 Preheat the oven to 400°F. Place the onion wedges and polenta cubes on a lightly oiled baking sheet and bake for 25 minutes or until the onion is tender and the polenta is crisp and golden, turning them regularly to prevent them sticking. Leave to cool slightly.

2 Meanwhile, make the dressing. Place olive oil, lemon juice and seasoning to taste in a bowl or screw-top jar. Stir or shake thoroughly to combine.

3 Place the spinach leaves in a serving bowl. Toss the avocado in the lemon juice to prevent it browning, then add to the spinach with the roasted onions.

4 Pour the dressing over the salad and toss gently to combine. Sprinkle the polenta croutons on top or hand them round separately and serve immediately.

HEALTH BENEFITS

Avocados have been traditionally regarded as a high fat food that should be avoided. However, although they do contain high amounts of fat, it is beneficial, monounsaturated fat, and new research has revealed that regularly eating avocados can actually decrease the level of cholesterol in the body. Avocados also have a valuable mineral content and eating them can improve the condition of your skin and hair.

COOK'S TIP

If you can't find ready made polenta, you can make your own using instant polenta grains. Simply cook according to the package instructions, then pour into a tray and leave to cool and set.

Feta and Mint Potato Salad

FETA CHEESE, yogurt and fresh mint combine perfectly with warm new potatoes in this salad.

INGREDIENTS

1 1/4 pounds new potatoes
4 ounces feta cheese, crumbled

For the dressing
1 cup plain live yogurt
1/2 cup fresh mint leaves
2 tablespoons mayonnaise
salt and freshly ground black pepper
Serves 4

1 Steam the potatoes over a saucepan of boiling water for about 20 minutes until tender, then drain well and tip into a large bowl.

2 Meanwhile, make the dressing. Place the yogurt and mint in a food processor for a few minutes until the mint leaves are finely chopped. Transfer the dressing to a small bowl.

3 Stir in mayonnaise and season to taste. Spoon the dressing over the warm potatoes and scatter with feta cheese. Serve immediately.

COOK'S TIPS

New potatoes are simply young potatoes (any variety). They have not had time to convert their sugar fully into starch and have a crisp waxy texture and thin, undeveloped wispy skins. They are also excellent for boiling or pan-roasting.

HEALTH BENEFITS

Potatoes are often considered to be fattening, but it is usually the method of preparation that is to be blamed. Steaming adds no calories and preserves the vitamin C content.

Apple and Beet Salad with Red Leaves

BITTER LEAVES are complemented by sweet-flavored apples and beet in this summer salad.

INGREDIENTS

1/3 cup whole unblanched almonds
2 red apples, cored and diced
juice of 1/2 lemon
4 cups red salad leaves, such as lollo rosso, oak leaf and radicchio
7 ounces cooked beets in natural juice, sliced

For the dressing
2 tablespoons olive oil
1 tablespoon walnut oil
1 tablespoon red or white wine vinegar
salt and freshly ground black pepper
Serves 4

1 Toast the almonds in a dry frying pan for 2–3 minutes until golden brown, tossing frequently to color them evenly and prevent them burning.

2 Meanwhile, make the dressing. Put the olive and walnut oils, vinegar and seasoning in a bowl or screw-top jar. Stir or shake thoroughly to combine.

3 Toss the apples in lemon juice to prevent them browning, then place in a large bowl and add the salad leaves, beets and almonds. Pour over the dressing and toss gently.

HEALTH BENEFITS

Red fruits and vegetables have high levels of vitamins C and E and beta carotene.

Sesame Noodle Salad

TOASTED SESAME oil adds a nutty flavor to this Asian-style salad. Best served warm, it is substantial enough to serve as a main meal.

INGREDIENTS

9 ounces medium egg noodles

1 cup sugar snap peas or snow peas, sliced diagonally

2 carrots, cut into julienne strips

2 tomatoes, seeded and diced

2 tablespoons fresh cilantro, chopped

1 tablespoon sesame seeds

3 scallions, shredded

fresh cilantro, to garnish

For the dressing

2 teaspoons light soy sauce

2 tablespoons toasted sesame seed oil

1 tablespoon sunflower oil

1 1/2-inch piece fresh root ginger, finely grated

1 garlic clove, crushed

Serves 2–4

1 Place the noodles in a saucepan of lightly salted boiling water and bring back to a boil. Cook for 2 minutes, then add the sugar snap peas or snow peas and cook for a further 2 minutes. Drain and rinse under cold running water.

HEALTH BENEFITS

Garlic is highly antiseptic, particularly in its raw form, and, like ginger, can help to ward off colds and flu and stimulate circulation.

2 Meanwhile, make the dressing. Combine the soy sauce, sesame and sunflower oils, ginger and garlic in a screw-top jar or bowl. Shake or mix to combine thoroughly.

3 Place the noodles and the peas or snow peas in a bowl and add the carrots, tomatoes and cilantro. Pour the dressing over the top, and toss with your hands to combine. Sprinkle with the sesame seeds and top with the scallions and cilantro.

Japanese Salad

HIJIKI IS a mild-tasting seaweed and, combined with radishes, cucumber and beansprouts, it makes a delicate, refreshing salad.

INGREDIENTS

1/2 cup hijiki

1 1/4 cups radishes, sliced into very thin rounds

1 small cucumber, cut into thin sticks

1/2 cup beansprouts

For the dressing

1 tablespoon sunflower oil

1 tablespoon toasted sesame oil

1 teaspoon light soy sauce

2 tablespoons rice vinegar or 1 tablespoon wine vinegar

1 tablespoon mirin

Serves 4

1 Soak the hijiki in a bowl of cold water for 10–15 minutes until rehydrated. Drain, rinse under cold running water and drain again. It should almost triple in volume.

2 Place the hijiki in a saucepan of water. Bring to a boil, then reduce the heat and simmer for about 30 minutes or until tender.

3 Meanwhile, make the dressing. Place sunflower and sesame oils, soy sauce, vinegar and mirin in a bowl or screw-top jar. Stir or shake thoroughly to combine.

4 Arrange the hijiki in a shallow bowl or platter with the radishes, cucumber and beansprouts. Pour over the dressing and toss lightly.

HEALTH BENEFITS

Hijiki is treasured as one of nature's richest sources of minerals, the balance of which is said to counteract high blood pressure. The seaweed has a distinguished reputation in Japan for enhancing beauty and adding luster to hair.

Roasted Beets with Horseradish Dressing

FRESH BEETS are enjoying a well-deserved renaissance. Roasting gives them a delicious sweet flavor, which contrasts wonderfully with a sharp, tangy dressing.

INGREDIENTS

1 pound baby beets, preferably
   with leaves
1 tablespoon olive oil

For the dressing
2 tablespoons lemon juice
2 tablespoons mirin
8 tablespoons olive oil
2 tablespoons creamed horseradish
salt and freshly ground black pepper
Serves 4

1 Cook the beets in boiling salted water for 30 minutes. Drain, add the olive oil and toss gently. Preheat the oven to 400°F.

2 Place the beets on a baking sheet and roast for 40 minutes or until tender when pierced with a knife.

3 Meanwhile, make the dressing. Whisk together the lemon juice, mirin, olive oil and horseradish until smooth and creamy. Season.

4 Cut the beets in half, place in a bowl and add the dressing. Toss gently and serve immediately.

HEALTH BENEFITS

Beets have a reputation for containing cancer-fighting compounds and enhancing the immune system. They are a powerful blood-purifier and are rich in iron, vitamins C and A, and folates, which are essential for healthy cells.

COOK'S TIP

This salad is probably at its best served warm, but you can make it in advance, if you wish, and serve it at room temperature. Add the dressing to the beets just before serving.

SIDE DISHES

These delicious dishes make enticing and interesting
accompaniments to all sorts of main courses.

Sautéed Potatoes

THESE ROSEMARY-SCENTED, crisp golden potatoes are a favorite in French households.

INGREDIENTS
3 pounds baking potatoes
4–6 tablespoons oil or clarified butter
2 or 3 sprigs of fresh rosemary, leaves removed and chopped
salt and freshly ground black pepper
Serves 6

1 Peel the potatoes and cut them into 1-inch pieces. Place them in a bowl, cover with cold water and let soak for 10–15 minutes. Drain the potatoes, rinse and drain again, then dry thoroughly in a dish towel.

2 Heat about 4 tablespoons of the oil or butter over medium-high heat until very hot but not smoking. Add the potatoes and cook for 2 minutes without stirring, so that they seal completely and brown on one side.

3 Shake the pan and toss the potatoes to brown on another side. Season with salt and pepper.

4 Add a little more oil or butter and continue cooking the potatoes over medium-low to low heat, stirring and shaking the pan frequently, for 20–25 minutes, until tender when pierced with a knife. About 5 minutes before the end of cooking, sprinkle the potatoes with the chopped rosemary.

Straw Potato Cake

THESE FRIED grated potatoes resemble straw, hence the name of the dish. You could make several small cakes instead of a large one, if you prefer—simply adjust the cooking time accordingly.

INGREDIENTS
1 pound baking potatoes
1 1/2 tablespoons melted butter
1 tablespoon vegetable oil, plus extra if needed
salt and freshly ground black pepper
Serves 4

1 Peel the potatoes and grate them coarsely, then immediately toss them with melted butter and season with salt and pepper.

2 Heat the oil in a large nonstick frying pan. Add the potato mixture and press down to form an even layer that covers the pan. Cook over medium heat for 7–10 minutes, until the bottom is well browned.

3 Loosen the potato cake by shaking the pan or running a thin spatula under it.

4 To turn the potato cake over, invert a large baking sheet over the frying pan and, holding it tightly against the pan, turn them both over together. Lift off the frying pan, return it to the heat and add a little oil if it looks dry. Slide the potato cake into the frying pan and continue cooking until crisp and browned on both sides. Serve hot.

Puffy Creamed Potatoes

THIS ACCOMPANIMENT consists of creamed potatoes incorporated into mini Yorkshire puddings. Serve them with a vegetable casserole or, for a meal on its own, serve two or three per person and accompany with salads.

INGREDIENTS

10 ounces potatoes
creamy milk and butter for mashing
1 teaspoon fresh parsley, chopped
1 teaspoon fresh tarragon, chopped
2/3 cup all-purpose flour
1 egg
about 1/2 cup milk
oil or sunflower margarine, for baking
salt and freshly ground black pepper

Makes 6

1 Boil the potatoes until tender and mash with a little milk and butter. Stir in the chopped parsley and tarragon and season with salt and pepper. Preheat the oven to 400°F.

2 Process the flour, egg, milk and a pinch of salt in a food processor or a blender to make a smooth, thick batter.

3 Place about 1/2 teaspoon oil or a small pat of sunflower margarine in the bottom of each of six ramekins and place in the oven on a baking sheet for 2–3 minutes, until the oil is very hot.

4 Working quickly, pour a small amount of batter (about 4 teaspoons) into each ramekin. Add a heaped tablespoon of mashed potatoes on top and then pour an equal amount of the remaining batter into each dish. Place the ramekins in the oven and bake for 15–20 minutes, until the puddings are puffy and golden brown.

5 Using a thin spatula, carefully ease the puddings out of the ramekins and arrange on a large, warm serving dish. Serve at once.

Potatoes Dauphinois

RICH, CREAMY and satisfying, this is a comforting dish to serve when it's cold outside.

INGREDIENTS

1 1/2 pounds potatoes, peeled and
   thinly sliced
1 garlic clove
2 tablespoons (1/4 stick) butter
1 1/4 cups light cream
1/4 cup milk
salt and white pepper

Serves 4

1 | Preheat the oven to 300°F. Place the potato slices in a bowl of cold water to remove the excess starch. Drain the slices thoroughly and pat dry with paper towels.

2 Cut the garlic in half and rub the cut side around the inside of a wide, shallow ovenproof dish. Butter the dish generously. Blend the cream and milk in a bowl.

3 Cover the bottom of the dish with a layer of potatoes. Dot a little butter over the potato layer, season with salt and pepper and then pour a little of the cream and milk mixture over the potatoes.

4 Continue making layers until all the ingredients have been used up, ending with a layer of cream. Bake for about 1 1/4 hours. Do not turn the potatoes or they may break up. If the dish browns too quickly, cover with a lid or with a piece of foil. The potatoes are ready when they are very soft and the top is golden brown.

Spicy Potatoes and Cauliflower

THIS DISH, a variant of the traditional Indian aloo gobhi, is simplicity itself to make and can be eaten as a main course with Indian breads or rice, a raita such as cucumber and yogurt, and a fresh mint relish.

INGREDIENTS

8 ounces potatoes

5 tablespoons peanut oil

1 teaspoon ground cumin

1 teaspoon ground coriander

1/4 teaspoon ground turmeric

1/4 teaspoon cayenne pepper

1 fresh green chile, seeded and finely
   chopped

1 medium cauliflower, broken up into small
   florets

1 teaspoon cumin seeds

2 garlic cloves, cut into shreds

1–2 tablespoons cilantro, finely chopped

salt

Serves 2

1 Cook the potatoes in their skins in boiling salted water for about 20 minutes, until just tender. Drain and let cool. When cool enough to handle, peel and cut into 1-inch cubes.

2 Heat 3 tablespoons of the oil in a frying pan or wok. When hot, add the ground cumin, coriander, turmeric, cayenne pepper and chile. Let the spices sizzle for a few seconds.

3 Add the cauliflower and about 1/4 cup water. Cook over medium heat, stirring constantly, for 6–8 minutes. Add the potatoes and stir-fry for 2–3 minutes. Season with salt, then remove from the heat.

4 Heat the remaining oil in a small frying pan. When hot, add the cumin seeds and garlic and cook until lightly browned. Pour the mixture over the vegetables. Sprinkle with the chopped cilantro and serve at once.

Garlic Mashed Potatoes

THESE CREAMY mashed potatoes have a wonderful aroma. Although two bulbs seems like a lot of garlic, the flavor is sweet and subtle when garlic is cooked in this way.

INGREDIENTS

2 garlic bulbs, separated into cloves, unpeeled
8 tablespoons (1 stick) unsalted butter
3 pounds baking potatoes
$^1/_2$–$^3/_4$ cup milk
salt and white pepper
Serves 6–8

1 Bring a small saucepan of water to a boil over high heat. Add the garlic cloves and boil for 2 minutes, then drain and peel.

2 In a heavy frying pan, melt half of the butter over low heat. Add the blanched garlic cloves, then cover and cook gently for 20–25 minutes, until very tender and just golden, shaking the pan and stirring occasionally. Do not allow the garlic to scorch or brown.

3 Remove the pan from the heat and cool slightly. Spoon the garlic and any butter from the pan into a blender or food processor fitted with a metal blade and process until smooth. Transfer to a small bowl, press plastic wrap onto the surface to prevent a skin from forming and set aside.

4 Peel and quarter the potatoes, place in a large saucepan and add enough cold water to just cover them. Salt the water generously and bring to a boil over high heat.

5 Cook the potatoes until tender, then drain and work through a food mill or press through a sieve back into the saucepan. Return the pan to medium heat and, using a wooden spoon, stir the potatoes for 1–2 minutes to dry them out completely. Remove from the heat.

6 Warm the milk over medium-high heat until bubbles form around the edge. Gradually beat the milk, remaining butter and reserved garlic puree into the potatoes, then season with salt, if needed, and white pepper.

Roasted Potatoes, Peppers and Shallots

THIS POPULAR dish from the Deep South is often served in elegant New Orleans restaurants.

INGREDIENTS

1¼ pounds waxy potatoes

12 shallots

2 yellow bell peppers

olive oil

2 sprigs of fresh rosemary

salt and freshly ground black pepper

Serves 4

1 Preheat the oven to 400°F. Wash the potatoes and blanch for 5 minutes in boiling water. Drain and allow to cool slightly.

2 When the potatoes are cool enough to handle, peel them and halve lengthwise. Peel the shallots, allowing them to fall into their natural segments. Cut each pepper lengthwise into 8 strips, discarding the seeds and pith.

3 Oil a shallow ovenproof dish. Arrange potatoes and peppers in alternating rows. Stud with shallots.

4 Cut the rosemary sprigs into 2-inch lengths and tuck among the vegetables. Season the dish generously with olive oil, salt and pepper and bake, uncovered, for 30–40 minutes, until all are tender.

COOK'S TIP

Waxy potatoes are used here because they retain moisture and don't fall apart. You can substitute red or green bell peppers, or a combination, for the yellow ones.

Baked Sweet Potatoes

GIVE SWEET potatoes a Cajun flavor with salt, three different kinds of pepper and lavish quantities of butter. Serve half a potato per person as an accompaniment, or a whole one as a supper dish with a green salad peppered with watercress.

INGREDIENTS

3 pink-skinned sweet potatoes, about 1 pound each
6 tablespoons (³/4 stick) butter, sliced
black, white and cayenne peppers
salt

Serves 3–6

Wash the potatoes and leave the skins wet. Rub salt into the skins, prick them all over with a fork and place on the middle shelf of the oven. Turn on the oven to 400°F and bake for about an hour, until the flesh yields and feels soft when pressed.

COOK'S TIP

Sweet potatoes cook more quickly than ordinary ones, so there is no need to preheat the oven.

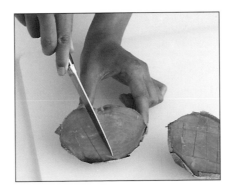

2 The potatoes can either be served in halves or whole. For halves, split each one lengthwise and make close crisscross cuts in the flesh of each half. Then spread with slices of butter and work the butter and seasonings roughly into the cuts with a knife point.

3 Alternatively, make an incision along the length of each potato if they are to be served whole. Open them slightly and put in butter slices along the length, seasoning with the peppers and a pinch of salt.

Thai Fragrant Rice

THIS LOVELY, soft, fluffy rice dish, perfumed with fresh lemongrass, is a classic Thai accompaniment to red and green curries.

INGREDIENTS

1 stalk of lemongrass
2 limes
1 cup brown basmati rice
1 tablespoon olive oil
1 onion, chopped
1-inch piece of fresh ginger root, peeled and
    finely chopped
1 1/2 teaspoons coriander seeds
1 1/2 teaspoons cumin seeds
3 cups vegetable stock
1/4 cup cilantro, chopped
lime wedges, to serve

Serves 4

1 Finely chop the lemongrass using a sharp knife.

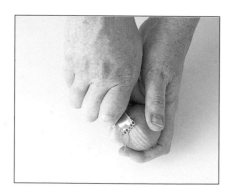

2 Remove the zest from the limes using a zester or fine grater. Avoid removing the pith with the zest.

3 Rinse the rice in plenty of cold water until the water runs clear. Drain through a sieve.

4 Heat the oil in a large pan and add the onion, ginger, spices, lemongrass and lime zest and cook gently for 2–3 minutes.

COOK'S TIP

Other varieties of rice, such as white basmati or long-grain, can be used for this dish, but you will need to adjust the cooking times accordingly.

5 Add the rice and cook for another minute, then add the stock and bring to a boil. Reduce the heat to very low and cover the pan. Cook gently for 30 minutes, then check the rice. If it is still crunchy, cover the pan again and cook for 3–5 minutes more. Remove from the heat.

6 Stir in the chopped cilantro, fluff up the rice, cover and let sit for 10 minutes. Serve with lime wedges.

Rice with Seeds and Spices

A CHANGE from plain rice and a colorful accompaniment to spicy curries. Basmati rice gives the best texture and flavor, but you can use ordinary long-grain rice, if you prefer. Remember to alter the cooking time accordingly.

INGREDIENTS

1 teaspoon sunflower oil
1/2 teaspoon ground turmeric
6 cardamom pods, lightly crushed
1 teaspoon coriander seeds, lightly crushed
1 garlic clove, crushed
1 cup basmati rice
1 2/3 cups vegetable stock
1/2 cup plain yogurt
1 tablespoon sunflower seeds, toasted
1 tablespoon sesame seeds, toasted
salt and freshly ground black pepper
cilantro leaves, to garnish

Serves 4

1 Heat the oil in a nonstick frying pan and sauté the spices and garlic for about 1 minute, stirring all the time.

COOK'S TIP

Seeds are particularly rich in minerals, so they are a good addition to all kinds of dishes. Light toasting will improve their flavor.

2 Add the basmati rice and vegetable stock, bring to a boil, then cover and simmer for 15 minutes, or until just tender. Turn down the heat slightly.

3 Stir in the plain yogurt and the toasted sunflower and sesame seeds. Season the rice with salt and pepper and serve hot, garnished with cilantro leaves.

Red Fried Rice

THIS VIBRANT rice dish owes its appeal as much to the bright colors of red onion, red bell pepper and tomatoes as it does to their flavors.

INGREDIENTS

3/4 cup basmati rice

2 tablespoons peanut oil

1 small red onion, chopped

1 red bell pepper, seeded and chopped

8 ounces cherry tomatoes, halved

2 eggs, beaten

salt and freshly ground black pepper

Serves 2

1 Wash the rice several times under cold running water to remove the starch. Drain well. Bring a large pan of water to a boil. Add the rice and cook for 10–12 minutes.

2 Meanwhile, heat the oil in a wok until very hot. Add the onion and pepper and stir-fry for 2–3 minutes. Add the cherry tomatoes and continue stir-frying for 2 minutes more.

3 Pour in the beaten eggs all at once. Cook for 30 seconds without stirring, then stir to break up the egg as it sets.

4 Drain the cooked rice thoroughly. Add to the wok and toss it with the vegetable and egg mixture, over the heat for 3 minutes. Season with salt and pepper and serve immediately.

Herbed Rice Pilaf

A QUICK and easy dish to make, this simple pilaf is delicious to eat. Serve with a selection of fresh seasonal vegetables, such as broccoli florets and carrots.

INGREDIENTS

8 ounces mixed brown basmati and wild rice

1 tablespoon olive oil

1 onion, chopped

1 garlic clove, crushed

1 teaspoon ground cumin

1 teaspoon ground turmeric

1/2 cup golden raisins

3 cups vegetable stock

2–3 tablespoons fresh mixed herbs, chopped

salt and freshly ground black pepper

sprigs of fresh herbs and 1/4 cup pistachio nuts, chopped, to garnish

Serves 4

1 Wash the rice under cold running water, then drain well. Heat the oil, add the onion and garlic and cook gently for 5 minutes, stirring the mixture occasionally.

2 Add the spices and rice and cook gently for 1 minute, stirring. Stir in the raisins and stock, bring to a boil, cover and simmer gently for 20–25 minutes, stirring occasionally.

3 Stir in the chopped mixed herbs and season with salt and pepper. Spoon the pilaf into a warmed serving dish and garnish with fresh herb sprigs and a sprinkling of chopped pistachio nuts. Serve immediately.

Cheese-Topped Roast Baby Vegetables

THIS IS a simple way to bring out the flavor of baby vegetables.

INGREDIENTS

2 1/4 pounds mixed baby vegetables, such as eggplant, onions or shallots, zucchini, corn, button mushrooms

1 red bell pepper, seeded and cut into large chunks

1–2 garlic cloves, finely chopped

1–2 tablespoons olive oil

2 tablespoons fresh mixed herbs, chopped

8 ounces cherry tomatoes

4 ounces mozzarella cheese, coarsely grated

salt and freshly ground black pepper

black olives, to garnish (optional)

Serves 6

1 Preheat the oven to 425°F. Cut the eggplant and onions or shallots in half lengthwise.

2 Place the baby vegetables, pepper and garlic in a shallow ovenproof dish. Season with salt and pepper, drizzle with the oil and toss the vegetables to coat. Bake for 20 minutes, until tinged brown at the edges, stirring once.

3 Stir in the herbs, scatter the tomatoes over the top and sprinkle with the mozzarella cheese. Bake for another 5–10 minutes, until the cheese has melted and is bubbling. Serve at once, garnished with black olives, if you like.

Chinese Brussels Sprouts

IF YOU are bored with plain boiled Brussels sprouts, try pepping them up Chinese-style with this unusual stir-fried method.

INGREDIENTS

1 pound Brussels sprouts
1 teaspoon sesame or sunflower oil
2 scallions, sliced
1/2 teaspoon Chinese five-spice powder
1 tablespoon light soy sauce
Serves 4

1 Trim the Brussels sprouts, then shred them finely using a large, sharp knife or a food processor.

2 Heat the oil and add the sprouts and scallions. Cook for 2 minutes, without allowing the mixture to brown. Add the five-spice powder and soy sauce, then cook, stirring, for 2–3 minutes, until just tender.

COOK'S TIP

Serve the stir-fried brussels sprouts hot, as part of a selection of Chinese dishes. Chinese meals are made up of lots of small dishes, served together.

Festive Brussels Sprouts

THIS RECIPE originated in France, where it is a popular side dish at Christmas-time.

INGREDIENTS

8 ounces chestnuts

1/2 cup milk

1 1/4 pounds (4 cups) small, tender Brussels sprouts

2 tablespoons (1/4 stick) butter

1 shallot, finely chopped

2–3 tablespoons dry white wine or water

Serves 4–6

1 Using a small, sharp knife, score a cross in the bottom of each chestnut. Take care to hold the chestnut steady so the knife does not slip. Bring a saucepan of water to a boil over medium-high heat, then drop in the chestnuts and boil for 6–8 minutes. Remove pan from the heat.

2 Using a slotted spoon, remove a few chestnuts from the pan, leaving the others immersed in the water until ready to peel. Before the chestnuts cool, remove the outer shell with a knife and then carefully peel off the inner skin.

3 Rinse the pan, return the peeled chestnuts to it and add the milk. Add enough water to completely cover the chestnuts. Simmer over medium heat for 12–15 minutes, until the chestnuts are just tender. Drain and set aside.

4 Remove any wilted or yellow leaves from the Brussels sprouts. Trim the root ends but leave intact, or the leaves will separate. Using a small knife, score a cross in the bottom of each sprout so they cook evenly.

5 In a large, heavy frying pan, melt the butter over medium heat. Stir in the chopped shallot and cook for 1–2 minutes, until just softened, then add the Brussels sprouts and wine or water. Cook, covered, over medium heat for 6 8 minutes, shaking the pan and stirring occasionally, adding a little more water if necessary.

6 Add the poached chestnuts and toss gently to combine, then cover and cook for 3–5 minutes more, until the chestnuts and Brussels sprouts are tender.

Szechuan Eggplant

THIS MEDIUM-HOT dish is also
known as "fish fragrant eggplant"
in China, because the eggplant is
cooked with flavorings that are
often used with fish. Serve hot with
rice or noodles.

INGREDIENTS

2 small eggplants

1 teaspoon salt

3 dried red chiles

peanut oil, for deep-frying

3–4 garlic cloves, finely chopped

1/2-inch piece of fresh ginger root,
    finely chopped

4 scallions, cut into 1-inch lengths (white
    and green parts separated)

1 tablespoon Chinese rice wine or medium-
    dry sherry

1 tablespoon light soy sauce

1 teaspoon sugar

1/4 teaspoon ground roasted Szechuan
    peppercorns

1 tablespoon Chinese rice vinegar

1 teaspoon sesame oil

Serves 4

1 Trim the eggplant and cut into strips
about 1 1/2 inches wide and 3 inches
long. Place the eggplant strips in a
colander and sprinkle with the salt. Set
aside for 30 minutes, then rinse
thoroughly under cold running water.
Pat dry with paper towels.

2 Meanwhile, soak the chiles in
warm water for 15 minutes.
Drain, then cut each chile into four
pieces, discarding the seeds.

3 Half-fill a wok with oil and heat to
350°F. Deep-fry the eggplant until
golden brown. Drain on paper towels.
Pour off most of the oil from the wok.
Reheat the oil and add the garlic,
ginger and white scallion parts.

4 Stir-fry for 30 seconds. Add the
eggplant and toss, then add the
rice wine or sherry, soy sauce, sugar,
ground peppercorns and rice vinegar.
Stir-fry for 1–2 minutes. Sprinkle with
the sesame oil and green scallion parts
and serve immediately.

Sweet and Sour Onions

COOKED IN this way, sweet pearl onions make an unusual and tasty side dish. This simple and tasty recipe originated in the Provence region of France.

INGREDIENTS

1 pound pearl onions, peeled

1/4 cup wine vinegar

3 tablespoons olive oil

3 tablespoons sugar

3 tablespoons tomato paste

1 bay leaf

2 sprigs of fresh parsley

1/2 cup raisins

salt and freshly ground black pepper

Serves 6

1 Put all the ingredients in a saucepan with 1 1/4 cups water. Bring to a boil and simmer gently, uncovered, for 45 minutes, or until the onions are tender and most of the liquid has evaporated. Do not stir the mixture during cooking or the onions will break up.

2 Remove the bay leaf and parsley. Check the seasoning and add salt and pepper if necessary. Transfer the mixture to a serving dish and serve at room temperature.

Spinach with Raisins and Pine Nuts

RAISINS AND pine nuts are perfect partners. Here, tossed with wilted spinach and croutons, their contrasting textures and bursts of flavor make a delicious main-dish accompaniment.

INGREDIENTS

1/3 cup raisins

1 thick slice crusty white bread

3 tablespoons olive oil

1/3 cup pine nuts

1 1/4 pounds young spinach, stalks removed

2 garlic cloves, crushed

salt and freshly ground black pepper

Serves 4

1 Put the raisins in a small bowl with boiling water and let soak for 10 minutes. Drain.

2 Cut the bread into cubes and discard the crusts. Heat 2 tablespoons of the oil and sauté the bread until golden. Drain.

3 Heat the remaining oil in the pan. Sauté the pine nuts until they are beginning to color. Add the spinach and garlic and cook quickly, turning the spinach until it has just wilted.

4 Toss in the raisins and season with salt and pepper. Transfer to a warmed serving dish. Sprinkle with croutons and serve hot.

VARIATION

Use Swiss chard or beet greens instead of the spinach, and cook them a little longer.

Hot Parsnip Fritters on Baby Spinach

DEEP-FRYING BRINGS out the luscious sweetness of parsnips, and their flavor is perfectly complemented by walnut-dressed baby spinach leaves.

INGREDIENTS

2 large parsnips

1 cup all-purpose flour

1 egg, separated

1/2 cup milk

4 ounces baby spinach leaves, washed and dried

2 tablespoons olive oil

1 tablespoon walnut oil

1 tablespoon sherry vinegar

oil for deep-frying

1 tablespoon coarsely chopped walnuts

salt, freshly ground black pepper, and cayenne pepper

Serves 4

1 Peel the parsnips, bring to a boil in a pan of salted water and simmer for 10–15 minutes, until tender but not at all mushy. Drain, cool and cut diagonally into slices about 2 inches long and 1/4–1/2 inch thick.

2 Put the flour in a bowl and make a well in the center. Put the egg yolk in the well and mix in with a fork. Add the milk while continuing to mix in the flour. Season with salt and black and cayenne peppers, and beat with a whisk until the batter is smooth.

3 Put the spinach leaves in a bowl. Mix the oils and vinegar for the walnut dressing. Season with salt and pepper to taste.

4 When you are ready to serve, beat the egg white to soft peaks, fold in a little of the yolk batter, then fold the white into the batter. Heat the oil for frying.

5 Shake the dressing vigorously and toss with the salad. Arrange the salad on four plates and sprinkle it with the chopped walnuts.

6 Dip the parsnip slices in batter and fry until puffy and golden. Drain on paper towels and keep warm. Arrange the fritters on top of the mixed salad.

Parsnip and Chestnut Croquettes

THE DISTINCTIVE sweet, nutty taste of chestnuts blends perfectly with the sweet but earthy flavor of parsnips. Fresh chestnuts need to be peeled, but canned unsweetened chestnuts are nearly as good for this recipe.

INGREDIENTS

*1 pound parsnips, cut roughly into
    small pieces*
*4 ounces shelled fresh or canned
    whole chestnuts*
2 tablespoons butter
1 garlic clove, crushed
1 tablespoon cilantro, chopped
1 egg, beaten
1 1/2–2 ounces fresh white bread crumbs
vegetable oil, for frying
salt and freshly ground black pepper
sprig of cilantro, to garnish
Makes 10–12

1 Place the parsnips in a saucepan with enough water to cover. Bring to a boil, cover and simmer for 15–20 minutes.

2 Place the chestnuts in a pan of water, bring to a boil and simmer for 8–10 minutes. Drain, place in a bowl and mash roughly into a pulp using a fork.

3 Melt the butter in a saucepan and cook the garlic for 30 seconds. Drain the parsnips and mash with the garlic butter. Stir in the chestnuts and chopped cilantro. Season with salt and pepper.

4 Take about 1 tablespoon of the mixture at a time and form into small croquettes, about 3 inches long. Dip each croquette into the beaten egg and then roll in the bread crumbs.

5 Heat a little oil in a frying pan and fry each of the croquettes for 3–4 minutes, until crisp and golden, turning frequently so they brown evenly.

6 Drain the croquettes on sheets of paper towel, wiping away any excess oil, and serve at once, garnished with sprigs of cilantro.

Balti Baby Vegetables

THERE IS a wide and wonderful selection of baby vegetables available in supermarkets these days, and this simple recipe does full justice to their delicate flavor and attractive appearance. Serve as part of a main meal or even as a light appetizer.

INGREDIENTS

10 new potatoes, halved

12–14 baby carrots

12–14 baby zucchini

2 tablespoons corn oil

15 pearl onions

2 tablespoons chili sauce

1 teaspoon garlic pulp

1 teaspoon ginger pulp

1 teaspoon salt

14-ounce can chickpeas, drained

10 cherry tomatoes

1 teaspoon crushed red pepper and
   2 tablespoons sesame seeds, to garnish

Serves 4–6

1 Bring a medium pan of salted water to a boil and add the new potatoes and baby carrots. After 12–15 minutes, add the zucchini and boil for another 5 minutes, or until all the vegetables are just tender.

2 Remove from the heat, drain the vegetables well and set aside.

3 Heat the oil in a deep, round-bottomed frying pan or wok and add the onions. Cook until the onions turn golden brown. Lower the heat and add the chili sauce, garlic, ginger and salt, taking care not to burn the spice mixture.

4 Add the chickpeas and stir-fry over medium heat until the moisture has been absorbed.

5 Add the cooked vegetables and cherry tomatoes and continue cooking over medium heat, stirring with a slotted spoon, for about 2 minutes.

6 Garnish with crushed red pepper and sesame seeds and serve immediately.

VARIATION

By varying the vegetables chosen and experimenting with different combinations, this recipe can form the basis for a variety of delicious vegetable accompaniments. Try different vegetables, such as baby corn, green beans, snow peas, okra, sugar snap peas and cauliflower florets.

Fried Noodles, Bean Sprouts and Asparagus

SOFT FRIED noodles contrast beautifully with crisp bean sprouts and asparagus in this superquick recipe.

INGREDIENTS

4 ounces dried Chinese egg noodles

4 tablespoons vegetable oil

1 small onion, chopped

1-inch piece of fresh ginger root, peeled and grated

2 garlic cloves, crushed

6 ounces young asparagus spears, trimmed

4 ounces bean sprouts

4 scallions, sliced

3 tablespoons soy sauce

salt and freshly ground black pepper

Serves 2

1 Bring a pan of salted water to a boil. Add the noodles and cook for 2–3 minutes, until just tender. Drain and toss with 2 tablespoons of the oil.

2 Heat the remaining oil in a wok or frying pan until very hot. Add the onion, ginger and garlic and stir-fry for 2–3 minutes. Add the asparagus and then stir-fry for 2–3 minutes more.

3 Add the egg noodles and bean sprouts and stir-fry for 2 minutes. Toss the mixture gently.

4 Stir in the scallions and soy sauce. Season with salt and pepper, adding salt sparingly, as the soy sauce will probably supply enough salt in itself. Stir-fry the mixture for 1 minute, then serve immediately.

Deep-Fried Root Vegetables with Spiced Salt

ALL KINDS of root vegetables may be finely sliced and deep-fried to make chips. Serve as an accompaniment to an Asian-style meal or simply by themselves as a snack.

INGREDIENTS

1 carrot
2 parsnips
2 raw beets
1 sweet potato
peanut oil, for deep-frying
1/4 teaspoon cayenne pepper
1 teaspoon sea salt flakes

Serves 4–6

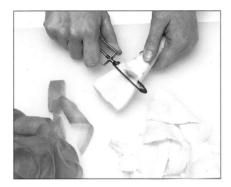

1 Peel all the vegetables, then slice the carrot and parsnips into long, thin ribbons and the beets and sweet potato into thin rounds. Pat dry all the vegetables on paper towels.

COOK'S TIP

To save time, you can slice the vegetables using a mandoline or a blender or food processor with a thin slicing disk attachment.

2 Half-fill a wok with oil and heat to 350°F. Add the vegetable slices in batches and deep-fry for 2–3 minutes, until golden and crisp. Fry only a few slices at a time, or the oil will cool down and the slices will not crisp. Remove and drain on paper towels.

3 Place the cayenne pepper and sea salt in a mortar and grind together to a coarse powder.

4 Pile up the vegetable chips on a serving plate and sprinkle with the spiced salt.

Split Pea and Shallot Mash

GREATLY UNDERRATED and underused, split peas can make a fantastic puree. When this is enlivened with herbs and spices, the puree makes an excellent alternative to mashed potatoes, and is particularly good with winter pies and nut roasts. It can also be served with warmed pita bread, accompanied by diced tomatoes and a splash of olive oil.

INGREDIENTS

1 cup yellow split peas

1 bay leaf

8 sage leaves, roughly chopped

1 tablespoon olive oil

3 shallots, finely chopped

heaping 1 teaspoon cumin seeds

1 large garlic clove, chopped

4 tablespoons (1/2 stick) butter, softened

salt and freshly ground black pepper

Serves 4–6

1 Place the split peas in a bowl and cover with cold water. Leave to soak overnight, then rinse and drain.

2 Place the peas in a saucepan, cover with fresh cold water and bring to a boil. Skim off any foam that rises to the surface, then reduce heat. Add bay leaf and sage, simmer for 30–40 minutes until the peas are tender. Add more water during cooking, if necessary.

3 Meanwhile, heat the oil in a frying pan and cook the shallots, cumin seeds and garlic for 3 minutes or until the shallots soften, stirring occasionally. Add the mixture to the split peas while they are still cooking.

4 Drain the split peas, reserving the cooking water. Remove the bay leaf, then place the split peas in a food processor or blender with the butter and season well.

5 Add 7 tablespoons of the reserved cooking water and blend until the mixture forms a coarse puree. Add more water if the mash seems to be too dry. Adjust seasoning and serve warm.

HEALTH BENEFITS

Split peas, like other pulses, are an excellent source of protein, fiber, minerals and B vitamins. They are particularly good for diabetics as they can help to control blood sugar levels.

Root Vegetable Gratin with Indian Spices

SUBTLY SPICED with curry powder, turmeric, coriander and mild chili powder, this rich gratin is substantial enough to serve on its own for lunch or supper. It also makes a good accompaniment to a vegetable or bean curry.

INGREDIENTS

2 large potatoes, total weight about 1 pound

2 sweet potatoes, total weight about 10 ounces

6 ounces celery root

3 shallots, chopped

2/3 cup light cream

2/3 cup low-fat milk

1 tablespoon unsalted butter

1 teaspoon curry powder

1 teaspoon ground turmeric

1/2 teaspoon ground coriander

1 teaspoon mild chili powder

salt and freshly ground black pepper

fresh Italian parsley, chopped, to garnish

Serves 4

1 Thinly slice the potatoes, sweet potatoes and celery root, using a sharp knife or the slicing attachment on a food processor. Immediately place the vegetables in a bowl of cold water to prevent them discoloring.

COOK'S TIP

The cream adds richness to this gratin; use low-fat milk, if you prefer.

2 Preheat the oven to 350°F. Heat half the butter in a heavy-based saucepan, add the curry powder, turmeric, coriander and half the chili powder. Cook for 2 minutes, then leave to cool slightly. Drain the vegetables, then pat dry with paper towels. Place in a bowl, add the spice mixture and the shallots, and mix well.

HEALTH BENEFITS

This gratin contains ground spices, which boost a sluggish digestion and have a beneficial effect on the circulation.

3 Arrange the vegetables in a baking dish, seasoning between the layers. Mix together the cream and milk, pour the mixture over the vegetables, then sprinkle the remaining chili powder on top.

4 Cover with waxed paper and bake for about 45 minutes. Remove the waxed paper, dot with remaining butter and bake for 50 minutes more until the top is golden. Serve garnished with chopped fresh parsley.

Vegetables Provençal

THE FLAVORS of the Mediterranean shine through in this delicious side dish.

INGREDIENTS

1 onion, sliced
2 leeks, sliced
2 garlic cloves, crushed
1 red bell pepper, seeded and sliced
1 green bell pepper, seeded and sliced
1 yellow bell pepper, seeded and sliced
12 ounces zucchini, sliced
8 ounces mushrooms, sliced
14-ounce can tomatoes, chopped
2 tablespoons ruby port
2 tablespoons tomato paste
1 tablespoon ketchup
14-ounce can chickpeas
1 cup pitted black olives
3 tablespoons fresh mixed herbs, chopped
salt and freshly ground black pepper
fresh mixed herbs, chopped, to garnish

Serves 6

1 Put the onion, leeks, garlic, peppers, zucchini and mushrooms in a large saucepan.

2 Add the tomatoes, port, tomato paste and ketchup and mix well.

3 Rinse and drain the chickpeas and add to the pan.

4 Cover, bring to a boil and simmer gently for 20–30 minutes, stirring occasionally, until the vegetables are cooked and tender but not mushy or overcooked.

5 Remove the lid and increase the heat slightly for the last 10 minutes of the cooking time, to thicken the sauce, if you like.

6 Stir in the olives and herbs and season with salt and pepper. Serve immediately, garnished with chopped mixed herbs.

COOK'S TIP

This dish is also delicious served cold. It can be prepared in advance for a picnic, stored in the refrigerator, and served with plain yogurt or a refreshing tzatziki.

Mixed Vegetables with Aromatic Seeds

A HEALTHY diet should include plenty of vegetables to provide fiber as well as vitamins and minerals. Here, spices transform everyday vegetables.

INGREDIENTS

1 1/2 pounds small new potatoes

1 small cauliflower

6 ounces green beans

4 ounces frozen peas

small piece of fresh ginger

2 tablespoons sunflower oil

2 tablespoons cumin seeds

2 tablespoons black mustard seeds

2 tablespoons sesame seeds

juice of 1 lemon

ground black pepper

cilantro, to garnish (optional)

Serves 4 – 6

1 Scrub the potatoes, cut the cauliflower into small florets, and trim and halve the green beans.

2 Cook the vegetables in separate pans of lightly salted boiling water until tender, allowing 15–20 minutes for the potatoes, 8– 10 minutes for the cauliflower and 4–5 minutes for the beans and peas. Drain thoroughly.

3 Using a small, sharp knife, peel and finely chop the fresh ginger.

4 Heat the oil. Add the ginger and seeds. Fry until they start to pop.

5 Add the vegetables and stir-fry for 2–3 minutes. Sprinkle over the lemon juice and season with pepper. Garnish with cilantro, if using.

COOK'S TIP

Other vegetables could be used, such as zucchini, leeks or broccoli. Buy whatever looks freshest and do not store vegetables for long periods as their vitamin content will deteriorate.

Root Vegetable Casserole

POTATOES, CARROTS and parsnips are all complex carbohydrates and make a hearty, sustaining vegetable dish, high in fiber and vitamin C. The carrots are also an excellent source of beta-carotene, which is converted to vitamin A in the body.

INGREDIENTS

8 ounces carrots

8 ounces parsnips

1 tablespoon sunflower oil

pat of butter

1 tablespoon raw or brown sugar

1 pound baby new potatoes, scrubbed

8 ounces small onions, peeled

1 2/3 cups vegetable stock

1 tablespoon Worcestershire sauce

1 tablespoon tomato paste

1 teaspoon whole-grain mustard

2 bay leaves

salt and ground black pepper

chopped parsley, to garnish

Serves 4 – 6

COOK'S TIP

Other vegetables could be added, such as leeks, mushrooms, sweet potato or celery. When they are in season, shelled chestnuts make a delicious addition.

1 Peel the carrots and parsnips, then cut into large chunks.

2 Heat the oil, butter and sugar in a pan. Stir until the sugar dissolves.

3 Add the potatoes, onions, carrots and parsnips. Sauté for 10 minutes, until the vegetables look glazed.

VARIATION

Use boiling onions or sweet pearl onions for this dish if they are available, or, if not, find the smallest onions you can.

4 Mix the vegetable stock, Worcestershire sauce, tomato paste and mustard in a pitcher. Stir well, then pour over the vegetables. Add the bay leaves. Bring to a boil, then lower the heat, cover and cook gently for about 30 minutes, until the vegetables are tender

5 Remove the bay leaves, add salt and pepper to taste and serve, sprinkled with the parsley.

Spicy Chickpeas

CHICKPEAS ARE used and cooked in a variety of ways all over the Indian subcontinent. Tamarind gives this spicy dish a deliciously sharp, tangy flavor.

INGREDIENTS

1 1/4 cups dried chickpeas
2 ounces tamarind pulp
1/2 cup boiling water
3 tablespoons corn oil
1/2 teaspoon cumin seeds
1 onion, finely chopped
2 garlic cloves, crushed
1-inch piece of fresh ginger root, peeled
    and grated
1 fresh green chile, finely chopped
1 teaspoon ground cumin
1 teaspoon ground coriander
1/4 teaspoon ground turmeric
1/2 teaspoon salt
8 ounces tomatoes, peeled and
    finely chopped
1/2 teaspoon garam masala
chopped fresh chiles and chopped onion,
    to garnish

Serves 4

1 Put the chickpeas in a large bowl and cover with plenty of cold water. Let soak overnight.

2 Drain the chickpeas and place in a large saucepan with double the volume of cold water. Bring to a boil and boil vigorously for 10 minutes. Skim off any scum. Cover and simmer for 1 1/2–2 hours, or until the chickpeas are soft. (If you choose to use canned chickpeas, omit this step.)

3 Meanwhile, break up the tamarind and soak in the boiling water for about 15 minutes. Rub the tamarind through a sieve into a bowl, discarding any seeds and fiber.

COOK'S TIP

To save time, make double the quantity of tamarind pulp and freeze in ice-cube trays. It will keep for up to 2 months.

4 Heat the oil in a large saucepan and sauté the cumin seeds for 2 minutes, until they splutter. Add the onion, garlic, ginger and chile and sauté for 5 minutes.

5 Add the cumin, coriander, turmeric and salt and sauté for 3–4 minutes. Add the tomatoes and tamarind pulp. Bring to a boil and simmer for 5 minutes.

6 Add the chickpeas and garam masala. Cover and simmer for about 45 minutes. Garnish with chopped chiles and onion.

Frijoles

A TRADITIONAL Mexican bean dish
that tastes great with tortillas and
vegetable chili.

INGREDIENTS

1¼–1½ cups dried red kidney, pinto
   or black beans, picked over and rinsed
2 onions, finely chopped
2 garlic cloves, chopped
1 bay leaf
1 or more small fresh green chiles
2 tablespoons corn oil
2 tomatoes, peeled, seeded and chopped
salt
sprigs of fresh bay leaves, to garnish

Serves 6–8

1 Put the dried beans in a pan and add
enough cold water to cover them by
1 inch.

2 Add half the onion, half the garlic,
the bay leaf and the chile or
chiles. Bring to a boil and boil
vigorously for about 10 minutes. Put
the beans and liquid into an
earthenware pot or large saucepan,
cover and cook over low heat for
30 minutes. Add boiling water if the
mixture starts to become dry.

3 When the beans begin to wrinkle,
add 1 tablespoon of the corn oil
and cook for another 30 minutes, or
until the beans are tender. Add salt to
taste and cook for 30 minutes more,
but try to avoid adding any more
water.

4 Remove the beans from the heat.
Heat the remaining oil in a small
frying pan and sauté the remaining
onion and garlic together until the
onion is soft. Add the tomatoes and
cook for a few minutes more.

5 Spoon 3 tablespoons of the beans
out of the pot or pan and add
them to the tomato mixture. Mash to a
paste. Stir into the beans to thicken the
liquid. Cook for just long enough to
heat through, if necessary. Serve the
beans in small bowls and garnish with
fresh bay leaves.

Peas with Pearl Onions and Cream

IDEALLY, USE fresh peas and fresh pearl onions. Frozen peas are an acceptable substitute if fresh ones aren't available, but frozen onions tend to be insipid and are not worth using. Alternatively, use the white parts of scallions.

INGREDIENTS

6 ounces pearl onions

1 tablespoon (^{1}/8 stick) butter

2 pounds fresh peas (about
   12 ounces shelled or frozen)

^{2}/3 cup heavy cream

2 tablespoons all-purpose flour

2 teaspoons fresh parsley, chopped

1–2 tablespoons lemon juice (optional)

salt and freshly ground black pepper

Serves 4

1 Peel the onions and halve them if necessary. Melt the butter in a flameproof casserole and cook the onions for 5 6 minutes over moderate heat, until they begin to be flecked with brown on the surface.

2 Add the peas and stir-fry for a few minutes. Add ^{1}/2 cup water and bring to a boil. Partially cover and simmer for about 10 minutes, until the peas and onions are tender. There should be a thin layer of water on the bottom of the pan—add a little more water if necessary or, if there is too much liquid, remove the lid and increase the heat until the liquid is reduced.

3 Using a small whisk, blend the cream with the flour. Remove the pan from the heat and stir in the combined cream and flour mixture and the chopped parsley. Season with salt and pepper.

4 Cook the mixture over gentle heat for 3–4 minutes, until the sauce is thick. Taste and adjust the seasoning; add a little lemon juice to sharpen, if desired.

Red Cabbage in Port and Red Wine

A SWEET and sour, spicy red cabbage dish, with the added crunch of pears and walnuts. Even non-cabbage eaters will come back for more!

INGREDIENTS

1 tablespoon walnut oil
1 onion, sliced
2 whole star anise
1 teaspoon ground cinnamon
pinch of ground cloves
1 pound red cabbage, finely shredded
2 tablespoons dark brown sugar
3 tablespoons red wine vinegar
1 1/4 cups red wine
2/3 cup port
2 pears, cut into 1/2-inch cubes
1/2 cup raisins
1/2 cup walnut halves
salt and freshly ground black pepper
Serves 6

1 Heat the oil in a large pan. Add the onion and cook gently for about 5 minutes, until softened.

COOK'S TIP

You can braise this dish in a low oven for up to 1 1/2 hours. Check occasionally and stir. Remove when tender and add the walnut halves last.

2 Add the star anise, cinnamon, cloves and cabbage and cook for about 3 minutes more.

3 Stir in the brown sugar, vinegar, red wine and port. Cover the pan; simmer gently for 10 minutes, stirring occasionally.

4 Stir in the cubed pears and raisins and cook for another 10 minutes, or until the cabbage is tender. Season with salt and pepper. Mix in the walnut halves and serve.

Beet and Celeriac Casserole

BEAUTIFUL RUBY-RED slices of beets mixed with celeriac make a stunning light accompaniment to any main-course dish.

INGREDIENTS

12 ounces raw beets

12 ounces raw celeriac

4 sprigs of fresh thyme, chopped

6 juniper berries, crushed

1/2 cup fresh orange juice

1/2 cup vegetable stock

salt and freshly ground black pepper

Serves 6

1 Preheat the oven to 375°F. Peel and slice the raw beets very finely. Quarter and peel the raw celeriac and slice very finely. Try to cut all slices to an even thickness.

2 Fill a 10-inch cast-iron ovenproof or flameproof frying pan with alternate layers of beet and celeriac slices, sprinkling with thyme, juniper and salt and pepper between each layer.

3 Mix the orange juice and stock together and pour over the vegetables. Place over medium heat and bring to a boil. Boil for 2 minutes.

4 Cover with foil and place in the oven for 15–20 minutes. Remove the foil and raise the oven temperature to 400°F. Cook for another 10 minutes.

Runner Beans with Garlic

DELICATE AND fresh-tasting flageolet beans and sautéed garlic add a distinctly French flavor to this simple side dish.

INGREDIENTS

1 1/4 cups flageolet beans

1 tablespoon olive oil

2 tablespoons (1/4 stick) butter

1 onion, finely chopped

1–2 garlic cloves, crushed

3–4 tomatoes, peeled and chopped

12 ounces runner beans, prepared
  and sliced

2/3 cup white wine

2/3 cup vegetable stock

2 tablespoons fresh parsley, chopped

salt and freshly ground black pepper

Serves 4

1 Place the flageolet beans in a large saucepan of water, bring to a boil and simmer for 3/4–1 hour, until tender.

2 Heat the olive oil and butter in a large frying pan and sauté the onion and garlic for 3–4 minutes, until soft and golden.

3 Add the chopped tomatoes to the onions in the pan and continue cooking over gentle heat until they are soft.

COOK'S TIP

If fresh flageolet beans are not available, use canned and omit step 1 from the method.

4 Stir the flageolet beans into the onion and tomato mixture, then add the runner beans, wine, stock and a little salt. Stir. Cover and simmer for 5–10 minutes.

5 Increase the heat to reduce the liquid, then stir in the parsley, more salt, if necessary, and pepper.

Lima Beans in Chile Sauce

TRY THIS fabulous dish of lima beans with a tomato and chile sauce for warming up those winter evenings.

INGREDIENTS

1 pound lima or fava beans, thawed
   if frozen
2 tablespoons olive oil
1 onion, finely chopped
2 garlic cloves, chopped
12 ounces tomatoes, peeled, seeded
   and chopped
1 or 2 drained canned jalapeño chiles,
   seeded and chopped
salt
cilantro, chopped, to garnish

Serves 4

1 Cook the beans in a saucepan of boiling water for 15–20 minutes, until tender. Drain and keep hot, to one side, in the covered saucepan while you prepare the sauce.

2 Heat the olive oil in a frying pan and sauté the onion and garlic until the onion is soft but not brown. Add the tomatoes and cook until the mixture thickens.

3 Add the jalapeños and cook over medium heat for 1–2 minutes. Season with salt.

4 Pour the mixture over the reserved beans and check that they are hot. If not, return everything to the frying pan and cook over low heat for just long enough to heat through. Place in a warmed serving dish, garnish with cilantro and serve.

Glazed Carrots with Cider

THIS DISH is extremely simple to make. The carrots are cooked in the minimum of liquid to bring out the best of their flavor, and the cider adds a pleasant sharpness.

INGREDIENTS

I pound young carrots

2 tablespoons (1/4 stick) butter

I tablespoon brown sugar

1/2 cup cider

4 tablespoons vegetable stock or water

I teaspoon Dijon mustard

I tablespoon fresh parsley, finely chopped

Serves 4

I Trim the tops and bottoms of the carrots and peel them. Using a sharp knife, cut them into julienne strips.

COOK'S TIP

If the carrots are cooked before the liquid in the saucepan has reduced, transfer the carrots to a serving dish and rapidly boil the liquid until thick. Pour over the carrots and sprinkle with parsley.

2 Melt the butter in a frying pan, add the carrots and sauté for 4–5 minutes, stirring frequently. Sprinkle the brown sugar over the carrots and cook, stirring, for I minute, or until the sugar has dissolved.

3 Add the cider and stock or water, bring to a boil and stir in the mustard. Partially cover the pan and simmer for 10–12 minutes, until the carrots are just tender. Remove the lid and continue cooking until the liquid has reduced to a thick sauce.

4 Remove the saucepan from the heat, stir in the chopped fresh parsley and then spoon into a warmed serving dish.

DESSERTS, CAKES and BAKED GOODS

Most of us like to finish a meal with a dessert, and this chapter offers a tempting array of sweet treats as well as a mouthwatering selection of flavored breads.

Raspberry Yogurt and Amaretti Scrunch

THIS PUDDING looks stunning, but is actually very simple to make. The raspberries give a luscious swirl of color and the amaretti biscuits make a crunchy contrast to the creamy yogurt.

INGREDIENTS

1 1/2 cups raspberries, frozen or fresh

2 1/2 cups thick plain live yogurt

2 tablespoons clear honey

rind of 1 small lemon, finely grated

1 1/2 cups amaretti biscuits, broken
    into pieces

crystallized rose petals, for decoration
    (optional)

Serves 4–6

If using frozen raspberries, allow them to partly defrost. If using fresh ones, partly freeze them.

2 Place the yogurt in a large bowl and stir in the honey and lemon rind. Add the raspberries and fold in gently, being careful not to over mix. Chill for 1 hour.

3 Stir in the amaretti biscuits just before serving. Decorate with crystallized rose petals, if you wish.

HEALTH BENEFITS

Raspberries are extremely cleansing for the body and can relieve menstrual cramps and cystitis.

Tropical Fruit with Hot Rum and Cinnamon Sauce

DARK RUM and cinnamon give this hot fruit dessert a distinctly Caribbean flavor. It is best eaten as soon as it is ready, so prepare the fruit ahead of time, then cook between courses – this will only take a few minutes.

INGREDIENTS

2 tablespoons (1/4 stick) unsalted butter

1 medium pineapple, peeled, cored
    and sliced

1 mango, peeled, stoned and cut into
    1/2-inch cubes

1 papaya, peeled, halved, pitted and sliced

2 bananas, thickly sliced

2 tablespoons clear honey or maple syrup

1 teaspoon ground cinnamon

4 tablespoons dark rum

plain live yogurt or yogurt ice, to serve

Serves 4

Melt the butter in a large heavy-based frying pan. Add the sliced pineapple and cook for 3 minutes or until it starts to brown, turning it occasionally.

HEALTH BENEFITS

Papaya contains the enzyme papain, which can help to stimulate the digestion. Like pineapple and mango, papaya is rich in both vitamin C and beta carotene.

2 Add the prepared mango, papaya and bananas to the pan and cook for 1 minute, turning occasionally.

3 Stir in the honey or maple syrup, cinnamon and rum, and cook for a further 2 minutes or until the sauce thickens and the fruit is tender. Serve immediately with yogurt or yogurt ice.

Pan-fried Apple Slices with Walnut Shortcake

SOFT, CARAMELIZED apples and crisp nutty shortcake make a perfect combination. Serve warm with a spoonful of yogurt or a scoop of vanilla ice cream.

INGREDIENTS

2 tablespoons (¼ stick) unsalted butter

4 dessert apples, cored and thinly sliced

2 tablespoons light brown sugar

2 teaspoons ground ginger

1 teaspoon ground cinnamon

½ teaspoon ground nutmeg

For the walnut shortbread

⅔ cup whole wheat flour

⅔ cup unbleached all-purpose flour

¼ cup oatmeal

1 teaspoon baking powder

¼ teaspoon salt

¼ cup superfine sugar

8 tablespoons (1 stick) unsalted butter

¼ cup shelled walnuts, finely chopped

1 tablespoon milk, plus extra for brushing

light brown sugar, for sprinkling

Serves 4

1 Preheat the oven to 350°F and grease one or two baking sheets. To make the walnut shortcake, sift together the flours, adding any bran left in the sieve, and mix with the oatmeal, baking powder, salt and sugar. Rub in the butter with your finger tips until the mixture resembles fine bread crumbs.

2 Add the chopped walnuts, then stir in enough of the milk to form a soft dough.

3 Gently knead the dough on a floured work surface. Form into a round, then roll out to a ¼-inch thickness. Using a 3-inch fluted cutter, stamp out eight rounds – you may have some dough left over.

4 Place the shortcake rounds on the prepared baking sheets. Brush the tops with milk and sprinkle with sugar. Bake for 12–15 minutes until golden, then transfer to a wire rack and leave to cool.

5 To prepare the apples, melt the butter in a heavy-based frying pan. Add the apples and cook for 3–4 minutes over gentle heat until softened. Increase the heat to medium, add the sugar and spices, and stir well. Cook for a few minutes, stirring frequently, until the sauce turns golden brown and caramelizes.

6 Place two shortcake rounds on each of four individual serving plates and spoon over the warm apples and sauce. Serve immediately.

HEALTH BENEFITS

• Recent studies have shown that eating walnuts regularly can greatly reduce the risk of heart disease and lower the level of blood cholesterol in the body.

• There is much truth in the adage: "an apple a day keeps the doctor away." Apples have many health-giving properties. They help cleanse the blood, remove impurities in the liver and inhibit the growth of harmful bacteria in the digestive tract. Apples are also known to treat skin diseases and arthritis.

COOK'S TIP

To prevent the apples browning after they are sliced, place them in a large bowl of water mixed with about 1 tablespoon lemon juice.

Coconut Rice Puddings with Broiled Oranges

STICKY RICE pudding is a specialty of many South-east Asian countries. In these little desserts, Thai jasmine rice is cooked with rich and creamy coconut milk.

INGREDIENTS

scant 1 cup jasmine rice

1²/3 cups coconut milk

¹/2 teaspoon grated nutmeg, plus extra
    for sprinkling

large pinch of salt

4 tablespoons sugar

oil, for greasing

2 oranges, skin and pith removed and cut
    into thin rounds

orange peel twists, to decorate

Serves 4

1 Rinse and drain the rice. Place in a saucepan, cover with water, and bring to a boil. Cook for 5 minutes until the grains are just beginning to soften. Drain well.

2 Place the rice in a muslin-lined steamer, then make a few holes in the muslin to allow the steam to get through. Steam the rice for 15 minutes or until tender.

HEALTH BENEFITS

• Rice is gluten-free and therefore can be eaten by coeliacs. Although more refined than brown rice, jasmine rice is a useful source of energy.

3 Put the steamed rice in a heavy-based saucepan with the coconut milk, nutmeg, salt and sugar, and cook over gentle heat until the mixture begins to simmer. Simmer for about 5 minutes until the mixture is thick and creamy, stirring frequently to prevent the rice sticking.

4 Spoon the rice mixture into four lightly oiled ³/4-cup molds or ramekins and leave to cool.

5 When ready to serve, heat the broiler to high. Line a cookie sheet or the broiler rack with foil and place the orange slices on top. Sprinkle the oranges with a little grated nutmeg, then broil for 6 minutes until lightly golden, turning the slices halfway through cooking.

6 When the rice mixture is completely cold, run a knife around the edge of the molds or ramekins and turn out the rice. Decorate with orange peel twists and serve with the warm orange slices.

Date, Fig and Orange Pudding

THIS LIGHT steamed pudding avoids the use of suet, which is usually made from hydrogenated fat, often animal in origin. The addition of fresh orange juice and rind, and orange liqueur, gives an intense citrus tang.

INGREDIENTS

juice and rind of 2 oranges

2/3 cup pitted, dried dates, chopped

2/3 cup dried figs, chopped

2 tablespoons orange liqueur (optional)

12 tablespoons (1 1/2 sticks) unsalted butter, plus extra for greasing

3/4 cup light brown sugar

3 eggs

2/3 cup self-rising whole wheat flour

1 cup unbleached self-rising flour

2 tablespoons corn syrup (optional)

Serves 6

1 Reserve a few strips of orange rind for decoration and put the rest in a saucepan with the orange juice. Add chopped dates, figs and orange liqueur, if using. Cook, covered, over gentle heat for 8–10 minutes, until the fruit is soft.

2 Leave the fruit mixture to cool, then transfer to a food processor or blender and process until smooth. Press through a strainer to remove the fig seeds, if you wish.

3 Cream the butter and sugar until pale and fluffy, then beat in the fig puree. Beat in the eggs, then fold in the flours and mix until combined.

HEALTH BENEFITS

The healing qualities of figs have been recognized for thousands of years and, as a result, the fruit has been used to treat almost every known disease. Widely known as a gentle laxative, figs also contain vitamins B_6 and C, calcium and iron. Dates contain their fair share of vitamin B_6 and iron and provide a useful source of potassium.

4 Grease a 5-cup pudding basin, and pour in the corn syrup, if using. Tilt the bowl to cover the inside with a layer of syrup. Spoon in the pudding mixture. Cover the top with waxed paper, with a pleat down the center, and then with pleated foil, and tie down with string.

5 Place the bowl in a large saucepan, and pour in enough water to come halfway up the sides of the bowl. Cover with a tight-fitting lid and steam for 2 hours. Check the water occasionally and top up if necessary. Turn out and decorate with the reserved orange rind.

Lemon and Almond Tart

THIS REFRESHING, tangy tart has a rich, creamy lemon filling set off by a caramelized sugar top. Serve warm or cold with a dollop of crème fraîche or plain yogurt.

INGREDIENTS

2 eggs
¹/4 cup superfine sugar
rind, finely grated and juice of
    4 unwaxed lemons
¹/2 teaspoon vanilla extract
¹/2 cup ground almonds
¹/2 cup light cream

For the pastry

2 cups unbleached spelt flour
³/4 cup confectioner's sugar, plus extra
    for dusting
9 tablespoons (1¹/8 sticks) butter
1 egg, beaten
a pinch of salt

Serves 8–10

1 Preheat the oven to 350°F. To make the pastry, sift together the flour and sugar in a bowl. Rub in the butter with your finger tips until the mixture resembles fine bread crumbs. Add the egg and salt, then mix to a smooth dough.

2 Knead the dough lightly on a floured work surface and form into a smooth flat round. Wrap the dough in plastic wrap and chill for 15 minutes.

3 Roll out the dough on a lightly floured work surface and use to line a 9-inch loose-bottomed tart pan. Prick the pastry base and chill for a further 15 minutes.

4 Line the pie case with baking parchment. Tip in some baking beans and bake blind for 10 minutes. Remove the paper and beans and return the pastry case to the oven for 10 minutes more or until it is light golden.

5 Meanwhile, make the filling. Beat the eggs with the sugar until the mixture leaves a thin ribbon trail. Gently stir in the lemon rind and juice, vanilla extract, almonds and cream.

6 Carefully pour the filling into the pie case and level the surface. Bake for about 25 minutes or until the filling is set.

7 Heat the broiler to high. Sift a thick layer of confectioners' sugar over the tart and broil until the sugar caramelizes. Decorate the tart with a little extra sifted confectioners' sugar before serving warm or cold.

HEALTH BENEFITS

• The high level of vitamin C in lemons is widely known but they also contain good amounts of calcium, iron and potassium.
• Lemons are a natural antiseptic and have been used for centuries to treat skin problems. They are also used to cleanse the body of toxins.

COOK'S TIP

• Spelt flour is a type of wheat flour that is available in some large supermarkets and health food stores. If you can't find it, then use unbleached all-purpose flour instead.

Baked Ricotta Cakes with Red Sauce

THESE HONEY and vanilla-flavored desserts take only minutes to make. The fragrant fruity sauce provides a contrast of both color and flavor.

INGREDIENTS

generous 1 cup ricotta cheese

2 egg whites, beaten

4 tablespoons clear honey, plus extra to taste

1 teaspoon vanilla extract

4 cups mixed fresh or frozen fruit, such as strawberries, raspberries, blackberries and cherries

fresh mint leaves, to decorate (optional)

Serves 4

1 Preheat the oven to 350°F. Place the ricotta cheese in a bowl and break it up with a wooden spoon.
Add the beaten egg whites, honey and vanilla extract and mix thoroughly until the mixture is smooth and well combined.

2 Lightly grease four ramekins. Spoon the ricotta mixture into the prepared ramekins and level the tops. Bake for 20 minutes or until the ricotta cakes are risen and golden.

3 Meanwhile, make the fruit sauce. Reserve about a quarter of the fruit for decoration. Place the rest of the fruit in a saucepan, with a little water if the fruit is fresh, and heat gently until softened. Leave to cool slightly and remove any cherry stones, if using cherries.

COOK'S TIP

The red berry sauce can be made a day in advance. Chill until ready to use. Frozen fruit doesn't need extra water, as there are usually plenty of ice crystals clinging to the berries.

4 Press the fruit through a strainer, then taste and sweeten with honey if it is too tart. Serve the sauce, warm or cold, with the ricotta cakes. Decorate with the reserved berries and mint leaves, if using.

HEALTH BENEFITS

• Ricotta contains about 4 per cent fat, compared with 35 per cent in a hard cheese like Cheddar. It is a good source of vitamin B_{12}, calcium and protein.

• All berries are rich in the anti-cancer compound ellagic acid, which is a powerful antioxidant.

Apricot Panettone Pudding

PANETTONE MAKES a rich addition to this "almost no-butter" version of a traditional bread and butter pudding.

INGREDIENTS

unsalted butter, for greasing

12 ounces panettone, sliced into triangles

1/3 cup unsulfured dried apricots, chopped

1/4 cup pecan nuts

2 1/4 cups milk

1 teaspoon vanilla extract

1 large egg, beaten

2 tablespoons maple syrup

grated nutmeg

light brown sugar, for sprinkling

Serves 6

1 Butter a 4-cup baking dish. Arrange half the panettone in the dish, scatter over half the pecan nuts and all the apricots, then add another layer of panettone on top.

2 Heat the milk and vanilla extract in a small saucepan until it just simmers. Put the egg and maple syrup in a large bowl, grate in 1/2 teaspoon nutmeg, then whisk in the hot milk.

3 Preheat the oven to 400°F. Pour the egg mixture over the panettone, lightly pressing down the bread so that it is submerged. Leave the pudding to stand for 10 minutes.

4 Scatter over the reserved pecan nuts and sprinkle with the light brown sugar and nutmeg. Bake for 40–45 minutes until risen and golden.

HEALTH BENEFITS

Dried apricots have an even higher concentration of beta carotene than fresh ones. This powerful antioxidant is known to lower the risk of cataracts, heart disease and some forms of cancer.

Indian Rice Pudding

THIS CREAMY pudding is scented with saffron, cardamom and freshly grated nutmeg. Shelled pistachio nuts give a subtle contrast in color and add a delicious crunch to the dessert. This pudding is the perfect way to end a spicy meal.

INGREDIENTS

3/4 cup brown short grain rice

1 1/2 cups boiling water

2 1/2 cups milk

6 cardamom pods, bruised

1/2 teaspoon nutmeg, freshly grated

pinch of saffron strands

4 tablespoons maize malt syrup

1 tablespoon clear honey

1/2 cup pistachio nuts, chopped

Serves 4

1 | Wash the rice under cold running water and place in a saucepan with a boiling water. Bring to a boil and boil, uncovered, for 15 minutes.

COOK'S TIP

Maize malt syrup is a natural alternative to refined sugar and can be found in health food stores.

2 Pour the milk over the rice, then reduce the heat and simmer, partially covered, for 15 minutes.

3 Add the cardamom pods, grated nutmeg, saffron, maize malt syrup and honey, and cook for a further 15 minutes, or until the rice is tender, stirring occasionally.

4 Spoon the rice into small serving bowls and sprinkle with pistachio nuts before serving hot or cold.

HEALTH BENEFITS

• *Brown rice is unrefined and therefore, unlike white polished rice, retains most of its fiber and nutrients. It is a good source of B vitamins and vitamin E.*

• *Pistachio nuts are densely packed with nourishment, being rich in protein, vitamins and minerals. However, because of their high fat content, they go rancid quickly, so buy them in a store with a high turnover of stock and keep them in a cool dry place. Due to their high fat content, pistachio nuts should be eaten in moderation.*

Winter Fruit Poached in Mulled Wine

FRESH APPLES and pears are combined with dried apricots and figs, and cooked in a fragrant, spicy wine until tender and intensely flavored.

INGREDIENTS

1 1/4 cups red wine
1 1/4 cups fresh orange juice
rind, finely grated and juice of 1 orange
3 tablespoons clear honey or barley
    malt syrup
3 small cinnamon sticks
4 cloves
4 cardamom pods, split
2 pears, such as Comice or William, peeled,
    cored and halved
8 dried figs
12 dried unsulfured apricots
2 eating apples, peeled, cored and
    thickly sliced

Serves 4

1 Put the wine, the fresh and squeezed orange juice and half the orange rind in a saucepan with the honey or syrup and spices. Bring to a boil, then reduce the heat and simmer for 2 minutes, stirring occasionally.

HEALTH BENEFITS

• The combination of fresh and dried fruit ensures a healthy amount of vitamins and minerals, particularly vitamins C, beta carotene, potassium and iron. The fruit is also rich in fiber.

• Cardamom and cinnamon soothe indigestion and, along with cloves, can offer relief from colds and coughs.

2 Add the pears, figs and apricots to the pan and cook, covered, for 25 minutes, occasionally turning the fruit in the wine mixture. Add the apples and cook for a further 12–15 minutes until the fruit is tender.

3 Remove the fruit from the pan and discard the spices. Cook the wine mixture over a high heat until reduced and syrupy, then pour it over the fruit. Serve decorated with the reserved strips of orange rind, if wished.

Apricot and Almond Tart

FLAKY, RICH gluten-free pastry encases an apricot and almond filling to make this tempting dessert. Serve with Mediterranean-style yogurt or crème fraîche.

INGREDIENTS

^{1}/2 cup soft margarine
^{1}/2 cup sugar
1 egg, beaten
^{1}/3 cup ground rice
^{1}/2 cup ground almonds
few drops of almond extract
1 pound fresh apricots, halved and pitted
sifted confectioner's sugar, for dusting
apricot slices and fresh mint sprigs, to
    decorate (optional)

For the pastry

1 cup brown rice flour
1 cup gluten-free cornmeal
pinch of salt
^{1}/2 cup soft margarine
2 tablespoons sugar
1 egg yolk

Serves 6

1 To make the pastry, place the rice flour, cornmeal and pinch of salt in a bowl and stir to mix. Lightly rub in the soft margarine until the mixture resembles bread crumbs.

VARIATION

For a change, use ground hazelnuts and vanilla extract in place of the ground almonds and almond extract.

2 Add the 2 tablespoons sugar, stir in the egg yolk and add enough chilled water to make a smooth, soft but not sticky dough. Wrap the dough and chill for 30 minutes.

3 Preheat the oven to 350°F. Line a 9^1/2-inch loose-bottomed tart pan with the pastry by pressing it gently over the bottom and up the sides of the pan, making sure there are no holes in the pastry. Trim the edge with a sharp knife.

4 To make the almond filling, place the margarine and sugar in a mixing bowl and cream together, using a wooden spoon, until the mixture is light and fluffy.

5 Gradually add the beaten egg, beating well after each addition. Fold in the ground rice and almonds and the almond extract and mix well to incorporate them.

6 Spoon the almond mixture into the pastry shell, spreading it evenly, and arrange the apricot halves over the top, cut side down.

7 Place on a baking sheet and bake for 40–45 minutes, until the filling and pastry are cooked and lightly browned. Serve warm or cold, dusted with confectioner's sugar and decorated with apricots and sprigs of mint, if you like.

COOK'S TIP

If you do not require a gluten-free dessert, this tart also tastes delicious with ordinary sweet shortcrust pastry.

Baked Fruit Compote

INGREDIENTS
2/3 cup dried figs
1/2 cup dried apricots
1/2 cup dried apple rings
1/4 cup prunes
1/2 cup dried pears
1/2 cup dried peaches
1 1/4 cups unsweetened apple juice
1 1/4 cups unsweetened orange juice
6 cloves
1 cinnamon stick
flaked almonds, toasted, to decorate
Serves 6

1 Preheat the oven to 350°F. Place the figs, apricots, apple rings, prunes, pears and peaches in a shallow ovenproof dish and stir to mix them together.

2 Mix together the apple and orange juices and pour over the fruit. Add the whole cloves and cinnamon stick and stir gently to mix.

3 Bake for about 30 minutes, until the fruit mixture is hot, stirring once or twice during cooking. Set aside and let soak for 20 minutes, then remove and discard the cloves and cinnamon stick.

4 Spoon into serving bowls and serve warm or cold, decorated with toasted flaked almonds.

COOK'S TIP

Use other mixtures of unsweetened fruit juices, such as pineapple and orange or grape and apple. Dried fruit contains quite a lot of concentrated sugar so it doesn't need any additional sweetenings.

VARIATION

The hot compote tastes delicious served with a dollop of fresh cream or vanilla ice cream.

Mango Yogurt Ice

INGREDIENTS
1 pound ripe mango flesh, chopped
1 1/4 cups low-fat peach or apricot yogurt
2/3 cup Mediterranean-style yogurt
2/3 cup low-fat plain yogurt
2–4 tablespoons sugar
fresh mint sprigs, to decorate
Serves 6

1 Place the mango flesh in a blender or food processor and blend until smooth. Transfer to a bowl.

2 Add all three yogurts and blend until thoroughly mixed.

3 Stir in enough of the sugar to sweeten to taste and stir to mix.

4 Pour the mixture into a shallow plastic container. Cover and chill for 1 1/2–2 hours, until it is mushy in consistency. Turn the mixture into a chilled bowl and beat until smooth.

5 Return the mixture to the plastic container, cover and freeze until the ice is firm. Transfer the ice to the refrigerator about 30 minutes before serving to allow it to soften a little. Serve in scoops decorated with mint sprigs.

COOK'S TIP

Replace the mango with other fruits of a similar texture and delicate taste such as peach or apricot.

Creamy Lemon Rice Pudding

THIS IS a creamy baked rice pudding with a difference, being subtly flavored with lemon. It is wonderful served warm or cold with fresh strawberries or pineapple.

INGREDIENTS

$^1/_4$ cup short-grain white rice

$2^1/_2$ cups low-fat milk

2 tablespoons sugar

zest of 1 lemon, finely grated

1 tablespoon butter, cut into small pieces

orange and lemon zest, pared, to decorate

For serving

8 ounces prepared fresh fruit, such
  as strawberries or pineapple

6 tablespoons reduced fat crème
  fraîche (optional)

Serves 4

1 Lightly grease a 1-quart ovenproof dish. Add the rice and pour in the milk, then set aside for about 30 minutes, to allow the rice to soften a little while it absorbs the milk. Preheat the oven to 300°F.

2 Add the sugar, grated lemon zest and butter to the rice and milk and stir gently to mix. Bake for 2–2$^1/_2$ hours, until the top of the pudding is lightly browned.

3 Decorate with pared orange and lemon zest and serve warm or cold with the fresh fruit.

4 If serving cold, allow the pudding to cool, remove and discard the skin, then chill. Fold in the crème fraîche just before serving, if desired.

Peach and Raspberry Crumble

INGREDIENTS

$^3/_4$ cup brown rice flour

4 tablespoons soft margarine

$^1/_4$ cup buckwheat flakes

$^1/_4$ cup millet flakes

$^1/_4$ cup hazelnuts, roughly chopped

scant $^1/_3$ cup light brown sugar

1 teaspoon ground ginger

3 fresh peaches, pitted and cut
  into wedges

1$^1/_3$ cups raspberries

4 tablespoons fresh orange juice

Serves 4

1 Preheat the oven to 350°F. Grease a 5-cup pie dish. Place the rice flour in a bowl and rub in the margarine using your fingertips until the mixture resembles bread crumbs.

2 Stir in the buckwheat flakes, millet flakes, hazelnuts, $^1/_4$ cup of the sugar and the ginger. Mix well.

3 Mix the peaches, raspberries, orange juice and remaining sugar together and place in the dish. Sprinkle the crumble over the top, pressing it down lightly. Bake for 30–45 minutes, until the crumble is lightly browned. Serve warm or cold.

VARIATIONS

Use almonds or walnuts in place of the hazelnuts and substitute ground cinnamon for the ground ginger.

Firm, ripe nectarines or thinly sliced dessert apples could be used in place of the peaches, if you like.

Fruit Fondue with Hazelnut Dip

INGREDIENTS

selection of fresh fruits for dipping, such as
   clementines, kiwi fruit, grapes, physalis
   and whole strawberries
1/2 cup low-fat soft cheese
2/3 cup low-fat plain yogurt
1/4 cup hazelnuts, chopped
1 teaspoon vanilla extract
1 teaspoon superfine sugar
Serves 2

COOK'S TIP

For a truly indulgent addition, offer a bowl
of melted milk or dark chocolate, placed
alongside the hazelnut dip.

1 First prepare the fruits. Peel and segment
the clementines. Then peel the kiwi fruit
and cut into wedges. Wash the grapes and
peel back the papery casing on the physalis.

2 Beat the soft cheese with the yogurt,
vanilla extract and sugar in a bowl. Stir
in three-quarters of the hazelnuts. Spoon
the dip into a glass serving dish set on a
platter or small pots on individual plates and
scatter over the remaining hazelnuts.
Arrange the prepared fruits around the dip
and serve immediately.

Yogurt Sundaes with Passionfruit Coulis

HERE IS a sundae you can enjoy every
day! The frozen yogurt has less fat
and fewer calories than traditional
ice cream and the fruits provide
vitamins A and C.

INGREDIENTS

12 ounces strawberries, halved
2 passionfruits, halved
2 teaspoons confectioner's sugar (optional)
2 ripe peaches, pitted and chopped
8 scoops (about 12 ounces) vanilla or
   strawberry frozen yogurt
Serves 4

COOK'S TIP

Serve the sundaes with brandy snap
cookies or other rolled cookies, stuck in
the yogurt.

1 Puree half the strawberries. Scoop out
the passionfruit pulp and add it to the
coulis. Sweeten, if necessary.

2 Spoon half the remaining strawberries
and half the chopped peaches into
four tall sundae glasses. Top each dessert
with a scoop of frozen yogurt. Set aside a
few choice pieces of fruit for decoration,
and use the rest to make another layer on
the top of each sundae. Top each with a final
scoop of frozen yogurt.

3 Pour over the passionfruit coulis and
decorate the sundaes with the
reserved strawberries and pieces of peach.
Serve immediately.

Mango and Orange Sorbet

FRESH AND tangy, and gloriously vibrant in color, this sorbet is the perfect finale for a spicy meal.

INGREDIENTS

1/2 cup sugar
2 large mangoes
juice of 1 orange
1 egg white (optional)
thinly pared strips of fresh unwaxed orange
    rind, to decorate

Serves 2–4

1 Gently heat the sugar and 1 1/4 cups water in a pan until the sugar has dissolved. Bring to a boil, then reduce the heat and simmer for 5 minutes. Leave to cool.

2 Cut away the two sides of the mango close to the stone. Peel, then cut the flesh from the stone. Dice the fruit and discard the stone.

3 Process the mango flesh and orange juice in a food processor with the sugar syrup until smooth.

4 Pour the mixture into a freezer-proof container and freeze for 2 hours until semi-frozen. Whisk the egg white, if using, until it forms stiff peaks, then stir it into the sorbet. Whisk well to remove any ice crystals and freeze until solid.

5 Transfer the sorbet to the refrigerator 10 minutes before serving, then serve, decorated with orange rind.

HEALTH BENEFITS

Mangoes and oranges aid the digestion, boost the immune system and are said to cleanse the blood. They are also an excellent source of vitamins C and A.

Rhubarb and Ginger Yogurt Ice

THIS DELICATE pink yogurt ice is flavored with honey and ginger.

INGREDIENTS

scant 1 1/2 cups set plain live yogurt
scant 1 cup mascarpone cheese
3 cups rhubarb, trimmed
    and chopped
3 tablespoons stem ginger syrup
2 tablespoons clear honey
3 pieces stem ginger, finely chopped

Serves 6

1 In a bowl, whisk together the yogurt and mascarpone.

2 Pour the yogurt mixture into a shallow freezer-proof container and freeze for 1 hour.

3 Meanwhile, put rhubarb, preserved ginger syrup and honey in a large saucepan and cook over low heat for 15 minutes, or until the rhubarb is soft. Leave to cool, then puree in a food processor or blender.

4 Remove the semi-frozen yogurt mixture from the freezer and fold in the rhubarb and stem ginger puree. Beat well until smooth. Add the chopped stem ginger.

5 Return the yogurt ice to the freezer and freeze for 2 hours more. Remove from the freezer and beat again, then freeze until solid. Serve scoops of the yogurt ice on individual plates or in bowls.

HEALTH BENEFITS

• *Rhubarb is rich in potassium and is an effective laxative. However, it is also high in oxalic acid, which is reputed to inhibit the absorption of iron and calcium and can exacerbate joint problems, such as arthritis. The leaves are poisonous and should never be eaten.*
• *Stem ginger retains many of the health-giving qualities of fresh ginger. It aids digestion and is effective in treating gastrointestinal disorders.*

COOK'S TIP

Take the yogurt ice out of the freezer and transfer it to the refrigerator 15 minutes before serving to let it soften.

Spiced Apple Crumble

ANY FRUIT can be used in this popular dessert, but you can't beat the combination of blackberry and apple. Hazelnuts and cardamom seeds give the topping extra flavor.

INGREDIENTS

butter, for greasing
1 pound cooking apples
1 cup blackberries
zest, grated and juice of 1 orange
1/3 cup light brown sugar
custard, to serve

For the topping

1 1/2 cups all-purpose flour
5 tablespoons (5/8 stick) butter
1/3 cup sugar
1/4 cup hazelnuts, chopped
1/2 teaspoon cardamom seeds, crushed

Serves 4–6

1 Preheat the oven to 400°F. Generously butter a 5-cup baking dish. Peel and core the apples, then slice them into the prepared baking dish. Level the surface, then scatter the blackberries over. Sprinkle the orange zest and light brown sugar evenly over the top of the fruit, then pour the orange juice over. Set the fruit mixture aside while you make the crumble topping.

2 Make the topping. Sift the flour into a bowl and rub in the butter until the mixture resembles coarse bread crumbs. Stir in the sugar, hazelnuts and cardamom seeds. Scatter the topping over the top of the fruit.

3 Press the topping around the edges of the dish to seal in the juices. Bake for 30–35 minutes, or until the crumble is golden. Serve hot, with custard.

Baked Stuffed Apples

THIS TRADITIONAL apple dessert is exceptionally simple and speedy. Bake the apples in the oven on the shelf under the Sunday roast for a delicious end to the meal.

INGREDIENTS

4 large cooking apples
1/2 cup light brown sugar
6 tablespoons (3/4 stick) butter, softened
zest, grated and juice of 1/2 orange
1/4 teaspoon ground cinnamon
2 tablespoons ratafia biscuits (almond-paste cookies) or other dessert cookies, crushed
1/2 cup pecans, chopped
1/2 cup deluxe mixed glacé fruit, chopped

Serves 4

1 Preheat the oven to 350°F. Wash and dry the apples. Remove the cores with an apple corer, then carefully enlarge each core cavity to twice its size by shaving off more flesh with the corer. Score each apple around its equator, using a sharp knife. Stand the apples in a baking dish.

2 Mix the brown sugar, butter, orange zest and juice, cinnamon and ratafia crumbs. Beat well, then stir in the nuts and glacé fruit. Divide the filling among the apples, piling it high. Shield the filling in each apple with a small piece of foil. Bake for 45–60 minutes, until each apple is tender.

Lemongrass Skewers with Lime Cheese

The lemongrass skewers give the fruit a subtle citrus tang. Almost any soft fruit can be used.

INGREDIENTS

4 long fresh lemongrass stalks

1 mango, peeled, pitted and cut into chunks

1 papaya, peeled, seeded and cut into chunks

1 star fruit, cut into thick slices and halved

8 fresh bay leaves

a nutmeg

1/4 cup maple syrup

1/3 cup demerara sugar

For the lime cheese

2/3 cup cottage cheese or low-fat cream cheese

1/2 cup heavy cream

zest , grated and juice of 1/2 lime

2 tablespoons confectioners' sugar

Serves 4

1 Prepare the grill or preheat the broiler. Cut the top of each lemongrass stalk into a point with a sharp knife. Discard the outer leaves, then use the back of the knife to bruise the length of each stalk to release the aromatic oils. Thread each stalk, skewer-style, with the fruit pieces and bay leaves.

2 Support a piece of foil on a baking sheet and roll up the edges to make a rim. Grease the foil, lay the kebabs on top and grate a little nutmeg over each. Drizzle the maple syrup over and dust liberally with the demerara sugar. Broil for 5 minutes, until lightly charred.

3 Meanwhile, make the lime cheese. Mix together the cheese, cream, grated lime zest and juice and confectioner's sugar in a bowl. Serve at once with the lightly charred fruit kebabs.

COOK'S TIP

Only fresh lemongrass will work as skewers for this recipe.

Coconut Jelly with Star Anise Fruits

INGREDIENTS

1 cup cold water

1/3 cup sugar

1 tablespoon powdered gelatin

1 2/3 cups canned coconut milk

For the syrup and fruit

1 cup water

3 star anise

1/4 cup sugar

1 star fruit, sliced

12 lychees, peeled and pitted

1 cup blackberries

Serves 4

1 Heat the water and sugar in a pan until the sugar has dissolved. Sprinkle the gelatin over and stir occasionally, until dissolved. Stir in the coconut milk, remove from the heat and set aside to cool.

2 Grease a 7-inch square cake pan. Line with plastic wrap. Pour in the coconut milk mixture and chill until set.

3 To make the syrup, combine the water, star anise and sugar in a pan. bring to a boil, stirring, then lower the heat and simmer for 10–12 minutes, until syrupy. Place the fruit in a heatproof bowl and pour the hot syrup over it. Cool first, then chill.

4 To serve, cut the coconut jelly into diamonds and remove from the pan. Arrange the coconut jelly on individual plates, adding a few of the fruits and their syrup to each portion.

Tropical Fruit Gratin

THIS OUT-OF-THE-ORDINARY gratin is strictly for grown-ups. A colorful combination of fruit is topped with a simple sabayon before being flashed under the broiler.

INGREDIENTS

2 tamarillos

1/2 sweet pineapple

1 ripe mango

1 1/2 cups blackberries

1/2 cup sparkling white wine

1/2 cup sugar

6 egg yolks

Serves 4

1 Cut each tamarillo in half lengthwise and then into thick slices. Cut the zest and core from the pineapple and take spiral slices off the outside to remove the eyes. Cut the flesh into chunks. Peel the mango, cut it in half and cut the flesh from the pit in slices.

2 Divide all the fruit, including the blackberries, among four 5 1/2-inch gratin dishes set on a baking sheet and set aside. Heat the wine and sugar in a saucepan until the sugar has dissolved. Bring to a boil and cook for 5 minutes.

3 Put the egg yolks in a large heatproof bowl. Place the bowl over a pan of simmering water and beat until pale. Slowly pour in the hot sugar syrup, beating all the time, until the mixture thickens. Preheat the broiler.

4 Spoon the mixture over the fruit. Place the baking sheet holding the dishes on a low shelf under the hot broiler until the topping is golden.

Broiled Pineapple with Papaya Sauce

INGREDIENTS

1 sweet pineapple

melted butter, for greasing and brushing

2 pieces drained preserved ginger in syrup, cut into fine matchsticks, plus 2 tablespoons of the syrup from the jar

2 tablespoons demerara sugar

pinch of ground cinnamon

fresh mint sprigs, to decorate

For the sauce

1 ripe papaya, peeled and seeded

3/4 cup apple juice

Serves 6

1 Peel the pineapple and take spiral slices off the outside to remove the eyes. Cut it crossways into six slices, each 1 inch thick. Line a baking sheet with a sheet of foil, rolling up the sides to make a rim. Grease the foil with melted butter. Preheat the broiler.

2 Arrange the pineapple slices on the lined baking sheet. Brush with butter, then top with the ginger matchsticks, sugar and cinnamon. Drizzle the ginger syrup over. Broil for 5–7 minutes, or until the slices are golden and lightly charred on top.

3 Meanwhile, make the sauce. Cut a few slices from the papaya and set aside, then puree the rest with the apple juice in a blender or food processor.

4 Press the puree through a strainer placed over a bowl, then stir in any juices from cooking the pineapple. Serve the pineapple slices with a little of the sauce drizzled around each plate. Decorate with the reserved papaya slices and the mint sprigs.

COOK'S TIP

Try the papaya sauce with savory dishes such as grilled chicken and game birds.

Banana and Pecan Bread

BANANAS AND pecans just seem to belong together. This is a moist and delicious tea bread.

INGREDIENTS

8 tablespoons (1 stick) butter, softened

1 cup light brown sugar

2 large eggs, beaten

3 ripe bananas

3/4 cup pecans, coarsely chopped

2 cups self-rising flour

1/2 teaspoon ground apple pie spice

Makes a 2-pound loaf

1 Preheat the oven to 350°F. Generously grease a 9 x 5 x 3-inch loaf pan and line it with baking parchment. Cream the butter and brown sugar in a large mixing bowl until the mixture is light and fluffy. Gradually add the eggs, beating after each addition, until well combined.

2 Peel and then mash the bananas with a fork. Add them to the creamed mixture with the chopped pecans. Beat until well combined.

COOK'S TIP

If the mixture shows signs of curdling when you add the eggs, stir in a little of the flour to stabilize it.

3 Sift flour and spice together and fold into the banana mixture. Spoon into the pan, and bake for 1–1 1/4 hours, or until a skewer inserted into the middle of the loaf comes out clean. Cool for 10 minutes in the pan, then invert on a wire rack. Remove the pan and lining paper and let cool.

Date and Walnut Brownies

THESE RICH brownies are great for an afternoon snack, but they also make a fantastic dessert. Reheat slices briefly in the microwave oven and serve with crème fraîche.

INGREDIENTS

12 ounces semisweet chocolate, broken into squares

1/2 pound (2 sticks) butter, diced

3 large eggs

1/2 cup granulated sugar

1 teaspoon pure vanilla extract

3/4 cup all-purpose flour, sifted

1 1/2 cups fresh dates, peeled, pitted and chopped

1 3/4 cups walnut pieces

confectioner's sugar, for dusting

Makes 12

1 Preheat the oven to 375°F. Generously grease a 12 x 8-inch baking pan and line with baking parchment.

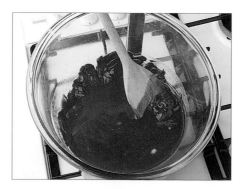

2 Put the chocolate and butter in a large heatproof bowl over a pan of hot water and leave until both have melted. Stir until smooth, then lift the bowl out and cool slightly.

3 In a separate bowl, beat the eggs, granulated sugar and vanilla. Beat into the chocolate mixture, then fold in the flour, dates and nuts. Pour into the pan.

4 Bake 30–40 minutes, until firm and the mixture comes away from the sides of the pan. Cool in the pan. Turn out, remove paper and dust with sugar.

Dutch Apple Cake

INGREDIENTS

2¼ cups self-rising flour

2 teaspoons baking powder

I teaspoon ground cinnamon

generous ½ cup sugar

4 tablespoons (½ stick) butter, melted

2 eggs, beaten

⅔ cup milk

For the topping

2 crisp, juicy eating apples

I tablespoon (⅛ stick) butter, melted

¼ cup demerara sugar

½ teaspoon ground cinnamon

Makes 8–10 slices

VARIATION

Add a few golden raisins or raisins to the apples if you like.

I Preheat the oven to 400°F. Grease and line an 8-inch round cake pan. Sift the flour, baking powder and cinnamon into a large mixing bowl. Stir in the sugar. In a separate bowl, whisk the melted butter, eggs and milk together, then stir the mixture into the dry ingredients.

2 Pour the cake mixture into the prepared pan, smooth the surface, then make a shallow hollow in a ring around the edge of the mixture.

3 Make the topping. Peel and core the apples, slice them into wedges and slice the wedges thinly. Arrange the slices around the hollow in the cake mixture. Brush with the melted butter, then scatter the demerara sugar and ground cinnamon over the top.

4 Bake for 45–50 minutes, or until the cake has risen well, is golden and a skewer inserted into the center comes out clean. Serve immediately with cream, or remove from the pan and cool before slicing.

Pear and Polenta Cake

POLENTA GIVES the light sponge that tops the sliced pears a nutty corn flavor that complements the fruit. Serve with custard or cream.

INGREDIENTS

¾ cup turbinado sugar

4 ripe pears

juice of ½ lemon

2 tablespoons honey

3 eggs

seeds from I vanilla bean

½ cup sunflower oil

I cup self-rising flour

⅓ cup instant polenta

Makes 10 slices

I Preheat the oven to 350°F. Generously grease and line an 8½-inch round cake pan. Scatter 2 tablespoons of the turbinado sugar over the bottom of the prepared pan.

2 Peel and core the pears. Cut them into chunks and toss in the lemon juice. Arrange them on the bottom of the prepared cake pan. Drizzle the honey over the pears and set aside.

3 Mix together the eggs, seeds from the vanilla bean and the remaining turbinado sugar in a bowl.

4 Beat the egg mixture until thick and creamy, then gradually beat in the oil. Sift together the flour and polenta and fold into the egg mixture.

5 Pour the mixture carefully into the pan over the pears. Bake for about 50 minutes, or until a skewer inserted into the center comes out clean. Cool in the pan for 10 minutes, then turn the cake out onto a plate, peel off the lining paper, invert and slice.

Date and Walnut Spice Cake

THIS DELICIOUSLY moist and richly spiced cake is topped with a sticky honey and orange glaze. Serve it as a dessert with a generous spoonful of plain yogurt or cream, flavored with grated orange rind.

INGREDIENTS

8 tablespoons (1 stick) unsalted butter, plus
    extra for greasing

3/4 cup dark brown sugar

2 eggs

1 1/2 cups unbleached self-rising flour,
    plus extra for dusting

1 teaspoon bicarbonate of soda

1/2 teaspoon nutmeg, freshly grated

1 teaspoon mixed spice

pinch of salt

3/4 cup buttermilk

1/3 cup ready-to-eat stoned
    dates, chopped

1/4 cup shelled walnuts, chopped

For the topping

4 tablespoons clear honey

3 tablespoons fresh orange juice

1 tablespoon orange rind, coarsely grated,
    plus extra to decorate

Serves 8

1 Grease and lightly flour a 9-inch spring-form cake pan. Preheat the oven to 350°F.

HEALTH BENEFITS

• Dried dates offer a more concentrated source of nutrients than fresh ones, including iron, potassium, niacin and magnesium. They also provide soluble fiber, making them a gentle laxative.

• According to a recent American study, a handful of walnuts a day has been found to lower blood cholesterol and therefore helps reduce the risk of heart disease.

2 Cream together butter and sugar with a wooden spoon until fluffy and creamy. Add the eggs, one at a time, and beat well to combine.

3 Sift together the flour, bicarbonate of soda, spices and salt. Gradually add this to the creamed mixture, alternating with the buttermilk. Add the dates and walnuts, and stir well.

COOK'S TIP

To make your own buttermilk substitute, mix 1 tablespoon lemon juice with 1 cup low-fat milk.

4 Spoon the mixture into the prepared cake pan and level the top. Bake for 50 minutes or until a skewer inserted into the center of the cake comes out clean. Leave to cool for 5 minutes, then turn out on to a wire rack to cool completely.

5 To make the topping, heat the honey, orange juice and rind in a small heavy-based saucepan. Bring to a boil and boil rapidly for 3 minutes, without stirring, until syrupy. Make small holes in the top of the warm cake using the skewer, and pour over the hot syrup. Decorate with the orange rind.

Rich Lemon Poppyseed Cake

THE CLASSIC combination of poppy seeds and lemon is used for this light cake, which has a delicious lemon curd and cream filling.

INGREDIENTS

1 1/2 cups (3 sticks) unsalted butter, plus
    extra for greasing
1 3/4 cups golden superfine sugar
3 tablespoons poppy seeds
4 teaspoons lemon rind, finely grated
4 heaped tablespoons luxury
    lemon curd
6 eggs, separated
1/2 cup low-fat milk
3 cups unbleached self-rising flour, plus
    extra for flouring pans
confectioner's sugar, to decorate

For the filling
1/2 cup luxury lemon curd
2/3 cup thick cream, whipped
Serves 8

1 Butter and lightly flour two 9-inch spring-form cake pans. Preheat the oven to 350°F.

VARIATION

Replace the lemon curd and cream filling with a tangy lemon syrup. Boil 3 tablespoons lemon juice, 1 tablespoon lemon rind and 2 tablespoons superfine sugar for 3 minutes until the mixture becomes syrupy and glossy. Make a single cake using half the ingredients. Pour the syrup over the warm cake and leave to cool before cutting into wedges to serve.

2 Cream together the butter and sugar with a wooden spoon until light and fluffy. Add the poppy seeds, lemon rind, lemon curd and egg yolks and beat well, then add the milk and mix well. Gently fold in the flour until combined.

3 Whisk the egg whites using a hand-held electric mixer until they form soft peaks. Carefully fold the egg whites into the cake mixture until just combined. Divide the cake mixture between the prepared pans.

4 Bake for 40–45 minutes until a skewer inserted into the center of the cakes comes out clean and the tops are golden.

5 Leave the cakes to cool in the pans for 5 minutes, then remove from the pans and leave to cool completely on wire racks. To finish, spread one cake with the lemon curd and spoon the cream evenly over the lemon curd. Put the second cake on top, press down gently, then dust with confectioner's sugar before serving.

Sponge Layer Cake

SERVE THIS light, classic sponge cake sandwiched together with your favorite jam. For special occasions, fill the cake with prepared fresh fruit, such as raspberries or sliced peaches, as well as jam and whipped dairy cream or fromage frais.

INGREDIENTS

3/4 cup (12 tablespoons) soft margarine

3/4 cup sugar

3 eggs, beaten

1 1/2 cups pancake and baking mix, sifted

4 tablespoons jam

2/3 cup whipped cream or framage frais

1–2 tablespoons confectioner's sugar, for dusting

Makes one 7-inch cake

1 Preheat the oven to 350°F. Lightly grease and line the bottom of two 7-inch cake pans.

2 Place the margarine and sugar in a bowl and cream together until pale and fluffy.

3 Add the eggs, a little at a time, beating well after each addition. Fold in half the baking mix, using a metal spoon, then fold in the rest.

4 Divide the mixture between the two cake pans and level the surfaces with the back of a spoon.

5 Bake for 25–30 minutes, until the cakes have risen, feel just firm to the touch and are golden brown. Turn out and cool on a wire rack.

6 When the cakes are cool, sandwich them with the jam and whipped cream or fromage frais. Dust the top of the cake with sifted confectioner's sugar and serve cut into slices. Store the cake in the refrigerator in an airtight container or wrapped in foil.

VARIATION

Replace 2 tablespoons of the baking mix with sifted cocoa powder. Sandwich the cakes with chocolate butter icing.

Chunky Chocolate and Banana Muffins

LUXURIOUS BUT not overly sweet, these muffins are simple and quick to make. Serve warm while the chocolate is still gooey.

INGREDIENTS

6 tablespoons low-fat milk

2 eggs

10 tablespoons (1 1/4 sticks) unsalted butter, melted

2 cups unbleached all-purpose flour

pinch of salt

1 teaspoon baking powder

3/4 cup superfine sugar

5 ounces semi-sweet chocolate, cut into large chunks

2 small bananas, mashed

Makes 12

1 Place 12 paper cases in a deep muffin pan. Preheat the oven to 400°F. Place the milk, eggs and butter in a bowl and whisk until combined.

HEALTH BENEFITS

Bananas are rich in potassium, which is vital for muscle and nerve function. They are also a good source of energy.

2 Sift together the flour, salt and baking powder into a separate bowl. Add the sugar and chocolate to the flour mixture and then stir to combine. Slowly stir in the milk mixture, but do not beat it. Fold in the mashed bananas.

3 Spoon the batter into the paper cases. Bake for 20 minutes until golden. Cool on a wire rack.

Apricot and Hazelnut Oat Cookies

THESE COOKIE-CUM-FLAPJACKS have a chewy, crumbly texture. They are sprinkled with apricots and toasted hazelnuts, but any combination of dried fruit and nuts can be used.

INGREDIENTS

8 tablespoons (1 stick) unsalted butter, plus extra for greasing

scant 1/2 cup superfine sugar

1 tablespoon clear honey

1 cup self-rising flour, sifted

1 cup rolled oats

scant 1/2 cup dried unsulfured apricots, chopped

For the topping

2 tablespoons dried unsulfured apricots, chopped

1/4 cup shelled hazelnuts, toasted and chopped

Makes 9

1 Lightly grease a baking sheet. Preheat the oven to 325°F. Put the butter, sugar and honey in a small heavy-based saucepan and cook over gentle heat, until the butter melts and the sugar dissolves, stirring occasionally. Remove the pan from the heat.

HEALTH BENEFITS

Oats provide soluble fiber, which is believed to lower blood cholesterol levels.

2 Put the flour, oats and apricots in a bowl, add the honey mixture and mix with a wooden spoon to form a sticky dough. Divide the dough into nine pieces and place on the baking sheet. Press into 1/2-inch thick rounds. Scatter over the apricots and hazelnuts and press into the dough.

3 Bake for 15 minutes until golden and slightly crisp. Leave to cool on the cookie sheet for 5 minutes, then transfer to a wire rack.

Chocolate Chip Cookies

INGREDIENTS

6 tablespoons soft margarine
1/4 cup light brown sugar
1/4 cup sugar
1 egg, beaten
few drops of vanilla extract
3/4 cup rice flour
3/4 cup gluten-free cornmeal
1 teaspoon gluten-free baking powder
pinch of salt
2/3 cup semisweet chocolate chips, or a
    mixture of milk and white
    chocolate chips

Makes 16

1 Preheat the oven to 375°F. Lightly grease two baking sheets. Place the margarine and sugars in a bowl and cream together until light and fluffy.

2 Beat in the egg and vanilla extract. Fold in the rice flour, cornmeal, baking powder and salt, then fold in the chocolate chips.

3 Place spoonfuls of the mixture on the prepared baking sheets, leaving space for spreading between each one. Bake for 10–15 minutes, until the cookies are lightly browned.

4 Remove the cookies from the oven and let cool for a few minutes, then transfer to a wire rack using a metal spatula. Let cool completely before serving. Once cool, store the cookies in an airtight container for up to a week, or pack into plastic bags and freeze.

VARIATIONS

Add 1/4 cup of your favorite nuts such as walnuts or pecans to the mixture if desired.

Cherry Coconut Munchies

YOU'LL FIND it hard to stop at just one of these munchies, which make a wonderful morning or afternoon treat. If desired, drizzle 1–2 ounces melted chocolate over the cold munchies and allow to set before serving.

INGREDIENTS

2 egg whites
1 cup confectioner's sugar, sifted
1 cup ground almonds
generous 1 cup dried, unsweetened coconut
few drops of almond extract
1/3 cup candied cherries, finely chopped

Makes 20

1 Preheat the oven to 300°F. Line two baking sheets with baking parchment. Place the egg whites in a bowl and beat until stiff.

2 Fold in the confectioners' sugar, then fold in the almonds, coconut and almond extract to form a sticky dough. Fold in the chopped cherries.

3 Place heaped teaspoonfuls of the mixture on the prepared baking sheets. Bake for 25 minutes, until pale golden. Cool on the baking sheets for a few minutes, then transfer to a wire rack until completely cool.

VARIATIONS

Use ground hazelnuts in place of the almonds and omit the almond extract. Alternatively, retain the almonds and cherries but cut the amount by one third and add 1/3 cup chocolate chips to the mixture.

COOK'S TIP

These munchies will keep for up to a week if stored in an airtight container.

Golden Raisins and Cinnamon Bars

THESE SPICY, chewy bars are hard to
resist and make a great treat,
especially for children.

INGREDIENTS

$^{1}/_{2}$ cup (8 tablespoons) soft margarine

2 tablespoons light brown sugar

1 ounce plain toffees

$^{1}/_{4}$ cup honey

$1^{1}/_{2}$ cups golden raisins

2 teaspoons ground cinnamon

6 ounces rice crispies

Makes 16

1 Lightly grease a shallow 9 x 11-inch
cake pan. Place the margarine, sugar,
toffees and honey in a pan and heat
gently, stirring, until melted. Bring to the
boil. Remove the pan from the heat.

2 Stir in the raisins, cinnamon and
rice crispies and mix well. Transfer
the mixture to the prepared pan and
spread the mixture evenly, pressing it
down firmly.

3 Allow to cool, then chill until firm.
Once firm, cut into bars, remove
from the pan and serve. Store the bars
in an airtight container in the refrigerator.

VARIATION

*For an extra-special treat, melt
3 ounces semisweet or milk chocolate
and spread or, using a teaspoon or paper
piping bag, drizzle it over the cold rice
crispie mixture. Allow to set before
cutting into the bars.*

Apricot and Orange Muffins

SERVE THESE fruity muffins freshly
baked and warm.

INGREDIENTS

1 cup cornmeal

$^{3}/_{4}$ cup rice flour

1 tablespoon baking powder

pinch of salt

4 tablespoons soft margarine, melted

$^{1}/_{4}$ cup light brown sugar

1 egg, beaten

scant 1 cup low-fat milk

zest, finely grated of 1 orange

$^{1}/_{2}$ cup dried apricots, chopped

Makes 8 large or 12 medium muffins

1 Preheat the oven to 400°F. Lightly
grease or line an 8- or 12-cup muffin
pan. Place the cornmeal, rice flour,
baking powder and salt in a bowl
and mix.

2 Stir together the melted
margarine, sugar, egg, milk and
orange zest, then pour the mixture
over the dry ingredients. Fold the
ingredients gently together—just
enough to combine them. The
mixture will look quite lumpy, which is
correct, as overmixing will result in
heavy muffins.

3 Fold in the chopped, dried
apricots, then spoon the mixture
into the prepared muffin pan, dividing it
equally among the cups.

4 Bake for 15–20 minutes, until the
muffins have risen and are golden
brown and springy to the touch. Turn
them out on to a wire rack to cool.

5 Serve the muffins warm or cold,
on their own or cut in half and
spread with a little low-fat spread.
Store in an airtight container for up to
one week or seal in plastic bags and
freeze for up to three months.

Wholemeal Apple, Apricot and Walnut Loaf

INGREDIENTS

2 cups whole wheat flour

1 teaspoon baking powder

pinch of salt

1/2 cup sunflower or low-fat margarine

1 cup light brown sugar

2 large eggs, lightly beaten

rind, grated and juice of 1 orange

1/2 cup walnuts, chopped

1/3 cup dried apricots, chopped

1 large cooking apple

oil, for greasing

Makes 10–12 slices

1 Preheat the oven to 350°F. Grease a 2-pound loaf pan and line the bottom and sides with wax paper.

2 Sift the flour, baking powder and salt into a large mixing bowl, then turn the bran remaining in the sifter into the mixture. Add the margarine, sugar, eggs, orange rind and juice. Stir, then beat with a hand-held electric beater until smooth.

3 Stir in the walnuts and apricots. Quarter, peel and core the apple, chop it coarsely and add it to the mixture. Stir, then spoon the mixture into the prepared pan and level the top.

Spiced Banana Muffins

WHOLE WHEAT muffins, with banana for added fiber, make a tasty treat at any time of the day. They are delicious served warm with butter, but, if preferred, slice off the tops and fill with a teaspoon of jam or marmalade.

INGREDIENTS

3/4 cup whole wheat flour

1/2 cup all-purpose flour

2 teaspoons baking powder

pinch of salt

1 teaspoon mixed ground cinnamon, nutmeg, and allspice

1/4 cup light brown sugar

1/4 cup polyunsaturated or low-fat margarine

1 egg, beaten

2/3 cup low-fat milk

rind of 1 orange, grated

1 ripe banana

1/4 cup rolled oats

scant 1/4 cup hazelnuts, chopped

Makes 12

1 Preheat the oven to 400°F. Line a muffin pan with 12 large paper cups. Sift together both flours, the baking powder, salt and mixed spices into a bowl, then turn the bran remaining in the sifter into the bowl. Stir in the sugar.

2 Melt the margarine and pour it into a mixing bowl. Cool slightly, then beat in the egg, milk and grated orange rind.

3 Gently fold in the dry ingredients. Mash the banana with a fork, then stir it gently into the mixture, being careful not to overmix.

VARIATION

You can substitute the banana with chopped apples or pears for a change, if desired.

4 Spoon the mixture into the paper cases. Combine the oats and hazelnuts and sprinkle a little of the mixture over each muffin.

5 Bake for 20 minutes, until the muffins are well risen and golden, and a skewer inserted in the center comes out clean. Transfer to a wire rack and serve warm or cold.

Fruit, Nut and Seed Teabread

CUT INTO slices and spread with a little butter, jam or honey, this tea bread makes an ideal breakfast bread but is just as good for tea.

INGREDIENTS

²/3 cup dried dates, chopped

¹/2 cup dried apricots, chopped

1 cup golden raisins

¹/2 cup light brown sugar

2 cups pancake and baking mix

1 teaspoon baking powder

2 teaspoons apple-pie spice

3 ounces mixed nuts, such as walnuts and
    hazelnuts, chopped

3 ounces mixed seeds, such as millet,
    sunflower and sesame seeds

2 eggs, beaten

²/3 cup low-fat milk

Makes a 2-pound loaf

1 Preheat the oven to 350°F. Lightly grease a 13 x 4 x 4-inch loaf pan. Place the chopped dates and apricots and raisins in a large mixing bowl and stir in the sugar.

2 Place the baking mix, baking powder, spice, mixed nuts and seeds in a separate bowl and mix well.

3 Stir the eggs and milk into the fruit, then add the flour mixture and beat together until well mixed.

4 Spoon into the prepared pan and level the surface. Bake for about 1 hour, until the tea bread is firm to the touch and lightly browned.

5 Allow to cool in the pan for a few minutes, then turn out onto a wire rack to cool completely. Serve warm or cold, cut into slices, either on its own or spread with butter and jam. Wrap the tea bread in foil to store.

COOK'S TIP

You can also use this mixture to make muffins. Fill muffin cups ⅔ full and bake for about 15 minutes, or until the muffin is firm and the top springs back.

Gingerbread

INGREDIENTS

1/2 cup light brown sugar

6 tablespoons soft margarine

1/4 cup golden syrup or light corn syrup

1/4 cup molasses

7 tablespoons low-fat milk

1 egg, beaten

1 1/2 cups flour

1/2 cup chickpea (gram) flour

pinch of salt

2 teaspoons ground ginger

1 teaspoon ground cinnamon

1 1/2 teaspoons baking powder

Makes a 2-pound loaf

1 Preheat the oven to 325°F. Lightly grease and line a 13 x 4 x 4-inch loaf pan. Place the sugar, margarine, syrup and molasses in a saucepan and heat gently until melted and blended, stirring occasionally.

2 Remove the pan from the heat, let cool slightly, then mix in the milk and egg.

3 Mix the flours, salt, spices and baking powder in a large bowl.

4 Make a well in the center, pour in the liquid mixture and beat well.

5 Pour the mixture into the prepared pan and bake for 1–1 1/2 hours, until firm to the touch and lightly browned.

6 Allow to cool in the pan for a few minutes, then turn out onto a wire rack to cool completely. Store it in an airtight container or wrapped in foil.

VARIATION

Fold 2 ounces finely chopped preserved ginger into the raw cake mixture, if desired. Add 1–2 teaspoons extra ground ginger for a more pronounced flavor.

Cheese and Potato Biscuits

THE UNUSUAL addition of creamy mashed potato gives these whole wheat biscuits a light moist crumb and a crisp crust. A sprinkling of mature Cheddar and sesame seeds adds the finishing touch.

INGREDIENTS

1 cup whole wheat flour
1/2 teaspoon salt
4 teaspoons baking powder
3 tablespoons (3/8 stick) unsalted butter,
    plus extra for greasing
2 eggs, beaten
1/4 cup low-fat milk or buttermilk
1 1/3 cups cooked, mashed potato
3 tablespoons fresh sage, chopped
1/2 cup mature vegetarian
    Cheddar, grated
sesame seeds, for sprinkling

Makes 9

1 Preheat the oven to 425°F. Grease a baking sheet.

2 Sift the flour, salt and baking powder into a bowl. Rub in the butter using your finger tips until the mixture resembles fine bread crumbs, then mix in half the beaten egg and all the milk or buttermilk. Add the mashed potato, sage and half the Cheddar, and mix to a soft dough using your hands.

3 Turn out dough on to a floured work surface and knead lightly until smooth. Roll out the dough to 3/4 inch thick, then stamp out nine biscuits using a 2 1/2-inch fluted cutter.

VARIATIONS

• Use unbleached self-rising flour instead of whole wheat flour and baking powder, if you wish.
• Fresh rosemary, basil or thyme can be used in place of the sage.

4 Place the biscuits on the prepared baking sheet and brush with the remaining beaten egg. Sprinkle remainder of the cheese and the sesame seeds on top and bake for 15 minutes until golden. Transfer to a wire rack and leave to cool.

HEALTH BENEFITS

Fresh sage is thought to assist the digestion of rich food and also acts as a stimulant to the central nervous system.

Whole Wheat Sunflower Bread

SUNFLOWER SEEDS give a nutty crunchiness to this whole wheat loaf. Serve with a chunk of cheese and rich tomato chutney.

INGREDIENTS

4 cups whole wheat bread flour

1/2 teaspoon rapid-rise dried yeast

1/2 teaspoon salt

1/2 cup sunflower seeds, plus extra
  for sprinkling

Makes 1 loaf

1 Grease and lightly flour a 1-pound loaf pan. Mix together the flour, yeast, salt and sunflower seeds in a large bowl. Make a well in the center and gradually stir in 1 1/4 cups warm water. Mix vigorously with a wooden spoon to form a soft, sticky dough. The dough should be quite wet and sticky, so don't be tempted to add any extra flour.

2 Cover the bowl with a damp dish towel and leave to rise in a warm place for 45–50 minutes or until doubled in bulk.

3 Preheat the oven to 400°F. Turn out the dough on to a floured work surface and knead for 10 minutes—the dough will still be quite sticky.

HEALTH BENEFITS

High in protein, sesame seeds also provide calcium as well as vitamin E and the B complex vitamins.

4 Form the dough into an oblong and place in the loaf pan. Sprinkle the top with sunflower seeds. Cover with a damp dish towel and leave to rise again for 15 minutes more.

5 Bake for 40–45 minutes until golden—the loaf should sound hollow when tapped underneath. Leave for 5 minutes, then turn out of the pan and leave to cool on a wire rack.

Spicy Millet Bread

THIS IS a delicious spicy bread with a golden crust. Cut into wedges, as you would a cake, and serve warm with a thick vegetable soup.

INGREDIENTS

1/2 cup millet

5 1/2 cups unbleached bread flour

2 teaspoons salt

1 teaspoon sugar

1 teaspoon dried chili flakes
(optional)

1/4-ounce sachet rapid-rise dried yeast

2 tablespoons (1/4 stick) unsalted butter

1 onion, roughly chopped

1 tablespoon cumin seeds

1 teaspoon ground turmeric

Makes 1 loaf

1 Bring scant 1 cup water to a boil, add the millet, cover and simmer gently for 20 minutes until the grains are soft and the water is absorbed. Remove from the heat and leave to cool until just warm.

2 Mix together the flour, salt, sugar, chili flakes, if using, and yeast in a large bowl. Stir in the millet, then add 1 1/2 cups warm water and mix to form a soft dough.

HEALTH BENEFITS

Millet is a versatile—and much underrated—grain. If eaten on a regular basis as part of a varied healthy diet, it can help lower the risk of heart disease and certain cancers.

3 Turn out the dough on to a floured work surface and knead for 10 minutes. If the dough seems a little dry, knead well until the dough is smooth and elastic.

4 Place the dough in an oiled bowl and cover with oiled plastic wrap or a dish towel. Leave to rise in a warm place for 1 hour, until doubled in bulk.

5 Meanwhile, melt the butter in a heavy-based frying pan, add the onion and fry for 10 minutes until softened, stirring occasionally. Add the cumin seeds and turmeric, and fry for a further 5–8 minutes, stirring constantly, until the cumin seeds begin to pop. Set aside.

COOK'S TIP

To test if a dough has risen properly, make a small indentation in the top with your index finger. If the indentation does not spring back entirely, then rising is complete; if it springs back at once, the dough is not ready and should be left for another 15 minutes before retesting.

6 Punch down the dough by pressing down with your knuckles to deflate the dough, then shape it into a round. Place the onion mixture in the middle of the dough and bring the sides over the filling to make a package, then seal well.

7 Place the loaf on an oiled baking sheet, seam-side down, cover with oiled plastic wrap and leave in a warm place for 45 minutes until doubled in bulk. Preheat the oven to 425°F.

8 Bake the bread for 30 minutes until golden. It should sound hollow when tapped underneath. Leave to cool on a wire rack.

Polenta and Bell Pepper Bread

FULL OF Mediterranean flavor, this satisfying, sunshine-colored bread is best eaten while still warm, drizzled with a little extra virgin olive oil and served with soup.

INGREDIENTS

1 1/2 cups polenta

1 teaspoon salt

3 cups unbleached bread flour, plus extra for dusting

1 teaspoon sugar

1/4-ounce sachet rapid-rise dried yeast

1 red bell pepper, roasted, peeled and diced

1 tablespoon olive oil

Makes 2 loaves

1 Mix together the polenta, salt, flour, sugar and yeast in a large bowl. Stir in the diced red pepper until it is evenly distributed, then make a well in the center of the mixture. Grease two loaf pans.

2 Add 1 1/4 cups warm water and the oil and mix to a soft dough. Knead for 10 minutes until smooth and elastic. Place in an oiled bowl, cover with oiled plastic wrap and leave to rise in a warm place for 1 hour, or until doubled in bulk.

HEALTH BENEFITS

Weight for weight, red bell peppers contain about three times as much vitamin C as fresh oranges.

COOK'S TIP

Cook the pepper in the oven or under a broiler until charred, then place in a plastic bag and leave until cool enough to peel.

3 Punch down the dough, knead lightly, then divide in two. Shape each piece into an oblong and place in the pans. Cover with oiled plastic wrap and leave to rise for 45 minutes. Preheat the oven to 425°F.

4 Bake for 30 minutes until golden —the loaves should sound hollow when tapped underneath. Leave for 5 minutes, then cool on a wire rack.

Fruit Soda Bread

THIS TRADITIONAL Irish bread is quick to make as it does not require prolonged kneading or rising. It is best eaten while still warm on the day of baking.

INGREDIENTS

2 cups unbleached all-purpose flour

2 cups whole wheat flour

1 teaspoon salt

1 teaspoon bicarbonate of soda

heaped 1 tablespoon sugar

3/4 cup raisins

1/4 cup ready-to-eat stoned prunes, chopped

1 egg, lightly beaten

1 1/4 cups buttermilk

Serves 4

1 Preheat the oven to 400°F. Sift together the plain and whole wheat flours, salt and bicarbonate of soda into a large bowl, adding any bran left in the sifter. Add the sugar and dried fruit, and mix well to combine.

2 Make a well in the center and add the egg and buttermilk. Mix first with a wooden spoon and then with your hands until it forms a soft, slightly sticky dough. If the dough is too dry, add a little more buttermilk.

HEALTH BENEFITS

Dried fruit is recognized as a good source of fiber as well as minerals, such as potassium and iron.

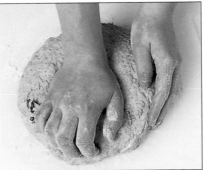

3 Turn out the dough on to a lightly floured work surface and knead lightly until smooth. Form into a flat round, about 1 1/2 inches thick.

4 Place on a greased baking sheet and dust the loaf with flour.

5 Cut a large deep cross, almost through to the bottom of the dough round. Bake for 30–35 minutes until risen and golden. The bread should sound hollow when tapped underneath. Transfer to a wire rack and leave to cool.

Rosemary and Rock Salt Focaccia

ENRICHED WITH olive oil and flavored with rosemary, garlic and black olives, this popular Italian bread takes its name from the Italian word for hearth—which is where it was traditionally baked.

INGREDIENTS

2 cups unbleached bread flour, sifted

1/2 teaspoon salt

1/4-ounce sachet rapid-rise dried yeast

4 garlic cloves, finely chopped

2 sprigs of rosemary, leaves removed and chopped

10 black olives, pitted and roughly chopped (optional)

1 tablespoon olive oil

For the topping

6 tablespoons olive oil

2 teaspoons rock salt

1 sprig of rosemary, leaves removed

Makes 1 loaf

1 Mix together the flour, salt, yeast, garlic, rosemary and olives, if using, in a large bowl. Make a well in the center and add the olive oil and 2/3 cup warm water. Mix thoroughly to form a soft dough.

HEALTH BENEFITS

The oil in olives is monounsaturated and this type of oil is believed to reduce blood cholesterol levels. Olives also provide good amounts of iron and the antioxidant, vitamin E.

2 Turn out the dough on to a floured work surface and knead for 10–15 minutes. Put the dough in an oiled bowl and cover with oiled plastic wrap or a dish towel. Leave to rise in a warm place for 45 minutes, until the dough has doubled in bulk.

3 Turn out the dough and knead lightly again. Roll out to an oval shape, about 1/2-inch thick.

4 Place the dough on a greased baking sheet, cover loosely with oiled plastic wrap or a dish towel and leave in a warm place for 25–30 minutes to rise again.

5 Preheat the oven to 400°F. Make indentations with your fingertips all over the top of the bread. Drizzle two-thirds of the olive oil over the top, then sprinkle with the rock salt and rosemary.

6 Bake for 25 minutes until golden. The bread should sound hollow when tapped underneath. Transfer to a wire rack and spoon the remaining olive oil over the top.

VARIATIONS

• *To make sun-dried tomato focaccia, omit the rosemary leaves and olives, and add 1 1/2 cups chopped and drained sun-dried tomatoes in oil to the dry ingredients. Add 1 tablespoon sun-dried tomato paste and 1 tablespoon of the oil from the sun-dried tomatoes to the dough when adding the oil and water, then mix well.*

• *To make saffron focaccia, add a few strands of saffron to the warm water and leave to stand for 5 minutes before adding to the flour. Alternatively, add a pinch of saffron powder to the flour.*

Index

acorn squash, 38
aduki bean sprouts, 56
aduki beans, 80, 83
agar-agar, 60
orange jelly, 60
alfalfa sprouts, 56
allergies, nut, 103
allspice, 106
almond oil, 121
almonds, 100
apricot and almond tart, 462
lemon and almond tart, 456
amaranth, 76
apples, 18–19
   apple and beet salad with red leaves, 392
   apple and blackcurrant pancakes, 148
   apple, onion, and Gruyère tart, 350
   baked apples, 19
   baked stuffed apples, 472
   cranberry and apple juice, 132
   Dutch apple cake, 480
   pan-fried apple slices with walnut
      shortbread, 452
   red cabbage and apple casserole, 258
   spiced apple crumble, 472
   whole-wheat apple, apricot, and walnut loaf,
      494
apricots, 18
   apricot and almond muesli, 141
   apricot and almond tart, 462
   apricot and ginger compote, 144
   apricot and hazelnut oat cookies, 486
   apricot panettone pudding, 459
   spiced apricot puree, 127
   warm bagels with poached apricots, 149
   whole-wheat apple, apricot, and walnut loaf,
      494
arugula, 51
   fennel, orange, and arugula salad, 388
   arugula and tomato pizza, 355
   arugula, pear, and Parmesan salad, 382
arame, 59
asparagus, 40
   asparagus tart with ricotta, 318
   asparagus rolls with herb butter sauce, 207
   asparagus soup, 164
   asparagus with eggs, 209
   asparagus with tarragon hollandaise, 318
   fried noodles, beansprouts, and asparagus,
      428
   Spanish asparagus and orange salad, 369
   teriyaki soba noodles with tofu and
      asparagus, 325
avocados, 44
   avocado, red onion, and spinach salad with
      polenta croutons, 391
   fresh spinach and avocado salad, 365
   gazpacho with avocado salsa, 160
   rice and beans with avocado salsa, 324

bagels with poached apricots, 149
balsamic vinegar, 122
Balti baby vegetables, 426
bananas, 29
   banana and pecan bread, 478

banana and strawberry smoothie, 132
   cheese and banana toasties, 152
   chunky chocolate and banana muffins, 486
   date, banana and walnut yogurt, 134
   oaty pancakes with caramel bananas and
      pecan nuts, 147
   spiced banana muffins, 495
barley, 74
   lemon barley water, 75
basil, 52
   pesto, 53
basmati rice, 67
bay leaves, 52
bean sprouts, 56
   fried noodles, beansprouts, and asparagus,
      428
beancurd skins and sticks, 87–8
beans, 80–5
   beans with mushrooms, 253
   brown bean salad, 379
   corn and bean tamale pie, 340
   Jamaican black bean pot, 262
   mushroom and bean pâté, 197
   omelet with beans, 228
   rice and beans with avocado salsa, 324
   Silvio's bean and pasta soup, 161
   spicy bean and lentil loaf, 226
   sweet and sour mixed bean hot pot, 260
   vegetable chili, 283
   white bean salad with roasted red bell pepper
      dressing, 398
   white bean soup, 177
beet, 30
berries, 24–5
biryani, parsnip, eggplant, and cashew, 266
black bean sauce, 88
black beans, 80, 83
Jamaican black bean pot, 262
black-eyed beans, 80, 83
black peppercorns, 110

blackberries, 24–5
blackcurrants, 25
   apple and blackcurrant pancakes, 148
blinis, buckwheat, with mushroom caviar, 204

blueberries, 24
bok choy with soy sauce, 419
Bolognese, mushroom, 278
borlotti beans, 81, 83
Boston lettuce, 50
bran, 62, 71
brassicas, 34–6
bread: cannellini bean and rosemary bruschetta,
      155
   fruit soda bread, 503
   griddled tomatoes on soda bread, 150
   Lebanese flatbread, 188
   panzanella, 396
   polenta and pepper bread, 502
   rosemary and rock salt focaccia, 504
   spicy millet bread, 500
   whole-wheat sunflower bread, 499
   zucchini, mushroom, and pesto panino, 156
   brioches, chive scrambled eggs in, 154
broccoli, 34
brown bean salad, 379
brown lentils, 78–9
brownies, date and walnut, 478
brunches, 131–57
bruschetta, cannellini bean and rosemary, 155
Brussels sprouts, 36
   Chinese Brussels sprouts, 416
   festive Brussels sprouts, 417
buckwheat, 75–6
   buckwheat blinis with mushroom caviar, 204
   buckwheat pasta, 113
bulgur, 63
   bulgur and fava bean salad, 367
butter, 95
buttermilk, 91
butternut squash, 38
butternut squash and sage pizza, 352
button mushrooms, 48

cabbage, 35–6
   mixed cabbage stir-fry, 36
   whole-wheat pasta with caraway cabbage,
      274
cakes: date and walnut spice cake, 482
   Dutch apple cake, 480
   gingerbread, 497
   pear and polenta cake, 480
   rich lemon poppyseed cake, 483
calzone, eggplant, shallot, and tomato, 360
chamomile tea, 125
canned beans, 84
cannellini beans, 81, 83
   cannellini bean and rosemary bruschetta, 155
   cannellini bean puree, 80
cannelloni, broccoli and ricotta, 272
caramelized onion tart, 344
caraway, 106
cardamom, 106
carob, 126–7
carotenoids, 30
carrageenan, 61
carrots, 30
   carrot and cilantro soup, 165
   glazed carrots with cider, 444
   spiced carrot dip, 187

cauliflower, 34
    broccoli and cauliflower gratin, 445
    cauliflower and broccoli with tomato sauce, 274
    cauliflower and mushroom gougère, 314
    spicy potatoes and cauliflower, 406
cayenne, 106
celeriac, 31
    beet and celeriac casserole, 441
    celeriac and blue cheese roulade, 303
celery, 41
    curried celery soup, 168
celery seeds, 106–7
cellophane noodles, 116–17
cèpes, 49
    cèpes with a parsley dressing, 384
cereal grains, 62–5
chanterelles, 48
cheat's lasagne with mixed mushrooms, 268
cheese, 94–7
    apple, onion, and Gruyère tart, 350
    baked leeks with cheese and yogurt, 231
    baked onions stuffed with feta, 234
    baked squash with Parmesan, 252
    broccoli and cauliflower gratin, 445
    broiled goat cheese salad, 370
    cauliflower and mushroom gougère, 314
    celeriac and blue cheese roulade, 303
    cheese and potato scones, 498
    cheese-topped roast baby vegetables, 414
    chestnut, Stilton, and ale pie, 351
    corn and cheese beggar's purses, 342
    eggplant, smoked mozzarella, and basil rolls, 236
    feta and mint potato salad, 392
    fried mozzarella, 200
    goat cheese soufflé, 302
    Greek cheese and potato patties, 201
    Jerusalem artichoke soup with Gruyère toasts, 172
    onion tarts with goat cheese, 234
    Parmesan and poached egg salad, 372
    penne with fennel, tomato, and blue cheese, 219
    potato, red onion, and feta frittata, 296
    potted Stilton with herbs and Melba toast, 196
    red onion and goat cheese pastries, 346
    roasted tomato and mozzarella salad with basil dressing, 374
    Roquefort tartlets, 203
    tomato and feta cheese salad, 371
    vegetable hot pot with cheese triangles, 250

watercress, pear, walnut, and Roquefort salad, 396
cherries, 19
    cherry coconut munchies, 488
chestnut mushrooms, 48
chestnuts, 100–1
chickpea sprouts, 56
chickpeas, 82–3
    chickpea falafel with cilantro dip, 189
    eggplant and chickpea tagine, 263
    garlic, chickpea, and spinach soup, 175
    hummus with pan-fried zucchini, 194
    sesame seed-coated falafel with tahini yogurt dip, 245
    spicy chickpeas, 436
chicory, 40–1
chilies, 43, 107
    chili, tomato, and spinach pizza, 358
    crispy spring rolls with sweet chili dip, 190
    lima beans in chili sauce, 443
    rice noodles with vegetable chili sauce, 242
    spicy potato wedges with chili dip, 193
    vegetable chili, 283
    zucchini fritters with chili jam, 269
Chinese Brussels sprouts, 416
chives, 52
    chive scrambled eggs in brioches, 154
chocolate: chocolate chip cookies, 488
    chunky chocolate and banana muffins, 486
cider vinegar, 123
cilantro, 52–3
    chickpea falafel with cilantro dip, 189
    cilantro omelet parcels with Oriental vegetables, 229
    cilantro ravioli with pumpkin filling, 322
    tomato, scallion, and cilantro salad, 383
cinnamon, 107
citrus fruits, 22–3
citrus rind, 23
citrus shake, 132
cloves, 107
coconut, 101
    cherry coconut munchies, 488
    coconut milk: coconut jelly with star anise fruits, 474
    coconut rice puddings with broiled oranges, 456
    spiced red lentil and coconut soup, 182
coffee, 124
conchiglie, spinach and ricotta, 280
coriander, 107
corn, 45, 73
    corn and bean tamale pie, 340
    corn and cheese beggar's purses, 342
    corn cakes with broiled tomatoes, 239
cornmeal, 73–4
corn oil, 119
corn pasta, 113
cos lettuce, 50
cottage cheese, 94
couscous, 64
    couscous salad, 378
    spiced couscous with halloumi and zucchini ribbons, 327
cow's milk, 90
cracked wheat, 63
cranberries, 24
    cranberry and apple juice, 132
    cranberry oat bars, 492
cream, 90
cream cheese, 94
crème fraîche, 91

croquettes, parsnip and chestnut, 425
crumbles: peach and raspberry, 466
    spiced apple, 472
cucumber, 39
    marinated cucumber salad, 387
cumin, 108
curly endive, 50
currants, 25
    currants (dried), 27
curries: curried celery soup, 168
    curried eggs, 208
    eggplant curry, 332
    mushroom and okra curry, 328
    vegetable Kashmiri, 264
    vegetable korma, 333

dairy foods, 90–7
dandelion and lemon verbena tea, 125
dates, 27
    date and walnut brownies, 478
    date and walnut spice cake, 482
    date, banana, and walnut yogurt, 134
    date, fig, and orange pudding, 455
    porridge with date puree and pistachio nuts, 144
dill, 53
dips, 184–93
    chili, 193
    cilantro, 189
    eggplant, 188
    guacamole, 184
    lima bean, watercress, and herb, 185
    saffron, 186
    spiced carrot, 187
    sweet chili, 190
dried fruit, 21, 127
    baked fruit compote, 464
    fruit, nut, and seed teabread, 496
    fruity sesame porridge, 138
    trail mix, 138
    vine fruits, 27
dried mushrooms, 49
dulse, 60
durum wheat pasta, 112
Dutch apple cake, 480

egg noodles, 116
eggplant, 42–3
    breaded eggplant with pilaf vinaigrette, 210
    eggplant and chickpea tagine, 263
    eggplant curry, 332
    eggplant dip with crispy bread, 188

eggplant, lemon, and caper salad, 388
eggplant, shallot, and tomato calzone, 360
eggplant, smoked mozzarella, and basil rolls,
    236
parsnip, eggplant, and cashew biryani, 266
Szechuan eggplant, 418
vegetable moussaka, 270
eggs, 98–9
    asparagus with eggs, 209
    baked eggs with creamy leeks, 233
    chive scrambled eggs in brioches, 154
    curried eggs, 208
    Parmesan and poached egg salad, 372
    puree of lentils with baked eggs, 304
elderflower tea, 125
enoki mushrooms, 49

fajitas, vegetable, 232
falafel: chickpea falafel with cilantro dip, 189
    sesame seed-coated with tahini yogurt dip,
        245
fava beans, 45, 81, 83
bulgur and fava bean salad, 367
fennel, 40
    baked fennel with a crumb crust, 446
    fennel, orange, and arugula salad, 388
    mushroom and fennel hot pot, 241
    penne with fennel, tomato, and blue cheese,
        219
fenugreek, 108
feta and mint potato salad, 392
feta cheese, 96
field blewitts, 48–9
field mushrooms, 48
figs, 27
    date, fig, and orange pudding, 455

flageolet beans, 82–3
    flageolet beans with garlic, 442
flour, 64–5
    rice flour, 71
    soy flour, 88
focaccia, rosemary and rock salt, 504
fondue, fruit with hazelnut dip, 468
fonduta with steamed vegetables, 309
fool, tofu fruit, 87
freezing herbs, 55
French beans, 45
French onion soup, classic, 176
frijoles, 438
frittata: frittata with sun-dried tomatoes, 243
    potato, red onion, and feta frittata, 296

sliced frittata with tomato sauce, 225
fritters: hot parsnip fritters on baby spinach, 424
    zucchini fritters with chili jam, 269
fromage frais, 94
fruit, 18–29
    coconut jelly with star anise fruits, 474
    crunchy fruit layer, 140
    fruit fondue with hazelnut dip, 468
    fruit puree, 25
    lemon grass skewers with lime cheese, 474
    three fruit compôtes, 137
    tofu fruit fool, 87
    tropical fruit gratin, 476
    tropical fruit with hot rum and cinnamon
        sauce, 450
    winter fruit poached in mulled wine, 461
    fruit juice, 127
    fruit, nut, and seed teabread, 496
    fruit salads: melon, pineapple, and grape
        cocktail, 136
    three fruit compotes, 137
    fruit soda bread, 503
    fruit teas, 124
    fruity rice salad, 386
fusilli with peppers and onions, 216

gado gado, 385
galangal, 108
garlic, 46–7
    garlic, chickpea, and spinach soup, 175
    garlic mashed potatoes, 407
    garlic mushrooms with a parsley crust, 206
gazpacho with avocado salsa, 160
ginger, 108–9
gingerbread, 497
globe artichokes, 41
    broccoli, chili, and artichoke pasta, 320
    mixed vegetables with artichokes, 258
    sweet and sour artichoke salad, 368
gnocchi, potato, 256
goat cheese, 96
goat milk, 90
gooseberries, 25
gougère, cauliflower and mushroom, 314
grain syrups, 127
grains, 62–77
    sprouted, 56–7
granola, 142
grapefruit, 22
    grapefruit and strawberry compote, 137
grapes, 26
grapeseed oil, 120
gratins: broccoli and cauliflower, 445
    potato, spinach, and pine nut, 315
    root vegetable gratin with Indian spices, 431
    tropical fruit, 476
Greek cheese and potato patties, 201
Greek salad, 364
green beans, 45
    Oriental green beans, 420
green lentils, 78–9
green peppercorns, 110
green tea, 124
grits, 74
groundnut oil, 119–20
guacamole, 184
    tortilla wrap with tabbouleh and guacamole,
        246

halloumi cheese, 96
haricot beans, 82–3
harvest vegetable and lentil casserole, 291

hazelnut oil, 121
hazelnuts, 101
    fruit fondue with hazelnut dip, 468
    trail mix, 138
hemp seeds, 105
herbs, 52–5
    drying, 55
    freezing, 55
herbal infusions, 55
herbal tisanes, 125
herbed rice pilaf, 414
herb omelet, 99
hijiki, 60
hoisin sauce, 88
hollandaise, tarragon, 318
hominy, 74
honey, 126
horseradish, 33
    roasted beet with horseradish dressing, 399
hot-and-sour soup, 178
hummus with pan-fried zucchini, 194

iceberg lettuce, 50
Indian rice pudding, 460
infusions, herbal, 55
Italian pea and basil soup, 182

Jamaican black bean pot, 262
Japanese rice products, 70
Japanese salad, 394
Japanese-style noodle soup, 179
Japanese sushi rice, 71
jasmine rice, 66
jelly: coconut jelly with star anise fruits, 474
    orange jelly, 60
Jerusalem artichokes, 32
    Jerusalem artichoke soup with Gruyère
        toasts, 172
julienne strips, citrus rind, 23

kaffir limes, 53
kamut, 76
kebabs, marinated tofu, 87
kecap manis, 88
kidney beans see red kidney beans
kiwi fruit, 28
kombu, 59

lasagne: cheat's lasagne with mixed mushrooms,
    268
laver, 58
leafy vegetables, 34, 36–7
Lebanese flatbread, 188
leeks, 47
    baked eggs with creamy leeks, 233
    baked leeks with cheese and yogurt, 231
    leek, mushroom, and lemon risotto, 284
    leek soufflé, 305
    pea, leek, and broccoli soup, 167
legumes, 78–9, 85
lemon, 22–3
    creamy lemon rice pudding, 466
    lemon and almond tart, 456
    lemon barley water, 75
    lemon balm, 53
    lemon grass, 109
    lemon grass skewers with lime cheese, 474
    rich lemon poppyseed cake, 483
lentil sprouts, 56
lentils, 78–9
    creamy lemon Puy lentils, 236
    fresh tomato, lentil, and onion soup, 181

harvest vegetable and lentil casserole, 291
puree of lentils with baked eggs, 304
spiced lentils and rice, 150
spiced red lentil and coconut soup, 182
spicy bean and lentil loaf, 226
tomato and lentil dahl with toasted almonds, 247
lettuce, 50
lima beans, 81, 83
lima beans in chili sauce, 443
lima bean, watercress, and herb dip, 185
limes, 23
linseeds, 105
lollo rosso, 50
long grain rice, 66

macadamia nuts, 101
mace, 110
Mâche (lamb's lettuce), 51
maize, 73
malt vinegar, 122
mangoes, 28
griddled pineapple and mango on toasted panettone with vanilla yogurt, 146
mango and orange sorbet, 470
mango yogurt ice, 464
maple syrup, 127
margarine, 95
marjoram, 53
marrows, 39
masa harina, 73

Mediterranean one-crust pie, 345
melon, 26–7
melon, pineapple, and grape cocktail, 136
milk, 90–1
millet, 75
spicy millet bread, 500
minestrone with pesto, 170
mint, 54
miso, 89
molasses, 126
morels, 49
moussaka, vegetable, 270
mozzarella, 96
muesli: apricot and almond, 141
luxury, 142
muffins: chunky chocolate and banana, 486
spiced banana, 495
mung bean sprouts, 56
mung beans, 83–5
mushrooms, 48–9

dried mushrooms, 49
baked portobello mushrooms, 240
beans with mushrooms, 253
beet, wild mushroom, and potato casserole, 254
buckwheat blinis with mushroom caviar, 204
cauliflower and mushroom gougère, 314
cheat's lasagne with mixed mushrooms, 268
fresh cèpes with a parsley dressing, 384
garlic mushrooms with a parsley crust, 206
leek, mushroom, and lemon risotto, 284
lemon, thyme, and aduki bean-stuffed mushrooms with pine nut tarator, 326
mushroom and bean pâté, 197
mushroom and fennel hot pot, 241
mushroom and okra curry, 328
mushroom Bolognese, 278
mushroom croustades, 199
mushroom, nut, and prune jalousie, 349
mushroom hunter's omelet, 157
pepper and wild mushroom pasta salad, 380
risotto with mushrooms, 288
spinach and wild mushroom soufflé, 294
wild mushroom and broccoli tart, 336
wild mushroom and Fontina tarts, 348
wild mushroom soup, 162
zucchini, mushroom, and pesto panino, 156
mustard, 109–10

nectarines, 20
new spring vegetable salad, 377
non-dairy cheeses, 94, 97
non-dairy milks, 92
noodles, 116–7
fried noodles, beansprouts, and asparagus, 428
Japanese-style noodle soup, 179
peanut noodles, 220
rice noodles with vegetable chili sauce, 242
sesame noodle salad, 394
teriyaki soba noodles with tofu and asparagus, 325
tofu stir-fry with egg noodles, 222
nori, 58
rolled sushi with mixed filling, 61
nut butter, 102
nutmeg, 110
nuts, 100–3
allergies, 103
nut milk, 92
roasting and skinning, 103
fruit, nut, and seed teabread, 496
mushroom, nut, and prune jalousie, 349
savory nut loaf, 227

oak leaf lettuce, 50
oat milk, 92
oats, 72
apricot and almond muesli, 141
apricot and hazelnut oat cookies, 486
baked portobello mushrooms, 240
cranberry oat bars, 492
fruity sesame porridge, 138
granola, 142
oaty pancakes with caramel bananas and pecan nuts, 147
porridge with date puree and pistachio nuts, 144
oils, 118–21
okra: mushroom and okra curry, 328
olive oil, 118–9
olives: marinated vegetable antipasto, 192

omelets: cilantro omelet parcels, 229
herb omelet, 99
mushroom hunter's omelet, 157
omelet with beans, 228
onions, 46
apple, onion, and Gruyère tart, 350
baked onions stuffed with feta, 234
caramelized onion tart, 344
classic French onion soup, 176
onion and thyme tart, 341
onion tarts with goat cheese, 234
peas with pearl onions and cream, 439
polenta pan-pizza with red onions, garlic mushrooms, and mozzarella, 354
red onion and goat cheese pastries, 346
sweet and sour onions, 422
oolong tea, 124
oranges, 22
citrus shake, 132
coconut rice puddings with broiled oranges, 454
date, fig, and orange pudding, 455
fennel, orange, and arugula salad, 388
mango and orange sorbet, 470
orange and prune compote, 137
orange jelly, 60
Spanish asparagus and orange salad, 369
orchard fruits, 18-21
oregano, 54
Oriental green beans, 420
oyster mushrooms, 49
pancakes: apple and blackcurrant pancakes, 148
oaty pancakes with caramel bananas and pecan nuts, 147
panettone pudding, apricot, 459
panzanella, 396
papaya, 28
pappardelle and Provençal sauce, 215
paprika, 110
Parmesan and poached egg salad, 372
Parmesan cheese, 97
parsley, 54
parsnips, 31
hot parsnip fritters on baby spinach, 424
parsnip and chestnut croquettes, 425
parsnip, eggplant, and cashew biryani, 266
passionfruit, 28
yogurt sundaes with passionfruit coulis, 468
pasta, 112–5
broccoli, chili, and artichoke pasta, 320
cilantro ravioli with pumpkin filling, 322
fusilli with peppers and onions, 216

mushroom Bolognese, 278
pasta primavera, 218
penne with fennel, tomato, and blue cheese, 219
pepper and wild mushroom pasta salad, 380
ravioli with ricotta and spinach, 276
rustic buckwheat pasta and Fontina cheese bake, 320
Silvio's bean and pasta soup, 161
spinach and ricotta conchiglie, 280
summer tomato pasta, 214
sun-dried tomato and Parmesan carbonara, 224
whole-wheat pasta with caraway cabbage, 274
whole-wheat pasta salad, 381
pastries: red onion and goat cheese pastries, 346
red pepper and watercress phyllo parcels, 316
pâté, mushroom and bean, 197
pattypan squash, 38
peaches, 20
crunchy fruit layer, 140
peach and raspberry crumble, 466
peanut butter: gado gado, 385
warm vegetable salad with peanut sauce, 390
peanut oil, 119–20
peanut noodles, 220
pears, 20–1
arugula, pear, and Parmesan salad, 382
cheese-stuffed pears, 202
pear and kiwi fruit compote, 137
pear and pecan salad with blue cheese, 376
pear and polenta cake, 480
watercress, pear, walnut, and Roquefort salad, 396
peas, 45
fresh pea soup, 166
Italian pea and basil soup, 182
pea, leek, and broccoli soup, 167
peas with pearl onions and cream, 439
peas, dried, 78
split pea and zucchini soup, 180
split pea and shallot mash, 430
pecan nuts, 102
banana and pecan bread, 478
pear and pecan salad with blue cheese, 376
pepper, 110
peppermint tea, 125
peppers, 44
peeling, 44
fusilli with peppers and onions, 216
mixed pepper pipérade, 153

pepper and wild mushroom pasta salad, 380
polenta and pepper bread, 502
Provençal stuffed peppers, 290
red fried rice, 413
red pepper and watercress phyllo parcels, 316
red pepper risotto, 287
roasted potatoes, peppers, and shallots, 408
sweet and sour peppers with pasta bows, 366
vegetable fajitas, 232
white bean salad with roasted red bell pepper dressing, 398
pesto, 53
zucchini, mushroom, and pesto panino, 156
minestrone with pesto, 170
tomato pesto toasts, 198
phyllo: phyllo vegetable pie, 338
red pepper and watercress phyllo parcels, 316
phytochemicals, 35
pies: chestnut, Stilton, and ale pie, 351
corn and bean tamale pie, 340
Mediterranean one-crust pie, 345
mushroom, nut, and prune jalousie, 349
phyllo vegetable pie, 338
spring vegetable boxes with Pernod sauce, 310
pine nuts, 102
pineapple, 28
broiled pineapple with papaya sauce, 476
citrus shake, 132
griddled pineapple and mango on toasted panettone with vanilla yogurt, 146
pink peppercorns, 110
pink pickled ginger, 109
pinto beans, 82–3
pipérade, mixed pepper, 153
pistachio nuts, 102–3
pizzas: arugula and tomato, 355
butternut squash and sage, 352
chili, tomato, and spinach, 358
pizza with fresh vegetables, 353
polenta pan-pizza with red onions, garlic mushrooms, and mozzarella, 354
ricotta and Fontina, 356
pods and seeds, 45
polenta, 73
avocado, red onion, and spinach salad with polenta croutons, 391
corn and bean tamale pie, 340
layered polenta bake, 297
pear and polenta cake, 480
polenta and pepper bread, 502
polenta pan-pizza with red onions, garlic mushrooms, and mozzarella, 354
popcorn, 74
poppy seeds, 104–5
porridge: fruity sesame porridge, 138
porridge with date puree and pistachio nuts, 144
portabello mushrooms, 48
potatoes, 32
beet, wild mushroom, and potato casserole, 254
cheese and potato scones, 498
feta and mint potato salad, 392
garlic mashed potatoes, 407
Greek cheese and potato patties, 201
potato gnocchi, 256
potato, red onion, and feta frittata, 296
potato rösti and tofu with fresh tomato and ginger sauce, 312
potato, spinach, and pine nut gratin, 315
potatoes Dauphinois, 405

puffy creamed potatoes, 404
roasted potatoes, peppers, and shallots, 408
root vegetable gratin with Indian spices, 431
sautéed potatoes, 402
spicy baked potatoes, 230
spicy potato wedges with chili dip, 193
spicy potatoes and cauliflower, 406
straw potato cake, 402
Provençal stuffed peppers, 290
prunes: mushroom, nut, and prune jalousie, 349
pudding rice, 70
pulses, 80–5
sprouted, 56–7
pumpkin, 38
peeling, 39
cilantro ravioli with pumpkin filling, 322
pumpkin seeds, 105
pumpkin soup, 170
Puy lentils, 78–9

quark, 94
quinces, 21
quinoa, 74–5

radicchio, 51
radishes, 33
Japanese salad, 394
raisins, 27
ramen noodles, 116
rapeseed oil, 120
raspberries, 24
peach and raspberry crumble, 466
puree, 25
raspberry yogurt and amaretti scrunch, 450
rhubarb and raspberry sundaes, 492
raspberry leaf tea, 125
raspberry vinegar, 122
ratatouille, 238
ravioli: cilantro ravioli with pumpkin filling, 322
ravioli with ricotta and spinach, 276
red cabbage: red cabbage and apple casserole, 258
red cabbage in port and red wine, 440
red fried rice, 413
red kidney beans, 82–3
beans with mushrooms, 253
corn and bean tamale pie, 340
frijoles, 438
rice and beans with avocado salsa, 324
spicy bean and lentil loaf, 226
vegetable chili, 283

red lentils, 78–9
red rice, 67
redcurrants, 25
rhubarb: rhubarb and ginger yogurt ice, 470
    rhubarb and raspberry sundaes, 492
rice, 66–71
    coconut rice puddings with broiled oranges, 454
    creamy lemon rice, 466
    fruity rice salad, 386
    herbed rice pilaf, 414
    Indian rice pudding, 460
    leek, mushroom, and lemon risotto, 284
    parsnip, eggplant, and cashew biryani, 266
    red fried rice, 413
    red pepper risotto, 287
    rice and beans with avocado salsa, 324
    rice with seeds and spices, 412
rice bran, 71
rice flakes, 71
rice flour, 71
rice milk, 92
rice noodles, 116
rice vinegar, 123
ricotta, 94
risotto, 68–9
    risotto alla Milanese, 282
    risotto with mushrooms, 288
    rolled sushi with mixed filling, 61
    Thai fragrant rice, 410
    vegetable pilaf, 286
root vegetables, 30–3
    deep-fried root vegetables with spiced salt, 429
    roasted root vegetable soup, 173
    root vegetable casserole, 435
    root vegetable gratin with Indian spices, 431
Roquefort tartlets, 203
rosehip tea, 125
rosemary, 54
    rosemary and rock salt focaccia, 504
    rosemary tea, 125
rösti, potato, 312
roulades: celeriac and blue cheese, 303
    sweet potato, 300
rye, 72–3

safflower oil, 119
saffron, 110
saffron dip, 186
sage, 54
salad dressings, 120
salads, 50–1, 363–99
    apple and beet with red leaves, 392
    arugula, pear, and Parmesan, 382
    avocado, red onion, and spinach, 391
    broiled goat cheese, 370
    brown bean, 379
    bulgur and fava bean, 367
    classic Greek, 364
    eggplant, lemon, and caper, 388
    fennel, orange, and arugula, 388
    feta and mint potato, 392
    fresh cèpes with a parsley dressing, 384
    fresh spinach and avocado, 365
    fruity rice, 386
    gado gado, 385
    Japanese, 394
    marinated cucumber, 387
    mixed herb salad with toasted mixed seeds, 374
    new spring vegetable, 377

panzanella, 396
Parmesan and poached egg, 372
pear and pecan with blue cheese, 376
pepper and wild mushroom pasta, 380
roasted beet with horseradish dressing, 399
roasted tomato and mozzarella with basil dressing, 374
sesame noodle, 394
Spanish asparagus and orange, 369
sweet and sour artichoke, 368
    sweet and sour peppers with pasta bows, 366
tomato and feta cheese, 371
tomato, scallion, and cilantro, 383
tortilla wrap with tabbouleh and guacamole, 246
warm vegetable salad with peanut sauce, 390
watercress, pear, walnut, and Roquefort, 396
white bean salad with roasted red bell pepper dressing, 398
whole-wheat pasta, 381
salsa verde, roasted vegetables with, 292
salt, 111
sauces: soy bean sauces, 88
    Provençal sauce, 215
scones, cheese and potato, 498
sea vegetables, 58–61

sesame oil, 120
sesame seeds, 104
sesame seed-coated falafel with tahini yogurt dip, 245
sherry vinegar, 122
shiitake mushrooms, 49
shoot vegetables, 40–1
shoyu, 88
smetana, 91
soba noodles, 117
soda bread, fruit, 503
somen noodles, 116
sorbet, mango and orange, 470
sorghum, 77
sorrel, 51
soufflés: goat cheese, 302
    leek, 305
    spinach and wild mushroom, 294
soups, 162–81
    asparagus, 164
    carrot and coriander, 165
    classic French onion, 176
    cream of zucchini, 174
    curried celery, 168

fresh pea, 166
fresh tomato, lentil, and onion, 181
garlic, chickpea, and spinach, 175
gazpacho with avocado salsa, 160
hot-and-sour, 178
Italian pea and basil, 182
Japanese-style noodle, 179
Jerusalem artichoke soup with Gruyère toasts, 172
minestrone with pesto, 170
pea, leek, and broccoli, 167
pumpkin, 170
roasted root vegetable, 173
Silvio's bean and pasta, 161
spiced red lentil and coconut, 182
split pea and zucchini, 180
tomato and fresh basil, 163
white bean, 177
wild mushroom, 162
soured cream, 91
soy sauce, 88
soy beans, 83, 86–9
soy cheese, 97
soy cream, 92–3
soy milk, 92
soy oil, 119
Spanish asparagus and orange salad, 369
spices, 106–11
    grinding, 111
    toasting, 111
spinach, 37
    avocado, red onion, and spinach salad with polenta croutons, 391
    cheese and spinach tart, 343
    chili, tomato, and spinach pizza, 358
    fresh spinach and avocado salad, 365
    garlic, chickpea, and spinach soup, 175
    hot parsnip fritters on baby spinach, 424
    potato, spinach, and pine nut gratin, 315
    ravioli with ricotta and spinach, 276
    spinach and ricotta conchiglie, 280
    spinach and wild mushroom soufflé, 294
    spinach with raisins and pine nuts, 423
spinach beet, 37
split pea and shallot mash, 430
spreads, 95
spring greens, 37
spring rolls with sweet chili dip, 190
spring vegetable boxes with Pernod sauce, 310
spring vegetable stir-fry, 420
sprouted seeds, 56–7
squashes, 38
    baked squash with Parmesan, 252
    butternut squash and sage pizza, 352
stem ginger, 109
stock, basic vegetable, 33
store cupboard ingredients, 100–27
straw potato cake, 402
strawberries, 24
sultanas, 27
summer herb ricotta tart, 346
summer squashes, 38-9
sunflower oil, 119
sunflower seeds, 104
    whole-wheat sunflower bread, 499
sushi, 71
    rolled sushi with mixed filling, 61
swedes, 31
sweet and sour artichoke salad, 368
sweet and sour mixed bean hot pot, 260
sweet and sour onions, 422
sweet and sour peppers with pasta bows, 366

sweet potatoes, 33
    baked sweet potatoes, 409
    sweet potato roulade, 300
sweeteners, 126–7
Swiss chard, 37
syrups, 127
Szechuan eggplant, 418

tabbouleh, tortilla wrap with, 246
tagliatelle: sun-dried tomato and Parmesan
        carbonara, 224
tamari, 88-9
tarragon, 54–5
tarts: apple, onion, and Gruyère tart, 350
    apricot and almond tart, 462
    asparagus tart with ricotta, 318
    caramelized onion tart, 344
    cheese and spinach tart, 343
    lemon and almond tart, 456
    onion and thyme tart, 341
    onion tarts with goat cheese, 234
    Roquefort tartlets, 203
    summer herb ricotta tart, 346
    wild mushroom and broccoli tart, 336
    wild mushroom and Fontina tarts, 348
teabreads: banana and pecan bread, 478
    fruit, nut, and seed teabread, 496
    whole-wheat apple, apricot and walnut loaf,
        494
teas, 124–5
tempeh, 87
    Thai tempeh cakes with sweet dipping sauce,
        244
teriyaki soba noodles with tofu and asparagus,
        325
terrines: broccoli and chestnut, 306
    broiled vegetable, 308
Thai fragrant rice, 410
Thai tempeh cakes with sweet dipping sauce,
        244
thyme, 55
    thyme tea, 125
tisanes, 124–5
toast: cheese and banana toasties, 152
tomato pesto toasts, 198
tofu, 86–7
    marinated tofu kebabs, 87
    potato rösti and tofu with fresh tomato and
        ginger sauce, 312
teriyaki soba noodles with tofu and asparagus,
        325
tofu fruit fool, 87
tofu stir-fry with egg noodles, 222

tomatoes, 42
    arugula and tomato pizza, 355
    cauliflower and broccoli with tomato sauce,
        274
    chili, tomato, and spinach pizza, 358
    corn cakes with broiled tomatoes, 239
    fresh tomato, lentil, and onion soup, 181
    frittata with sun-dried tomatoes, 243
    griddled tomatoes on soda bread, 150
    penne with fennel, tomato, and blue cheese,
        219
    red fried rice, 413
    red pepper risotto, 287
    roasted tomato and mozzarella salad with
        basil dressing, 374
    sliced frittata with tomato sauce, 225
    summer tomato pasta, 214
    sun-dried tomato and Parmesan carbonara,
        224
    tomato and feta cheese salad, 371
    tomato and fresh basil soup, 163
    tomato and lentil dahl with toasted almonds,
        247
    tomato pesto toasts, 198
    tomato, scallion, and cilantro salad, 383
    zucchini in rich tomato sauce, 446
tortillas: tortilla wrap with tabbouleh and
        guacamole, 246
    vegetable fajitas, 232
trail mix, 138
tropical fruit, 28–9
tropical fruit gratin, 476
tropical fruit with hot rum and cinnamon
        sauce, 450
tubers, 30–3
turmeric, 111
turnips, 32

udon noodles, 116

Valencia rice, 68
vanilla, 111
vegetable fruits, 42–4
vegetables, 30–51
    balti baby vegetables, 426
    basic vegetable stock, 33
    broiled vegetable terrine, 308
    cheese-topped roast baby vegetables, 414
    cilantro omelet parcels with Oriental
        vegetables, 229
    deep-fried root vegetables with spiced salt,
        429
    fonduta with steamed vegetables, 309

    harvest vegetable and lentil casserole, 291
    marinated vegetable antipasto, 192
    mixed vegetables with aromatic seeds, 434
    mixed vegetables with artichokes, 258
    phyllo vegetable pie, 338
    pizza with fresh vegetables, 353
    ratatouille, 238
    rice noodles with vegetable chili sauce, 242
    roasted root vegetable soup, 173
    roasted vegetables with salsa verde, 292
    root vegetable casserole, 435
    root vegetable gratin with Indian spices, 431
    spring vegetable stir-fry, 420
    stir-fried vegetables with cashew nuts, 221
    vegetable chili, 283
    vegetable fajitas, 232
    vegetable hot pot with cheese triangles, 250
    vegetable Kashmiri, 264
    vegetable korma, 333
    vegetable moussaka, 270
    vegetable pilaf, 286
    vegetables Provençal, 432
    zingy vegetable juice, 132
vinegars, 122–3

wakame, 59
walnuts, 103
watermelon, 26–7
wheat, 62–5
    wheat berries, 62–3
    wheat berry sprouts, 56
    wheat flakes, 63
    wheat flour, 64–5
    wheat germ, 63
    wheat noodles, 116–7
    wheatgrass, 62
white beans: omelet with beans, 228
white bean salad with roasted red bell pepper
        dressing, 398
white bean soup, 177
white peppercorns, 110
whitecurrants, 25
whole-wheat apple, apricot, and walnut loaf,
        494
whole-wheat pasta, 113
whole-wheat pasta salad, 381
whole-wheat pasta with caraway cabbage, 274
wild rice, 67
wine, 26
winter fruit poached in mulled wine, 461
wine vinegar, 122
winter fruit poached in mulled wine, 461
winter squashes, 38

yellow bean sauce, 88
yellow lentils, 78
yogurt, 92–3
    banana and strawberry smoothie, 132
    date, banana, and walnut yogurt, 134
    mango yogurt ice, 464
    mixed berry yogurt shake, 134
    raspberry yogurt and amaretti scrunch, 450
    rhubarb and ginger yogurt ice, 470
    yogurt sundaes with passionfruit coulis, 468

zucchini, 38–9
    cream of zucchini soup, 174
    hummus with pan-fried zucchini, 194
    split pea and zucchini soup, 180
    zucchini fritters with chili jam, 269
    zucchini in rich tomato sauce, 446
    zucchini, mushroom, and pesto panino, 156

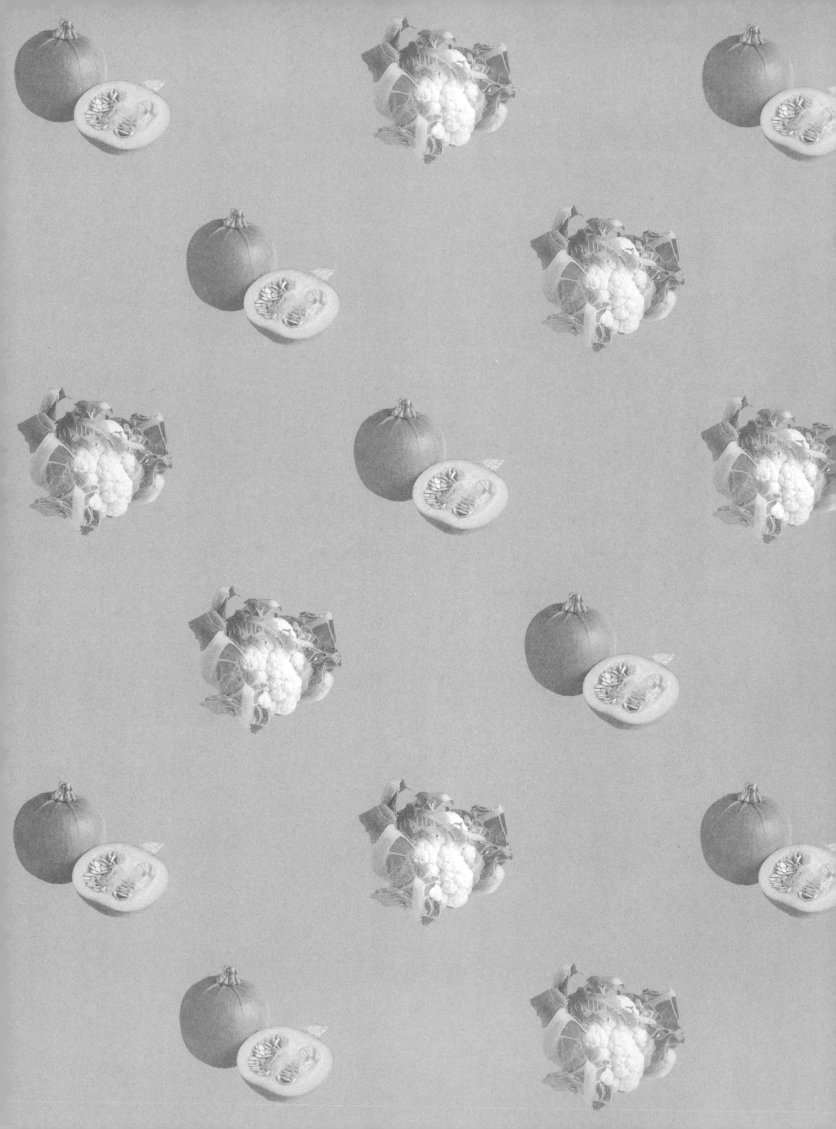